OXFORD MONOGRAPHS IN
INTERNATIONAL LAW

General Editor: Professor Ian Brownlie CBE, QC, FBA
Chichele Professor of Public International Law in the University of Oxford and Fellow of All Souls College, Oxford

THE CONCEPT OF INTERNATIONAL OBLIGATIONS *ERGA OMNES*

OXFORD MONOGRAPHS IN INTERNATIONAL LAW

The aim of this series of monographs is to publish important and original pieces of research on all aspects of public international law. Topics which are given particular prominence are those which, while of interest to the academic lawyer, also have important bearing on issues which touch the actual conduct of international relations. None the less the series is wide in scope and includes monographs on the history and philosophical foundations of international law.

RECENT TITLES IN THIS SERIES

The Human Rights Committee: Its Role in the Development of the International Covenant on Civil and Political Rights
DOMINIC McGOLDRICK

Human Rights in States of Emergency in International Law
JAIME ORAÁ

China's Practice in the Law of the Sea
JEANETTE GREENFIELD

The International Law of Maritime Boundaries and the Practice of States in the Mediterranean Sea
FARAJ ABDULLAH AHNISH

Human Rights in the Private Sphere
ANDREW CLAPHAM

Land and Maritime Zones of Peace in International Law
SURYA SUREDI

The Concept of International Obligations *Erga Omnes*

MAURIZIO RAGAZZI
LL.M. (*Columbia*), D. PHIL. (*Oxon*)
Counsel, Legal Department
The World Bank

CLARENDON PRESS · OXFORD
1997

Oxford University Press, Great Clarendon Street, Oxford OX2 6DP
Oxford New York
Athens Auckland Bangkok Bogota Bombay
Buenos Aires Calcutta Cape Town Dar es Salaam
Delhi Florence Hong Kong Istanbul Karachi
Kuala Lumpur Madras Madrid Melbourne
Mexico City Nairobi Paris Singapore
Taipei Tokyo Toronto Warsaw
and associated companies in
Berlin Ibadan

Oxford is a trade mark of Oxford University Press

Published in the United States
by Oxford University Press Inc., New York

British Library Cataloguing in Publication Data
Data available

Library of Congress Cataloging in Publication Data
Ragazzi, Maurizio.
The concept of international obligations erga omnes / Maurizio Ragazzi.
p. cm.
(Oxford monographs in international law)
Includes bibliographical references.
1. International obligations. 2. Government liability (International law).
3. International offenses. I. Title. II. Series.
JX5402.R34 1997 341.3'7—dc21 97–8003
ISBN 0–19–826480–1

1 3 5 7 9 10 8 6 4 2

Typeset by Hope Services (Abingdon) Ltd.
Printed in Great Britain
on acid-free paper by
Bookcraft Ltd. Midsomer Norton, Somerset

‘He has showed you, O man, what is good;
and what does the Lord require of you
but to do justice, and to love kindness,
and to walk humbly with your
God?’

(Micah 6, 8)

To Grace,
my spouse
in Christ

In Memory

Ospitale of Bondeno is a village near Ferrara, in the north-eastern part of Italy. In this village, there is a Marian shrine. By its side, there is a tiny graveyard where four tombstones remind the living of the sacrifice of four young men, my grandfather among them, who gave their lives for their fellow men in order that light might shine in the darkness of hatred and death.

The words on the four tombstones were written by a teacher of the local school. To this day, these words have touched my heart. They introduce in an appropriate way, I think, a work on international obligations *erga omnes*, a lofty concept by which the International Court has honoured justice and human solidarity as well as the sacrifice of the many who have died for these ideals.

CARLO RAGAZZI	7/3/1911 – 23/4/1945
Spezzato	Broken
non piegato	not bent
per l'umanità intera	for the whole of humanity
vincitore di luce	conqueror of light
riposa	rests

ELIA TASSI	26/3/1920 – 23/4/1945
Riposa	Rests
mite sereno forte	meek peaceful strong
nel tempo	in the course of time
da tirannide costretto	forced by tyranny
sua vita dona	offers his life
perché vita si abbia	in order that there be life

PROBINO MAESTRI	31/7/1921 – 23/4/1945
Riposa	Rests
nel silenzio della morte	in the silence of death
ai superstiti	to the survivors
il suo animo puro	his pure soul
parla ancora	continues to speak
di libertà e di vita	of freedom and life

TURNO PLACATI 24/10/1927 – 23/4/1945

La sua spoglia	His mortal remains
abbandona	abandons
giovane esuberante	young exuberant
lo spirito innalza	his spirit lifts up
alla morte la sua vita	to death his life
per vita donare	in order that life be given

Editor's Preface

Dr Ragazzi's study constitutes a significant contribution to the literature of general international law. The problems of *erga omnes* obligations present a major intellectual challenge. In meeting this challenge, the author has produced a careful and comprehensive analysis of the sources and has tackled the difficult question of the relation between obligations *erga omnes* and the concept of *jus cogens*. This book will retain its status as the definitive work for quite some time.

All Souls College,
Oxford

IAN BROWNLIE

16th January 1997

Preface

The subject of this work is the concept of international obligations *erga omnes*, a category of international obligations which appeared on the agenda as a result of a dictum by the International Court of Justice in the *Barcelona Traction* case. While there are several writings on certain aspects of obligations *erga omnes* (mainly on their corresponding rights of protection), to the writer's knowledge there is as yet no monograph on the concept itself. The present work is meant to fill this gap.

At the outset, it is legitimate to ask whether a monograph on the concept of international obligations *erga omnes* is at all justified. From a theoretical perspective, the subject is certainly important. The latest edition of Oppenheim's classic treatise on international law dedicates to obligations *erga omnes* a relevant part of its opening paragraph on the very concept of international law.[1] In his general course at the Hague Academy, Weil (who cannot really be regarded as an enthusiastic supporter of the concept) acknowledged that obligations *erga omnes* have become a key component of the conceptual apparatus of contemporary international law.[2] From a practical perspective, it is a fact (as this work will show) that, since the International Court's dictum, the concept of obligations *erga omnes* has become ever more influential in the practice of States, in international case law and in the work of the International Law Commission. These considerations alone would justify a monograph on the subject.

Despite the importance of the concept in theory and practice, obligations *erga omnes* remain to a large extent, as Brownlie remarked, 'very mysterious indeed'.[3] This mystery has multiple facets, as it pertains to the criteria for identifying obligations *erga omnes* besides the few examples given by the International Court in its dictum, the correlative rights to obligations *erga omnes*, and the remedies available in case of their breach. Not all of these aspects of the mystery, though, will be addressed in this study. Hence the need to delimit its scope.

First of all, this work is about the *concept* of obligations *erga omnes*. This means that it does not aim at providing a list of these obligations (assuming that the production of this list is at all possible at the present stage in

[1] *Oppenheim's International Law. Peace*, i, 9th edn. Jennings and Watts (London, 1992), pp. 4–7.

[2] 'On peut sans exagération y voir l'une des pièces maîtresses de l'arsenal conceptuel du droit international d'aujourd'hui.' (Weil, 'Le droit international en quête de son identité. Cours général de droit international public', 237 Hague *Recueil* (1992, VI), p. 287.)

[3] 'To What Extent are the Traditional Categories of *Lex Lata* and *Lex Ferenda* still viable? Presentation', Cassese and Weiler (eds.), *Change and Stability in International Law-Making* (Berlin and New York, 1988), p. 71.

the development of the concept), but at discussing their characteristics and criteria of identification. At the same time, however, this attention to the concept will not result in a research based on abstract propositions rather than on the study of the available evidence. On the contrary, while the enquiry into broad issues of the theory of law and international law has been a necessary premise of this work, the writer has made a deliberate effort to refer constantly to the practice of States, international case law and the work of the International Law Commission, and to resort to considerations of principle only when the state of the authorities is ambiguous.[4]

Secondly, this work is about the concept of obligations *erga omnes* as a particular kind of international *obligations*, with the consequence that the discussion of the corresponding rights and remedies will be restricted to what is necessary to elucidate the concept. In other words, the writer will try to bring the concept of obligation 'emphatically to the fore',[5] instead of insisting on those corollaries to obligations *erga omnes* that, while attracting considerable interest in the literature, are still highly controversial and are likely to remain so unless the essence of the concept is more clearly grasped. For the same reason, this work will restrict the study of *actio popularis* to the question whether *actio popularis* is necessarily implied by the International Court's dictum on obligations *erga omnes*, and will omit all discussion of international crimes. Thus, obligations *erga omnes* will be examined here as a subject to be studied on its own merits.

This approach will not lead the writer, though, to advance any new general theory of international obligations. While the evolution of the concept of obligations *erga omnes* may sooner or later induce international lawyers to reconsider the current theories of international obligation, a similar exercise can only be undertaken when the time is ripe. In this respect, the writer is convinced, with Ago, that scientific progress develops one step at a time.[6]

Even within these boundaries, the subject of this study is neither self-contained nor easily manageable. The concept of obligations *erga omnes* cuts across the whole spectrum of international law, and the relevant materials vary both in origin and content. In a way, the research for this work has evolved like a detective story, with important clues being collected from different (and sometimes unexpected) sources. Among these, the pleadings and oral arguments of the parties before the International Court have a

[4] 'the more precedents there are . . . the less occasion is there for investigating principles' (McNair, *Dr Johnson and the Law* (Cambridge, 1948), p. 102 (quoting Samuel Johnson)).

[5] This expression is used, for different purposes than the present ones, in Kelsen, *Introduction to the Problems of Legal Theory*, English trans. Litschewski Paulson and Paulson (Oxford, 1992), p. 43.

[6] 'We can recall another rule that Ago taught through a polite precept, besides his own example, by quoting his own words: "remember that scientific progress consists of small steps forward". By this he meant that imagination is helpful, provided that it does not run too fast.' (Ziccardi, 'Il diritto nell'insegnamento di Roberto Ago', 78 *Riv. dir. int.* (1995), pp. 306–7.)

prominent place, because they often articulate the legal positions of States to an extent that is otherwise difficult to find in diplomatic correspondence, and invariably provide elements for discussion irrespective of any partisan spirit by which they may be pervaded.

In selecting the relevant areas of research, the writer will explore some emerging subjects (such as the international law of the environment and development), but will work above all in the 'old quarries' (such as sources, State responsibility and international transactions), because 'it is here that the richest seams are still to be found'.[7]

The particular nature of the subject, which is that of universal obligations binding on all States, calls for attention to legal materials from various countries and in different languages, to the extent allowed by the writer's access to them. For the same reason, the many references contained in this work to the collected courses of the Hague Academy of International Law are justified not only by the quality of this collection but also by its international character.[8]

Notes on Style

By analogy with the orthography adopted in the drafting of the Vienna Convention on the Law of Treaties for the expression 'jus cogens', the Latin word 'jus' and its inflexions (such as 'juris') are written with an initial 'j' instead of 'i', unless they are part of a quotation, in conformity with medieval (as opposed to classic Roman) usage. (See the *Oxford English Dictionary*, 2nd edn. (Oxford, 1989), viii, under 'j'.)

The words 'State' and 'Power', as philosophical concepts indicating a political unit, are capitalized and are sometimes used as shorthand for 'subject of international law'. This does not imply, however, that only States are international legal persons.

Unless otherwise indicated, the writer is responsible for all translations from a foreign language into English. Transliteration from Russian adheres substantially (except for minor typographical changes) to the 'British' System for (Modern) Cyrillic (*British Standard for Transliteration of Cyrillic and Greek Characters*, B.S. 2979:1958). For typographical reasons, the accentuation in certain languages (such as Spanish) has been simplified.

[7] Jennings, 'General Course on Principles of International Law', 121 Hague *Recueil* (1967, II), p. 327.

[8] On the international character of the collection, and of the Hague Academy, see Dupuy, R. J., 'La contribution de l'Académie au développement du droit international', 138 Hague *Recueil* (1973, I), p. 51; Jennings, 'Fifty Years of Hague Academy Lectures on Public International Law', *The Hague Academy of International Law. Jubilee Book. 1923-1973* (Leiden, 1973), p. 100.

Quotations from and references to Scripture adhere to the text of the 'Revised Standard Version', as it appears in May, H. G. and Metzger (eds.), *The New Oxford Annotated Bible with the Apocrypha* (New York, 1977).

The footnotes give a complete citation of every work that is cited for the first time. Then, an abbreviated form of citation is used. To retrieve a full citation more easily, the reader should turn to the bibliography at the end of this work rather than go back to the first citation in the text.

While the writer is currently a member of the Legal Department of the World Bank, the opinions expressed in this work are those of the writer and should not be attributed to the institution with which the writer is associated.

Acknowledgements

While I alone am responsible for the opinions expressed in this work, I am pleased to acknowledge at least some of the many debts of gratitude I have incurred in the course of the 'long vigils and labours' (if I may borrow this expression from a famous fellow-citizen) that this study has required.[9]

Ian Brownlie, CBE, QC, FBA, Chichele Professor of Public International Law in the University of Oxford, was the supervisor, from beginning to end, of the doctoral thesis completed in Trinity Term, 1995 of which the present work is a slightly revised version. His contribution to the substance and presentation of this work was considerable. His teaching on legal reasoning and technique was invaluable. His patience and kindness were never failing.

Oscar Schachter, Hamilton Fish Professor Emeritus of International Law and Diplomacy at Columbia University, inspired my interest in obligations *erga omnes* when I was a Fulbright student at Columbia Law School. He has nourished my love for international law with his scholarship and friendship.

Giovanni Battaglini, Professor Emeritus of International Law at Ferrara University (Italy), was my first teacher of international law and with paternal affection encouraged me to pursue my studies at the Universities of Columbia and Oxford.

I am also grateful to C. R. Seppala, Esq.; the late Sir Robert McIntosh and Lady Dorothy; J. Oraa, Professor of International Law at Deusto University; J. G. Merrills, Professor of Public International Law at the University of Sheffield; Dr M. W. Janis, Exeter College, Oxford; D. D. Prentice, Allen & Overy Professor of Corporate Law at the University of Oxford; J. M. Eekelaar, B.C.L., Reader in Law at the University of Oxford; M. Mendelson, QC, Professor of International Law at University College (London); Dr C. D. Gray, St. Hilda's College, Oxford; S. Smith, M.A.; Mrs D. Leandri (née Wilde); all the members of Pembroke College, a college that I began to love while reading, at Columbia Law School, of the influence exercised by the *Commentaries* of Sir William Blackstone (who studied at Pembroke) on Chancellor Kent (who was the first Professor of Law at Columbia). May I express my deep gratitude to the Oxford University Press (and particularly to Miss Michaela Coulthard and Ms Myfanwy Milton, Assistant Editors, Law; Ms Alison Morley, Barrister; Mr Chris Rycroft, Commissioning Editor, Law; Mr Richard Hart, former Chief Editor, Law) for their courtesy and careful preparation of this text for publication.

[9] 'longhe vigilie e fatiche' (Ariosto, *Opere minori*, Segre ed. (Milan, 1954), p. 762 (Ariosto's letter to the Doge of Venice, dated 25 October 1515)).

My studies in Oxford were generously sponsored by these institutions: Consiglio Nazionale delle Ricerche, The British Council (FCOSAS), Cassa di Risparmio di Ferrara, Fondazione Rui, ENAM, Pembroke College.

I conducted the greatest part of my research at the Bodleian law library and the Codrington library, Oxford, to whose librarians I am much indebted. Additional materials were provided by my visits over the years to several other law libraries, including those of the Peace Palace (The Hague, The Netherlands), Columbia University (New York, U.S.A.), Bibliothèque Interuniversitaire Cujas (Paris, France), Max-Planck-Institut für ausländisches öffentliches Recht und Völkerrecht (Heidelberg, Germany), Bologna University (Bologna, Italy) and Deusto University (Bilbao, Spain).

My wife, Grazia Ragazzi (née Mangano), B.Th. (*Angelicum*, Rome), CCRS (*Cantab*), M.Th. and doctoral candidate (*Institut Catholique*, Paris), shared with me every joy and pain of this work. The dedication of the final product to her acknowledges our mutual love always and her faithful support for the project, especially on the (frequent) occasions when I felt discouraged by its complexity.

My parents, Luciano Ragazzi and Lea Ragazzi (née Conti), have constantly been a source of love and support. In my filial devotion for them, may I remember the soul of Stefania, my sister.

The Revd Vincent Lucas, former parish priest of St Gregory and St Augustine Church, helped me to regain my spiritual sight and fed me while I was in Oxford with the Bread that lasts.

MR

On 21 November 1996, feast of the
Presentation of the Blessed Virgin Mary

Table of Contents

Abbreviations

A.F.D.I.	*Annuaire français de droit international*
A.J.I.L.	*American Journal of International Law*
Ann. suisse	*Annuaire suisse de droit international* (since 1991, *Revue suisse de droit international et de droit européen*)
Ann. Institut	*Annuaire de l'Institut de droit international*
Brownlie, *Basic Documents*	*Basic Documents in International Law*, 4th edn. (Oxford, 1995)
Brownlie, *Principles*	*Principles of Public International Law*, 4th edn. (Oxford, 1990)
B.Y.I.L.	*British Year Book of International Law*
C.J.T.L.	*Columbia Journal of Transnational Law*
G.Y.I.L.	*German Yearbook of International Law*
Hague *Recueil*	*Recueil des cours de l'Académie de droit international de l'Haye*
Heidelberg *Encycl.*	Bernhardt (ed.), *Encyclopedia of Public International Law* (12 instalments, Amsterdam, 1981–90) (the instalments are now being consolidated in a five-volume revised edition)
I.C.J. Pleadings	*International Court of Justice: Pleadings, Oral Arguments, Documents*
I.C.J. Reports	Reports of Judgments, Advisory Opinions and Orders of the International Court of Justice
I.C.L.Q.	*International and Comparative Law Quarterly*
I.L.M.	*International Legal Materials*
I.L.R.	*International Law Reports* (continuation of the *Annual Digest*)
J.D.I.	*Journal du droit international*
Keesing's	*Keesing's Record of World Events* (continuation of *Keesing's Contemporary Archives*)
L.N.O.J.	*League of Nations Official Journal*
L.N.T.S.	*League of Nations Treaty Series*
N.Y.U.J.I.L.P.	*New York University Journal of International Law and Politics*

Nouv. rec. gén.	de Martens (ed.), *Nouveau recueil général de traités* (Series I, 20 vols. (1843–75); Series II, 35 vols. (1876–1908); Series III (1909–))
Oppenheim's International Law	*Oppenheim's International Law. Peace*, i, 9th edn. Jennings and Watts (London, 1992)
P.C.I.J.	Publications of the Permanent Court of International Justice
P.Y.I.L.	*Polish Yearbook of International Law*
R.D.I.L.C.	*Revue de droit international et de législation comparée* (vols. 1–30 (1869–98); 2nd series, vols. 1–16 (1899–1914); 3rd series, vols. 1– (1920–))
R.G.D.I.P.	*Revue générale de droit international public*
R.I.A.A.	United Nations, Reports of International Arbitral Awards
Riv. dir. int.	*Rivista di diritto internazionale*
Suppl. rec.	de Martens (ed.), *Supplément au recueil des principaux traités*
Third Restatement	*Restatement of the Law. The Foreign Relations Law of the United States (Third Restatement)*
U.N.T.S.	*United Nations Treaty Series*
Y.I.L.C.	United Nations, *Yearbook of the International Law Commission*
Z.a.ö.R.V.	*Zeitschrift für ausländisches öffentliches Recht und Völkerrecht*

Table of Cases

(Within each sub-division, cases are listed in alphabetical order, while the different phases of the same case are listed in chronological order)

Permanent Court of International Justice

International Court of Justice

Other Courts and Arbitral Tribunals

Table of Documents

TREATIES
(Listed in chronological order)

Other Documents
(Listed in alphabetical order)

ICJ Pleadings
(Listed in alphabetical order)

REPORTS TO INTERNATIONAL LAW COMMISSION
(Listed by author in alphabetical order,
and chronologically within each sub-division)

1

The Appearance of the Concept of Obligations *Erga Omnes* on the Agenda: The Dictum of the International Court in the *Barcelona Traction* Case

And they were all amazed,
so that they questioned among themselves, saying,
'What is this?
A new teaching! With authority . . .'
(Mark 1,27)

I. Introduction

The classic passage on obligations *erga omnes*[1] is contained in two paragraphs from the judgment in the *Barcelona Traction* case (Second Phase), which the International Court delivered on 5 February 1970. These paragraphs read in their entirety as follows:

33. When a State admits into its territory foreign investments or foreign nationals, whether natural or juristic persons, it is bound to extend to them the protection of the law and assumes obligations concerning the treatment to be afforded them. These obligations, however, are neither absolute nor unqualified. In particular, an essential distinction should be drawn between the obligations of a State towards the international community as a whole, and those arising vis-à-vis another State in the field of diplomatic protection. By their very nature the former are the concern of all States. In view of the importance of the rights involved, all States can be held to have a legal interest in their protection; they are obligations *erga omnes*.

34. Such obligations derive, for example, in contemporary international law, from the outlawing of acts of aggression, and of genocide, as also from the principles and rules concerning the basic rights of the human person, including protection from slavery and racial discrimination. Some of the corresponding rights of protection

[1] The Latin expression '*erga omnes*' means 'towards all'. The term '*omnes*' can have either a collective or a distributive connotation. (See Glare (ed.), *Oxford Latin Dictionary* (Oxford, 1982), pp. 1248–9 ('omnis').) As applied to the concept of obligations *erga omnes*, this double connotation raises the issue whether the international community as such can be bound by obligations *erga omnes* and be the bearer of the corresponding rights of protection. This issue, however, does not belong to this study, but to one on international legal personality or on the enforcement of corresponding rights of protection of obligations *erga omnes*.

have entered into the body of general international law (*Reservations to the Convention on the Prevention and Punishment of the Crime of Genocide, Advisory Opinion, I.C.J. Reports 1951*, p. 23); others are conferred by international instruments of a universal or quasi-universal character.[2]

The authoritative text of the judgment in the *Barcelona Traction* case is in French.[3] In this language, the passage on obligations *erga omnes* reads as follows:

33. Dès lors qu'un Etat admet sur son territoire des investissements étrangers ou des ressortissants étrangers, personnes physiques ou morales, il est tenu de leur accorder la protection de la loi et assume certaines obligations quant à leur traitement. Ces obligations ne sont toutefois ni absolues ni sans réserve. Une distinction essentielle doit en particulier être établie entre les obligations des Etats envers la communauté internationale dans son ensemble et celles qui naissent vis-à-vis d'un autre Etat dans le cadre de la protection diplomatique. Par leur nature même, les premières concernent tous les Etats. Vu l'importance des droits en cause, tous les Etats peuvent être considérés comme ayant un intérêt juridique à ce que ces droits soient protégés; les obligations dont il s'agit sont des obligations *erga omnes*.

34. Ces obligations découlent par exemple, dans le droit international contemporain, de la mise hors la loi des actes d'agression et du génocide mais aussi des principes et des règles concernant les droits fondamentaux de la personne humaine, y compris la protection contre la pratique de l'esclavage et la discrimination raciale. Certains droits de protection correspondants se sont intégrés au droit international général (*Réserves à la convention pour la prévention et la répression du crime de génocide, avis consultatif, C.I.J. Recueil 1951*, p. 23); d'autres sont conférés par des instruments internationaux de caractère universel ou quasi universel.[4]

When examining a judgment rendered by the International Court, it is advisable to refer to both the English and the French texts, because (as the International Court itself has remarked) the two texts are 'mutually supportive', by reason of the very process of drafting.[5] In any event, one should

[2] *Barcelona Traction, Light and Power Company, Limited*, Second Phase, Judgment, I.C.J. Reports 1970, p. 32, paras. 33–4.

[3] Ibid., p. 51, para. 103. The parties before the International Court can agree to conduct a case in English or French. Without this agreement (which, so far, has only been concluded in the *Asylum* case), the parties may submit their pleadings in either English or French. The International Court then gives its decision in both languages and determines which text is authoritative. See Article 39 of the Statute of the International Court. (*Gen. Ass., Off. Recs., Second Session of the General Assembly, Resolutions, 16 September–29 November 1947*, pp. 105–10, reproduced in Brownlie (ed.), *Basic Documents in International Law*, 4th edn. (Oxford, 1995), pp. 438–55.) For comment, see Mani, *International Adjudication: Procedural Aspects* (The Hague, 1980) pp. 155–7; Tabory, *Multilingualism in International Law and Institutions* (Alphen aan den Rijn and Rockville, 1980), pp. 18–20.

[4] I.C.J. Reports 1970, p. 32, paras. 33–4.

[5] See the International Court's observations on this point, prompted by a report of the United Nations Joint Inspection Unit and reproduced in Rosenne, 'Publications of the International Court of Justice', 81 *A.J.I.L.* (1987), pp. 687–8.

avoid drawing hasty conclusions from textual arguments based on the translation from the authoritative text.[6] For example, it has been suggested in the literature that, by writing that a distinction 'should be drawn' between obligations *erga omnes* and other obligations, the International Court was using hypothetical language in the sense that obligations *erga omnes* would only be 'a concept *de lege ferenda*'.[7] This interpretation of the International Court's passage, though, is untenable, both because the French original uses the indicative mood rather than the conditional ('[u]ne distinction essentielle doit . . . être établie')[8] and because the use of the conditional in a particular line cannot be isolated from the rest of the passage, where (like the English version in the present instance) the indicative mood is used consistently.

A more appropriate starting point in the study of the International Court's passage on obligations *erga omnes* is the context in which the passage appeared. The *Barcelona Traction* case arose out of the adjudication in bankruptcy by a Spanish court of the Barcelona Traction Light and Power Company, Limited, a Canadian company.[9] Belgium had initially instituted proceedings before the International Court in 1958, by which it sought reparation for the damage inflicted on the Barcelona Traction company as a result of acts allegedly committed by organs of the Spanish State in violation of international law. Three years later, Belgium requested that the proceedings be discontinued in order that the parties might settle their dispute out of court. Spain did not oppose this request, and the International Court removed the case from its list.[10]

[6] According to Rosenne, 'experience has shown the need for care in using that version of a judgment or of an individual or dissenting opinion, which is not the authoritative text.' (*The Law and Practice of the International Court*, 2nd revised edn. (Dordrecht, 1985), p. 601, note 1.)

[7] Willisch, *State Responsibility for Technological Damage in International Law* (Berlin, 1987), p. 40.

[8] Nor does the presence of the modal auxiliary 'should' (in English) or 'doit' (in French) justify the inference drawn by Willisch. The best grammars confirm in theory and show by way of examples how the use of modal verbs is subject to variations and nuances of meaning. See Quirk, Greenbaum, Leech and Svartik, *A Comprehensive Grammar of the English Language* (London, 1985), paras. 4.49–4.50, and (for the auxiliaries 'ought to' and 'should') para. 4.56; Grevisse, *Le bon usage. Grammaire française*, 13th edn. Goosse (Paris, 1993), para. 789, and (for the auxiliary 'devoir') para. 791(c).

[9] For a summary of the case, see Wallace, C. D., 'Barcelona Traction Case', Heidelberg *Encycl.*, ii, pp. 30–3; Eisemann, Coussirat-Coustère and Hur, *Petit manuel de la jurisprudence de la Cour internationale de justice*, 4th edn. (Paris, 1984), pp. 95–105. For a more extensive discussion, see Miaja de la Muela, *Aportacion de la Sentencia del Tribunal de la Haye en el caso Barcelona Traction (5 de febrero de 1970) a la jurisprudencia internacional* (Valladolid, 1970). See also Higgins, R. 'Aspects of the Case Concerning the Barcelona Traction, Light and Power Company, Ltd.', 11 *Virginia Journal of International Law* (1971), pp. 327–43; Seidl-Hohenveldern, 'Der Barcelona-Traction-Fall', 22 *Österreichische Zeitschrift für öffentliches Recht* (1971), pp. 255–310.

[10] *Barcelona Traction, Light and Power Company, Limited*, Order of 10 April 1961, I.C.J. Reports 1961, p. 9.

After negotiations for a settlement broke down, Belgium filed a new application in 1962. Having the benefit of knowing the preliminary objections raised by Spain in response to the first application, Belgium modified its earlier submissions. It now sought reparation for damage suffered, not by the Barcelona Traction company, but by Belgian nationals who were allegedly the owners of a substantial number of shares of the company. Spain responded by filing four preliminary objections. The first and the second objections concerned the jurisdiction of the International Court, while the third and the fourth objections related to the admissibility of the Belgian application. By a judgment delivered in 1964, the International Court dismissed the preliminary objections to jurisdiction and joined the third and fourth objections to the merits.[11] In its judgment of 1970, at the end of the second phase of the *Barcelona Traction* case, the International Court upheld the third preliminary objection put forward by Spain, namely that Belgium did not have legal standing to bring the action. On this ground, the International Court rejected the Belgian claim[12] without pronouncing on any other aspects of the case.[13]

The judgment in the *Barcelona Traction* case has not been immune from criticism.[14] On the specific passage relating to obligations *erga omnes*, some

[11] *Barcelona Traction, Light and Power Company, Limited*, Preliminary Objections, Judgment, I.C.J. Reports 1964, p. 6. At the time of the proceedings, preliminary objections were governed by Article 62 of the Rules of Court. Article 62 was then renumbered as Article 67 after the 1972 amendments of the Rules, and again renumbered as Article 79 after the 1978 revision. (The Rules, as revised in 1978, are reproduced in 17 *I.L.M.* (1978), pp. 1286–304.) On the changes introduced by these revisions, see the considerations developed by Judge Shahabuddeen in his separate opinion in *Certain Phosphate Lands in Nauru (Nauru* v. *Australia)*, Preliminary Objections, Judgment, I.C.J. Reports 1992, pp. 271–6. On preliminary objections, see Rosenne, *Law and Practice*, pp. 437–68. On the distinction between preliminary objections to jurisdiction and preliminary objections to admissibility, see Shihata, *The Power of the International Court to Determine its own Jurisdiction: Compétence de la Compétence* (The Hague, 1965), pp. 107–12; Oda, 'The International Court of Justice Viewed from the Bench (1976–1993)', 244 Hague *Recueil* (1993, VII), pp. 47–50.

[12] It was not merely a declaration of inadmissibility of the claim, but an outright rejection of it. In his separate opinion, Judge Morelli wrote as follows: 'Belgium's right is thereby denied, not because such a right might hypothetically belong to a State other than Belgium (in other words, not for lack of capacity on the part of Belgium), but rather because no such right can be invoked by any State, since no rule exists from which it could derive.' (I.C.J. Reports 1970, p. 228.)

[13] The fourth preliminary objection on the exhaustion of local remedies was addressed, though, in several separate opinions attached to the International Court's judgment.

[14] For example, Thirlway has written that this is a 'generally disappointing decision' ('The Law and Procedure of the International Court of Justice 1960–1989', 61 *B.Y.I.L.* (1990), p. 35). Carreau has written that, in the *Barcelona Traction* case (and in other cases), the International Court gave 'des solutions contestables et contestées' (*Droit international*, 4th edn. (Paris, 1994), p. 612). Taking a more subtle position, Henkin has written that '[i]n its own terms, the Court's judgment may not have been unsound. . . But if *Barcelona Traction* can be justified by its origins, it may not serve the purposes of international justice, as the shareholders, principal parties in interest, may be without adequate protection and remedy.' ('"Nationality" at the Turn of the Century', Beyerlin, Bothe, Hofmann and Petersmann (eds.), *Recht zwischen Umbruch und Bewahrung. Völkerrecht, Europarecht, Staatsrecht. Festschrift für Rudolf Bernhardt* (Berlin, 1995), p. 97.)

writers have raised doubts whether this reference to obligations *erga omnes* was necessary, or even appropriate, for the International Court to reach its conclusions on legal standing. McCaffrey, a former member of the International Law Commission, has expressed the view that this reference was a 'gratuitous statement', which was made in the context of a case 'whose facts and legal issues hardly required such a pronouncement'.[15] In even stronger terms, Mann has written that *obiter dicta* like that on obligations *erga omnes* 'convey the impression of having been studiously planted in the text or artificially dragged into the arena'.[16]

As a result of the widespread acceptance of the concept in the international practice, case law and literature, these remarks have become irrelevant. However, to the extent that they bring into question (at least implicitly) the origins of the concept of obligations *erga omnes*, they call for comment. The first issue to consider is the distinction between the *ratio decidendi* of a case and *obiter dictum*, which is the premise upon which McCaffrey and Mann have criticized the International Court's pronouncement on obligations *erga omnes*.

II. The Distinction between *Ratio Decidendi* and *Obiter Dictum*: (a) Preliminary Considerations

The distinction between *ratio decidendi* and *obiter dictum* is traditional in the common law.[17] One of the rules of the doctrine of precedent (*stare decisis*) is that the only part of a decision that is binding for future cases is the

[15] '*Lex Lata* or the Continuum of State Responsibility', Weiler, Cassese and Spinedi (eds.), *International Crimes of State. A Critical Analysis of the ILC's Draft Article 19 on State Responsibility* (Berlin and New York, 1989), p. 243.

[16] 'The Doctrine of Jus Cogens in International law', Ehmke, Kaiser, Kewenig, Meessen and Rüfner (eds.), *Festschrift für Ulrich Scheuner zum 70 Geburtstag* (Berlin, 1973), p. 418. On the same page, in note 70, Mann reports the view that the dictum on obligations *erga omnes* was a reaction against the International Court's judgment in the *South West Africa* cases (Second Phase) (on which, see Chapters 7 and 10, below). The same point has been made by several other writers without, however, drawing negative conclusions on the dictum on obligations *erga omnes* similar to those drawn by Mann. See, for example, Crawford, 'The General Assembly, the International Court and Self-Determination', Lowe and Fitzmaurice, M. (eds.), *Fifty Years of the International Court of Justice. Essays in Honour of Sir Robert Jennings* (Cambridge, 1996), pp. 588–9.

[17] On this distinction, see Cross and Harris, *Precedent in English Law*, 4th edn. (Oxford, 1991), pp. 39–96. See also Allen, *Law in the Making*, 7th edn. (Oxford, 1964), pp. 259–68; Raz, *The Authority of Law. Essays on Law and Morality* (Oxford, 1979), pp. 183–9. These references to works by common lawyers are not meant to exclude the fact that this distinction, and more generally the acknowledgement of the value of precedents, also have a place in the civil law tradition. See Zweigert and Kötz, *Introduction to Comparative Law*, 2nd edn., English trans. Weir (Oxford, 1987), i, pp. 267–73. See also the considerations developed in Kriele, 'Das Präjudiz im kontinental-europäischen und anglo-amerikanischen Rechtskreis', *La sentenza in Europa. Metodo, tecnica e stile* (Padua, 1988), pp. 62–80; Taruffo, 'Dimensioni del precedente giudiziario', *'Scintillae iuris'. Studi in memoria di Gino Gorla*, i (Milan, 1994), pp. 383–404.

ratio decidendi.[18] Essentially, the *ratio decidendi* includes what is necessary to decide the issues before the court, while all propositions of law which are not part of the *ratio decidendi* are *obiter dicta*.

Brownlie defines *obiter dicta* as those

> lesser propositions of law stated by tribunals or by individual members of tribunals; propositions not directed to the principal matters in issue.[19]

Jennings has correctly pointed out that, in international law, the doctrine of precedent has not been fully worked out.[20] If so, one could legitimately raise the question whether there is any place at all, in international law, for a dichotomy between *ratio decidendi* and *obiter dictum*. This issue has several ramifications, which cannot (and need not) be explored here. For the purposes of the present analysis, it will be sufficient to note, once again with Jennings,[21] that the expression '*obiter dictum*' is often used in the international literature and that, by implication, one can also speak of the '*ratio decidendi*' of an international decision.

The distinction between *ratio decidendi* and *obiter dictum* is clearer in theory than in practice, and the two expressions are bound to remain, like many other key terms of legal discourse, in a 'penumbra of uncertainty'.[22] An element of uncertainty is that not all *obiter dicta* have the same weight. Some may be wholly gratuitous, whereas others, while not strictly necessary to arrive at the decision of a case, may address a specific point raised by the parties in the course of the proceedings.[23] To assess the weight and authority of a dictum,[24] it is therefore necessary to consider its background, circumstances and subsequent developments.

[18] On the doctrine of precedent, as on other issues, one can profitably refer to the writings of Lord Denning. See *The Discipline of Law* (London, 1979), pp. 283–314.

[19] *Principles of Public International Law*, 4th edn. (Oxford, 1990), p. xlvii.

[20] 'Judicial Reasoning at an International Court', *Universität des Saarlands. Vorträge Reden und Berichte aus dem Europa-Institut*, Ress ed., No. 236 (Saarbrücken, 1991), pp. 6–7. While denying the binding force of precedents in international law, Franck has noted that 'the narrowest point of law can have the widest conceptual implications' (*Fairness in International Law and Institutions* (Oxford, 1995), p. 317). See also Abi-Saab, 'Cours général de droit international public', 207 Hague *Recueil* (1987, VII), pp. 129–30 and, more extensively, Shahabuddeen, *Precident in the World Court* (Cambridge, 1996).

[21] 'The Judiciary, International and National, and the Development of International Law', 45 *I.C.L.Q.* (1996), pp. 9–10.

[22] Hart, *The Concept of Law*, 2nd edn. (Oxford, 1994), p. 135.

[23] In *Slack* v. *Leeds Industrial Co-operative Society* [1923] 1 Ch. 431, 451, Sterndale MR wrote that '[d]icta are of different kinds and of varying degrees of weight. Sometimes they may be called almost casual expressions of opinion upon a point which has not been raised in the case, and is not really present in the judge's mind . . . Some dicta, however, are of a different kind; they are, although not necessary for the decision of the case, deliberate expressions of opinion given after consideration upon a point clearly brought and argued before the Court . . . [M]uch greater weight attaches to them than to the former class.' (The passage, in its entirety, is reproduced in Allen, *Law in the Making*, p. 261.)

[24] For reasons of convenience, the term 'dictum', unlike the expression '*obiter dictum*', is not in italics.

In international law, to underestimate the importance of *obiter dicta* would be an even greater mistake. In his separate opinion in the *Barcelona Traction* case (Second Phase), Judge Fitzmaurice acknowledged that comments made by the International Court by way of *obiter dicta* cannot have the authority of a judgment. Yet, he remarked, in the absence of international legislation, judicial pronouncements 'of one kind or another' are the principal instrument for the clarification and development of international law.[25] Sir Hersch Lauterpacht has put forward another reason for the importance of *obiter dicta* in international adjudication, namely the need that the International Court, whose jurisdiction rests on consent, examine all the arguments developed by the parties. This favours a 'full measure of exhaustiveness' of international decisions.[26] (The application of this test of exhaustiveness varies, of course, in each particular case, in the sense that a judgment must invariably be 'supported by a stated process of reasoning' but 'need not enter meticulously into every claim and contention' put forward by either party.)[27]

To sum up, the remark that the International Court's pronouncement on obligations *erga omnes* was *obiter dictum* is true, but does not dispose of the question of its significance. The next two sections will assess the value of this dictum in light of its background, circumstances and subsequent developments.

III. The Distinction between *Ratio Decidendi* and *Obiter Dictum*: (b) Background and Circumstances of the Dictum on Obligations *Erga Omnes*

Lord Devlin once remarked that 'new categories in the law do not spring into existence overnight'.[28] While made in a completely different context, this observation accurately reflects the origins of the concept of obligations *erga omnes*.

The very expression 'obligation *erga omnes*' predates the dictum of the International Court. In 1957, while writing on the legal effects of treaties for third States, Schwarzenberger remarked that

[25] I.C.J. Reports 1970, p. 64, para. 2. On the influence of statements pronounced by the International Court, see the observations of Gaja and Brownlie in Cassese and Weiler (eds.), *Change and Stability*, pp. 77 and 92, respectively.

[26] Lauterpacht, H., *The Development of International Law by the International Court* (London, 1958), pp. 37–45. A classic case of judicial articulation of a principle (the principle of the persistent objector) by way of *obiter dictum* in response to the arguments of the parties will be discussed in Chapter 3, below.

[27] *Application for Review of Judgment No. 158 of the United Nations Administrative Tribunal*, Advisory Opinion, I.C.J. Reports 1973, p. 210, para. 95.

[28] *Hedley Byrne & Co. Ltd.* v. *Heller & Partners Ltd.* [1964] A.C. 465, 525, *per* Lord Devlin.

[i]nternational servitudes, the effect of treaties of cession on third parties and the problem of individuals as bearers of international duties have been discussed in previous chapters. Treaties in any of these fields hardly bear out the view that, in this manner, obligations *erga omnes* can be automatically created.[29]

A few years later, Lachs (at that time a member of the International Law Commission) used the expression in the course of a debate on draft Article 62 ('Treaties providing for obligations or rights of third States') of the Vienna Convention on the Law of Treaties. He noted that

[t]reaties establishing objective regimes and obligations *erga omnes* should be dealt with separately from Article 62, paragraph 2.[30]

This latter precedent is important, if one considers that Lachs was later elected to the International Court and took part in the decision on the merits in the *Barcelona Traction* case. His specific contribution to the drafting of the dictum on obligations *erga omnes* has been highlighted in the international literature.[31]

Without using the expression, several writers may be regarded as having foreshadowed the concept of obligations *erga omnes*. For example, Schachter has noted that certain views expressed by Judge Jessup in the *South West Africa* cases (Second Phase) were a 'presage' to the International Court's dictum on obligations *erga omnes*.[32] In his dissenting opinion, Judge Jessup had written that

States may have a general interest—cognizable in the International Court—in the maintenance of an international régime adopted for the common benefit of the international society.[33]

Like Judge Lachs, Judge Jessup was a member of the International Court at the time of the *Barcelona Traction* case (Second Phase); his earlier views

[29] *International Law as Applied by International Courts and Tribunals*, i (London, 1957), p. 459. (Footnotes have been omitted.)

[30] *Y.I.L.C.* (1964, I), p. 83, para. 29.

[31] For example, McWhinney has written that the dictum on obligations *erga omnes* is Lachs's '(generally acknowledged, and celebrated) personal addition' to the International Court's judgment in the *Barcelona Traction* case. (*Judge Manfred Lachs and Judicial Law-Making. Opinions on the International Court of Justice, 1967–1993* (The Hague, 1995), p. 25, and also pp. 36–8 (where McWhinney elaborates on the same point).) Similar remarks have been made by Rosalyn Higgins ('Fundamentals of International Law', Jasentuliyana (ed.), *Perspectives on International Law (A Publication on the Occasion of the Fiftieth Anniversary of the United Nations and Contribution to the Decade of International Law)* (London, 1995), p. 19; René-Jean Dupuy ('Authors Recollect Judge Lachs', ibid., p. 531); and Pierre-Marie Dupuy ('The Judicial Policy of the International Court of Justice', Salerno (ed.), *Il ruolo del giudice internazionale nell' evoluzione del diritto internazionale e comunitario* (Padua, 1995), p. 71).

[32] 'Philip Jessup's Life and Ideas', 80 *A.J.I.L.* (1986), p. 892.

[33] I.C.J. Reports 1966, p. 373. This reference to a 'general interest' of States in maintaining an objective regime must be distinguished from Jessup's discussion, in a different context, of a broader 'principle of community interest in the prevention of breaches of international law' (*A Modern Law of Nations. An Introduction* (New York, 1948; reimpressed in 1968 with a new Preface by the author), p. 12).

are undoubtedly helpful in understanding the background of the dictum on obligations *erga omnes*.[34]

Similarly, Cassese has written that the concept of 'joint obligations' put forward by Sperduti in 1958 is 'the same' as that embodied in the International Court's dictum in the *Barcelona Traction* case.[35] Cassese was referring to a passage in which Sperduti indicated the existence of

> rare . . . norms giving rise to joint obligations, whereby a wrong caused by a subject results in the violation of an obligation towards the community . . .[36]

There is an evident element of analogy between these words and the International Court's dictum on obligations *erga omnes*. However, Cassese was perhaps overstating his point because, by the expression 'joint obligations', Sperduti meant to refer to a wider category than that of obligations *erga omnes*, including not only customary rules but also conventional ones.[37] In this sense, 'joint obligations', which apply either to all States or to a limited number of States by way of consent, may be regarded as being similar to, but not 'the same' as, obligations *erga omnes*.[38]

All these statements from different authors belonging to different legal traditions confirm the observation, made by Fitzmaurice in another context, that 'no one section of humanity has a monopoly of ideas and discoveries'.[39] Thus, if the writer is allowed to borrow a vivid expression from Roman law, he would sum up this brief discussion and conclude that, while the 'mother' of the dictum (namely, the International Court) is certain, the identity of its 'father' is not equally sure.[40]

This uncertainty calls for greater attention to the circumstances of the dictum, and in particular to the arguments put forward by the parties in the course of the proceedings. In its third preliminary objection, Spain alleged that Belgium lacked any capacity to bring an action before the International

[34] Schachter was even more explicit, when he wrote that '[i]t seems likely in light of Jessup's earlier opinions that he had an important role in the Court's formulation of the *erga omnes* principle.' ('Philip Jessup's Life and Ideas', p. 892.)

[35] 'Note sull'opera di Giuseppe Sperduti', 77 *Riv. dir. int.* (1994), p. 317, note 7 ('It cannot be denied that the same concept [of 'joint obligations', in Italian 'vincoli solidali'] is the basis of the famous dictum of the International Court of Justice on obligations *erga omnes* . . .').

[36] *Lezioni di diritto internazionale* (Milan, 1958), p. 140 ('Rare . . . norme istitutive di vincoli solidali nel senso che in virtù di esse una lesione arrecata ad un soggetto si concreta nella violazione di un dovere verso la collettività . . .').

[37] Ibid., p. 152. See also Sperduti's dissenting opinion, as a member of the European Commission on Human Rights, cited in section VI of Chapter 10, below.

[38] This remark, of course, is not meant to deny Sperduti's contribution to the development of the specific concept of obligations *erga omnes*, after the International Court's dictum, in his role as rapporteur of the Institute of International Law. (See section II of Chapter 8, below.)

[39] 'The Contribution of the Institute of International Law to the Development of International Law', 138 Hague *Recueil* (1973, I), p. 212.

[40] '*(Mater)* semper certa est, etiam si vulgo conceperit: pater vero is est, quem nuptiae demonstrant.' (*The Digest of Justinian*, Mommsen and Krueger eds., English trans. ed. by Watson (Philadelphia, 1985), i, p. 44) (D.2.4.5, *Paulus libro quarto ad edictum*.)

Court on behalf of the Barcelona Traction, which was a Canadian company. In support of its objection, Spain argued that the international obligations on the protection of foreign nationals are strictly bilateral, although a State is bound at one time towards several States on the basis of obligations having the same contents. In this context, and in response to the Belgian allegation of denial of justice by the Spanish courts, Spain expressed the view that

> denial of justice is always a damage inferred on a particular State, the State to which the injured person belongs, and not States in general. Another State cannot bring a claim and invoke the international responsibility for such damage: *no State is authorized to intervene and safeguard the rights of other States.*[41]

Elaborating on this point, Ago (who was counsel for Spain) explained that

> denial of justice committed against a particular person is not a kind of crime towards the international community as a whole or towards each one of its members; it is an international delict committed by a State towards the State to which the person in question belongs.[42]

Thus, in rejecting the Belgian allegation of denial of justice,[43] Spain examined the possibility that, in the case of an international 'crime', any State may invoke the international responsibility of another State irrespective of the nationality of the injured person. While the expression 'obligations *erga omnes*' cannot be found anywhere in the pleadings and oral arguments (or, at least, the present writer did not find it),[44] the premises for

[41] *I.C.J. Pleadings, Barcelona Traction, Light and Power Company, Limited (New Application: 1962)*, i, pp. 194–5 ('Exceptions préliminaires présentées par le Gouvernement Espagnol'). The French original reads as follows: 'un déni de justice est un préjudice causé à un Etat déterminé, à l'Etat national de la personne intéressée et non pas à la généralité des Etats. Un autre Etat ne peut pas s'en plaindre et ne peut pas faire valoir une responsabilité internationale comme conséquence d'un tel fait: *aucun Etat n'est autorisé à intervenir pour sauvegarder les droits des autres.*'

[42] Ibid., ii, p. 212. The French original reads as follows: 'le déni de justice commis à l'égard d'une personne déterminée n'est pas une sorte de crime envers la communauté internationale tout entière ou envers chacun de ses membres; c'est un délit international commis par un Etat envers l'Etat national de la personne en question.'

[43] On the concept of denial of justice, see Brownlie, *Principles*, pp. 529–30. See also Fitzmaurice, 'The Meaning of the Term "Denial of Justice"', 13 *B.Y.I.L.* (1932), pp. 93–114.

[44] In reviewing the pleadings of a case such as the *Barcelona Traction*, a student comes across similar difficulties to those encountered by the judges called to master its written case-file, which alone amounted to 60,776 pages. (See Sette Camara, 'Behind the World Bench', *International Law in an Evolving World. Liber Amicorum in Tribute to Professor Eduardo Jiménez de Aréchaga* (Montevideo, 1994), p. 1071.) Several members of the International Court have lamented the excessive length of pleadings and oral arguments. See, for example, Jennings, 'New Problems at the International Court of Justice', ibid., pp. 1062–5; Guillaume, 'The Future of International Judicial Institutions', 44 *I.C.L.Q.* (1995), pp. 853–4. Critical considerations on the same point are developed in Bowett, Crawford, Sinclair and Watts, 'The International Court of Justice: Efficiency of Procedures and Working Methods. Report of the Study Group established by the British Institute of International and Comparative Law as a contribution to the UN Decade of International Law', 45 *I.C.L.Q.* (1996), Supplement, pp. S4–9 (paras. 10–23).

the International Court's dictum were there. On the basis of these elements, it seems reasonable to conclude that the dictum was not a 'gratuitous statement', but reflected the International Court's attempt to provide a 'full measure of exhaustiveness' in its response to the arguments put forward by the parties in the course of the proceedings. (This conclusion is not meant to deny that broader considerations may *also* have been present to the International Court when pronouncing its dictum, but to underline that any such broader considerations cannot be regarded as *excluding* specific considerations relating to the *Barcelona Traction* case.)

The judgment in the *Barcelona Traction* case (Second Phase) was backed by a considerable degree of consent within the International Court, and only one judge appended a dissenting opinion. The passage on obligations *erga omnes* attracted the support of all judges. Judge *ad hoc* Riphagen, who was the only dissenting judge from the judgment of the International Court, wrote as follows:

> The Judgment seems to draw a distinction between *obligations* of a State *erga omnes*, obligations of a State which exist towards certain other States under general international law, and obligations of a State which only exist towards a State with which it has entered into 'treaty stipulations'. This distinction can of course be drawn. But it is still difficult to hold that this distinction would necessarily correspond to an *a priori* classification in accordance with the nature of the *interests* protected by such obligations, a classification which is already in itself a fairly doubtful one.[45]

Thus, despite some other sentences in his dissenting opinion that seem to qualify the view expressed in this passage,[46] Judge *ad hoc* Riphagen endorsed the concept of obligations *erga omnes*.[47] On this specific point, his disagreement from the majority of the International Court had more to do

[45] I.C.J. Reports 1970, p. 340. The French original reads as follows: 'L'arrêt semble faire une distinction entre les *obligations* d'un Etat *erga omnes*, les obligations d'un Etat qui existent envers certains autres Etats d'après le droit international général et des obligations d'un Etat qui n'existent envers un autre Etat qu'en raison de 'stipulations conventionnelles'. On peut, certes, faire cette distinction. Encore est-il difficile d'admettre que cette distinction correspondrait nécessairement à une classification à priori suivant la nature des *intérêts* protégés par ces obligations, classification qui est déjà en soi assez douteuse.'

[46] In an earlier passage, Judge *ad hoc* Riphagen had written that the distinction of principle between different types of obligations, drawn by the International Court in paras. 33, 34 and 87 of its judgment, 'seems very artificial and cannot in any case justify the *essential* legal consequences which the judgment attaches to this distinction' ('paraît bien artificielle et ne peut en aucun cas justifier les conséquences juridiques *essentielles* que l'arrêt attache à cette distinction'). (Ibid., pp. 338–9.)

[47] One should not neglect the relationship that always exists between a judgment (or an advisory opinion) and the opinions appended to it. See Jennings, 'The International Judicial Practice of the International Court of Justice', 59 *B.Y.I.L.* (1988), pp. 42–4; Bedjaoui, 'La "fabrication" des arrêts de la Cour internationale de Justice', *Le droit international au service de la paix, de la justice et du développement. Mélanges Michel Virally* (Paris, 1991), pp. 104–5.

with the criteria of identification of obligations *erga omnes*, and the practical consequences deriving from them, than with the concept itself.[48]

IV. The Distinction between *Ratio Decidendi* and *Obiter Dictum*: (c) Developments after the Dictum on Obligations *Erga Omnes*

After the *Barcelona Traction* case, references to the concept of obligations *erga omnes* have occurred both in judgments and advisory opinions rendered by the International Court[49] and pleadings of the parties.[50] Relevant materials for the study of the concept can also be found in the practice of States (apart from

[48] Several years after the judgment, in his capacity as Special Rapporteur on the codification of the law of State responsibility, Riphagen referred often to the concept of obligations *erga omnes*. Some of these references are cited later in this work.

[49] Some of the references appearing in the context of the *Nuclear Tests*, *Nicaragua*, *East Timor* and *Bosnia-Herzegovina* cases, as well as the *Namibia* and the two *Nuclear Weapons* advisory opinions, will be examined (or simply cited) in the course of this work, without, however, any pretension to exhaustiveness. These references should be sufficient to allow a different conclusion from that drawn by some writers, according to whom the International Court's dictum on obligations *erga omnes* is an isolated case. (See, for example, Cahier, 'Changements et continuité du droit international. Cours général de droit international public', 195 Hague *Recueil* (1985, VI), p. 295; Sinclair, 'State Responsibility and the Concept of Crimes of States', Weiler, Cassese and Spinedi (eds.), *International Crimes of State*, p. 225.)

[50] In addition to the pleadings and oral arguments which will be mentioned later in this work, references to the concept of obligations *erga omnes* (which will not be examined in this work) can be found, for example, in some written and oral statements relating to the *Legality of the Use by a State of Nuclear Weapons in Armed Conflict (Request for Advisory Opinion Submitted by the World Health Organization)*, and the *Legality of the Threat or Use of Nuclear Weapons (Request for Advisory Opinion Submitted by the General Assembly of the United Nations)*, such as: 'Request by the World Health Organization for an Advisory Opinion on the Legality of the Use of Nuclear Weapons in View of their Effects on Human Health and the Environment – Written Observations Submitted by the Government of Solomon Islands to the International Court of Justice' (10 June 1994), para. 3.89 (note 211), and 'Request by the United Nations General Assembly for an Advisory Opinion on the Legality of the Threat or Use of Nuclear Weapons – Written Observations Submitted by the Government of Solomon Islands to the International Court of Justice' (20 June 1995), para. 398 (note 212); 'Request by the World Health Organization for an Advisory Opinion on the Legality of the Use of Nuclear Weapons in View of their Effects on Human Health and the Environment – Further Written Observations Submitted by the Government of Solomon Islands to the International Court of Justice' (20 June 1995), paras. 4.94–6 (notes 68 and 74); oral submission presented by the representative of the Government of Mexico (H.E. Ambassador Sergio Gonzalez Galvez, Undersecretary of Foreign Relations) at the public sitting of 3 Nov. 1995 (uncorrected Verbatim Record, CR 95/25), p. 60; oral submission presented by the representative of the Government of the Philippines (Mr Merlin M Magallona, Agent) at the public sitting of 9 Nov. 1995 (uncorrected Verbatim Record, CR 95/28), pp. 78–9. (The writer is grateful to Mr Eduardo Valencia-Ospina, Registrar of the International Court, for providing him with a copy of the mimeographed text of the written observations, and to Dr Laurence Boisson de Chazournes, formerly Assistant Professor, Graduate Institute of International Studies, Geneva, for providing him with a copy of the uncorrected Verbatim Record.)

pleadings),[51] and in the judgments and advisory opinions of other courts.[52] Some of these instances will be discussed in the course of this work.

In the international literature, the picture is composite. In the legal writings of some countries, the concept is mentioned or examined in general treatises on public international law,[53] and in the very few works that have been expressly dedicated to the subject.[54] In the scientific production of

[51] See, for example, 'Letter dated 29 August 1980 from the Chairman of the Group of 77 to the President of the Conference' (Doc.A/Conf.62/106), *III United Nations Conference on the Law of the Sea. Official Records*, xiv, pp. 111–14.

[52] See, for example, Inter-American Court of Human Rights, *Interpretation of the American Declaration of the Rights and Duties of Man Within the Framework of Article 64 of the American Convention on Human Rights*, Advisory Opinion OC–10/89 of 14 July 1989, Series A No. 10, para. 38.

[53] Besides the pages from *Oppenheim's International Law* cited in the Preface, above, see for example Brownlie, *Principles*, pp. xlvii and 598 (including note 2); Cassese, *International Law in a Divided World* (Oxford, 1986), pp. 28–30; Ott, *Public International Law in the Modern World* (London, 1987), pp. 245 and 292; Wallace, R., *International Law. A Student Introduction*, 2nd edn. (London, 1992), p. 171; Henkin, Pugh, Schachter and Smit, *International Law Cases and Materials*, 3rd edn. (St. Paul, Minn., 1993), pp. 555–8; Combacau and Sur, *Droit international public*, 2nd edn. (Paris, 1995), pp. 533–5, 542–3, 686; Dupuy, P. M., *Droit international public*, 3rd edn. (Paris, 1995), pp. 284 (para. 356), 319–21 (para. 403), 363–4 (para. 457), 377 (para. 477) and 459–61 (para. 554); Nguyen Quoc Dinh, Daillier and Pellet, *Droit international public*, 5th edn. (Paris, 1994), pp. 734–5 (para. 483) and 898–901 (para. 585); Reuter, *Droit international public*, 6th edn. (Paris, 1983), pp. 269–71; Verdross and Simma, *Universelles Völkerrecht*, 3rd edn. (Berlin, 1984), pp. 40–1; Podesta Costa and Ruda, *Derecho internacional publico*, updated edn. (Buenos Aires, 1984), ii, pp. 203–4; Carrillo Salcedo, *Curso de derecho internacional publico* (Madrid, 1991), pp. 204–7; Diez de Velasco Vallejo, *Instituciones de derecho internacional publico*, i, 10th edn. (Madrid, 1994), pp. 78, 85, 709 and 728–31; Gonzalez Campos, Sanchez Rodriguez and Andres Saenz de Santa Maria, *Curso de derecho internacional publico*, 5th edn. (Madrid, 1992), pp. 301–6; Pastor Ridruejo, *Curso de derecho internacional publico y organizaciones internacionales*, 6th edn. (Madrid, 1996), pp. 68 and 573–7; Giuliano, Scovazzi and Treves, *Diritto internazionale. Parte generale*, 3rd edn. (Milan, 1991), pp. 484–92; Conforti, *Diritto internazionale*, 4th edn. (Naples, 1992), pp. 363–6; Da Silva Cunha, *Direito Internacional Publico. Introduçao e Fontes*, 5th edn. (Coimbra, 1991), p. 25. As will be seen from several citations throughout this work, references to the concept of obligations *erga omnes* appear also in many of the general courses given at the Hague Academy after 1970. Among these, the most extensive treatment is to be found in the general courses given by Schachter in 1982 (see its revised edition, published as a separate volume headed *International Law in Theory and Practice* (Dordrecht, 1991), pp. 196–8, 208–13, 342–5 and 381–3) and Weil in 1992 ('Le droit international', pp. 284–91 specifically, and the whole of chapter VII (pp. 261–312) for the wider phenomenon of what Weil calls 'supernorms', or 'normes à autorité renforcée').

[54] See Juste Ruiz, 'Las obligaciones "erga omnes" en derecho internacional publico', *Estudios de Derecho Internacional. Homenaje al Profesor Miaja de la Muela* (Madrid, 1979), i, pp. 219–33; Frowein, 'Die Verpflichtungen erga omnes im Völkerrecht und ihre Durchsetzung', *Völkerrecht als Rechtsordnung. Internationale Gerichtsbarkeit. Menschenrechte. Festschrift für Hermann Mosler* (Berlin, 1983), pp. 241–62; Picone, 'Obblighi reciproci ed obblighi *erga omnes* degli Stati nel campo della protezione internazionale dell'ambiente marino dall'inquinamento', Starace (ed.), *Diritto internazionale e protezione dell'ambiente marino* (Milan, 1983), pp. 15–135; Casado Raigon, 'Las obligaciones "erga omnes" en el derecho internacional contemporaneo', 6 *La Ley* (29 Jan. 1985, No. 1120), pp. 1–4; Annacker, *Die Durchsetzung von erga omnes Verpflichtungen vor dem Internationalen Gerichtshof* (Hamburg, 1994); ea., 'The Legal Régime of *Erga Omnes* Obligations in International Law', 46 *Austrian Journal of Public and International Law* (1994), pp. 131–66. To these writings, one should add Weil, 'Towards Relative Normativity in International Law?', 77 *A.J.I.L.* (1983), pp. 413–42 (an article dealing

some other countries, the concept has not yet found its 'consecration' in the general treatises,[55] but is occasionally discussed in monographs on various international topics.[56]

Most often, the subject of obligations *erga omnes* has been approached from the perspective of a particular area of the law (mainly, but not exclusively, the law of international human rights), or by reference to other concepts.[57] In particular, an extensive literature has been evolving on the

extensively, though not exclusively, with obligations *erga omnes*). In the *Encyclopedia of Public International Law*, there is regrettably no separate article on obligations *erga omnes*, but various articles are relevant to the concept, above all: Mosler, 'International Legal Community', Heidelberg *Encycl.*, vii, pp. 309–12; Jaenicke, 'International Public Order', ibid., vii, pp. 314–18; Frowein, 'Jus cogens', ibid., vii, pp. 327–30. For bibliographical references on the relationship between the concepts of obligations *erga omnes* and norms of *jus cogens*, and between the concepts of obligations *erga omnes* and *actio popularis*, see, respectively, sections I and VI of Chapter 10, below.

55 For example, with respect to the Russian (and formerly Soviet) literature, the writer could not find any reference to the concept of obligations *erga omnes* in Kudriavtsev (ed.), *Kurs mezhdunarodnogo prava v semi tomakh* (Moscow, 1989–93), or in any of the most recent editions of treatises on public international law such as Ignatenko (ed.), *Mezhdunarodnoe pravo*, 2nd edn. (Moscow, 1995); Kolosov and Kusnetsov (eds.), *Mezhdunarodnoe pravo* (Moscow, 1995). Likewise, in two examples from the literature of former socialist States, there is no discussion of the concept of obligations *erga omnes* in either Bierzanek and Symonides, *Prawo miedzynarodowe publiczne*, 3rd edn. (Warsaw, 1994), or Diaconu, *Curs de drept international public*, 2nd edn. (Bucharest, 1995).

56 See, for example, in the Russian literature, Lukashuk, *Funktsionirovanie mezhdunarodnogo prava* (Moscow, 1992), especially pp. 43–4 (including note 34 for bibliographical references), 101 and 114; Movchan, *Mezhdunarodnyi pravoporiadok* (Moscow, 1996), p. 70. In the Polish literature, see Czaplinski, *Skutki prawne nielegalnego uzycia sily w stosunkach miedzynarodowych* (Warsaw, 1993) (*International Legal Effects of the Illegal Use of Force*, in Polish, with English summary), pp. 104–6, 154–90 (with a discussion of the concepts of obligations *erga omnes*, *actio popularis* and international crimes in the context of the illegal use of force) and 229–3, paras. 3.3 and 4.4 (with an English summary of the chapters containing the pages of the book referred to above). See also Mik, 'On the Specific Character of State Obligations in the Field of Human Rights', 20 *P.Y.I.L.* (1993), pp. 129–33.

57 See, for example, International Law Association, *Report of the Sixty-first Conference held at Paris. August 26th to September 1st, 1984* (Aberystwyth, 1985), p. 82; Hanz, *Zur völkerrechtlichen Aktivlegitimation zum Schutze der Menschenrechte* (Munich, 1985), pp. 72–4 and 110–17; Bryde, 'Verpflichtungen Erga Omnes aus Menschenrechten', *Multilaterale Staatsverträge erga omnes und deren Inkorporation in nationale IPR-Kodifikationen—Vor- und Nachteile einer solchen Rezeption* (Heidelberg, 1986), pp. 165–90 (with English summary); Cocuzza, 'State Involvement in Terrorist Activities and Economic Sanctions: The Libyan Case', 7 *The Italian Yearbook of International Law* (1986–1987), pp. 209–15; Macdonald, 'The Principle of Solidarity in Public International Law', Dominicé, Patry and Reymond (eds.), *Etudes de droit international en l'honneur de Pierre Lalive* (Basel and Frankfurt, 1993), pp. 276–7 and 285; Vierdag, 'Some Remarks about Special Features of Human Rights Treaties', 25 *Netherlands Yearbook of International Law* (1994), p. 129; Francioni, 'Patrimonio comune della cultura. Sovranità e conflitti armati', 106 *Studi senesi* (1994), pp. 18–19; Provost, 'Reciprocity in Human Rights and Humanitarian Law', 65 *B.Y.I.L.* (1994), especially pp. 385–7; Oellers-Frahm, 'Die Einsetzung des "Internationalen Tribunals über Kriegsverbrechen im ehemaligen Jugoslawien" durch den Sicherheitsrat', Beyerlin, Bothe, Hofmann and Petersmann (eds.), *Recht. Festschrift Bernhardt*, pp. 747–9; Bleckmann, 'General Theory of Obligations under Public International Law', 38 *G.Y.I.L.* (1995), pp. 32-3; Weisburd, 'The Effect of Treaties and Other Formal International Acts On the Customary Law of Human Rights', 25 *Georgia Journal of International and Comparative Law* (1995/96), pp. 106–8;

relationship between the concepts of obligations *erga omnes* and international crimes of States.[58] Although some of the arguments developed by the parties in the *Barcelona Traction* case already foreshadowed a distinction between international delicts and international crimes (as was mentioned in the previous section of this chapter), it is indisputable that the dictum on obligations *erga omnes* has had a decisive influence on the refinement of this distinction by the International Law Commission in its codification of the law of State responsibility.[59] In particular, this influence is reflected in the list of examples of international crimes provided by the International Law Commission, which includes:

(a) a serious breach of an international obligation of essential importance for the maintenance of international peace and security, such as that prohibiting aggression;
(b) a serious breach of an international obligation of essential importance for safeguarding the right of self-determination of peoples, such as that prohibiting the establishment or maintenance by force of colonial domination;
(c) a serious breach on a widespread scale of an international obligation of essential importance for safeguarding the human being, such as those prohibiting slavery, genocide, *apartheid*;
(d) a serious breach of an international obligation of essential importance for the safeguarding and preservation of the human environment, such as those prohibiting massive pollution of the atmosphere or of the seas.[60]

To sum up, there is a tendency, in the international literature, to dilute the examination of obligations *erga omnes* by referring to other concepts

Nakatani, 'Economic Sanctions and Compliance: Theoretical Aspects' (paper submitted to the American Society of International Law/Japanese Association of International Law/Canadian Council of International Law (ASIL/JAIL/CCIL) Joint Meeting—Atlanta, 25 March 1996), para. 4.1.B.

[58] In addition to the writings on international crimes that are cited below in this section (most of which contain references to obligations *erga omnes*), see Picone, 'Interventi delle Nazioni Unite e obblighi *erga omnes*', Picone (ed.), *Interventi delle Nazioni Unite e diritto internazionale* (Milan, 1995), pp. 517–78; de Hoogh, *Obligations 'Erga Omnes' and International Crimes. A Theoretical Inquiry into the Implementation and Enforcement of the International Responsibility of States* (The Hague, 1996).

[59] This remark is made, for example, in Jiménez de Aréchaga, 'The Work and the Jurisprudence of the International Court of Justice 1947–1986', 58 *B.Y.I.L.* (1987), pp. 21–2; Ruda, 'Some of the Contributions of the International Court of Justice to the Development of International Law', 24 *N.Y.U.J.I.L.P.* (1991), pp. 53–5. In justifying the distinction between international crimes and international delicts, Ago's 'Fifth Report on State responsibility' (Doc.A/CN.4/291, and Add. 1 and 2) referred extensively to the concept of obligations *erga omnes*.

[60] Text adopted by the International Law Commission upon completion of its first reading of Part I of the draft Articles on State responsibility. The text of the draft Articles is reproduced in Brownlie, *Basic Documents*, pp. 426–37. Among the many writings on international crimes, see Graefrath, Oeser and Steiniger, 'Internationale Verbrechen—Internationale Delikte', 22 *Deutsche Aussenpolitik* (1977), pp. 90–101; Marek, 'Criminalizing State Responsibility', 14 *Revue belge de droit international* (1978–79), pp. 460–85; Dupuy, P. M., 'Observations sur le "crime international de l'Etat"', 84 *R.G.D.I.P.* (1980), pp. 449–86; Cardona Llorens, 'La responsabilidad internacional por violacion grave de obligaciones

and, when specifically discussing obligations *erga omnes*, to concentrate on their corresponding rights and remedies. As a result of this attitude, almost thirty years after the International Court's dictum in the *Barcelona Traction* case the very concept of obligations *erga omnes* still lacks a precise definition. Hence the need to address this topic.

The complexity and novelty of the subject suggest a cautious approach. Whenever definite answers would be premature, the writer will restrict his contribution to providing elements for discussion; whenever bolder statements are legitimate, the writer will put forward his views while respecting any contrary opinions. Perhaps the words used by Lesky in the preface to his history of Greek literature can be repeated here, because they capture the spirit that also animates the present work:

> An author's right to his own opinion can always be reconciled with the appreciation of other points of view, and often enough it becomes the scholar's duty to confess either that we simply do not know or that there is still doubt.[61]

esenciales para la salvaguarda de intereses fundamentales de la comunidad internacional (el "crimen internacional")', 8 *Anuario de derecho internacional* (1985), pp. 265–336; Carella, *La responsibilità dello Stato per crimini internazionali* (Naples, 1985); Cassese, 'Remarks on the Present Legal Regulation of Crimes of States', *International Law at the Time of its Codification. Essays in Honour of Roberto Ago* (Milan, 1987), iii, pp. 49–64; Conforti, 'In tema di responsabilità degli Stati per crimini internazionali', ibid., pp. 99–111; Rigaux, 'Le crime d'Etat. Réflexions sur l'article 19 du projet d'articles sur la responsabilité des Etats', ibid., pp. 301–25; Sahovic, 'Le concept du crime international de l'Etat et le développement du droit international', ibid., pp. 364–9; Gilbert, 'The Criminal Responsibility of States', 39 *I.C.L.Q.* (1990), pp. 345–69; Rosenstock, 'Crimes of States—an Essay', Ginther, Hafner, Lang, Neuhold and Sucharipa-Behrmann (eds.), *Völkerrecht zwischen normativen Anspruch und politischer Realität. Festschrift für Karl Zemanek zum 65. Geburtstag* (Berlin, 1994), pp. 319–34. More generally, on the responsibility for breach, and on the enforcement, of obligations *erga omnes*, see Starace, 'La responsabilité résultant de la violation des obligations à l'égard de la communauté internationale', 153 Hague *Recueil* (1976, IV), pp. 265–317; Frowein, 'Collective Enforcement of International Obligations', 47 *Z.a.ö.R.V.* (1987), pp. 73–8; id., *International Law in the Period after Decolonization* (Lagos, 1988), pp. 7–11; id., 'Reactions by Not Directly Affected States to Breaches of Public International Law', 248 Hague *Recueil* (1994, IV), especially pp. 405–22; Focarelli, 'Le contromisure pacifiche collettive e la nozione di obblighi *erga omnes*', 76 *Riv. dir. int.* (1993), pp. 52–72; Alland, *Justice privée et ordre juridique international. Etude théorique des contre-mesures en droit international public* (Paris, 1994), pp. 352–7. Those who (unlike the present writer) can read Japanese can also refer to Nakatani, 'The Functions and the Legality of Economic Sanctions under International Law—A Study of the Legal Consequences of International Wrongful Acts' (published in six parts in vols. 100 and 101 of *Kokka Gakkai Zassi—The Journal of the Association of Political and Social Sciences* (1987 and 1988)), especially chapter 1, sections 2 and 3; chapter 2, section 1.

[61] *A History of Greek Literature*, English trans. Willis and de Heer of the second German edition, 1963 (London, 1966), p. xiv. In the German original of the first edition, the passage reads as follows: 'Das Recht des Autors, seine eigene Stellung zu vertreten, ist mit der Würdigung anderer Sehweise durchaus vereinbar, und nicht selten wird auch das Einbekenntnis unseres Nichtwissens oder nicht gelöster Zweifel zur wissenschaftlichen Pflicht.' (*Geschichte der griechischen Literatur* (Bern, 1957–8), p. 8.)

V. Conclusions

The main conclusion that can be drawn from the analysis developed in this introductory chapter is that the International Court's pronouncement on obligations *erga omnes*, while *obiter dictum*, (a) addressed some arguments put forward by the parties in their pleadings, (b) was unanimously endorsed by the members of the International Court, and (c) has been acquiring increasing influence ever since the judgment in the *Barcelona Traction* case. From this, it follows that the real issue is to elucidate the concept of obligations *erga omnes* rather than undertake a fruitless discussion on the formal authority of the International Court's pronouncement in which it first appeared.

The dictum in the *Barcelona Traction* case identifies two characteristic features of obligations *erga omnes*. The first one is *universality*, in the sense that obligations *erga omnes* are binding on all States without exception. The second one is *solidarity*, in the sense that every State is deemed to have a legal interest in their protection. Of these two characteristic elements, the second one (solidarity) is linked with wider issues of enforcement and legal standing in international law. The first one (universality), which has been unduly neglected in the international literature (at least in the specific context of obligations *erga omnes*), raises complex theoretical problems. In particular, it appears difficult to reconcile this element with the structure of international society, which is composed of independent entities giving rise, as a rule, to legal relations on a consensual basis.

The concept of obligations *erga omnes* does not represent, though, the first attempt to go beyond reciprocal relations among States based on consent. Therefore, it is appropriate to examine, as a starting point of this work, a few selected 'prefigurations' of obligations *erga omnes*.

2

Selected Prefigurations of the Concept of Obligations *Erga Omnes*: (a) State Servitude, Permanent Dedication, International Status and Objective Regime

I. Introduction

The question that will be addressed in this chapter and the next is the following: to what extent do some notions of international law, which predate the judgment in the *Barcelona Traction* case, contain elements of analogy with the concept of obligations *erga omnes*? The assumption behind this question is that, while the concept of obligations *erga omnes* has a relatively short history, it has a much longer prehistory. This assumption seems to be justified in light of the considerations developed in Chapter 1, above, with respect to the background to the International Court's dictum.

The term 'prefigurations' in the heading of the present chapter is shorthand for certain notions employed to protect or promote the common interests of States, beyond strict considerations of reciprocity. There is no need to stress that these prefigurations will be discussed within the narrow limits of what may be helpful to understand better the concept of obligations *erga omnes*.

Any selection of prefigurations is bound to be somewhat arbitrary, as many more notions and institutions than those that will be discussed in this work can claim some affinities with the concept of obligations *erga omnes*. Despite this inevitable component of arbitrariness, the selection has been based on three main criteria.

The first criterion is that the only prefigurations that will be discussed here are those to which States have referred in their diplomatic relations or pleaded before international tribunals. This restriction is not meant to deny that the concept of obligations *erga omnes* also has a long prehistory in the world of ideas.[1] However, the very nature of the present monograph, which

[1] This observation is all the more relevant because, as will become clearer in the course of this work, the concept of obligations *erga omnes* aims at safeguarding and promoting those same human values which, as Peirano Basso has correctly remarked, belong to the very foundation of international law. ('Naturaleza y fundamento del derecho internacional publico', *International Law. Liber Jiménez de Aréchaga*, i, pp. 205–6.)

is a work of international law rather than jurisprudence or legal history, implies that this broader line of enquiry cannot be pursued here.

The second criterion is one of economy. Among the prefigurations, some writers[2] have referred, for example, to a passage from an advisory opinion in which the International Court wrote that the 'vast majority of the members of the international community' can bring about an entity endowed with 'objective international personality'.[3] Irrespective of the question whether this pronouncement is at all relevant to the concept of obligations *erga omnes* (a question that is further complicated by the intrinsic difficulties of interpretation of this pronouncement),[4] the fact is that its discussion would require a thorough analysis of the law of international legal persons, with the unavoidable consequence of spending long pages on tangential issues. For this reason, possible prefigurations such as this one will not be discussed in this work.

The third criterion is a practical one. As was mentioned in the introductory chapter, Schwarzenberger used the expression 'obligations *erga omnes*' in his examination of international servitudes, and Lachs used it in the context of objective regimes. These two notions of international servitude and objective regime are therefore obvious candidates for consideration in this chapter.[5] Their discussion will also refer, however briefly, to permanent dedication and international status.

II. The Concept of Servitude and, in Particular, of State Servitude

The concept of servitude has its origins in Roman law. In a wide sense (which apparently developed late), the term denotes all kinds of encumbrance over a piece of property, other than natural restrictions, that limit

[2] See, for example, Juste Ruiz, 'Las obligaciones "erga omnes"', pp. 220–1.

[3] *Reparation for Injuries Suffered in the Service of the United Nations, Advisory Opinion*, I.C.J. Reports 1949, p. 185 ('. . . the Court's opinion is that fifty States, representing the vast majority of the members of the international community, had the power, in conformity with international law, to bring into being an entity possessing objective international personality, and not merely personality recognized by them alone, together with capacity to bring international claims').

[4] Quadri has written that the International Court's pronouncement reproduced in footnote 3, above, is 'equivocal'. (*Diritto internazionale pubblico*, 5th edn. (Naples, 1968), p. 182.) On the legal personality of international organizations, including an examination of the above-cited passage from the *Reparation* case, see Amerasinghe, *Principles of the institutional law of international organizations* (Cambridge, 1996), pp. 67–104.

[5] The relevance of these concepts to a study of obligations *erga omnes* should not be surprising. Judge Weeramantry has highlighted the importance of the concept of sevitude (as a term of analogy) for the study of rights other than property rights (such as human rights). (See his separate opinion in *Application of the Convention on the Prevention and Punishment of the Crime of Genocide*, Preliminary Objections, I.C.J. Reports 1996 (mimeographed text), p. 9.)

the owner's rights.[6] In this sense, servitudes are rights *in rem* (absolute rights) or *in re aliena* (real rights).[7] As absolute rights, they are opposable to the world at large, apart from exemptions resting on a particular title.[8] As real rights, they give rise to a special relation between a person and a tangible thing and are not affected by changes of ownership, so that the right can be said to 'run' with the encumbered thing.

Servitudes are usually distinguished into two categories: real servitudes and personal servitudes. A real or praedial servitude ('*servitus praediorum*'), like an easement or profit in the common law,[9] is a burden laid upon a piece of land ('*praedium serviens*') for the benefit of another piece of land ('*praedium dominans*') belonging to a different owner. The essentials of a real servitude are the following: (a) the charge is not imposed for the benefit of an individual as such, but of an individual as the owner of the dominant estate, so that it can metaphorically be said that the relationship is between two pieces of land (this is the so-called 'praedial element'); (b) as it inheres in the land, the servitude passes over with the land (both dominant and servient estates) to third parties or successors; and (c) the dominant and servient owners must be different persons,[10] otherwise the servitude would terminate by operation of law (consolidation or confusion). If the dominant and servient tenements belong to the same owner, the right of property accounts for any utility derived from the servient estate. Sometimes, perpetuity ('*perpetua causa*') and vicinity ('*praedia vicina esse debent*') are also listed among the essential elements of a servitude, but on closer inspection they do not seem to be independent requisites; they are rather evidence that a relationship exists between two pieces of land.

[6] See Grosso, *Le servitù prediali nel diritto romano* (Turin, 1969), pp. 4–6. In classic Roman law, there were '*servitutes*', but no unified concept of '*servitus*' (Giorgianni, *L'obbligazione (la parte generale delle obbligazioni)* (Milan, 1968), p. 9).

[7] There is no agreement on terminology. See Austin, *Lectures on Jurisprudence or the Philosophy of Positive Law*, 5th edn. Campbell (London, 1885), pp. 364–92; *Salmond on Jurisprudence*, 12th edn. Fitzgerald (London, 1996), pp. 235–8; Hohfeld, *Fundamental Legal Conceptions as Applied in Judicial Reasoning and Other Legal Essays*, Cook ed. (New Haven, 1920), pp. 65–114; Honoré, 'Rights of Exclusion and Immunities against Divesting', 34 *Tulane Law Review* (1960), pp. 453–68; Lawson, 'Rights and Other Relations *in rem*', *Many Laws. Selected Essays* (Amsterdam, 1977), i, pp. 2–22.

[8] 'Title' denotes those 'facts or events by reason of which the right has become vested in its owner' (*Salmond on Jurisprudence*, p. 221). A similar definition appears in the *Dictionnaire de la Terminologie du Droit international* (Paris, 1960), p. 604.

[9] For the 'resemblance' between praedial servitudes in Roman law and easements and profits in the common law, see Buckland and McNair, *Roman Law and Common Law. A Comparison in Outline*, 2nd edn. revised by Lawson (Cambridge, 1965), pp. 127–42. On the concept of easement, and the distinction between easement and profit, see *Gale on Easements*, 15th edn. Maurice (London, 1986), pp. 3–36.

[10] '[*N*]*ulli enim res sua servit*' (*The Digest of Justinian*, i, p. 256 (D.8.2.26, *Paulus libro quinto decimum ad Sabimum*); 'you cannot have an easement over your own land' (*Metropolitan Ry. Co.* v. *Fowler* [1892] 1 Q.B. 165, 171, *per* Esher M.R.). A servitude requires also that the right-holder has no possession of the servient tenement, otherwise there would not be a servitude, but a lease.

The other category is that of personal servitudes. A personal servitude is an absolute right that inheres in a person as such, and not as the owner of a certain piece of property.[11] In a personal servitude, there is no praedial element. From this it follows that a personal servitude, in which the thing serves the interest of a person and not of another tenement, does not survive the death of the right-holder or, when the beneficiary is a legal person, the passage of a certain period of time. A sub-category of personal servitudes is that of public servitudes, which are burdens upon a piece of land for the benefit of the general public, a group of individuals or their representative body. Examples are the right of the public to a highway over private land or the right of the public to navigate a river, the bed of which belongs to a private person.[12]

Whether the concept of servitude has a place in international law is controversial.[13] In the international literature, references to the term date back

[11] In Roman law, examples of personal servitudes are '*usufructus*', '*usus*' and '*habitatio*', which, according to Paton (*A Textbook of Jurisprudence*, 4th edn. Paton and Derham (Oxford, 1972), p. 525), appear in postclassical writings.

[12] See *Salmond on Jurisprudence*, p. 427–8.

[13] See Klüber, *Droit des gens moderne de l'Europe*, i (Stuttgart, 1819), pp. 214–20; de Martens, *Précis du Droit des gens*, i (Paris, 1831), pp. 262–4; Heffter, *Le Droit international public de l'Europe*, French trans. Bergson (Berlin and Paris, 1857), pp. 98–102; Bluntschli, *Le Droit international codifié*, French trans. Lardy (Paris, 1870), pp. 199–202; Phillimore, *Commentaries upon International Law*, 3rd edn., i (London, 1879), pp. 388–92; Bello, D. A., *Principios de derecho internacional*, i (Madrid, 1883), pp. 110–13; Rivier, *Principes du Droit des gens*, i (Paris, 1896), pp. 294–303; Westlake, *International Law*, i (Cambridge, 1910), pp. 60–1 and 294–5; Fauchille, *Traité de Droit international public*, i (Paris, 1922), pp. 676–84; von Liszt, *Le Droit international. Exposé systématique*, French trans. Gidel and Alcindor of the 9th German edn. of 1913 (Paris, 1927), pp. 80–2 (and pp. 131–4 in the last German edition of this work, edited by Fleischmann in 1925); Scelle, *Précis de droit des gens. Principes et systématique*, i (Paris, 1932), pp. 113–17; Cavaglieri, *Corso di diritto internazionale*, 3rd edn. (Naples, 1934) pp. 297–9; Accioly, *Traité de droit international public*, French trans. Goulé of the first Portuguese edition, 1933–5 (Paris, 1940–2), i, pp. 252–5; Hyde, *International Law Chiefly as Interpreted and Applied by the United States*, i (Boston, 1947), pp. 510–15; Barros Jarpa, *Derecho internacional publico* (Santiago de Chile, 1955), pp. 239–43; Dahm, *Völkerrecht*, i (Stuttgart, 1958), pp. 547–53; Sereni, *Diritto internazionale*, ii (Milan, 1958), pp. 627–9; Moreno Quintana, *Tratado de derecho internacional*, i (Buenos Aires, 1963), pp. 325–6; Fenwick, *International Law*, 4th edn. (New York, 1965), pp. 458–82; Kelsen, *Principles of International Law*, 2nd edn. Tucker (New York, 1966), pp. 484–6; Cansacchi, *Istituzioni di diritto internazionale pubblico*, 6th edn. Cansacchi and Marazzi (Turin, 1967), pp. 157–60; François, *Grondlijnen van het Volkenrecht*, 3rd edn. (Zwolle, 1967), pp. 56–60, Verzijl, *International Law in Historical Perspective*, iii (Leiden, 1970), pp. 413–28; Monaco, *Manuale di diritto internazionale pubblico*, 2nd edn. (Turin, 1971), pp. 421–2; Rousseau, *Droit international public*, iii (Paris, 1977), pp. 43–6; McDougal and Reisman, *International Law in Contemporary Perspective: The Public Order of the World Community. Cases and Materials* (Mineola, New York, 1981), pp. 745–61; Arellano Garcia, *Derecho internacional publico*, i (Mexico City, 1983), pp. 778–80; Verdross and Simma, *Universelles Völkerrecht*, pp. 638–9; Brownlie, *Principles*, pp. 374–7; *Oppenheim's International Law*, i, pp. 670–6; Kapoor, *International Law*, 9th edn. (Allahabad, 1992), pp. 234–5; Nguyen Quoc Dinh, Daillier and Pellet, *Droit international public*, pp. 468–9 (para. 320); *Starke's International Law*, 11th edn. Shearer (London, 1994), pp. 179–80; Detter, *The International Legal Order* (Aldershot, 1994), pp. 342–4. Among the various monographs and articles, see Reid, *International Servitudes in Law and Practice* (Chicago, 1932); Mercier, *Les Servitudes Internationales* (Lausanne, 1939); Vali, *Servitudes of*

to classic works such as those by Grotius, Wolff and Vattel.[14] However, no generally accepted definition of the concept and scope of State servitude has ever emerged. Some, like Hall,[15] include in the definition the natural restrictions on territorial sovereignty (the so-called '*servitutes juris gentium necessariae*'), such as the right of innocent passage through the territorial sea or the rights and obligations of neighbourhood. Others, like Oppenheim,[16] restrict the definition to those encumbrances by which a State territory, or part of it, serves a certain purpose or interest of another State. Guggenheim,[17] while indicating some core elements attaching to the concept, does not commit himself to any definition. To sum up, if one were to compile a table of the views expressed in the international literature, it would be difficult to draw a coherent conclusion on what the expression 'State servitude' means and to which situations it applies.

Nor does a clearer idea derive from the analysis of the practice of States and international decisions. Verosta once cited an example of State servitude dating back to the sixth century.[18] However, apart from occasional references—for example, in the correspondence between Spain and Portugal on a question relating to fisheries,[19] or in the Proposal of the President of the United States to the Governments of Chile and Peru regarding the

International Law, 2nd edn. (London, 1958); Potter, 'The Doctrine of Servitudes in International Law', 9 *A.J.I.L.* (1915), pp. 627–41; McNair, 'So-called State Servitudes', 6 *B.Y.I.L.* (1925), pp. 111–27; Crusen, 'Les Servitudes Internationales', 22 Hague *Recueil* (1928, II), pp. 5–79; O'Connell, 'A Reconsideration of the Doctrine of International Servitude', 30 *The Canadian Bar Review* (1952), pp. 807–18; Wyrozumska, 'Problem istnienia w prawie miedzynarodowym publicznym sluzebnosci miedzynarodowego', 7 *Acta Universitatis Lodziensis. Folia Iuridica* (1982), pp. 71–96 (with English summary); Fastenrath, 'Servitudes', Heidelberg *Encycl.*, x, pp. 389–92; Marchisio, 'Servitù (diritto internazionale)', *Enciclopedia del diritto*, xlii (Milan, 1990), pp. 342–55. See also Lauterpacht, H., *Private Law Sources and Analogies of International Law* (London, 1927), pp. 119–24; Hostie, 'Examen de quelques règles du droit international dans le domaine des communications et du transit', 40 Hague *Recueil* (1932, II), pp. 446–9; Barile, *I diritti assoluti nell'ordinamento internazionale* (Milan, 1951), pp. 251–7.

[14] Grotius, *De jure belli ac pacis libri tres*, English trans. Kelsey of 1646 edition, Scott (ed.), *Classics of International Law* (Oxford, 1925), Bk. i, Ch. i, Section iv, and Bk. ii, Ch. iii, Section ii; Wolff, *Jus gentium methodo scientifica pertractatum*, English trans. Drake of 1764 edition, Scott (ed.), *Classics* (Oxford, 1934), Section 320; Vattel, *The Law of Nations or the Principles of Natural Law Applied to the Conduct and to the Affairs of Nations and of Sovereigns*, English trans. Fenwick of 1758 edition, Scott (ed.), *Classics* (Washington, D.C., 1902; reprinted New York and London, 1964), Bk. ii, Section 89.

[15] *A Treatise on International Law*, 8th edn. Higgins, A. P. (Oxford, 1924), pp. 203–5.

[16] *Oppenheim's International Law*, i, pp. 670–1. The definition given in the latest edition of Oppenheim's treatise is more cautious ('State servitudes is the term sometimes used to denote . . .') than the one given in the earlier edition (Oppenheim, *International Law. A Treatise*, i, 8th edn. Lauterpacht, H. (London, 1955), p. 536).

[17] *Traité de Droit international public*, i (Geneva, 1953), pp. 394–7.

[18] 'International Law in Europe and Western Asia between 100 and 650 A.D.', 113 Hague *Recueil* (1964, III), p. 610. (The example in question is a Roman–Persian treaty of 562 A.D.)

[19] See Bruns (ed.), *Fontes Juris Gentium*, Series B, Sectio i, Tomus ii, Pars i, p. 71.

territorial dispute of Tacna-Arica[20]—representatives of States have been reluctant to use the term. Perhaps, Sir William Snowdon Robson's remark that the idea of 'serving' another Government or property hurts the national pride[21] had some element of truth, and was not merely due to the 'forensic atmosphere' in which it was pronounced.[22]

On a few occasions, the question of State servitudes has arisen in cases before national[23] and international[24] tribunals. International tribunals have been very cautious: while not rejecting the concept as a matter of principle, they have invariably decided the disputes before them on other grounds. A classic example is the *North Atlantic Coast Fisheries Arbitration Case*,[25] which arose out of a difference between the United Kingdom and the United States on the interpretation and application of a treaty that granted certain fishing rights to the United States. After fully developed arguments by the parties, which probably constitute the most extensive discussion ever of State servitudes before an international tribunal,[26] the arbitral tribunal refused to regard the grant of fishing rights as a servitude.[27]

[20] The Proposal, dated 14 May 1929, is reproduced in 23 *A.J.I.L.* (1929), Suppl., pp. 183–4. In the Treaty that followed the Proposal ('Treaty between Chile and Peru for the Settlement of the Tacna-Arica Territorial Dispute with Supplementary Protocol, Lima, June 3, 1929', 130 *State Papers* (1929), i, pp. 463–6), the term 'servitude' does not appear. On the dispute, see Ulloa, *Derecho internacional publico*, 4th edn. (Madrid, 1957), pp. 497–510; Woolsey, 'The Tacna-Arica Settlement', 23 *A.J.I.L.* (1929), pp. 605–10.

[21] *Proceedings in the North Atlantic Coast Fisheries Arbitration before the Permanent Court of Arbitration at the Hague* (Washington, 1912), xi, pp. 1023–4.

[22] This reference to the 'forensic atmosphere' can be found in Lauterpacht, H., *Private Law Sources*, p. 241.

[23] See, for example, Supreme Court of Cologne (Seventh Civil Division), Dutch State Servitude in Prussia, 8 *A.J.I.L.* (1914), pp. 907–13; Appellate Court of Rome, *Foro Italiano* (1921), columns 309–11; Swiss Federal Court, *Canton of Thurgau* v. *Canton of St. Gallen*, 4 *Annual Digest* (1927–8), pp. 420–3.

[24] Apart from the cases to which more extensive reference will be made in this chapter, see the proceedings relating to the case of *Jurisdiction of the European Commission of the Danube*, P.C.I.J., Series C, No. 13(IV), i, p. 200; the opinion of Judge Nyholm in the *Free Zones of Upper Savoy and the District of Gex* case, Order of 19 August 1929, P.C.I.J., Series A, No. 22, p. 26; the dissenting opinion of Judge Moreno Quintana to the decision on the merits in the *Right of Passage over Indian Territory* case, I.C.J. Reports 1960, p. 90; the oral arguments in the same case, *I.C.J. Pleadings, Right of Passage over Indian Territory*, iv, pp. 266–9 (Bourquin), pp. 517–18 (Lalive d'Epinay), pp. 702–4 (Guggenheim).

[25] R.I.A.A., xi, p. 167.

[26] See *Proceedings in the North Atlantic Coast Fisheries Arbitration*, viii, pp. 16–31; xi, pp. 333–418, 1000–35 and 1284–8 (page numbers as in the original). Long extracts from the proceedings and the award are reproduced in Parry (ed.), *A British Digest of International Law*, 2b (London, 1967), pp. 378–405.

[27] The extent to which the arbitral award in the *North Atlantic Coast Fisheries Arbitration Case* amounts to an outright rejection of the concept of State servitude is discussed in *Oppenheim's International Law*, i, pp. 671–2. (See also Oppenheim, *International Law. A Treatise*, i, 8th edn. Lauterpacht, H., p. 537.) While both editions of Oppenheim's treatise take a cautious approach, the view that the arbitral award may be interpreted as rejecting the concept of State servitude is expressed, for example, in Cavaglieri, 'Règles générales du droit de la paix', 26 Hague *Recueil* (1929, I), p. 429.

While the concept has been and remains controversial, the situations in which it has been invoked present a real problem, which is relevant to the study of the concept of obligations *erga omnes*. The problem is to explain the grounds on which certain treaties have been held to establish obligations and confer rights valid for all States, irrespective of changes of sovereignty over the territories to which such rights and obligations relate. Two instances in which this problem has arisen are the *Wimbledon* case and a dispute relating to the Aaland Islands.

III. The Concept of Permanent Dedication to the Use of the Whole World (the *Wimbledon* Case)

In 1921 the *Wimbledon*, a British vessel chartered by a French company, was proceeding to the Polish city of Danzig with a cargo of military material for the Polish Government. To reach Danzig, the *Wimbledon* demanded access to the Kiel Canal, an artificial waterway connecting the Baltic Sea with the North Sea. While the Kiel Canal is entirely on German territory, the German Government had unilaterally opened it for passage by the merchant ships of all nations. With respect to all ships alike (including warships), Article 380 of the Peace Treaty of Versailles of 28 June 1919 provided that the Kiel Canal would remain 'free and open to the vessels of commerce and war of all nations at peace with Germany on terms of entire equality.'[28] The German authorities refused the *Wimbledon* access to the Kiel Canal on the ground that Poland and Russia were at war and that German neutrality regulations forbade the transit across Germany of war material destined for these two countries, even if neither country was at war with Germany.

Under Article 386 of the Peace Treaty of Versailles, 'any interested Power' could bring an action for breach of any conditions provided in Articles 380 to 386 of the Peace Treaty. Upon this jurisdictional ground, Great Britain, France, Italy and Japan, as Principal Allied Powers, instituted joint proceedings against Germany.[29] They asked the Permanent Court of International Justice to adjudge that Germany was wrong in refus-

[28] Relevant extracts from the Peace Treaty are reproduced in the Application instituting proceedings in the *Wimbledon* case before the Permanent Court of International Justice, Judgments, 1923, P.C.I.J., Series A, No. 1, p. 6. On the *Wimbledon* case, see von Münch, 'The Wimbledon', Heidelberg *Encycl.*, ii, pp. 293–6.

[29] On 22 May 1923, Poland applied for permission to intervene in the proceedings (Judgments, 1923, P.C.I.J., Series A, No. 1, pp. 9–10). The intervention of Poland was accepted by the Permanent Court on 28 June 1928 on the basis of Article 63 of the Statute of the Permanent Court, rather than Article 62 as Poland had originally requested (ibid., pp. 11–14). For comment, see Salvioli, 'La jurisprudence de la Cour permanente de Justice internationale', 12 Hague *Recueil* (1926, II), pp. 12–13. On the two different procedures of intervention under Articles 62 and 63, see the brief considerations developed in Scerni, 'La procédure de la Cour permanente de Justice internationale', 65 ibid. (1938, III), pp. 648–9.

ing the *Wimbledon* access to the Kiel Canal and that it should make reparation for the loss incurred by the vessel.

By a majority vote (Judges Anzilotti, Huber and Schücking dissenting), the Permanent Court held that the applicants' claim was well founded and that the German Government was bound to make good the prejudice suffered by the vessel. In its decision, the Permanent Court addressed the issue of the legal standing of the four applicant States and observed that

> each of the four Applicant Powers has a clear interest in the execution of the provisions relating to the Kiel Canal, since they all possessed fleets and merchant vessels flying their respective flags.[30]

This passage is interesting for the purposes of the present work, because there may seem to be an element of analogy between the notion of 'interested Power' and the concept of a State interested in the protection of obligations *erga omnes*. However, the analogy is only apparent. In fact, in the case of obligations *erga omnes*, a legal interest is deemed to be vested in all States by operation of general international law. On the contrary, in the *Wimbledon* case, the existence of a legal interest depended on the interpretation of a conventional rule, which alone was the ground for the institution of the legal proceedings.

The Permanent Court then addressed the central question of the case, namely whether Germany was entitled to refuse access to and passage through the Kiel Canal. On this point, the Permanent Court remarked that, by adopting Article 380, the parties to the Peace Treaty of Versailles had meant to facilitate the access to the Baltic for the benefit of all nations. As a means to this end, they had established an 'international regime' (in the French authoritative text of the judgment, a 'stipulation d'ordre international') for the Kiel Canal, by virtue of which the Kiel Canal would always remain open to foreign vessels.[31] In this context, the Permanent Court examined the argument, which was fully explored by Judge Schücking in his dissenting opinion,[32] according to which the right of passage through the Kiel Canal should be construed as a State servitude incumbent on Germany. If this was the case, then this servitude, like all restrictions on sovereignty, should be interpreted restrictively, with the result that the right of passage through the Kiel Canal could not affect the rights attaching to German neutrality.

[30] Judgments, 1923, P.C.I.J., Series A, No. 1, p. 20. The French authoritative text reads as follows: 'chaqune des Puissances demanderesses a un intérêt évident à l'exécution des stipulations qui concernent le Canal de Kiel, puisqu'elles ont toutes des flottes et des navires marchands battant leur pavillon.'

[31] Ibid., p. 23. Sometimes riparian States have been held to be under a duty to allow free navigation of a river even outside any contractual obligation. See the documents relating to the navigation of the river Po reproduced in McNair, *The Law of Treaties* (Oxford, 1961), pp. 318–20.

[32] Judgments, 1923, P.C.I.J., Series A, No. 1, p. 43.

The Permanent Court did not accept this argument. It noted that a restrictive interpretation of the limitations incumbent on Germany would be justified anyway, irrespective of whether these limitations were based on a servitude or on a contractual obligation. As a basis for the grant of a general right of passage through the Kiel Canal, the Permanent Court referred by analogy to the rules applicable to the Suez and Panama Canals. It remarked that, according to a general opinion,

> when an artificial waterway connecting two open seas has been permanently dedicated to the use of the whole world, such waterway is assimilated to natural straits in the sense that even the passage of a belligerent man-of-war does not compromise the neutrality of the sovereign State under whose jurisdiction the waters in question lie.[33]

On this ground, the Permanent Court concluded that the Kiel Canal was 'permanently dedicated to the use of the whole world', and therefore freedom of navigation in the Kiel Canal should prevail over other considerations put forward by the territorial sovereign.[34] In reaching its decision, the Permanent Court had thus introduced a new concept of 'permanent dedication'. But what does 'permanent dedication' really mean? Several interpretations have been proposed in the international literature.

Cahier has written that the Permanent Court probably meant that the rights of navigation for the benefit of all States derive from an international custom evolved by analogy with the rules applicable to international straits.[35] This explanation assumes that there is an international custom conferring on all States a right of free navigation in the Kiel Canal and, more generally, in international rivers and canals. This assumption, though, is questionable.[36]

[33] Judgments, 1923, P.C.I.J., Series A, No. 1, p. 28. The French authoritative text reads as follows: 'lorsqu'une voie d'eau artificielle mettant en communication deux mers libres, a été affecté d'une manière permanente à l'usage du monde entier, cette voie se trouve assimilée aux détroits naturels, en ce sens que le passage même d'un navire de guerre belligérant ne compromet pas la neutralité de l'Etat souverain sous la juridiction duquel se trouvent les eaux dont il s'agit.'

[34] The study of the subsequent developments relating to the Kiel Canal is outside the scope of the present discussion. However, it may be recalled that, by a Note dated 14 November 1936, the German Government repudiated Article 380 and the other clauses of the Peace Treaty of Versailles relating to waterways on German territory. In 1950, the Supreme Court of Germany, British Zone, wrote that this Note had put an end to internationalisation, 'at least *de facto*' (*Kiel Canal Collision* Case, 17 *I.L.R.* (1950), p. 133). See Lagoni, 'Kiel Canal', Heidelberg *Encycl.*, xii, pp. 200–2; Böhmer, 'One Hundred Years: The Kiel Canal in International Law', 38 *G.Y.I.L.* (1995), pp. 325–46.

[35] 'Le problème des effets des traités à l'égard des Etats tiers', 143 Hague *Recueil* (1974, III), p. 693.

[36] See Westlake, *International Law*, i, p. 157; Kaeckenbeeck, *International Rivers: A Monograph Based on Diplomatic Documents* (London, 1918), p. 23; Hall, *Treatise*, pp. 172–3; Winiarski, 'Principes généraux du droit fluvial international', 45 Hague *Recueil* (1933, III), p. 172; Giuliano, 'L'ordinamento internazionale e i fiumi navigabili d'interesse internazionale', 42 *Riv. dir. int.* (1959), pp. 205–6; Parry (ed.), *A British Digest*, 2b, pp. 55–190; Brownlie, *Principles*, pp. 271–4; *Oppenheim's International Law*, i, pp. 582–6.

McNair has suggested that dedication is based on certain legislative powers exercised by a large group of States, coupled with the granting, by the territorial sovereign (in this case, Germany), of rights *in rem* in regard of a strip of land (in this case, the Kiel Canal).[37] The problem with this argument is that the idea of 'legislative powers' vested in the international community is not immune from difficulties, as will be noted later in this chapter.

Baxter has added to permanent dedication an element of reliance by the international shipping community, with the consequence that, to establish a right of passage, a State would not need to give evidence of previous use by its own vessels.[38] This theory is ingenious, but ultimately leads back to the problem of how to construct an act of dedication and the reaction by the intended beneficiaries.[39]

To sum up, while avoiding the uncertain concept of State servitude, the Permanent Court introduced an equally controversial notion to explain the existence of perpetual rights to the benefit of all States.

Another attempt to account for the existence of rights and obligations valid for a wider circle of States than the contracting parties arose in the context of a dispute relating to the regime of demilitarization for the Aaland Islands,[40] which dates back to the time of the *Wimbledon* case.

[37] 'Treaties Producing Effects "Erga Omnes"', *Scritti di diritto internazionale in onore di Tomaso Perassi*, ii (Milan, 1957), pp. 27–30. Obieta has written that an international regime relating to a canal may be established 'by consent of the territorial sovereign given in a multilateral treaty, even if the treaty is not universal and in some cases, even if it does not secure acceptance from all the beneficiaries.' (*The International Status of the Suez Canal*, 2nd edn. (The Hague, 1970), p. 35.)

[38] *The Law of International Waterways* (Cambridge, Mass., 1964), pp. 182–4. There is here some analogy with the dedication of highways in municipal law, in that the common law requires that the express or presumed dedication to the public of a right of passage by the owner of land be accompanied by the acceptance of that right by the public. See Pratt and MacKenzie, *Law of Highways*, 21st edn. Parrish and Lord De Mauley (London, 1967), p. 16.

[39] For stringent criticism, see Brownlie, *Principles*, p. 280. On permanent dedication, see also Jennings, 'General Course', p. 373.

[40] See Menzel, 'Aland-Inseln', Strupp and Schlochauer (eds.), *Wörterbuch des Völkerrechts*, 2nd edn., i (Berlin, 1960), pp. 21–4; Modeen, 'Aaland Islands', Heidelberg *Encycl.*, xii, pp. 1–3. On the military importance of the archipelago, see Padelford and Andersson, 'The Aaland Islands Question', 33 *A.J.I.L.* (1939), pp. 484–7. On the present situation, see Erland, 'Some of the Main Points in the Proposed New Law of Autonomy for Aland', 57 *Nordic Journal of International Law* (1988), pp. 251–5. On the history of the legal questions concerning the Baltic area, see de Taube, 'Le statut juridique de la mer Baltique jusqu'au début du XIXe siècle', 53 Hague *Recueil* (1935, III), pp. 441–531; Pusta, 'Le statut juridique de la mer Baltique à partir du XIXe siècle', 52 ibid. (1935, II), pp. 109–89.

IV. The Concept of International Status in the General Interest of Europe (the Dispute on the Regime of Demilitarization for the Aaland Islands)

The Aaland Islands are an archipelago in the Baltic Sea. Their strategic position at the mouth of the Gulf of Bothnia accounts for the history of conflicting claims between the Baltic States to control these islands. The archipelago remained under Swedish sovereignty until 1809, when Sweden renounced its title to Finland (and to the Aaland Islands as an administrative unit of Finland) in favour of Russia.[41] Under Russian rule, the Aaland Islands were heavily fortified. On 30 March 1856, after the Russian defeat in the Crimean War, France, Great Britain and Russia concluded a Convention in which Russia declared that the Aaland Islands would not be fortified, and no military or naval base would be maintained or created there.[42] This Convention became an annex to the General Peace Treaty that Austria, France, Great Britain, Prussia, Russia, Sardinia and Turkey signed on the same day.[43] Sweden, which had not taken part in the Crimean War, was not a signatory to either agreement.

The events that took place in Russia in 1917 gave rise to important political changes in the Baltic area. Finland declared its independence,[44] and at about the same time a large majority of the population of the Aaland Islands invoked by plebiscite a right to reunite with Sweden.[45] In this context, a controversy arose between Sweden and Finland on whether the Aaland Islanders should be authorized to decide by plebiscite if they wanted to remain under Finnish sovereignty or reunite with Sweden.[46] Another controversial issue was demilitarization, particularly as the military status of the Aaland Islands was unclear after the Finnish declaration of independence and the disappearance of a recognized Government in Russia. An exchange of notes between Finland and Sweden did not settle the dis-

[41] 'Traité de paix entre la Suède et la Russie, signé à Friedrichshamn le 5/17 Sept. 1809 ratifié à Stockholm le 3 Oct. et à St. Petersbourg le 1/13 Oct. 1809', 5 *Suppl. rec.* (Series I, 1817), pp. 19–30 (Art. IV).

[42] 'Convention, annexée au traité de paix de Paris, conclue entre la Grande-Bretagne et la France d'une part et la Russie de l'autre, relative aux îles d'Aland; signée à Paris, le 30 mars 1856', 15 *Nouv. rec. gén.* (Series I, 1857), pp. 788–90 (Art. I).

[43] 'Traité général de paix entre l'Autriche, la France, la Grande-Bretagne, la Prusse, la Russie, la Sardaigne et la Porte Ottomane, signé à Paris, le 30 mars 1856', 15 *Nouv. rec. gén.* (Series I, 1857), pp. 770–81 (Art. XXXIII).

[44] On the independence and recognition of Finland, see Graham, 'The Diplomatic Recognition of the Border States. Part I: Finland', 3 *Publications of the University of California at Los Angeles in Social Sciences* (1936, No. 2), pp. i–viii and 81–230.

[45] The plebiscite took place on 31 December 1917. A new plebiscite, again in favour of reunion with Sweden, took place in June 1919.

[46] For a clear summary of the dispute and settlement relating to the Aaland Islands, see 'The Aaland Islands Settlement', *League of Nations Pamphlets Prepared by the Information Section, League of Nations Secretariat*, i (Political Activities 1924–1928) (Geneva, 1925), pp. 7–23.

pute.[47] Great Britain then brought the case before the Council of the League of Nations under Article XI, paragraph 2, of the Covenant of the League, which allowed third party intervention in circumstances affecting international peace.[48] Having examined the arguments of the parties, the Council decided to set up an *ad hoc* Committee of Jurists that would give an opinion on two preliminary legal questions, namely (a) whether the case of the Aaland Islands belonged to the domestic jurisdiction of Finland, and (b) what were the international obligations on demilitarization of the Aaland Islands.[49]

The composition and procedure of the Committee set up by the Council of the League of Nations leave little doubt that this was an *ad hoc* body of 'judicial' inquiry, which gave full guarantee of independent and informed advice and whose final report functionally corresponds to an advisory opinion of the Permanent Court.[50] (Indeed, Balfour declared on behalf of the Council of the League that the question of domestic jurisdiction would have been submitted to the Permanent Court of International Justice, had this body been in existence at that time.) The Committee was requested to give an opinion on legal issues alone; on the basis of the Committee's final report, the Council of the League set up a commission of inquiry (the 'Aaland Islands Commission') to examine the factual situation and recommend a solution of the dispute.[51]

Of the two legal questions submitted to the Committee of Jurists, the first one on domestic jurisdiction (which occupies the greater part of the

[47] 'Correspondence Relating to the Question of the Aaland Islands', *L.N.O.J.*, Special Supplement No. 1 (Aug. 1920).

[48] See the letter from Lord Curzon to the Secretary-General, reproduced in 5 *L.N.O.J.* (July-Aug. 1920), p. 250. On Article XI of the Covenant, see Kunz, 'L'article XI du Pacte de la Société des Nations', 39 Hague *Recueil* (1932, I), pp. 683–789. On third party intervention under Article XI of the Covenant, see Conwell-Evans, *The League Council in Action: A Study of the Methods Employed by the Council of the League of Nations to Prevent War and to Settle International Disputes* (Oxford, 1929), pp. 21–3.

[49] See the 'Resolution adopted at the seventh session of the Council of the League of Nations held in London from 9th to 12th July, 1920', 5 *L.N.O.J.* (July-Aug. 1920), pp. 249–50.

[50] The Committee comprised three members: Larnaude (President), Dean of the Faculty of Law at Paris; Struycken, Councillor of State of the Kingdom of The Netherlands; and Huber, Legal Adviser of the Swiss Political Department. Kaeckenbeeck, of the Legal Section of the Secretariat of the League of Nations, was the Secretary. In his general course at the Hague Academy, Kaufmann has underlined the link between certain conclusions reached by the Committee on the international status of the Aaland Islands and the legal writings of Max Huber, one of the members of the Committee. ('Règles générales du droit de la paix', 54 Hague *Recueil* (1935, IV), pp. 498–501.)

[51] 5 *L.N.O.J.* (Nov.-Dec. 1920), p. 86. Merrills has written that the technique of inquiry provides a wide range of solutions, from fact finding to near arbitration (*International Dispute Settlement*, 2nd edn. (Cambridge, 1991), p. 55). In the settlement of the Aaland Islands dispute, there was both 'judicial' and factual inquiry.

Committee's report)[52] need not be examined here.[53] It is the second question that is important for the present purposes, namely the question of the international obligations relating to the demilitarization of the Aaland Islands.

After finding that the provisions of 1856 relating to non-fortification were still in force, the Committee of Jurists addressed the question of the legal nature of demilitarization. Sweden was not a party to either the Convention or the Treaty of 1856, and yet it was claiming a right to call upon Finland to comply with the international obligations relating to the Aaland Islands. The main issue was therefore to explain the ground upon which Sweden had standing to claim compliance with the provisions on non-fortification of the archipelago. As a corollary to this question, there was also the problem of the ground upon which Finland, which did not even exist as an independent State in 1856, could be held to be under an international obligation not to fortify the Aaland Islands.

In its pleadings, the Swedish Government argued that the Convention of 1856 had established a real or praedial servitude ('servitude réelle') of non-fortification over the Aaland Islands.[54] The consequence was that Sweden would have a right to claim that the regime of demilitarization be respected, and that this regime would be automatically opposable (i.e. applicable) to any State (including Finland) acquiring sovereignty over the archipelago.[55]

[52] 'Report of the International Committee of Jurists entrusted by the Council of the League of Nations with the task of giving an advisory opinion upon the legal aspects of the Aaland Islands Question', *L.N.O.J.*, Special Supplement No. 3 (Oct. 1920), pp. 3–14. The second part of the report covers pp. 14–19.

[53] On this legal question, see Arangio-Ruiz, 'Le domaine réservé. L'organisation internationale et le rapport entre droit international et droit interne', 225 Hague *Recueil* (1990, VI), pp. 185–203. See also Rigo Sureda, *The Evolution of the Right of Self-Determination. A Study of United Nations Practice* (Leiden, 1973), pp. 29–34; 111–17; 233–7.

[54] See *Les îles d'Aland. Mémoires adressés par le Gouvernement Suédois au Conseil de la Société des Nations et à la Commission internationale de juristes, avec un appendice contenant le rapport de la Commission et celui du représentant britannique au Conseil, ainsi que la résolution adoptée en conséquence par le Conseil. (Juillet-septembre 1920.)* (Stockholm, 1920), pp. 186–92 (Swedish 'Mémoire' of 26 July 1920), and pp. 214–18 (Swedish 'Mémoire' of 11 Aug. 1920). (The writer is grateful to Mr Berndt Fredriksson, Assistant Under-Secretary at the Swedish Ministry for Foreign Affairs, for providing him with a copy of this volume.)

[55] De Staël-Holstein has remarked that in Northern Europe there is a traditional interest in servitudes ('Autour de la conception juridique des servitudes internationales', 15 *R.D.I.L.C.* (3rd series, 1934), p. 12). Among the writers who believe that the Convention of 1856 established a real servitude over the Aaland Islands see Rivier, *Principes*, pp. 299–300; Oppenheim, *International Law. A Treatise*, i, 8th edn. Lauterpacht, H., pp. 538–40 (a more cautious approach is taken in *Oppenheim's International Law*, i, pp. 672–3); Verzijl, *International Law*, iii, p. 418; De Staël-Holstein, 'La doctrine des servitudes internationales et son application en Scandinavie', 3 *R.D.I.L.C.* (3rd series, 1922), pp. 455–6. For the opposite view, see, among others, De Visscher, F., 'La question des îles d'Aland (*Suite*)', 2 *R.D.I.L.C.* (3rd series, 1921), pp. 249–56, and Söderhjelm, *Démilitarisation et neutralisation des Iles d'Aland en 1856 et 1921* (Helsingfors, 1928), pp. 39–48. Other writers refer to a personal (rather than real) servitude over the Aaland Islands. See Balladore Pallieri, *Diritto internazionale pubblico*, 8th edn. (Milan,

The Committee of Jurists expressed doubts on the very existence of State servitudes 'in the true technical sense of the term'. It then gave three reasons for rejecting the Swedish argument that there was a servitude on the Aaland Islands.[56] The first one was the difficulty of naming a dominant tenement in relation to the servient tenement represented by the Aaland Islands. As was mentioned earlier, the distinctive element of a real or praedial servitude is that one territory serves the needs of another territory belonging to a different owner. When this relationship of utility between two territories exists, it is easy to specify which is the dominant tenement and which is the servient one. But the diplomatic history of the Aaland Islands indicates that the interest in the demilitarization of the archipelago was not localized in any particular territory. For example, after Finland became independent, not only Sweden but also Russia claimed respect for the international regime of demilitarization.

The second reason was that, in any event, the Swedish territory could hardly be regarded as the dominant tenement, as Sweden was neither a party to the agreements of 1856 nor mentioned at all in those documents. While there have been, in international law, instances in which an obligation of non-fortification was undertaken to the benefit of a designated third party,[57] this was not the case in the Aaland Islands. In fact, the Convention of 1856 did not specify that the Swedish territory would benefit from the Russian obligation not to fortify the Aaland archipelago.[58]

1962), pp. 470–1. According to Mercier (*Les Servitudes Internationales*, p. 99), the Committee of Jurists implicitly acknowledged that there was a personal servitude over the archipelago to the benefit of the parties to the Convention of 1856.

56 'Report', pp. 16–17 and 19.

57 See, for example, the obligation not to fortify the Alsatian town of Huiningen to the advantage of the Swiss city of Basel, undertaken by France under a treaty to which Switzerland was not a party ('Traité définitif entre l'Autriche, la Grande-Bretagne, la Prusse, et la Russie d'une part, et la France de l'autre, signé à Paris le 20 Novembre 1815', 4 *Nouv. rec. gén.* (Series I, 1808–1819), p. 682). On this obligation, see Guggenheim et al. (eds), *Répertoire suisse de droit international public. Documentation concernant la pratique de la Confédération en matière de droit international public 1914–1939* (Basel, 1975), ii, pp. 1049–53, Section 5.37; Clauss, *Die Lehre von den Staatsdienstbarkeiten historisch-dogmatisch entwickelt* (Tubingen, 1894), pp. 15–17. On servitudes allegedly in favour of third States, see Udina, 'La succession des Etats quant aux obligations internationales autres que les dettes publiques', 44 Hague *Recueil* (1933, II), p. 728; Vali, *Servitudes*, pp. 310–11.

58 On similar grounds, the Committee wrote that the regime of demilitarization of the Aaland Islands could not be construed as a 'stipulation pour autrui' in favour of Sweden ('Report', p. 18). However, contrary to the Committee's conclusion, it seems that designation *ad nominem* is not required for a State to make use of a stipulation in its favour. (See Fitzmaurice, 'Fifth Report on the Law of Treaties' (Doc.A/CN.4/130), *Y.I.L.C* (1960, II), p. 81, Art. 20, para. 2; 'Research in International Law, Law of Treaties' (under the auspices of the Faculty of the Harvard Law School), 29 *A.J.I.L.* (1935), Supplement, p. 935.) It is true, however, that in its judgment in the *Free Zones of Upper Savoy and the District of Gex* case (P.C.I.J., Series A/B, No. 46, pp. 147–8), the Permanent Court of International Justice wrote that a stipulation favourable to a third party 'cannot be lightly presumed'. See also the views expressed by some of the judges in *Free Zones of Upper Savoy and the District of Gex*, Order of 19 August 1929, P.C.I.J., Series A, No. 22, pp. 26–7 (Judge Nyholm), pp. 36–9 (Deputy-

Finally, the third reason for rejecting the Swedish argument on State servitudes was that, if the Swedish territory were the dominant tenement and Sweden became the sovereign over the Aaland archipelago, the servitude relating to the Aaland Islands would automatically cease to exist by consolidation. However, this consequence would be contrary to the intention of the parties to the agreements of 1856.

Having thus rejected the Swedish argument that the demilitarization of the Aaland Islands should be construed as a State servitude, the Committee drew its own conclusions on the legal ground for the international obligations of non-fortification of the archipelago. The key element in the reasoning of the Committee was the general proposition, derived from the observation of the practice of States, that

> the Powers have, on many occasions since 1815, and especially at the conclusion of peace treaties, tried to create true objective law, a real political status the effects of which are felt outside the immediate circle of contracting parties.[59]

In light of this proposition, the Committee examined the intention of the parties to the agreements of 1856 and the subsequent events relating to the non-fortification of the Aaland archipelago. The political conditions under which the Convention on the Aaland Islands was signed, the decision to annex the Convention to the General Peace Treaty of 1856, the wording of the preliminary proceedings of the Treaty of 1856, and the preamble of the Convention on the Aaland Islands, were all pieces of evidence that the obligations undertaken by Russia went beyond the reciprocal interests of the contracting parties, and reflected 'permanent international interests'. From these elements, the Committee concluded that the provisions relating to the demilitarization of the Aaland Islands were

> laid down in European interests. They constituted a special international status relating to military considerations, for the Aaland Islands. It follows that until these provisions are duly replaced by others, every State interested has the right to insist upon compliance with them. It also follows that any State in possession of the Islands must conform to the obligations, binding upon it, arising out of the system of demilitarisation established by these provisions.[60]

Thus, the consequences from the international status for the Aaland Islands were clearly spelled out in the Committee's report: any State in possession of the archipelago would be bound to respect the obligations

Judge Negulesco), pp. 43–5 (Judge *ad hoc* Dreyfus). For the conflicting views on 'stipulation pour autrui' held by the parties to the case, see P.C.I.J., Series C, No. 17 (I), i, pp. 112–20, 339–55 (France) and pp. 196–206, 404–14 (Switzerland). For comment, see Beckett, 'Decisions of the Permanent Court of International Justice on Points of Law and Procedure of General Application', 11 *B.Y.I.L.* (1930), pp. 12–15. Among the writings on 'stipulation pour autrui', see Jiménez de Aréchaga, 'Treaty Stipulations in Favor of Third States', 50 *A.J.I.L.* (1956), pp. 338–57.

[59] 'Report', p. 17.

[60] Ibid., p. 19.

ensuing from the international status, and any interested State would be entitled to claim that these obligations be observed.[61]

As in the case of 'permanent dedication' discussed above, there are some elements of contact between the obligations ensuing from the international status of the Aaland Islands and obligations *erga omnes*. In its conclusions the Committee of Jurists stated that any State 'in possession of the Islands' must conform to the obligation of non-fortification. On the other hand, however, not every State without exception, but rather every 'interested' State, has legal standing to claim compliance with the obligations in question. In other words, the point of contact with obligations *erga omnes* is that the obligations relating to the demilitarization of the Aaland Islands exceed mere considerations of reciprocity and affect a circle of States wider than the contracting parties; the difference is that these obligations concern a number of directly interested States, and not *all* States as is the case of obligations *erga omnes*.

One may lead the analysis one step further and explore the reasoning followed by the Committee in reaching its conclusions. In its report, the Committee wrote that the general interest in the demilitarization of the Aaland archipelago was based on military considerations instrumental to the establishment of peaceful relations in the Baltic area. How could this general interest translate into rights and obligations of States other than those which were parties to the agreements providing for the demilitarization of the archipelago? Unfortunately, the Committee did not take a clear position on this. In the first passage from the Committee's report quoted earlier in this section, the Committee drew a parallel between the settlement for the Aaland Islands and certain repeated attempts by the great Powers to dictate international arrangements opposable to other States. However, this reference to precedents sheds hardly any light on the ground for the opposability of the obligations of non-fortification relating to the Aaland Islands. Attempts by the great Powers to dictate international arrangements took initially the form of a directorate of States,[62] and then of a system of

[61] The question of which States, according to the Committee, would be 'interested' in the international status of the Aaland Islands is beyond the scope of the present discussion. However, one would agree with Quéneudec's general remark that, when the expression 'interested States' is used, 'il est parfois presque impossible de déterminer précisément quel Etat peut être visé par cette expression'. ('La notion d'Etat intéressé en droit international', 255 Hague *Recueil* (1995), p. 349.)

[62] 'Protocole signé à Aix la Chapelle le 15 Novembre 1818 par les plénipotentiaires des cours d'Autriche, de France, de la Grande Bretagne, de Prusse et de Russie', 4 *Nouv. rec. gén.* (Series I, 1808–1819), pp. 554–5. (This protocol extended to France the agreement of the Powers reached at Chaumont on 1 March 1814, and confirmed at Paris on 20 November 1815.) On the 'directorate of States' see de la Brière, *La "Société des Nations"? Essai Historique et Juridique*, 2nd edn. (Paris, 1918), pp. 71–91; Dupuis, 'Les antécédents de la Société des Nations', 60 Hague *Recueil* (1937, II), pp. 67–106; Bourquin, 'La Sainte-Alliance, un essai d'organisation européenne', 83 Hague *Recueil* (1953, II), pp. 377–461.

international conferences, the so-called 'Concert of Europe'.[63] Occasionally, smaller States were invited to ratify arrangements agreed among the great Powers, but these acts of validation were regarded by the smaller States as being largely fictitious.[64] Practice was uncertain, and the predominance of the great Powers did not develop into an international norm conferring on them a legal right (and not just the political might) to make decisions on behalf of all members of the international community.[65]

Some writers have suggested that the general effects of the settlement for the Aaland Islands derive from certain established principles of international law. Sir Hersch Lauterpacht, for example, has written that the obligations of Finland relating to the demilitarization of the Aaland archipelago were based on the ordinary principles of State succession,[66] while Brierly has expressed the view that a general custom soon developed out of the agreements on the demilitarization of the Aaland Islands.[67]

Neither view is entirely convincing. As to the argument based on the principles of State succession, there is indeed a passage in the report on the

[63] Materials relating to the Concert of Europe are reproduced in Bruns (ed.), *Fontes*, Series B, Section 1, Tomus I, Pars 1, pp. 2–5. In the literature, see de la Brière, *La "Société des Nations"?*, pp. 92–104; Nys, 'Le concert européen et la notion de droit international', 1 *R.D.I.L.C.* (2nd series, 1899), pp. 273–313, and the helpful summary contained in Truyol y Serra, *Histoire du droit international public* (Paris, 1995), pp. 99–104. See also the brief considerations developed in Séfériadès, 'Principes généraux du droit international de la paix', 34 Hague *Recueil* (1930, IV), pp. 256–7.

[64] For example, in its protest of 7 October 1908 against the Austrian annexation of Bosnia and Herzegovina, Serbia relied on the provisions of the Treaty of Berlin but at the same time remarked that 'le traité de Berlin . . . nous avons été obligés de le subir en tant qu'il affectait notre sort . . .' (15 *R.G.D.I.P.* (1908), p. 37).

[65] See the dissenting opinion of Judge Negulesco in *Jurisdiction of the European Commission of the Danube*, Advisory Opinion, 1927, P.C.I.J., Series B, No. 14, p. 95. In the literature, see Gihl, *International Legislation: An Essay on Changes in International Law and in International Legal Situations*, English trans. Charleston (London, 1937), pp. 57–64; Rousseau, *Principes généraux du droit international public*, i (Paris, 1944), pp. 478–84; Oppenheim, *International Law. A Treatise*, i, 8th edn. Lauterpacht, H., pp. 275–6; Reuter, 'Principes de droit international public', 103 Hague *Recueil* (1961, II), pp. 445–53. For earlier views, see Mamiani, *D'un nuovo diritto europeo* (Torino, 1859), pp. 104–9 and 112–13; Rivier, *Principes*, i, p. 125; Fiore, *International Law Codified and its Legal Sanction or The Legal Organization of the Society of States*, English trans. Borchard (New York, 1918), pp. 222–3. For the view that the legal equality of States became obsolete as a result of the primacy of the great Powers, see Lawrence, *Essays on Some Disputed Questions in Modern International Law*, 2nd edn. (Cambridge, 1885), p. 227, and more cautiously Manning, *Commentaries on the Law of Nations*, revised edn. Amos (London and Cambridge, 1875), pp. 100–1. A different question is whether the Concert of Europe might be regarded as the forerunner of the process of organization of the international community. Compare Bluntschli, *Droit international codifié*, pp. 97–8 (art. 103), and Westlake, *International Law*, i, pp. 321–3, with Streit, 'Les grandes puissances dans le droit international', 2 *R.D.I.L.C.* (2nd series, 1900), pp. 13–25.

[66] *Development of International Law*, p. 312, note 50. This position is shared by Cahier, 'Le problème des effets des traités à l'égard des Etats tiers', pp. 666–7.

[67] 'Règles générales du droit de la paix', 58 Hague *Recueil* (1936, IV), pp. 222–4. Among the modern treatises of international law, a similar view is adopted in Giuliano, Scovazzi and Treves, *Diritto internazionale. Parte generale*, pp. 329–31.

Aaland Islands in which the Committee of Jurists remarked that one of the conditions for the recognition of Finland (and of new States generally) was that Finland should respect its international obligations under general international law and international settlements affecting its territory.[68] However, this would account for the obligations of Finland but not for the wider effects of the settlement for the Aaland Islands, and above all the conferment of rights on Sweden.

Likewise, to explain the general effects of the regime for the Aaland Islands on the basis of the emergence of an international custom after the First World War, or consent to this regime by the States that were not parties to the agreements of 1856, is somewhat 'illusory'.[69] It is true that in 1918 Finland, Sweden and Germany agreed to remove all the fortifications erected on the Aaland Islands,[70] but to infer from this that these Powers were not previously bound by the regime of demilitarization, and became bound only as a consequence of this agreement and an emerging custom, begs the question. The Committee of Jurists stated that the agreement of 1918 was merely 'evidence' of an international settlement for the Aaland Islands that was already binding on these States. In addition, when the great Powers and the Baltic States, except for the former Soviet Union, signed a new Convention that guaranteed the international status of the Aaland archipelago and superseded the Convention of 1856 among its parties, Finland confirmed 'as far as needed' ('en tant que de besoin') the Russian undertaking not to fortify the Aaland Islands.[71] This wording is extremely cautious and does not seem to undermine the conclusion reached by the Committee that demilitarization had already been achieved by virtue of the agreements of 1856.[72]

An interesting reinterpretation of the Committee's conclusions is contained in the separate opinion that Judge McNair attached to the advisory

[68] 'Report', p. 18.

[69] This term is used in Ross, *A Textbook of International Law. General Part* (London, 1947), p. 84.

[70] 'Agreement between Finland, Germany and Sweden concerning the Demolition of the Fortifications and other Military Establishments erected on the Aaland Islands, signed in Stockholm, December 30, 1918', 113 *State Papers* (1920), pp. 993–1002.

[71] See Art. 1 of the 'Convention relative à la non-fortification et à la neutralisation des Iles d'Aland, signée à Genève, le 20 octobre 1921', 12 *Nouv. rec. gén.* (Series III, 1923–1924), pp. 65–70. (For commentary, see De Visscher, F., 'La Convention relative à la Non-Fortification et à la Neutralisation des Iles d'Aland', 2 *R.D.I.L.C.* (3rd series, 1921), pp. 568–86; Erich, 'La question des zones démilitarisées', 26 Hague *Recueil* (1929, I) pp. 632–50.) Later, Finland undertook not to fortify the Aaland Islands towards the former Soviet Union in the 'Agreement between Finland and the Soviet Union concerning the Aland Islands, signed in Moscow, October 11, 1940', 144 *State Papers* (1940–1942), pp. 395–7. On the present situation, see Hannikainen, 'The Continued Validity of the Demilitarised and Neutralised Status of the Aland Islands', 54 *Z.a.ö.R.V.* (1994), pp. 614–51.

[72] In the preamble to the new Convention, the parties declared their intention to '. . . compléter, sans y porter atteinte, l'effet de l'engagement pris par la Russie dans la Convention du 30 mars 1856 . . .'.

opinion rendered by the International Court in 1950 on the *International Status of South West Africa*.[73] This was the first of a series of six instances in which the International Court was called to address legal issues relating to the mandate for South West Africa (now Namibia).[74] In 1949, the General Assembly of the United Nations asked the International Court to consider certain effects that the dissolution of the League of Nations had brought about with respect to the mandate for South West Africa.[75] This request raised difficult problems, particularly as the mandate, while established by treaty, pursued an international object in the general interest of humanity (a 'sacred trust of civilization').

In his separate opinion, Judge McNair wrote that the reasoning of the Committee of Jurists in its report on the Aaland Islands was relevant to the case at hand. After referring to the passages from the Committee's report that have been reproduced above, he drew this general conclusion:

> From time to time it happens that a group of great Powers, or a large number of States both great and small, assume a power to create by a multipartite treaty some new international régime or status, which soon acquires a degree of acceptance and durability extending beyond the limits of the actual contracting parties, and giving it an objective existence. This power is used when some public interest is involved, and its exercise often occurs in the course of the peace settlement at the end of a great war.[76]

A comparison between these words and the passages from the report of the Committee of Jurists reproduced above shows clear elements of similarity in the language used, but also important differences. First of all, in Judge McNair's view, an international regime can be established not only by the great Powers, but also by a large number of States, 'great and small'. This introduces an element of 'democracy' into the whole process, which is more in conformity with the present reality of the international community. Secondly, Judge McNair clearly indicated the ground on which the effects of an international status are opposable to third States: an international status soon acquires general effects by way of 'acceptance'. Finally, Judge McNair referred to a 'public interest' behind an international status, a concept which is much wider than the 'European interests' lying behind the international settlement for the Aaland Islands.

To sum up, in his separate opinion, Judge McNair put forward a more articulate definition of an international status than that proposed by the Committee in the dispute concerning the Aaland Islands. However, while

[73] I.C.J. Reports 1950, p. 128.

[74] For bibliographical references on the question of the mandate for South West Africa, see Chapter 7, below.

[75] The text of the resolution by which the General Assembly submitted its questions to the International Court is reproduced in I.C.J. Reports 1950, pp. 129–30.

[76] Ibid., p. 153.

providing some answers to the issues that the Committee of Jurists had left open, Judge McNair's opinion gives rise at the same time to new questions: what degree of acceptance is needed in order that an international status may be opposable to third States? Is the international status opposable to those States that have not accepted it, or even expressly objected to it? Is an international status established by a large number of States politically more acceptable, for the dissenting minority, than an international status established by the 'great Powers'?

These and other questions confronted the members of the International Law Commission when, some years after Judge McNair's separate opinion, they considered the concept of objective regime in the context of their work of codification that would eventually lead to the adoption of the Vienna Convention on the Law of Treaties.[77]

V. The Concept of Objective Regime in the Work of Codification of the Law of Treaties

In the Commentary that accompanied its draft articles on the law of treaties, the International Law Commission defined the content of objective regime as 'obligations and rights valid *erga omnes*'.[78] According to the International Law Commission, an objective regime could be established, for example, by a treaty providing for the demilitarization or neutralization of a certain territory or the freedom of navigation on international waterways. In other words, it could be established by treaties such as those relating to the non-fortification of the Aaland Islands or the dedication of the Kiel Canal.

The issue of objective regimes first emerged in the work of codification of the law of treaties when the Special Rapporteur Fitzmaurice submitted his fifth report to the International Law Commission. Sir Gerald Fitzmaurice's starting point was the 'absolutely firm and unequivocal principle' that treaties do not produce either rights or obligations for a third State without its consent (*pacta tertiis neque nocent neque prosunt*), subject to certain qualifications.[79] He then examined these qualifications

[77] 1155 *U.N.T.S.* 331. The Vienna Convention was adopted on 23 May 1969 and entered into force on 27 January 1980. Seventy-seven States have become parties (*Multilateral Treaties Deposited with the Secretary-General. Status as at 31 December 1995* (New York, 1996), p. 839). For commentary, see Sinclair, *The Vienna Convention on the Law of Treaties*, 2nd edn. (Manchester, 1984); Reuter, *La Convention de Vienne sur le droit des traités* (Paris, 1970).

[78] 'Draft Articles on the Law of Treaties with Commentaries, Adopted by the International Law Commission at its Eighteenth Session', *U.N.C.L.T., Off. Recs., First and second sessions, Vienna, 26 March–24 May 1968 and 9 April–22 May 1969, Documents of the Conference* (New York, 1971), p. 51 (Article 34, Commentary (4)).

[79] 'Fifth Report', p. 73, para. 3. The principle *pacta tertiis* is now codified in Article 34 of the Vienna Convention on the Law of Treaties. For the practice of States confirming this

analytically,[80] but did not provide any draft article that would list admissible exceptions, including objective regimes. This reflected his general idea that the codification of the law of treaties should take the form of an expository code rather than an international convention.[81]

Fitzmaurice's successor as Special Rapporteur, Sir Humphrey Waldock, took an altogether different approach to the codification of the law of treaties and went back to the original idea that the draft articles should take the form of an international convention.[82] This explains, at least in part, his different treatment of the concept of objective regime. In his third report, Waldock submitted to the International Law Commission an article headed 'Treaties providing for objective regimes' (draft Article 63).[83] The first paragraph of this draft article reads as follows:

> A treaty establishes an objective regime when it appears from its terms and from the circumstances of its conclusion that the intention of the parties is to create in the general interest general obligations and rights relating to a particular region, State, territory, locality, river, waterway, or to a particular area of sea, sea-bed, or airspace; provided that the parties include among their number any State having territorial competence with reference to the subject-matter of the treaty, or that any such State has consented to the provision in question.

The following paragraphs of draft Article 63 added that (a) a third State which had expressly or impliedly consented to an objective regime, or had

principle, see Kiss (ed.), *Répertoire de la pratique française en matière de droit international public*, i (Paris, 1962), pp. 500–13; Ago (ed.), *La prassi italiana di diritto internazionale, Prima Serie (1861–1887)*, i (New York, 1970), pp. 53–5; Guggenheim et al. (eds.), *Répertoire suisse*, i (Basel, 1975), pp. 139–45 (Sections 1.63–7). See also McNair, *Law of Treaties*, pp. 315–18 and 320–1. Among the judgments and arbitral awards, see *Islands of Palmas Case*, *R.I.A.A.*, ii, p. 829; *Affaire de l'île de Clipperton*, ibid., p. 1110; *Affaire Pablo Najera*, *R.I.A.A.*, v, p. 466; *Status of Eastern Carelia*, Advisory Opinion, 1923, P.C.I.J., Series B, No. 5, p. 27; *Certain German Interests in Polish Upper Silesia*, Merits, Judgment No. 7, 1926 P.C.I.J., Series A, No. 7, pp. 28–9; *Territorial Jurisdiction of the International Commission of the River Oder*, Judgment No. 16, 1929, P.C.I.J., Series A, No. 23, p. 19; *Aerial Incident of 27 July 1959 (Israel* v. *Bulgaria)*, Judgment, I.C.J. Reports 1959, pp. 136–8.

[80] See Fitzmaurice, 'Fifth Report', Articles 14 and 26 ('Case of the use of maritime or land territory under a treaty or international regime'), 17 ('General duty of all States to respect and not impede or interfere with the operation of lawful and valid treaties entered into between other States'), 18 ('General duty of all States to recognize and respect situations of law or of fact established under lawful and valid treaties') and 29 ('*In favorem* effects resulting from the application of the principle of respect for lawful and valid international acts').

[81] '(First) Report on the Law of Treaties' (Doc.A/CN.4/101), *Y.I.L.C.* (1956, II), pp. 105–6, paras. 3–4. Jennings has remarked that this idea reflected Fitzmaurice's proposition that treaties are sources of obligations, but not of law. (Jennings, 'Recent Developments in the International Law Commission: Its relation to the Source of International Law', 18 *I.C.L.Q.* (1964), pp. 388–9.)

[82] Apparently, Waldock agreed to become Special Rapporteur on condition that the Commission would adhere to this original idea. See Ago's intervention reproduced in *U.N.G.A., Off. Recs., Twentieth Session, Sixth Committee, Legal Questions, Summary Records of Meetings 22 September – 17 December 1965*, 851st Meeting, p. 76, para. 43.

[83] 'Third Report on the Law of Treaties' (Doc.A/CN.4/167 and Add. 1–3), *Y.I.L.C.* (1964, II), Article 63, p. 26.

not protested against it in due time,[84] would be regarded as having impliedly accepted the regime (paragraph 2); (b) a State accepting the regime would be bound by any general obligations it contained and would be entitled to exercise any general rights it conferred (paragraph 3); and (c) an accepting State would also have a say in the modification or revocation of the regime, provided that it had a substantial interest in its functioning (paragraph 4).

Waldock's definition of objective regime contains some characteristic elements that make it easy to distinguish this definition from the concepts of permanent dedication and international status discussed above, on the one hand, and from the concept of obligations *erga omnes*, on the other. Unlike the case of permanent dedication or international status, in a treaty purporting to establish an objective regime relating to a territory the State or group of States having 'territorial competence' must be a party to the treaty. In other words, there is no question of imposing an objective regime on a State such as Germany in the *Wimbledon* case or Finland in the settlement for the Aaland archipelago. Waldock also remarked in his Commentary that territorial competence helps to distinguish treaties establishing objective regimes from other treaties intended to have general effects, such as general law-making treaties, which produce general effects by operation of custom.[85]

On the other hand, according to Waldock's definition, a treaty establishing an objective regime would not give rise to obligations *erga omnes*, but rather to 'general obligations' that would not be opposable to a State that had raised timely objections to them.

Despite these qualifications to the universal opposability of an objective regime, the International Law Commission ultimately decided to delete draft Article 63 from the text of the Vienna Convention. Many of its members complained that an article along the lines proposed by Waldock might still, in appearance if not in substance, endorse the practices by which the great Powers had tried in the past to impose their will on the other members of the international community, or at least afford a majority of States an instrument for putting pressure on the dissenting States and forcing them to accept an objective regime. This would obviously be incompatible with the basic principle of the equality of States.[86] The International Law Commission concluded that, at least for the purposes of the Vienna Convention, the provision regarding treaties intended to create rights in

[84] i.e. 'within a period of X years of the registration of the treaty [providing for the objective regime] with the Secretary-General of the United Nations . . .' (para. 2(b)).

[85] See Waldock, 'Third Report', p. 33, paras. 19–20. On law-making treaties, see McNair, 'The Function and Differing Legal Character of Treaties', 11 *B.Y.I.L.* (1930), pp. 101–5; Scelle, *Précis*, ii (Paris, 1934), especially pp. 367–79; Vitta, E., 'Le traité multilatéral peut-il être considéré comme un acte législatif?', 6 *A.F.D.I.* (1960), pp. 225–38.

[86] See *Y.I.L.C.* (1964, I), p. 101, para. 22 (Jiménez de Aréchaga); p. 103, para. 46 (Tunkin); p. 103, para. 52 (Bartos); p. 104, para. 65 (Tabibi); and p. 105, para. 72 (Liu).

favour of third States (Article 36 of the Vienna Convention),[87] and the provision reserving the possibility that a conventional rule may develop into an international custom (Article 38 of the Vienna Convention),[88] would offer an adequate legal basis for the general effects of objective regimes.

After the adoption of the Vienna Convention, the issue of objective regimes has surfaced again, notably in the work of codification on the succession of States in respect of treaties.[89] The issue has continued to attract considerable interest among international writers, in the context also of the

[87] See Nahlik, 'Traités internationaux et Etats tiers. Historique d'une codification', 4 *Thesaurus Acroasium* (1977), pp. 9–30. On treaties conferring rights on third States, and more generally on treaties and third States, see Roxburgh, *International Conventions and Third States. A Monograph* (London, 1917); Kojanec, *Trattati e terzi stati. Limiti soggettivi di validità delle norme positive dell'ordinamento internazionale* (Padua, 1961); Smets, *Les effets des traités internationaux à l'égard des Etats tiers* (Paris, 1965–1966); *Völkerrechtlicher Vertrag und Drittstaaten* (*Treaties and Third States*, in German, with English summaries of the Reports) (Heidelberg, 1988). See also Salvioli, 'I terzi nel diritto internazionale', 12 *Riv. dir. int.* (1918), pp. 229–41; Ballreich, 'Verträge zugunsten und zu lasten Dritter', Strupp and Schlochauer (eds.), *Wörterbuch*, iii, pp. 544–7; Roucounas, 'Le traité et les Etats tiers (Quelques approches subjectives et objectives)', 17 *Revue Hellénique de Droit International* (1964), pp. 299–365; Braud, 'Recherches sur l'Etat tiers en droit international public', 72 *R.G.D.I.P.* (1968), pp. 17–96; Schweisfurth, 'International Treaties and Third States', 45 *Z.a.ö.R.V.* (1985), pp. 653–74.

[88] On the interaction between treaty and custom, see the important considerations developed by the International Court in *North Sea Continental Shelf*, Judgment, I.C.J. Reports 1969, pp. 32–41, and *Military and Paramilitary Activities in and against Nicaragua (Nicaragua v. United States of America)*, Merits, I.C.J. Reports 1986, pp. 92–6. In the literature, see Baxter, 'Treaties and Custom', 129 Hague *Recueil* (1970, I), pp. 25–106; Jiménez de Aréchaga, 'International Law in the Past Third of a Century', 159 Hague *Recueil* (1978, I), pp. 12–23; Schachter, 'Entangled Treaty and Custom', Dinstein (ed.), *International Law at a Time of Perplexity. Essays in Honour of Shabtai Rosenne* (Dordrecht, 1989), pp. 717–36. More extensively, see Thirlway, *International Customary Law and Codification* (Leiden, 1972); Villiger, *Customary International Law and Treaties* (Dordrecht, 1985).

[89] See Waldock, 'First Report on succession of States and Governments in respect of treaties' (Doc.A/CN.4/202), *Y.I.L.C.* (1968, II), pp. 92–3; Vallat, 'First Report on succession of States in respect of treaties' (Doc.A/CN.4/278 and Add.1–6), ibid. (1974, II), Part I, pp. 73–87; 'Draft articles adopted by the Commission: second reading', ibid. (1974, I), pp. 203–23; 'Draft articles on succession of States in respect of treaties with commentaries adopted by the International Law Commission at its twenty-sixth session', *United Nations Conference on Succession of States in Respect of Treaties, Official Records*, iii ('Documents of the Conference') (New York, 1979), pp. 26–37 (Articles 11 and 12); ibid., ii ('Summary records of the plenary meetings and of the meetings of the Committee of the whole') (New York, 1978), pp. 113–51. For comment, see Reuter, *Introduction to the Law of Treaties*, English trans. Mico and Haggenmacher (London and New York, 1989), pp. 97–9, paras 191–2. See also, in a different context, Bedjaoui, 'First Report on succession of States in respect of rights and duties resulting from sources other than treaties' (Doc.A/CN.4/204), *Y.I.L.C.* (1968, II), pp. 112–14. On succession to objective regimes, see Fitzmaurice, 'The juridical clauses of the peace treaties', 73 Hague *Recueil* (1948, II), p. 260; Castrén, 'Aspects récents de la succession d'Etats', 78 ibid. (1951, I), pp. 448–9; Zemanek, 'State succession after decolonisation', 116 ibid. (1965, III), pp. 239–43; *The Effects of Independence on Treaties. A Handbook Published after the auspices of The International Law Association* (London, 1967), pp. 352–60; O'Connell, *State Succession in Municipal Law and International Law*, (Cambridge, 1967), ii, pp. 12–17.

Antarctic Treaty.[90] However, the political acceptability of objective regimes continues to be controversial, and the concept remains, as acknowledged by Riphagen, 'somewhat nebulous'.[91]

VI. Conclusions

The prefigurations discussed in this chapter show that, for a long time before the International Court's dictum in the *Barcelona Traction* case, efforts had been made to regulate by treaty the common interests of States in such a way that rights and obligations might potentially be valid *erga omnes*, or at least for a wider circle of States than the parties to the treaty in question. The explanations provided in support of these efforts have been largely unsatisfactory. Some of the concepts which have occasionally been relied upon, such as State servitude, permanent dedication, and international status, are question-begging. Others, such as objective regime, end up falling back on the idea of consent.

Despite these limitations, the comparison between these prefigurations and the concept of obligations *erga omnes* has proved useful for several reasons. First of all, the foregoing analysis confirms that the concept of

[90] See Schachter, 'International Legislation', Sills (ed.), *International Encyclopedia of the Social Sciences*, vii (New York, 1972), pp. 551–8; Mosler, *The International Society as a Legal Community* (Aalphen aan den Rijn and Germantown, 1980), pp. 221–45; Klein, *Statusverträge im Völkerrecht: Rechtsfragen territorialer Sonderregime* (Berlin, 1980); Wyrozumska, 'Treaties Establishing Territorial Regimes', 15 *P.Y.I.L.* (1986), pp. 251–76; Vasciannie, 'Part XI of the Law of the Sea Convention and Third States: Some General Observations', 48 *Cambridge Law Journal* (1989), pp. 85–97; Subedi, 'The Doctrine of Objective Regimes in International Law and the Competence of the United Nations to Impose Territorial or Peace Settlements on States', 37 *G.Y.I.L.* (1994), pp. 162–205. With respect to the Antarctic Treaty (402 *U.N.T.S.* 71), see Battaglini, *La condizione dell'Antartide nel diritto internazionale* (Padua, 1971), pp. 10–11, 384–9, 411–19; Brownlie, 'Legal Status of Natural Resources in International Law (Some Aspects)', 162 Hague *Recueil* (1979, I), p. 293; Auburn, *Antarctic Law and Politics* (London, 1981), pp. 115–29; Arrow, 'Seabeds, Sovereignty and Objective Regimes', 7 *Fordham International Law Journal* (1984), pp. 221–6; Simma, 'The Antarctic Treaty as a Treaty Providing for an "Objective Regime"', 19 *Cornell International Law Journal* (1986), pp. 189–209; Francioni and Scovazzi (eds.), *International Law for Antarctica* (Milan, 1987), especially the contributions of Brunner, Charney, Francioni and Simma; Triggs (ed.), *The Antarctic Treaty Regime: Law, Environment and Resources* (Cambridge, 1987), especially the contributions of Orrego Vicuna, Lady Fox and Triggs; Orrego Vicuna, *Antarctic Mineral Exploitation. The Emerging Legal Framework* (Cambridge, 1988), pp. 423–47 and 479–97; Golitsin, *Antarktika: tendentsii razvitiia rezhima* (Moscow, 1989), pp. 143–57; Guillaume, 'Le statut de l'Antarctique: Réflexions sur quelques problèmes récents', *Humanité et droit international. Mélanges René-Jean Dupuy* (Paris, 1991), pp. 171–7. Of great interest also are the message of the Swiss Federal Council reproduced in 47 *Ann. suisse* (1990), pp. 130–1, and the 'Views of States' relating to the United Nations document headed 'Question of Antarctica. Study requested under General Assembly resolution 38/77. Report of the Secretary-General' (Doc.A/39/583 (Part II)).

[91] 'Fourth Report on the content, forms and degrees of State responsibility (Part 2 of the draft articles)' (Doc.A/CN.4/366), Y.I.L.C. (1983, II, Part 1), p. 16, para. 85.

obligations *erga omnes* is not outlandish, as the question of rights and obligations valid for all States had been around for quite some time before the International Court's dictum. Secondly, some at least of these prefigurations make use of ideas ('whole world', 'objective law', 'public interest') for which there are similar expressions in the dictum on obligations *erga omnes* ('international community as a whole', 'by nature', 'concern of all States'). Thirdly, with respect to the issue of political acceptability, these prefigurations show how the international community has historically been reluctant to accept any concept that would be instrumental (or would appear to be instrumental) to the attempts by the great Powers or a majority of States to impose obligations on the other States.

Another prefiguration of obligations *erga omnes* that must now be examined is a closer one in time (at least with respect to its consecration in the Vienna Convention on the Law of Treaties) to the dictum of the International Court: the concept of *jus cogens*.

3

Selected Prefigurations of the Concept of Obligations *Erga Omnes*: (b) *Jus Cogens*

I. *Jus Cogens* in and beyond the Vienna Convention on the Law of Treaties

Among the grounds of invalidity of international agreements, the Vienna Convention on the Law of Treaties lists the conflict of a treaty with a peremptory norm of general international law (*jus cogens*). Article 53 of the Vienna Convention reads as follows:

A treaty is void if, at the time of its conclusion, it conflicts with a peremptory norm of general international law. For the purposes of the present Convention, a peremptory norm of general international law is a norm accepted and recognized by the international community of States as a whole as a norm from which no derogation is permitted and which can be modified only by a subsequent norm of general international law having the same character.[1]

[1] The literature on international *jus cogens* is extensive. For a selection, see, among the general treatises on international law, Brownlie, *Principles*, pp. 512–15; *Oppenheim's International Law*, i, pp. 7–8; Cassese, *International Law*, pp. 175–9; Nguyen Quoc Dinh, Daillier and Pellet, *Droit international public*, pp. 199–206 (paras. 128–32); Favre, *Principes du droit des gens* (Fribourg, 1974), pp. 226–34; Verdross and Simma, *Universelles Völkerrecht*, pp. 328–34; Takano, *Einführung in das Völkerrecht*, German trans. Richter of the second Japanese edition, 1969 (14th reprint, 1977), i (Cologne, 1979), pp. 55–61; ii (Cologne, 1984), pp. 39–42, 68–70 and 116; Tunkin, *Theory of International Law*, English trans. Butler (London, 1974), pp. 147–60; Pastor Ridruejo, *Curso*, pp. 66–70; Giuliano, Scovazzi and Treves, *Diritto internazionale. Parte generale*, pp. 372–6. Most of the general courses delivered at the Hague Academy since the sixties discuss the concept of *jus cogens*. See, for example, Quadri, 'Cours général de droit international public', 113 Hague *Recueil* (1964, III), pp. 335–42; Jennings, 'General Course', pp. 563–5; Monaco, 'Cours général sur des Principes de droit international public', 125 Hague *Recueil* (1968, III), pp. 202–12; Chaumont, 'Cours général de droit international public', 129 ibid. (1970, I), pp. 370–80; De Visscher, P., 'Cours général de droit international public', 136 ibid. (1972, II), pp. 102–11; Tunkin, 'International Law in the International System', 147 ibid. (1975, IV), pp. 85–94; Jiménez de Aréchaga, 'International Law', pp. 62–9; Dupuy, R. J., 'Communauté internationale et disparités de devéloppement. Cours général de droit international public', 165 Hague *Recueil* (1979, IV), pp. 196–205; Lachs, 'The Development and General Trends of International Law in Our Time (General Course in Public International Law)', 169 ibid. (1980, III), pp. 201–11; Truyol y Serra, 'Théorie du droit international public. Cours général', 173 ibid. (1981, IV), pp. 257–61; Virally, 'Panorama du droit international contemporain. Cours général de droit international public', 183 ibid. (1983, V), pp. 175–8; Cahier, 'Changements et continuité', pp. 195–200; Abi-Saab, 'Cours général', pp. 426–7; Thierry, 'L'évolution du droit international. Cours général de droit international public', 222 Hague *Recueil* (1990, III), pp. 58–70; Weil, 'Le droit international', pp. 261–82; Capotorti, 'Cours général de droit international public', 248 Hague *Recueil* (1994, IV),

A treaty may conflict with a peremptory norm that existed when the treaty was concluded or else with a peremptory norm that emerged after the conclusion of the treaty. Addressing this latter case, Article 64 of the Vienna Convention provides as follows:

If a new peremptory norm of general international law emerges, any existing treaty which is in conflict with that norm becomes void and terminates.[2]

The origins of the concept of *jus cogens* are usually traced back to some writings of the earlier part of this century,[3] but the concept has not been

pp. 119–20, 138–42 and 182–4. See also Mosler, *The International Society*, pp. 19–20 and 134–6; Schachter, *International Law*, pp. 342–5; Wang Tieya, 'International Law in China: Historical and Contemporary Perspectives', 221 Hague *Recueil* (1990, II), pp. 279–87; Conforti, *International Law and the Role of Domestic Legal Systems*, English trans. Provost and Van Praagh (Dordrecht, 1993), pp. 118–23; Higgins, R., *Problems and Process. International Law and How We Use It* (Oxford, 1994), pp. 20–2; Henkin, *International Law: Politics and Values* (Dordrecht, 1995), pp. 38–9; Carrillo Salcedo, *Soberania del estado y derecho internacional*, 2nd edn. (Madrid, 1976), pp. 257–85; id., *El derecho internacional en un mundo en cambio* (Madrid, 1984), pp. 204–12; Lukashuk, *Mekhanizm mezhdunarodno-pravovogo regulirovaniia* (Kiev, 1980), pp. 45–55. Among the monographs, see Sztucki, *Jus Cogens and the Vienna Convention on the Law of Treaties* (Vienna, 1974); Rozakis, *The Concept of Jus Cogens in the Law of Treaties* (Amsterdam, 1976); Diaconu, *Normele imperative in dreptul international ('jus cogens')* (Bucharest, 1977) (in Romanian, with English summary); Shestakov, *Imperativnye normy v sisteme sovremennogo mezhdunarodnogo prava* (Moscow, 1981); Aleksidze, *Nekotorye voprosy teorii mezhdunarodnogo prava. Imperativnye normy jus cogens* (Tbilisi, 1982) (*Some Theoretical Problems of International Law. Peremptory Norms Jus Cogens*, in Russian with English summary); Hannikainen, *Peremptory Norms (Jus Cogens) in International law—Historical Development, Criteria, Present Status* (Helsinki, 1988). See also *The Concept of Jus Cogens in Public International Law: Papers and Proceedings (Report of a Conference organized by the Carnegie Endowment for International Peace, Lagonissi (Greece), April 1966)* (Geneva, 1967) and the complex on *jus cogens* organized by the Hague Academy of International Law in 1981, and reproduced in 172 Hague *Recueil* (1981, III), pp. 9–218 (Gomez Robledo), pp. 219–70 (Aleksidze), pp. 271–313 (Gaja). Among the articles, see Miaja de la Muela, '"Ius cogens" y "ius dispositivum" en Derecho internacional publico', *Estudios juridico-sociales, Homenaje al Professor Luis Legaz y Lacambra*, ii (Santiago de Compostela, 1960), pp. 1121–53; Schwarzenberger, 'International jus cogens?', 45 *Texas Law Review* (1965), pp. 455–78; Verdross, 'Jus Dispositivum and Jus Cogens in International Law', 60 *A.J.I.L.* (1966), pp. 55–63; Virally, 'Réflexions sur le "jus cogens"', 11 *A.F.D.I.* (1966), pp. 3–29; Morelli, 'A proposito di norme internazionali cogenti', 52 *Riv. dir. int.* (1968), pp. 108–17; Mosler, 'Ius cogens im Völkerrecht', 25 *Ann. suisse* (1968), pp. 9–40; Marek, 'Contribution à l'étude du jus cogens en droit international', *Recueil d'études de droit international en hommage à Paul Guggenheim* (Geneva, 1968), pp. 426–59; Li Haopei, 'Jus Cogens and International Law', *Selected Articles from Chinese Yearbook of International Law* (Beijing, 1983), pp. 58–6.

[2] Most of the writings cited in footnote 1, above, also examine Article 64.

[3] In conformity with a widespread view, Roland and Boyer (*Locutions latines du droit français*, 3rd edn. (Paris, 1993), p. 214, under 'JUS COGENS / Droit impératif') identify the origins of the concept in the 'doctrine allemande de l'entre-deux-guerres', presumably intending to refer, by this expression, to several writings by German and Austrian authors, such as von der Heydte, 'Die Erscheinungsformen des zwischenstaatlichen Rechts: *jus cogens* und *jus dispositivum* im Völkerrecht', 16 *Zeitschrift für Völkerrecht* (1932), pp. 461–87; Verdross, 'Forbidden Treaties in International Law', 31 *A.J.I.L.* (1937), pp. 571–7. While these contributions must not be underestimated, during the same years writers from other countries were likewise studying the concept, or at least using the term. See, for example, Anzilotti, *Corso di diritto internazionale*, i, 3rd edn. (Rome, 1928), pp. 88–92 (pp. 96–101 in id., *Cours de*

utilized with any degree of consistency in the practice of States and by international tribunals in the period before the adoption of the Vienna Convention. For this reason, international lawyers have long discussed whether the provisions on *jus cogens* in the Vienna Convention codify or rather progressively develop the law, in the sense in which 'codification' and 'progressive development' are used in the Statute of the International Law Commission.[4] A rigid distinction between the two expressions has proved elusive,[5] and is not very helpful in analysing the concept of *jus cogens* either. What is important is the increasing acceptance of the concept in international law, both during the work of codification of the law of treaties and after the adoption of the Vienna Convention.

The concept that an international agreement in conflict with a norm of *jus cogens* is void was introduced into the draft of the Vienna Convention by the Special Rapporteur Sir Hersch Lauterpacht,[6] and subsequently refined by his successors, Sir Gerald Fitzmaurice[7] and Sir Humphrey

droit international, i, French trans. Gidel (Paris 1929)); Williams, J. F., 'La doctrine de la réconnaissance en droit international et ses dévéloppements récents', 44 Hague *Recueil* (1933, II), p. 282; Ripert, 'Les règles du droit civil applicables aux rapports internationaux (Contributions à l'étude des principes généraux du droit visés au Statut de la Cour permanante de Justice international)', ibid., p. 599; Salvioli, 'Les règles générales du droit de la paix', 46 ibid. (1933, IV), pp. 26–7; Ray, 'Des conflits entre principes abstraites et stipulations conventionnelles', 48 ibid. (1934, II), p. 701. Already in 1914, Anzilotti had distinguished between peremptory and dispositive norms of international law without, however, using the expression '*jus cogens*' ('Intorno agli effetti delle modificazioni del corso di un fiume sul confine fra due Stati', 8 *Riv. dir. int.* (1914), p. 78); for criticism, see Cavaglieri, 'Concetto e caratteri del diritto internazionale generale', 14 *Riv. dir. int.* (1921/22), p. 495, note 3. The origins of the term are debated. Dhokalia has remarked that the term '*jus cogens*' did not belong to classic Roman law, and has reported Jolowicz's view that the term was introduced by the German pandectists ('Problems Relating to *Jus Cogens* in the Law of Treaties', Agrawala (ed.), *Essays on the Law of Treaties (With special reference to India)* (Bombay, 1972), p. 150, including note 4). On the other hand, Reuter has written that '*jus cogens*' is a term 'venu du droit romain à travers le Common Law' (*Le développement de l'ordre juridique international: écrits de droit international* (Paris, 1995), p. 21 (reproducing an article which originally appeared in 1970).

[4] See Articles 1 and 15 of the Statute (*U.N., Off. Recs., Second Session of the General Assembly, Resolutions, 16 September–29 November 1947*, pp. 105–10). On the Statute and work of the International Law Commission, see Briggs, *The International Law Commission* (Ithaca, N.Y., 1965); Sinclair, *The International Law Commission* (Cambridge, 1987); Sucharitkul, 'The Role of the International Law Commission in the Decade of International Law', 3 *Leiden Journal of International Law* (1990, No. 3, Special Issue December 1990) pp. 15–42. On codification, see Movchan, *Kodifikatsiia i progressivnoe razvitie mezhdunarodnogo prava* (Moscow, 1972); Geck, 'The Codification of International Law in the United Nations: Promoting and Obstructing Factors and their Results', 17 *Law and State* (1978), pp. 21–44 (with extensive bibliography).

[5] See Brownlie, *Principles*, pp. 30–1. See also Ago, 'La codification du droit international et les problèmes de sa réalisation', *Recueil Guggenheim*, pp. 93–131; Lauterpacht, H. 'Codification and Development of International Law', 49 *A.J.I.L.* (1955), pp. 16–43; Schachter, *International Law*, pp. 66–74.

[6] '[First] Report on the Law of Treaties' (Doc.A/CN.4/63), *Y.I.L.C.* (1953, II), pp. 154–6 (Article 15).

[7] 'Third Report on the Law of Treaties' (Doc.A/CN.4/115), *Y.I.L.C.* (1958, II), pp. 40–1 (Article 17).

Waldock.[8] At the Vienna Conference, an overwhelming majority of States voted in favour of what would then become Articles 53 and 64 in the final text.[9] After the adoption of the Vienna Convention, and already before its entry into force, Article 53 acquired wide acceptance.[10]

In a few instances, though not as many as one would have expected or feared, States have challenged the validity of treaties allegedly in breach of *jus cogens*.[11] The International Court, and some of its members in their individual opinions, have referred to *jus cogens* in the context of areas of the law as varied as the rights of passage through a territory, the protection of fundamental human rights, humanitarian law, the law of the sea, self-determination, and the prohibition of the unlawful use of force.[12]

[8] The first reference was in the 'Second Report on the Law of Treaties' (Doc.A/CN.4/156 and Add. 1–3), *Y.I.L.C.* (1963, II), Articles 1(3)(c) and 13.

[9] Article 50 (which was then numbered as Article 53 in the final text) was adopted at the 20th plenary meeting of the Vienna Conference by eighty-seven votes to eight, with twelve abstentions (*U.N.C.L.T., Off. Recs., Second Session, Vienna, 9 April – 22 May 1969, Summary records of the plenary meetings and of the Committee of the Whole*, pp. 106–7). Article 64 was adopted at the Vienna Conference by eighty-four votes to eight, with sixteen abstentions. On the drafting history of Articles 53 and 64 of the Vienna Convention, see Rosenne, *The Law of Treaties: A Comparative Guide to the Legislative History of the Vienna Convention* (Leiden and Dobbs Ferry, 1970), pp. 290–3 and 330–2.

[10] See, for example, the 'Letter of Submittal to the President of the United States by the Department of State', *S. Exec. Doc. L., 92d Cong., 1st sess.* (1971), p. 1; 'Message relatif à l'adhesion de la Suisse à la Convention de Vienne de 1969 sur le droit des traités et à la Convention de Vienne de 1986 sur le droit des traités entre Etats et organisations internationales', *Feuille fédérale* (1986, II), pp. 703–4. (The writer is grateful to Dr Alexandre Fasel, formerly of Fribourg University, for providing him with a copy of this document.) On the wider issue of the influence of certain international agreements before their entry into force, see Sinclair, 'The Impact of the Unratified Codification Convention', Bos and Siblesz (eds.), *Realism in Law-Making: essays on international law in honour of Willem Riphagen* (Dordrecht, 1986), pp. 211–29.

[11] See Ronzitti, 'Trattati contrari a norme imperative del diritto internazionale?', *Studi in onore di Giuseppe Sperduti. Fonti internazionali e rapporti fra ordinamenti, l'individuo nel diritto internazionale, altri contributi* (Milan, 1984), pp. 209–72.

[12] See, for example, *Right of Passage over Indian Territory*, Merits, Judgment, I.C.J. Reports 1960, p. 133, para. 29 (dissenting opinion of Judge Fernandes); *South West Africa, Second Phase*, Judgment, I.C.J. Reports 1966, p. 298 (dissenting opinion of Judge Tanaka); *North Sea Continental Shelf*, Judgment, I.C.J. Reports 1969, pp. 41–2, para. 72; pp. 97–8 (separate opinion of Judge Padilla Nervo); p. 182 (dissenting opinion of Judge Tanaka); p. 229 (dissenting opinion of Judge Lachs); p. 248 (dissenting opinion of Judge Sörensen); *Barcelona Traction, Light and Power Company, Limited*, Second Phase, Judgment, I.C.J. Reports 1970, pp. 301–4, para. 11 and p. 325, para. 34 (separate opinion of Judge Ammoun); *Military and Paramilitary Activities in and against Nicaragua (Nicaragua* v. *United States of America)*, Jurisdiction and Admissibility, Judgment, I.C.J. Reports 1984, pp. 614–16, para. 88 (dissenting opinion of Judge Schwebel); *Military and Paramilitary Activities in and against Nicaragua (Nicaragua* v. *United States of America)*, Merits, Judgment, I.C.J. Reports 1986, pp. 100–1, para. 190; p. 153 (separate opinion of President Nagendra Singh); pp. 199–200 (separate opinion of Judge Sette-Camara); *Maritime Delimitation in the Area Between Greenland and Jan Mayen*, Judgment, I.C.J. Reports 1993, p. 109 (separate opinion of Judge Oda); pp. 135–6 and 200 (separate opinion of Judge Shahabuddeen); p. 217 (separate opinion of Judge Weeramantry); *East Timor (Portugal v. Australia)*, Judgment, I.C.J. Reports 1995, p. 131 (separate opinion of Judge Ranjeva); p. 266, para. 135 (dissenting opinion of Judge *ad hoc* Skubiszewski); *Legality of the Threat or Use of Nuclear Weapons*, Advisory Opinion, I.C.J. Reports 1996 (mimeographed

References to international *jus cogens* have also occurred in decisions of municipal courts[13] and international arbitral tribunals,[14] as well as two opinions rendered by the *ad hoc* Arbitration Commission on the former Yugoslavia.[15]

Another important development attaching to *jus cogens* is that the concept is currently utilized outside its original context of the invalidity of treaties among States. By reproducing the exact terms of Articles 53 and 64 of the Vienna Convention of 1969, the Vienna Convention on the Law of Treaties between States and International Organizations or between International Organizations has expanded the reach of the concept.[16] Moreover, beyond the law of treaties, *jus cogens* has been influential, for example, in the work of codification of the law on State responsibility.[17]

A new approach in the literature confirms that the concept of *jus cogens* has now been accepted as part of general international law. Whereas formerly writers used to discuss whether the very idea of peremptory norms is at all compatible with the international system, almost everybody now takes

text), p. 29, para. 83; pp. 4–5, para. 21 (declaration of President Bedjaoui); p. 5 (dissenting opinion of Vice-President Schwebel); p. 4 (dissenting opinion of Judge Shahabuddeen); pp. 13–14 (dissenting opinion of Judge Koroma); *Application of the Convention on the Prevention and Punishment of the Crime of Genocide*, Preliminary Objections, I.C.J. Reports 1996 (mimeographed text), pp. 41–2, para. 43 and p. 62, para. 68 (dissenting opinion of Judge *ad hoc* Kreca).

[13] See, for example, *Sener c/ Ministère public de la Confédération et Département fédéral de justice et police*, Arrêts du Tribunal Fédéral, 22 Mar. 1983, Ib 64 (c.6), p. 72; *Ch. c/ Office fédéral de la police et Département de la justice et police*, ibid., 17 Apr. 1985, Ib 138 (c.6), p. 145; *Lavi* v. *Asco and Others* (Belgium, Commercial Court of Brussels (Ninth Chamber), 2 May 1988), 91 *I.L.R.* (1993), p. 249; *S* v. *Banda and Others* (Bophuthatswana, Supreme Court, General Division, 6 Feb. 1989), 82 *I.L.R.* (1990), p. 388. See also the *Siderman* case (*Siderman de Blake* v. *Republic of Argentina*, 965 F.2d 699 (9th Cir. 1992)), discussed in Janis, *An Introduction to International Law*, 2nd edn. (Boston, 1993), p. 65.

[14] See, for example, *Beagle Channel Arbitration (Argentina* v. *Chile)*, 52 *I.L.R.* (1979), p. 93 (the five arbitrators were Sir Gerald Fitzmaurice (President), Dillard, Gros, Onyeama and Petrén). See also the *Texaco, Aminoil* and *Guinea-Bissau* v. *Senegal* cases, cited in Section III of Chapter 8, below.

[15] Opinion No. 1 on secession and dismemberment (dated 29 November 1991) and Opinion No. 2 on the right of ethnic minorities to self-determination (dated 11 January 1992) state that respect for fundamental human rights and the rights of the peoples and minorities are 'normes imperatives du droit international général'. Comments on certain aspects of Opinion No. 1 are developed below in this chapter.

[16] Doc.A/Conf.129/15, reproduced in 25 *I.L.M.* (1986), pp. 543–92. The Convention was adopted on 21 March 1986 and has not yet entered into force. For commentary, see Gaja, 'A "New" Vienna Convention on Treaties between States and International Organizations or between International Organizations: A Critical Commentary', 58 *B.Y.I.L.* (1987), pp. 253–69. On the provisions relating to *jus cogens*, see Zemanek, 'The United Nations Conference on the Law of Treaties Between States and International Organizations: The unrecorded history of its "general agreement"', Böckstiegel, Folz, Mössner and Zemanek (eds.), *Law of Nations. Law of International Organizations. World's Economic Law. Liber Amicorum honouring Ignaz Seidl-Hohenveldern* (Cologne, 1988), pp. 675–7.

[17] The references are innumerable. See, for example, Gaja, '*Jus Cogens* Beyond the Vienna Convention', 172 Hague *Recueil* (1981, III), pp. 290–301.

for granted a positive answer to this question,[18] and writers concentrate on the outstanding issues that the Vienna Convention has left open.[19] Among these issues, the three on which the present chapter will focus are (a) the definition of the particular content of *jus cogens*, (b) the tests of *jus cogens* under Article 53 of the Vienna Convention, and (c) the question of the opposability *erga omnes* of peremptory norms.

II. The Search for a Definition of the Particular Content of *Jus Cogens*

Except for the general acceptance of the peremptory character of the prohibition of aggression and the protection of some, but not all, human rights, the definition of the precise content of *jus cogens* is still uncertain. This uncertainty is regrettable for various reasons: it can be dangerous for the stability of treaties and provide States with an excuse for escaping from their international commitments,[20] or conversely it can deter a State from challenging the validity of a treaty even when this challenge would be wholly justified.[21] In other words, uncertainty may be, on the one hand, a pretext for claiming the nullity of a lawful treaty or, on the other hand, an obstacle to the declaration of invalidity of an unlawful one.

A partial attempt to overcome these risks was the introduction into the Vienna Convention of a procedural safeguard according to which, in case of dispute relating to the interpretation or application of Articles 53 and 64, any party to the relevant treaty may submit the dispute to arbitration or, failing an agreement to this effect, to the International Court (Article 66(a) of the Vienna Convention).[22] So far, there have been no instances in which

[18] This was not the case in the early eighties, when Lachs wrote, in his general course at the Hague Academy, that *jus cogens* was a new institution which 'cannot yet quite be taken for granted.' ('The Development and General Trends', p. 203.)

[19] See, for example, Christenson, '*Jus Cogens*: Guarding Interests Fundamental to International Society', 28 *Virginia Journal of International Law* (1988), pp. 585–648. For an inventory of the outstanding issues attaching to the concept of *jus cogens*, see the report submitted by Jacovides to the International Law Commission in 1993 (Doc.A/CN.4/454, pp. 17–26).

[20] Likewise, in his *General Principles of Law as Applied by International Courts and Tribunals* (London, 1953; reprinted Cambridge, 1987), p. xiv, Cheng stressed the need for a clear definition of the scope and substance of the 'general principles of law recognised by civilised states', lest they be exploited as 'an ideological cloak for self-interest'.

[21] The United Kingdom alluded to this problem in the *Fisheries Jurisdiction* case, *I.C.J. Pleadings, Fisheries Jurisdiction (United Kingdom* v. *Iceland)*, i, p. 261. See also the statement by Ethiopia during the codification of the law of treaties, *U.N.C.L.T., Off. Recs., First Session,* p. 314, para. 76.

[22] The need for submission of controversies concerning *jus cogens* to an impartial body was expressed in the declarations of the representatives of the United Kingdom, the United States, France, Sweden, Italy, Belgium, Canada, Chile, Portugal and the Federal Republic of Germany at the 108th meeting of the Committee of the Whole (*U.N.C.L.T., Off. Recs., First*

a party has submitted a dispute to the International Court pursuant to this provision. This may be due, at least in part, to the fact that several countries have attached reservations to Article 66 when ratifying, or acceding to, the Vienna Convention.[23] In addition, while in principle a procedural safeguard can contribute, by accretion of judicial pronouncements, to the definition of *jus cogens*, it is difficult to see how in practice the mechanism provided in it can apply outside the context of the Vienna Convention. For all these reasons, the best possible protection against the risk of abuse remains a clear definition of the content of *jus cogens*.

In its Commentary on draft Article 50, the International Law Commission explicitly stated that what gives peremptory character to an international norm is 'the particular nature of the subject-matter with which it deals'.[24] This comment reflects the idea of *jus cogens* shared by all the Special Rapporteurs on the law of treaties and summarized by Fitzmaurice, who wrote that a common feature of peremptory rules is that they involve 'not only legal rules but considerations of morals and of international good order'.[25] In other words, to be in conflict with *jus cogens*, a treaty must be in breach of a rule of law: a court or an arbitral tribunal can always refuse to apply a treaty which is contrary to the public morals ('*contra bonos mores*'), but in this case there is no need to resort to *jus cogens*.[26] At the same time, the idea of *jus cogens* embodied in Article 53 is that of rules of general international law which are peremptory not only because States have recognized that there must be no derogation from them, but also because of the values that these rules are called on to protect and promote.

Naming a few norms of *jus cogens* is easy. Almost everybody would agree with Waldock (Fitzmaurice's successor as Special Rapporteur) that treaties conflicting with the prohibition of the use or threat of force, treaties involving international crimes, and treaties contemplating or conniving at the

Session, pp. 472–3). Article 66(a) was the result of a compromise proposed by ten States (see *U.N.C.L.T., Off. Recs., Second Session*, pp. 187–94). In the literature, see Bernardini, 'Qualche riflessione su norme internazionali di *jus cogens* e giurisdizione della Corte nella Convenzione di Vienna sul diritto dei trattati', 14 *Comunicazioni e studi* (1975), pp. 81–100; Rosenne, *Developments in the Law of Treaties 1945–1986* (Cambridge, 1989), pp. 281–8.

[23] See the declarations, reservations and objections to the Vienna Convention reproduced in *Multilateral Treaties Deposited with the Secretary-General. Status as at 31 December 1995*, pp. 840–6. See also the interventions of the representatives of the United Kingdom and the former Soviet Union in *U.N.C.L.T., Off. Recs., Second Session*, pp. 190–1.

[24] 'Draft Articles on the Law of Treaties', p. 67, para. 2.

[25] 'Third Report', p. 41, para. 76. Such considerations are not always as self-evident as in the case of the prohibition of aggression or the protection of basic human rights. For example, according to Fitzmaurice, freedom of the seas belongs to *jus cogens* because the sea is *res communis* (ibid., p. 40, note 54).

[26] In his 'Third Report', Fitzmaurice clearly distinguished between 'legality of the object (conflict with international law)' (Article 17) and 'ethics of the object' (Article 20). On treaties *contra bonos mores*, see Monaco, 'Cours général', pp. 153–4, including the bibliographical references in note 8.

commission of acts of slave trade, piracy or genocide, are in breach of *jus cogens*.[27] These examples largely coincide with those of obligations *erga omnes* given in the *Barcelona Traction* case.

The real problem arises when one tries to go further than these classic examples. At the Vienna Conference, there were several proposals that, if accepted, would have given the concept of *jus cogens* a better identifiable content. The delegation of the United Kingdom proposed to define peremptory rules in protocols to the Vienna Convention.[28] The representative of the Holy See suggested that a principle of interpretation such as the primacy of human rights would give the concept of *jus cogens* a more concrete value.[29] Other representatives stated that international *jus cogens* consists of the fundamental principles of international law,[30] an idea to which it was objected that each individual principle should be assessed on its own merits.[31] Ultimately, the diverging political agenda of the various States, and their concern that a sample list of peremptory norms might lead to abuse, discouraged all attempts to include examples of *jus cogens* in the final text of the Vienna Convention.[32] The preferred solution was to indicate in Article 53 three tests which, in the drafters' view, would help to establish in a concrete instance whether or not a rule is peremptory. The next two sections of this chapter will examine these tests in some detail.

[27] 'Second Report on the Law of Treaties', p. 52 (draft Article 13), and p. 53, para. 4 (Commentary). However, with respect to the inclusion of acts of piracy among those prohibited by peremptory rules, Fitzmaurice remarked that acts committed or authorized by a Government may well be illegal under international law, but not strictly on the basis of piracy, which consists essentially of private and unauthorized acts ('Third Report', p. 40, note 57).

[28] A sub-amendment to this effect (A/Conf.39/C.1/L.312) was then withdrawn at the 57th meeting of the Committee of the Whole for tactical reasons (*U.N.C.L.T., Off. Recs., First Session*, p. 300).

[29] Ibid., pp. 258–9, para. 75.

[30] See the intervention of the representative of the former Czechoslovakia at the 781st meeting of the Sixth Committee of the United Nations General Assembly (Twenty-fifth session), and of the representative of Iraq at the 1180th meeting.

[31] See the intervention of the representative of the Netherlands at the 1183rd meeting of the Sixth Committee of the United Nations General Assembly (Twenty-fifth session).

[32] See the Comments of Governments on draft Article 37 (which then became Article 53 of the Vienna Convention), *Y.I.L.C.* (1966, II), pp. 20–3. In its Commentary on draft Article 50, the International Law Commission had argued that any attempt to draw up a list of peremptory rules would require a prolonged study of matters which fell outside the scope of the Vienna Convention, and remarked that the inclusion of certain rules, and the exclusion of others, might give rise to misunderstandings ('Draft Articles on the Law of Treaties', pp. 67–8, para. 3).

III. The Tests of *Jus Cogens* under Article 53 of the Vienna Convention: (a) Acceptance and Recognition of the Peremptory Character of a Norm by the International Community of States as a Whole

Article 53 is composed of two sentences. The first one provides that a treaty conflicting with a norm of *jus cogens* is void.[33] This special consequence is not immune from difficulties, even if it has been a distinctive feature of *jus cogens* since the first draft submitted to the International Law Commission by Sir Hersch Lauterpacht.[34] For example, Fitzmaurice has remarked that, if no impartial body has jurisdiction to declare that a treaty is invalid for breach of *jus cogens*, nothing prevents the parties from applying the treaty among themselves. In practice, a treaty in conflict with *jus cogens* would be 'unenforceable' but not 'void'.[35]

However, it is the second sentence of Article 53 that is important for the purposes of the present work. It provides that a norm of *jus cogens* must satisfy three tests: the norm must be (a) 'accepted and recognized by the international community of States as a whole' as a norm from which (b) 'no derogation is permitted', and which (c) 'can be modified only by a subsequent norm of general international law having the same character'. These tests will now be examined in this order, starting from acceptance and recognition by the international community of States as a whole.

Article 53 was finalized at the second session of the Vienna Conference. The draft originally adopted by the International Law Commission, which was the starting point for the work at the Vienna Conference, did not specify that a peremptory rule should be 'accepted and recognized by the international community of States as a whole'. This was a later addition. When a widespread agreement emerged against giving examples of peremptory norms in the Vienna Convention, the United States, on the one hand, and

[33] Article 71 of the Vienna Convention then indicates the consequences of the invalidity of a treaty conflicting with a norm of *jus cogens*.

[34] *Y.I.L.C.* (1953, II), p. 154.

[35] 'Third Report', p. 41, note 61. A similar argument is developed in Barile, *Lezioni di diritto internazionale* (Padua, 1983), p. 135. There is no need to consider here the complex topic that falls under the 'composite heading', as Jennings put it ('Treaties', Bedjaoui (ed.), *International Law: Achievements and Prospects* (Paris and Dordrecht, 1991), p. 150), of the invalidity of international treaties, which includes the issue of the invalidity of treaties conflicting with peremptory rules, and is part of the wider subject of the invalidity of international legal acts (on which, see Guggenheim, 'La validité et la nullité des actes juridiques internationaux', 74 Hague *Recueil* (1949, I), pp. 195–265). Likewise, there is no need to examine the question of the separability of treaty provisions conflicting with a peremptory rule. The solution embodied in the Vienna Convention on this point prohibits separability when the conflict is with a norm of *jus cogens*, but allows it when the conflict is with a norm of *jus cogens superveniens*. (For comment, see Sinclair, *Vienna Convention*, p. 167; for critical remarks on the indivisibility of treaties for breach of *jus cogens*, see Quadri, 'Cours général', pp. 337–8.)

Greece, Spain and Finland, on the other, submitted two amendments aimed at reducing the risk that States may abuse peremptory norms to free themselves of valid obligations. The amendment proposed by the United States provided that a norm of *jus cogens* should have to be 'recognized in common by national and regional legal systems of the world'.[36] However, the United States did not succeed in dispelling the suspicion, voiced by some delegations,[37] that the reference to municipal laws and regional legal systems would give a dissenting State the power of veto over the formation of a peremptory norm. In the end, the Committee of the Whole rejected this amendment.[38]

The amendment proposed by Greece, Spain and Finland was better received. According to this proposal, draft Article 50 (which, after further amendments, became Article 53 of the Vienna Convention) would read as follows:

A treaty is void if it conflicts with a peremptory norm of general international law recognized by the international community as a norm from which no derogation is permitted and which can be modified only by a subsequent norm of general international law having the same character.[39]

This draft differs from the final text of Article 53 because it requires that a peremptory norm be merely 'recognized' (instead of being 'accepted and recognized') by the international community. Why was the draft modified? The answer is straightforward. As Yasseen (the Chairman of the Drafting Committee at the Vienna Conference) explained,[40] the Drafting Committee amended the language originally proposed by Greece, Spain and Finland in order that the definition of *jus cogens* might be fully in accordance with Article 38, paragraph 1, of the Statute of the International Court, which reads as follows:

The Court, whose function is to decide in accordance with international law such disputes as are submitted to it, shall apply:

a. international conventions, whether general or particular, establishing rules expressly recognized by the contesting states;
b. international custom, as evidence of a general practice accepted as law;
c. the general principles of law recognized by civilized nations;

[36] Doc. A/Conf.39/c.1/L.302. The representative of the United States explained the meaning of this language to the Committee of the Whole. See *U.N.C.L.T., Off. Recs., First Session*, p. 330, paras. 26–9.

[37] Ibid., p. 315, para. 4 (Spain), and p. 327, para. 64 (Trinidad and Tobago). The United States amendment is also criticized in Tunkin, 'Jus Cogens in Contemporary International Law', 3 *The University of Toledo Law Review* (1971), pp. 113–14.

[38] The amendment was rejected by fifty-seven votes to twenty-four, with seven abstentions (*U.N.C.L.T., Off. Recs., First Session*, p. 333, para. 80).

[39] Doc.A/Conf.39/C.1/L.306 and Add.1 and 2. The original sponsor of the amendment was Greece.

[40] *U.N.C.L.T. Off. Recs., First Session*, p. 471, para. 4.

d. subject to the provisions of Article 59, judicial decisions and the teachings of the most highly qualified publicists of the various nations, as subsidiary means for the determination of rules of law.

This article, like its predecessor (Article 38, paragraph 1, of the Statute of the Permanent Court of International Justice), has traditionally been regarded as an authoritative statement of the sources of international law.[41] It provides for 'recognition' of international conventions and the general principles of law, and 'acceptance' of international customs. Therefore, the term 'acceptance' was added to the text of Article 53 to cover the possibility of the emergence of peremptory rules by way of custom. This amendment was justified in consideration of the fact that, pursuant to Article 53, and already draft Article 1(c) of Waldock's second report,[42] peremptory rules belong to 'general international law', with the consequence (based on the interpretation of 'general international law' as synonymous with 'customary international law') that international *jus cogens* would essentially be the product of custom, albeit with a special form of *opinio juris*.[43]

However, Janis has warned that, by equating 'general international law' with 'customary international law', one runs the risk of misinterpreting the

[41] Article 38, paragraph 1, of the Statute of the Permanent Court of International Justice clearly represented the drafters' view on the sources of international law. See *Cour Permanente de Justice Internationale. Comité Consultatif de Juristes. Procès Verbaux des Séances du Comité 16 juin – 24 juillet 1920 avec Annexes* (The Hague, 1920), pp. 337–8 (intervention of Ricci-Busatti). However, while it traditionally represents an authoritative statement on the sources (see Brierly, *The Law of Nations. An Introduction to the International Law of Peace*, 6th edn. Waldock (Oxford, 1963), p. 56), the Court 'is not limited by the strict enumeration of article 38, whose prescriptions it is free to interpret in accordance with the constant evolution of the concepts of justice, principles of law and teachings of publicists' (*South West Africa*, Second Phase, Judgment, I.C.J. Reports 1966, p. 464 (dissenting opinion of Judge Padilla Nervo)). General treatises of international law invariably have a chapter on the sources of international law (see, for example, Brownlie, *Principles*, pp. 1–31). Three classic monographs on the subject are Sörensen, *Les sources du droit international. Etude sur la jurisprudence de la Cour permanente de justice internationale* (Copenhagen, 1946); Parry, *The Sources and Evidences of International Law* (Manchester, 1965); Verdross, *Die Quellen des universellen Völkerrecht. Ein Einführung* (Freiburg, 1973). A more recent work is van Hoof, *Rethinking the Sources of International Law* (The Hague, 1983). See also Scelle, 'Essai sur les sources formelles du droit international', *Recueil sur les sources du droit en l'honneur de F. Geny*, iii (Paris, 1935), pp. 400–30; Gihl, 'The Legal Character and Sources of International Law', 1 *Scandinavian Studies in Law* (1957), pp. 51–92; Fitzmaurice, 'Some Problems Regarding the Formal Sources of International Law', *Symbolae Verzijl présentées au Professor J. H. W. Verzijl à l'occasion de son LXX-ième anniversaire* (The Hague, 1958), pp. 153–76; Abi-Saab, 'Les sources du droit international: un essai de déconstruction', *International Law. Liber Jiménez de Aréchaga*, pp. 29–49. For a critical account of the relationship between the theory of sources and legal positivism, see Ago, 'Positive Law and International Law', 51 *A.J.I.L.* (1957), pp. 696–700; Schachter, *International Law*, pp. 34–48. The question of the sources of the law has to be distinguished from the problem of the ultimate foundation of the law. See Fitzmaurice, 'The Foundation of the Authority of International Law and the Problem of Enforcement', 19 *The Modern Law Review* (1956), p. 9.

[42] See 'Second Report on the Law of Treaties', p. 39 (including the Commentary, para. 2).

[43] See, for example, Ago's intervention reproduced in *Y.I.L.C.* (1963, I), p. 71, para. 50. For a more subtly refined position, see Tunkin's intervention, ibid., p. 69, paras. 25–6.

very essence of *jus cogens*, which cannot be reduced to the idea of consent that lies behind conventional and customary rules alike.[44] More generally, it seems reasonable to suggest that a too rigid approach to the sources of international *jus cogens* would be misleading. The examples of peremptory norms most often cited, such as the prohibition of genocide or the protection from slavery, are those of rules having their origins in more than just one of the traditional sources listed in Article 38, paragraph 1, of the Statute of the International Court.[45] In addition, it is legitimate to question whether *jus cogens* can be really confined within the strict limits of the sources enumerated in Article 38 of the Statute of the International Court. On this point, during the codification of the law of treaties, some members of the International Law Commission had asked, without success, that the question of the role of United Nations resolutions in the formation of international *jus cogens* be specifically addressed. The International Law Commission decided not to address this issue because it would exceed its specific task.[46]

To sum up, the important point about the expression 'acceptance and recognition' is not to decide in the abstract which source(s) can produce norms of *jus cogens*, but to assess whether the 'intrinsic value' of a certain rule and the fact that it is 'rooted in the international conscience' (as Yasseen put it)[47] are reflected in the acceptance and recognition of that rule as a rule of *jus cogens*. Hence the importance of the tests of *jus cogens* indicated in Article 53.

The first test provides for a special degree of acceptance and recognition: a peremptory norm must be accepted and recognized as such by the 'international community of States as a whole'.[48] Unlike the draft submitted by

[44] 'The Nature of *Jus Cogens*', 3 *Connecticut Journal of International Law* (1988), pp. 360–1. There is no need to examine here the use of the expression 'general international law', and the relationship of this expression with that of 'customary international law'. For brief considerations on the subject, see Piza Escalante, 'La "opinion juris" como fuente autonoma del derecho internacional ("opinio juris" y "jus cogens")', 8 *Anuario hispano-luso-americano de derecho internacional* (1987), pp. 149–50; Cheng, 'How Should We Study International Law?', 13 *Chinese Yearbook of International Law and Affairs* (1994/95), pp. 223–4. See also the discussion among the members of the International Law Association's committee on 'The Formation of Rules of Customary (General) International Law', reproduced in International Law Association, *Report of the Sixty-third Conference held at Warsaw. August 21st to August 27th, 1988* (London, 1988), pp. 952–3 (Appendix to Second Report of the Rapporteur) and pp. 960–72 (especially the interventions of Mrazek, Murase, Detter de Lupis, Broms, Koulichev, Benedek and Mendelson).

[45] See Chapters 5 and 6, below.

[46] See the interventions at the 685th meeting, *Y.I.L.C.* (1963, I), pp. 73–8.

[47] *Y.I.L.C.* (1963, I), p. 63, para. 39 (683rd meeting), and ibid. (1966, I, Part 1), pp. 38–9, para. 29 (828th meeting).

[48] For comments on this expression, see Combacau and Sur, *Droit international public*, pp. 159–60; el Kadiri, *La position des Etats du tiers monde à la Conférence de Vienne sur le droit des traités* (Rabat, 1980), pp. 113–22; Movchan, 'Sovremennyi mezhdunarodnyi pravoporiadok', Graefrath (ed.), *Probleme des Völkerrechts* (Berlin, 1987), pp. 257–62 (in Russian, with English summary). Critical remarks on the concept of 'international community' are developed in Weil, 'Le droit international', pp. 306–12.

Greece, Spain and Finland, the final text of Article 53 expressly requires that the international community that accepts and recognizes a peremptory rule must be a community 'of States'.[49] Why did the Drafting Committee introduce this requirement? One cannot search for an answer to this question in the records of the Drafting Committee, as these have not been published.[50]

However, the preparatory work of the Vienna Convention of 1986 on Treaties between States and International Organizations or between International Organizations sheds some light on this point. As was mentioned earlier, Article 53 of this Convention reproduces exactly the text of Article 53 of the Vienna Convention of 1969. In the debates that preceded the adoption of the Vienna Convention of 1986, the International Law Commission considered whether an exclusive reference to the international community 'of States' (without any mention at all of international organizations) might not be unduly restrictive in the context of the codification of the law of treaties involving international organizations. The International Law Commission decided not to depart from the formulation of Article 53 of the Vienna Convention of 1969, because 'it is States that are called upon to establish or recognize peremptory norms', at least 'in the present state of international law'.[51] In other words, the International Law Commission was reluctant to depart from the traditional tenets of international law, especially the primary role of States in the production of international rules, including rules of *jus cogens*.

A more troublesome aspect of the expression 'international community of States as a whole' lies in its final words: what does 'as a whole' mean? Is it necessary that a peremptory norm be accepted and recognized as such by every single State of the international community? If not, when does a number of States short of unanimity constitute the international community 'as a whole'? During the work of codification of the Vienna Convention of 1969, Yasseen explained that the words 'as a whole' had been added in order that, if 'one State in isolation' or 'a very small number of States' were

[49] The dictum on obligations *erga omnes* uses the expression 'international community as a whole' but omits the words 'of States'.

[50] Apart from any other possible considerations specifically referring to the work of the Drafting Committee, the publication of the records of the International Law Commission, and of other subsidiary organs of the United Nations General Assembly, is subject to financial constraints. Convincing reasons for recommending the continued publication of the summary records of the meetings of the International Law Commission were articulated in a document adopted by the International Law Commission at its forty-sixth session, in 1994. ('Programme, procedures and working methods of the Commission, and its documentation' (Report of the Planning Group) (Doc.A/CN.4/L.502), pp. 3–5, paras. 12–16.)

[51] See 'Report of the International Law Commission on the work of its thirty-fourth session (Question of treaties concluded between States and international organizations or between two or more international organizations)', *Y.I.L.C.* (1982, II, Part 2), p. 56, para. 3 (Commentary to Article 53).

to reject the peremptory character of a norm, the other States would not be precluded from accepting and recognizing this norm as a norm of *jus cogens*.[52] Therefore, for a norm of *jus cogens* to arise, there is no need for the unanimous consent of all States.

Yasseen's clarification does not indicate, however, the degree of acceptance and recognition that must accompany the emergence of a peremptory norm. A few years after the adoption of the Vienna Convention, Ago (who was the Chairman of the Vienna Conference) proposed a few practical criteria that would help to interpret the expression 'as a whole'. He wrote that, for an international norm to be a norm of *jus cogens*, it is sufficient that the peremptory character be accepted and recognized by the 'basic components' of the international community, including Eastern and Western countries, developed and developing States, as well as countries belonging to different continents.[53]

This effort of defining more precisely the content of *jus cogens* is helpful, but does not dissipate all doubts. When Ago referred to the 'basic components' of the international community, the difference between East and West had a precise political meaning. Today, after the collapse of the communist regimes in the former Soviet Union and in Eastern Europe, the distinction between East and West (as a reflection of the ideological conflict between the capitalist and socialist systems) is quickly vanishing, so that this criterion may soon lose (if it has not already lost) all relevance. The other criteria too are somewhat elusive. The classification of a State as belonging to the 'developed' or 'developing' world varies with the idea of 'development' that is selected. Usually, 'development' is meant to have an economic connotation, but a broader concept of development, one which corresponds to the integral development of the human person and society, would arguably be more in accordance with the moral considerations that underlie the concept of *jus cogens*. (And even on the basis of a purely economic concept of development, a clear-cut division between 'developed' and 'developing' countries is not always easy to draw.)[54] Finally, that a State

[52] *U.N.C.L.T., Off. Recs, First Session*, p. 472, para. 12. See also Yasseen, 'L'interprétation des traités d'après la Convention de Vienne sur le droit des traités', 151 Hague *Recueil* (1976, III), pp. 40–1.

[53] Ago, 'Droit des traités à la lumière de la Convention de Vienne. Introduction', 134 ibid. (1971, III), p. 323 ('. . . il faut que la conviction du caractère impératif de la règle soit partagée par toutes les composantes essentielles de la communauté internationale et non seulement, par exemple, par les Etats de l'Ouest ou de l'Est, par les pays développés ou en voie de développement, par ceux d'un continent ou d'un autre.').

[54] On the difficulties inherent in the definition of a developing country, see Bulajic, 'A Changing World Calls for International Development Law', Sarcevic and van Houtte (eds.), *Legal Issues in International Trade* (London, 1990), pp. 15–17; Betz, 'Developing Countries', Wolfrum (ed.), *United Nations: Law, Policies and Practice*, new, revised English edn. (Munich and Dordrecht, 1995), i, pp. 398–406. Nor is the concept of 'Third World' any easier to define. (See, for example, Gros Espiel, 'La evolucion del concepto de los derechos humanos: criterios occidentales, socialistas y del tercer mundo', 5 *Anuario hispano-luso-americano de derecho internacional* (1979), pp. 82–3.)

belongs to a certain continent is an indisputable but not unchangeable fact. In the course of their existence, States may (and sometimes actually do) expand to, or withdraw from, a continent by acquiring or losing territory. In any event, being part of a certain continent appears to be less meaningful for norm-creating purposes than being, for example, a riparian State or a geographically disadvantaged State, irrespective of location in any particular continent.

To sum up, any selected criteria will be more or less helpful depending in part on the political evolution of the international community and in part on the content of the peremptory norm in question. This is exactly where the inherent limitation of the test of the 'international community of States as a whole' lies. International rules of *jus cogens* do not appear in a vacuum, but under certain historical conditions and for the purpose of achieving certain objectives: a State may be specially affected by an emerging peremptory rule,[55] while another may have a lesser interest or fewer opportunities to define its attitude.[56] Relatively few examples of *jus cogens* enjoy unanimous support; for many proposed peremptory rules, there are bound to be enthusiastic and lukewarm supporters, as well as open and hidden opponents. In contested cases, the test of acceptance and recognition 'by the international community of States as a whole' is not likely, of itself, to settle the issue whether a norm of *jus cogens* has in fact emerged, but merely change the terms of the dispute, which will now turn around the issue whether, in that particular instance, the peremptory character of the norm is supported by the 'international community of States as a whole'.[57]

The test that has now been examined leaves open another important question. Assuming that the international community of States as a whole has accepted and recognized a certain norm as peremptory, will this norm be opposable to those States which have persistently objected to its peremptory character? In other words, does the principle of the persistent objector apply to *jus cogens*? Before addressing this question in some detail, the next section will briefly consider the two other tests of norms of *jus cogens* under Article 53, namely impermissible derogation and the restrictions on subsequent modification.

[55] See, for example, the position of South Africa, until recently, on the prohibition of apartheid, discussed in Chapter 7, below.

[56] See Lachs, 'The Development and General Trends', p. 210.

[57] See, for example, the French criticism of the alleged peremptory character of the prohibition of atmospheric testing (section V of Chapter 10, below).

IV. The Tests of *Jus Cogens* under Article 53 of the Vienna Convention: (b) Impermissible Derogation and Restrictions on Subsequent Modification

Under Article 53 of the Vienna Convention, the second test that a norm must satisfy to acquire peremptory character is that the norm in question must be accepted and recognized as a norm 'from which no derogation is permitted'.

'Derogation' is a basic concept of the general theory of law and of international law.[58] Its scope within the body of Article 53 gave rise to a lively debate in the International Law Commission.[59] Commenting on a draft of what would later become Article 53, and on a proposal for additional amendments, Yasseen expressed the opinion that the prohibition of derogation from a norm of *jus cogens* would also imply the prohibition of 'unilateral' derogation, for example by means of a constitutional norm of municipal law. In this case, there would be 'derogation from a rule of general international law by a rule of internal law'.[60] Contrary to this view, Verdross suggested that one State acting alone cannot 'derogate' from an international norm in the technical sense. The prohibition envisaged in Article 53 would only cover derogation 'by bilateral or multilateral treaties', with the consequence that a State acting alone can breach, but not 'derogate' from, a norm of *jus cogens*.[61]

A compromise solution proposed by the Special Rapporteur Waldock, to the effect that no derogation from a norm of *jus cogens* would be permitted 'whether by agreement or otherwise', was rejected.[62] Waldock's suggestion reappeared later, in a different form, in the Commentary of the International Law Commission on the draft articles on the law of treaties. The Commentary explained that no derogation from a norm of *jus cogens* is permitted, 'even by' agreement between States.[63] In other words, whereas the main focus in Article 53 is 'derogation' in the strict sense, i.e. by treaty, the Commentary indicates a wider sense of the term 'derogation', in which

[58] On 'derogation', from a jurisprudential perspective, see Kelsen, *General Theory of Norms*, English trans. Hartney (Oxford, 1991), pp. 106–14. On 'derogation' from international norms, see Morelli, 'Norme dispositive di diritto internazionale', 11 *Riv. dir. int.* (1932), pp. 388–404 and 483–508.

[59] *Y.I.L.C.* (1963, I), especially at pp. 291–2 (717th meeting). For comment, see Gomez Robledo, 'Le *ius cogens* international: sa genèse, sa nature, ses fonctions', 172 Hague *Recueil* (1981, III), pp. 88–92.

[60] *Y.I.L.C.* (1963, I), p. 292, para. 31.

[61] Ibid., p. 292, para. 34, and also pp. 214–15, para. 79. On this point, Verdross may have been influenced by Kelsen. In his *General Theory of Norms*, whose German original appeared in 1979 but reflected earlier views of the author, Kelsen wrote that 'derogation is the repeal of the validity of an already valid norm by *another norm*' (p. 106).

[62] *Y.I.L.C.* (1963, I), p. 292, paras. 35 and 37.

[63] 'Draft Articles on the Law of Treaties', p. 68, para. 4.

it is entirely legitimate to inquire whether a State can 'derogate' unilaterally from a peremptory rule. Presumably, this would also cover the case of persistent objection to an emerging norm of *jus cogens*.

Different considerations apply to the third test indicated in Article 53, according to which a norm of *jus cogens* 'can be modified only by a subsequent norm of general international law having the same character'. Conceptually, the idea of 'modification' of a rule is distinct from the idea of 'derogation' from it. While derogation denotes that a norm has repealed the validity of another norm with respect to certain relations, there is modification when a norm is replaced by another which regulates the same subject in a different way.[64]

During the work of codification of the law of treaties, everybody agreed that the content of *jus cogens* cannot be defined once and for all, and is therefore subject to modification. As a consequence of this, two problems arise. The first one is that of the restrictions on the modification of *jus cogens* relating to the content of the peremptory rule in question.[65] The second problem arises in connection with the procedure by which modification can occur. The Commentary of the International Law Commission on draft Article 50 (which later became Article 53) specifies that modification will 'most probably' occur by general multilateral treaty.[66] This language, though, does not seem to rule out other possible ways of modification. In any event, both problems can be set aside for the purposes of the present work.

V. The Question of the Opposability *Erga Omnes* of Norms of *Jus Cogens*: (a) The Principle of the Persistent Objector

The role of custom in the creation of peremptory norms has already been mentioned earlier in this chapter. By comparison with conventional law, a distinctive feature of custom is its general sphere of validity, in the sense that customary norms (other than local customs)[67] are binding, as a rule, on all States.[68] In its judgment in the *North Sea Continental Shelf* cases, the International Court wrote that customary law

[64] See Kelsen, *General Theory of Norms*, p. 109. Neither 'derogation' nor 'modification' should be confused with the 'conflict of norms' (ibid., p. 213).

[65] See Lach's views on this point, briefly mentioned in section IV of Chapter 9, below.

[66] 'Draft Articles on the Law of Treaties', p. 68, para. 4.

[67] See Cohen-Jonathan, 'La coutume locale', 7 *A.F.D.I.* (1961), pp. 119–40.

[68] See, for example, Brownlie, *Principles*, p. 2; Guggenheim, *Traité*, i, p. 49; Morelli, *Nozioni di diritto internazionale*, 7th edn. (Padua, 1967), pp. 29–31; Wolfke, *Custom in Present International Law*, 2nd revised edn. (Dordrecht, 1993), pp. 160–8; Kelsen, 'Théorie du droit international coutumier', 1 *Revue internationale de la théorie du droit* (1939), pp. 253–74. See also *League of Nations. Acts of the Conference for the Codification of International Law, Held at The Hague from March 13th to April 12th, 1930. Meetings of the Committees, Vol. IV,*

must have equal force for all members of the international community and cannot therefore be the subject of any right of unilateral exclusion exercisable at will by any one of them in its own favour.[69]

From this principle of general opposability, it follows that a State is bound by an international custom irrespective of whether or not it has expressed its consent to be bound. This applies also when a State has not taken part in the formation of a customary rule either because during the process of formation the State in question did not exist or because it did not express its position on the emerging rule.[70] This principle is widely shared among international writers, including those from developing States[71] and the former socialist countries,[72] who are usually reckoned among the strongest proponents of the role of consent in the formation of international law. However, the presumption that a general custom is opposable to all States is rebuttable. First of all, two or more States are free to derogate by treaty from an international custom, unless this belongs to *jus cogens*. Secondly, after an international custom has come into being, a State which was originally bound by that custom may no longer be bound because the State has subsequently acquired a historic or prescriptive right. Derogation by treaty and prescriptive rights have in common that they exempt a State from a customary rule which was previously binding on it.

A third qualification to the principle of the general opposability of custom is the possibility that a State may express its objection to an emerging customary rule and evade its application from the very beginning, without ever becoming bound by that rule. According to an expression apparently introduced by Brownlie,[73] this qualification is known as the principle of the 'persistent objector' (or 'recalcitrant State').[74] The leading authority for this principle is a dictum of the International Court in the *Fisheries* case.

Minutes of the Third Committee, Responsibility of States for Damage caused in their Territory to the Person or Property of Foreigners, pp. 32–59; Smith, H. A. (ed.), *Great Britain and the Law of Nations*, i (London, 1932), pp. 1–13.

[69] I.C.J. Reports 1969, pp. 38–9, para. 63.

[70] See Kelsen, *Principles*, pp. 444–5.

[71] See, for example, Anand, 'Attitude of the Asian–African States toward Certain Problems of International Law', 15 *I.C.L.Q.* (1966), pp. 70–1; Wang Tieya, 'The Third World and International Law', MacDonald and Johnston (eds.), *The Structure and Process of International Law: Essays in Legal Philosophy Doctrine and Theory* (The Hague, 1983), pp. 961–3.

[72] See, for example, Tunkin, *Theory*, pp. 126–9; Lukashuk, *Mekhanizm*, p. 76; Danilenko, *Obychai v sovremennom mezhdunarodnom prave* (Moscow, 1988), p. 38.

[73] See the first edition of his *Principles of Public International Law* (Oxford, 1966), p. 8.

[74] In the context of the International Law Association's work on 'The Formation of Rules of Customary (General) International Law', another expression has been used, i. e. 'persistent dissenter'. There is no need here to take a position on the distinction between 'persistent objector' (to an emerging rule) and 'persistent dissenter' (from an existing rule), which was articulated by the committee's Rapporteur (Mendelson) and is reproduced in International Law Association, *Report of the Sixty-fifth Conference held at Cairo, Egypt. 21 to 26 April 1992* (Cairo, 1993), p. 384. In this work, the expressions 'persistent objector', 'persistent dissenter' and 'recalcitrant State' are used interchangeably.

This case was brought before the International Court by a unilateral application of the United Kingdom against Norway. The main issue was the validity, under international law, of the Norwegian system of drawing lines to delimit the exclusive zone reserved for Norwegian fishermen. The parties agreed that the criterion for delimitation was the low-water mark, but had different views on its application. In particular, the United Kingdom was challenging before the International Court the Norwegian system of straight lines drawn from certain outermost points of the rampart of rocks and small islands off the coast of Norway (the 'skjaergaard'). Norway had been using this system since the nineteenth century and had reaffirmed it by decree in 1935, although this system had resulted in several incidents involving British vessels off the coast of Norway.

In its judgment,[75] the International Court rejected all British claims and concluded that, in consideration of the 'geographic realities' and other factors, the Norwegian method of delimitation was in accordance with international law. It disposed of the arguments of the parties in terms of the historic rights of Norway and acquiescence by the other States. But it is another principle to which the International Court referred in its judgment that is of special interest here. Part of the British argument was that straight lines could only be drawn across bays and the length of these straight lines across bays (other than historic bays) must not exceed ten miles. In rejecting this contention, the International Court held that the alleged 'ten-mile rule' for bays was not a general rule of international law. It then added that

> [i]n any event the ten-mile rule would appear to be inapplicable as against Norway inasmuch as she has always opposed any attempt to apply it to the Norwegian coast.[76]

The point made by the International Court in this passage was that Norway had 'always' opposed the ten-mile rule, and therefore the question was not one of subsequent departure by Norway from a well established rule, but of consistent dissent from that rule since the very beginning of the

[75] See Brownlie, *Principles*, pp. 10–11. On the *Fisheries* case, see Waldock, 'The Anglo-Norwegian Fisheries Case', 28 *B.Y.I.L.* (1951) pp. 114–71; Wilberforce, 'Some Aspects of the Anglo-Norwegian Fisheries Case', 38 *Transactions of the Grotius Society* (1953), pp. 151–68; Lauterpacht, H., *Development of International Law*, pp. 45–6; 190–9; 362–72; id., 'Implications of the *Norwegian Fisheries* Case', Lauterpacht, E. (ed.), *International Law. Being the Collected Papers of Hersch Lauterpacht*, i (Cambridge, 1977), pp. 213–17 (reproducing an article which appeared in *The Times* on 8 January 1952); Rudolf, 'New States and International Law', 21 *Law and State* (1980), pp. 61–3. According to Brownlie, the decision in the *Fisheries* case shows 'to what extent judicial reasoning provides the necessary refinement of positivist materials' ('The Sources of the Law Governing Maritime Delimitation', *International Law. Liber Jiménez de Aréchaga*, ii, p. 736).

[76] *Fisheries*, Judgment, I.C.J. Reports 1951, p. 131. The French authoritative text reads as follows: 'De toute manière, la règle des dix milles apparaît comme inopposable à la Norvege, celle-ci s'étant toujours élevée contre toute tentative de l'appliquer à la côte norvégienne.'

process that had led to its emergence. This is the principle of the persistent objector.

It is not surprising to find an explicit reference to this principle in the judgment on the *Fisheries* case. At the time of the judgment, the President of the International Court was Jules Basdevant, a distinguished French lawyer in whose general course at the Hague Academy there is support for the principle, although the expression itself 'persistent objector' does not occur.[77] In addition (as will be shown later in this section), both Norway and the United Kingdom had specifically addressed the question of persistent objection in their pleadings before the International Court.

Before the judgment in the *Fisheries* case, little had been written on the principle of the persistent objector. It was only later that international lawyers (and Sir Gerald Fitzmaurice probably more than anybody else)[78] defined the principle in more precise terms. Since then, references to the principle have occurred in the context of international[79] and municipal decisions,[80] and today most writers accept it.[81]

[77] See Basdevant, 'Règles générales du droit de la paix', 58 Hague *Recueil* (1936, IV), p. 512 (including note 3). A similar remark to that made in the text can be found in Dupuy, P. M., 'A propos de l'opposabilité de la coutume générale: enquête brève sur l'"objecteur persistant"', *Le droit international. Mélanges Virally*, p. 264, note 20. On the role of the President of the International Court (with special reference, though, to the current Rules of Court), see Rosenne, 'The President of the International Court of Justice', Lowe and Fitzmaurice, M. (eds.), *Fifty Years. Essays Jennings*, pp. 406–23.

[78] Fitzmaurice, 'The Law and Procedure of the International Court of Justice, 1951–54: General Principles and Sources of Law', 30 *B.Y.I.L.* (1953), pp. 24–6; id., 'The General Principles of International Law Considered from the Standpoint of the Rule of Law', 92 Hague *Recueil* (1957, II), pp. 99–101.

[79] See *North Sea Continental Shelf*, Judgment, I.C.J. Reports 1969, p. 97 (Judge Padilla Nervo), p. 229 (Judge Lachs), p. 253 (Judge Sörensen); *Fisheries Jurisdiction (United Kingdom* v. *Iceland)*, Merits, Judgment, I.C.J. Reports 1973, p. 58 (Judge Dillard), pp. 89–90 (Judge Castro); *Nuclear Tests (Australia* v. *France)*, Judgment, I.C.J. Reports 1974, pp. 286–9, paras. 15–21 (Judge Gros); *Legality of the Threat or Use of Nuclear Weapons*, Advisory Opinion, I.C.J. Reports 1996 (mimeographed text), p. 1 (Vice-President Schwebel). Some writers, when discussing the principle of the persistent objector, refer also to a passage from the judgment of the International Court in the *Asylum* case (I.C.J. Reports 1950, p. 277). However, this case related to the existence of a local custom. Local customs do not produce general effects, and the claimant State must give evidence that the opposing State has consented to the rule. Therefore, the question of the persistent objector cannot really arise, in the strict sense, with respect to a local custom.

[80] See, for example, *Entscheidungen des Bundesverfassungsgerichts*, vol. 46, Beschluss vom 13. Dezember 1977 (2 BvM 1/76), Nr. 32 (Tübingen, 1978), pp. 388–9, para. 6. (The writer is grateful to Prof. Jochen Abr. Frowein, of Heidelberg University, for drawing his attention to this decision.) See also *Inter-Science Research and Development Services (Pty) Ltd* v. *Republica Popular de Mocambique* (Margo J, citing Friedman, Lissitzyn and Pugh, *Cases and Materials on International Law*, St. Paul, Minn., 1969), extract reproduced in *Annual Survey of South African Law* (1980), p. 59.

[81] Besides Fitzmaurice's writings cited above, see Stein, 'The Approach of the Different Drummer', 26 *Harvard International Law Journal* (1985), pp. 457–82; Dupuy, P. M., 'A propos de l'opposabilité de la coutume generale', pp. 257–72; Colson, 'How Persistent Must the Persistent Objector Be?', 61 *Washington Law Review* (1986), pp. 957–70; McClane, 'How Late in the Emergence of a Norm of Customary Law May a Persistent Objector Object?', 13

Fitzmaurice has summarized the conditions which must be present in order that the principle of the persistent objector (in Fitzmaurice's words, the principle of the 'negative' aspect of historic rights) can apply.[82] First of all, the objector must have enjoyed in the past wider rights than those now conferred on it by an emerging rule of international law. Secondly, the objector must have expressed its dissent from the emerging customary rule since the very beginning. Thirdly, the objector's dissent must be open and express, without ambiguities, and only in this way can the presumption that it is bound by the new rule be overcome. Fourthly, the objection must be 'persistent', i.e. it must be consistently maintained throughout the formative stage of the rule and after its coming into existence.

ILSA Journal of International Law (1989), pp. 1–26. For a critical assessment, see Charney, 'The Persistent Objector Rule', 56 *B.Y.I.L.* (1985), pp. 1–24; Abi-Saab, 'Cours général', pp. 180–2 and 378; id., 'The 1977 Additional Protocols and general international law: some preliminary reflections', Delissen and Tanja (eds.), *Humanitarian Law of Armed Conflict. Challenges Ahead. Essays in Honour of Frits Kalshoven* (Dordrecht, 1991), pp. 124–5; Condorelli, 'Custom', Bedjaoui (ed.), *International Law*, pp. 204–5. Among the general works, see Brownlie, *Principles*, p. 10; von der Heydte, *Völkerrecht. Ein Lehrbuch* (Cologne, 1958), p. 68; Virally, 'The Sources of International Law', Sörensen (ed.), *Manual of Public International Law* (London, 1968), pp. 135–7; Sörensen, 'Principes de droit international public', 101 Hague *Recueil* (1960, III), pp. 43–4; Waldock, 'General Course on Public International Law', 106 ibid. (1962, II), pp. 49–51; Giraud, 'Le droit international public et la politique', 110 ibid. (1963, III), p. 729; Bishop, 'General Course of Public International Law', 115 ibid. (1965, II), pp. 226–7; Jennings, 'General Course', pp. 335–6; Tunkin, *Theory*, p. 130; Rousseau, *Droit international public*, i, p. 320; Mosler, *The International Society*, pp. 118–19; Merrills, *Anatomy of International Law. A Study of the Role of International Law in the Contemporary World*, 2nd edn. (London, 1981), pp. 5–6; Verdross and Simma, *Universelles Völkerrecht*, pp. 352–3; Giuliano, Scovazzi and Treves, *Diritto internazionale. Parte generale*, pp. 210–12; Danilenko, *Law-Making in the International Community* (Dordrecht, 1993), pp. 109–13; Conforti, *International Law*, pp. 60–3; Marino Menéndez, *Derecho Internacional Publico. Parte general* (Madrid, 1993), pp. 214–15; Tomuschat, 'Obligations Arising for States without or against Their Will', 241 Hague *Recueil* (1993, IV), pp. 284–90; Seidl-Hohenveldern, *Völkerrecht*, 8th edn. (Cologne, 1994), p. 122; Diaconu, *Curs*, p. 52. Among earlier works (which did not use the expression 'persistent objector' but discussed the concept) see De Visscher, C., 'La codification du droit international', 6 Hague *Recueil* (1925, I), p. 363; Balladore Pallieri, 'La forza obbligatoria della consuetudine internazionale', 7 *Riv. dir. int.* (1928), pp. 354–6; François, 'Règles générales du droit de la paix', 66 Hague *Recueil* (1938, IV), p. 175; Sperduti, *La fonte suprema dell'ordinamento internazionale* (Milan, 1946), p. 206. See also MacGibbon, 'Some Observations on the Part of Protest in International Law', 30 *B.Y.I.L.* (1953), pp. 317–19; D'Amato, *The Concept of Custom in International Law* (Ithaca, N.Y., 1971), pp. 187–99; Akehurst, 'Custom as a Source of International Law', 47 *B.Y.I.L.* (1974/75), pp. 23–7, Unger, *Völkergewohnheitsrecht – objectives Recht oder Geflecht bilateraler Beziehungen: Seine Bedeutung für einen "persistent objector"*' (Munich, 1978) (criticizing Simma, *Das Reziprozitätselement in der Entstehung des Völkergewohnheitsrechts* (Munich, 1970)); Weil, 'Towards Relative Normativity', p. 434; Danilenko, 'The Theory of International Customary Law', 31 *G.Y.I.L.* (1988), pp. 41–3 (and more extensively, in Russian, the same author's *Obychai*, pp. 13–14 and 115–18); Wolfke, *Custom*, pp. 66–7. The different approaches to the principle of the persistent objector reflect the different theories on custom. See Arangio-Ruiz, 'Consuetudine (consuetudine internazionale)', *Enciclopedia Giuridica*, viii (Rome, 1988), pp. 5–6; Sur, 'Sources du droit international. La coutume', *Jurisclasseur de droit international* (1989), 'Fascicule 13', pp. 10–11.

[82] See Fitzmaurice's writings cited earlier in this section.

Under these stringent conditions, the principle of the persistent objector may be easily reconciled with the statement on the general effect of custom pronounced by the International Court in the *North Sea Continental Shelf* cases and reproduced earlier in this section. In this statement, the International Court ruled out the possibility that a State may exclude 'at will' the operation of a customary rule.[83] Now, the principle of the persistent objector does not allow a State to evade the application of a customary rule 'at will', but rather allows a State to preserve its rights if certain tight requirements are met. In a way, it is therefore no exception to that statement of the International Court.

Certain attitudes of Japan and the United States towards emerging rules of the new law of the sea have been regarded as applications of the principle of the persistent objector.[84] The examples, though, are few. In practice, it is difficult for a State either to prove that it has objected to a customary rule since the very beginning of that rule's formation or, even more so, that it is persisting in its objection. The process that leads to the formation of a customary rule is imperceptible. It is rarely (if ever) possible to identify a certain point in time when the process of formation started, and another when the rule can be said to have fully emerged. In these circumstances, the requirement that a State must have expressed its objection to the customary rule in question from the very beginning and without interruption will be difficult to meet.

In addition, when a few States object to an emerging custom, it is open to question whether the situation is one of an international custom with several persistent objectors, or whether the concurrent dissents have impeded the formation of that custom by lack of general practice.[85] On the other

[83] For a different interpretation of the passage, see Lang, *Le plateau continental de la Mer du Nord. Arrêt de la Cour International de Justice 20 Février 1969* (Paris, 1970), p. 90, para. 24.

[84] For a critical discussion of these and other examples, see Charney, 'The Persistent Objector Rule', pp. 11–16. For examples involving Japan, and the evolution of the Japanese position, see the 'Statement of the Japanese Government on High Seas Fisheries, July 13, 1951', reproduced in 16 *Ecology Law Quarterly* (1989), pp. 98–9; Yanai and Asomura, 'Japan and the Emerging Order of the Sea—Two Maritime Laws of Japan', 21 *Japanese Annual of International Law* (1977), p. 72; Oda and Owada, 'Annual Review of Japanese Practice in International Law XV (1976–77)', 28 ibid. (1985), pp. 94–142; Ogiso, 'Japan and the UN-Convention on the Law of the Sea', 25 *Archiv des Völkerrechts* (1987), pp. 71–3. For examples involving the U.S.A., see Stein, 'The Approach of the Different Drummer', p. 462; Colson, 'How Persistent Must the Persistent Objector Be?', pp. 958–61; Kelly, 'Law of the Sea: The Jurisdictional Dispute over Highly Migratory Species of Tuna', 26 *C.J.T.L.* (1988), pp. 504–7; Treves, 'Codification du droit international et pratique des Etats dans le droit de la mer', 223 Hague *Recueil* (1990, IV), pp. 66–74 and 159–62. For other examples, see I.C.J. Pleadings, *North Sea Continental Shelf*, i, pp. 400 and 509; *I.C.J. Pleadings, Fisheries Jurisdiction*, ii (*Federal Republic of Germany* v. *Iceland*), pp. 400–1, para. 25 (Reply of the F.R.G.). See also the case reported by Verzijl, *International Law*, i, pp. 37–8, and the considerations developed in O'Connell, *The International Law of the Sea*, Shearer ed., i (Oxford, 1982), p. 44.

[85] Article 38(1)(b) of the Statute of the International Court (reproduced in section III of this chapter) defines custom as the 'evidence of a general practice accepted as law'. On the requirement of generality of practice, see Brownlie, *Principles*, p. 6.

hand, when one State alone objects to a customary rule, this State will find it increasingly difficult to persist in its position. As Pearce Higgins remarked at the beginning of this century (and his observation is still valid today), the 'pressure of the public opinion of the world' has a mighty force, which 'cannot eventually be ignored'.[86] This is why so far only the big and medium-sized Powers, which are willing and capable to stand the pressure of the international community, have been able, in practice, to assert their persistent objection to a rule. This also explains why persistent objection is often no more than a temporary device for shaping special relations with other States before accepting the customary rule in question.

The foregoing considerations help to understand why there are in practice so few instances in which a State has claimed to be a persistent objector to an international custom. Apart from the inherent difficulties and external pressures that have been mentioned, the fact is that, when a State is critical of an emerging custom, it will tend to deny altogether that a new custom has emerged, rather than acknowledge that a custom exists against which that State is a persistent objector. By openly claiming the status of persistent objector, a State would end up endorsing the idea that an international custom contrary to its own interests is emerging or has already emerged,[87] and projecting the image of an isolated dissenter in the eyes the whole international community.

Despite these practical difficulties, several examples of persistent objection exist. Therefore, it is legitimate to raise this question: are there boundaries beyond which the principle of the persistent objector is inadmissible? In particular, does the principle of the persistent objector apply to all international customs alike or are there some to which it does not apply?[88] To answer these questions, a useful source is the pleadings in the *Fisheries* case, where the parties specifically addressed the problem of the limits attaching to the invocation of the status of persistent objector.

In its Counter-Memorial, Norway rejected the British argument that certain customary rules restrict the power of a coastal State to follow the straight baselines method. Norway added that, even assuming that these rules exist, they would not be opposable to Norway because of its persistent dissent.[89] The United Kingdom objected to the Norwegian contention

[86] *The Binding Force of International Law. Inaugural Lecture in International Law at the London School of Economics and Political Science. Session 1910–11* (Cambridge, 1910), pp. 11–12. See also Westlake, *International Law*, i, p. 17.

[87] See Treves, 'Military Installations Structures, and Devices on the Seabed', 74 *A.J.I.L.* (1980), p. 814, note 36.

[88] Qualifications to the principle of the persistent objector are discussed in Schachter, *International Law*, pp. 13–14; Thirlway, *International Customary Law and Codification*, p. 110; Kaplan and Katzenbach, *The Political Foundations of International Law* (New York and London, 1961), p. 255; Wengler, *Völkerrecht* (Berlin, 1964), i, pp. 179–80.

[89] *I.C.J. Pleadings, Fisheries*, i, pp. 381–4, paras. 256–61.

on factual and legal grounds. While agreeing with Norway that a customary rule is not opposable to a recalcitrant State, the United Kingdom remarked that the right of a State to dissent from an emerging rule is not absolute. In particular,

> where a fundamental principle is concerned, the international community does not recognize the right of any State to isolate itself from the impact of the principle.[90]

In the case before the International Court, the 'fundamental principle' in question was the freedom of the seas. The British Reply acknowledged that the rights of the whole international community relating to the high seas may occasionally come into conflict with the rights of a coastal State. This had occurred, for example, as a result of the Norwegian delimitation of its territorial waters. However, the United Kingdom believed that, in a case like this, the rights of the international community should prevail over the conflicting rights of a coastal State, in consideration also of certain 'majoritarian' trends in international law which the British argument mentioned but did not explore. In other words, in the instant case, where a 'fundamental principle' was at stake, the principle of the persistent objector would not be available to Norway.[91]

In its Rejoinder, Norway agreed with the United Kingdom that no State can object to a 'fundamental principle', but added that,

> in order that the argument be plausible, it is essential to delimit the term 'principle' and not to confuse the 'principles' with the technical rules which are only the superstructure thereof.[92]

Quoting from De Visscher's lectures at the Hague Academy,[93] Norway defined 'principles' as those international rules which are so fundamental that they do not depend on the will of States. But the customary rules relating to maritime delimitation were not, according to Norway, 'fundamental principles'. They were rather 'technical rules', dependent on the will of States. For this reason, Norway would be entitled to object to their application.

To sum up, the United Kingdom and Norway agreed that (a) a State can persistently object to the application of a customary rule, and (b) no persistent objection is admissible in case of 'fundamental principles'. They disagreed, however, on the particular content of the 'fundamental principles' that would be immune from persistent objection. In a way, the pleadings

[90] *I.C.J. Pleadings, Fisheries*, ii, p. 429.

[91] Ibid., ii, p. 428, and iv, p. 121 (statement of Sir Frank Soskice).

[92] 'Pour que la thèse soit plausible, il est essentiel de limiter le sens du mot "principe" et de ne point confondre les "principes" avec les règles techniques qui n'en forment que la superstructure.' (Ibid., iii, p. 292.)

[93] De Visscher, C., 'La codification du droit international', p. 342.

in the *Fisheries* case anticipated the terms of the controversy whether the principle of the 'persistent objector' applies to *jus cogens*.

VI. The Question of the Opposability *Erga Omnes* of Norms of *Jus Cogens*: (b) The Principle of the Persistent Objector and *Jus Cogens*

At the Vienna Conference, France worked out an amendment to draft Article 50 (which later became Article 53 of the Vienna Convention) under which a norm of *jus cogens* would not be opposable to a State that has not expressly accepted its peremptory character.[94] The French Government circulated this amendment among some Western delegations, but then refrained from insisting on its proposal when many of these delegations expressed their concern that the French amendment might threaten the compromise on the settlement of disputes involving norms of *jus cogens*.[95] As the French proposal was not discussed on its merits, it is difficult to draw from its circulation and subsequent withdrawal any indication of the relationship between the principle of the 'persistent objector' and *jus cogens*. Thus, in addressing this question, one has to look for arguments outside the work of codification of the Vienna Convention.

The very concept of *jus cogens* makes it reasonable to argue that peremptory rules do not admit of any persistent objection. If the purpose of peremptory rules is to allow the common interest of States to prevail over the conflicting interest of a single State or a small number of States, this purpose would be frustrated if that State or small number of States were allowed to escape the application of a peremptory rule on the ground of persistent objection.

A considerable number of writers are in fact against the admissibility of persistent objection to a norm of *jus cogens*,[96] even if others take a more

[94] The text of the proposed amendment reads as follows: 'Toutefois une telle norme n'est pas opposable à un Etat qui peut faire la preuve qu'il ne l'a pas acceptée expressément en tant que telle.' (Deleau, 'Les positions françaises à la Conférence de Vienne sur le droit des traités', 15 *A.F.D.I.* (1969), p. 19.)

[95] See section II of this chapter, above.

[96] See Brownlie, *Principles*, p. 11, note 56; Bos, *A Methodology of International Law* (Amsterdam, 1984), pp. 246 and 250; van Hoof, *Rethinking the Sources*, pp. 160–2; Rozakis, *The Concept of Jus Cogens*, pp. 76–80; Juste Ruiz, *Derecho internacional publico?* (Valencia, 1986), pp. 208–9. See also De Azevedo Soares, *Licoes de direito internacional publico*, 4th edn. (Coimbra, 1988), p. 111; Gomez Robledo, 'Le *ius cogens* international', pp. 106–8; Rao, 'International Custom', 19 *Indian Journal of International Law* (1979), pp. 519–20; Ronzitti, 'La disciplina dello jus cogens nella Convenzione di Vienna sul diritto dei trattati', 15 *Comunicazioni e studi* (1978), pp. 256–7; Barberis, 'Réflexions sur la coutume international', 36 *A.F.D.I.* (1990), p. 39; Henkin, 'Human Rights and State "Sovereignty" (Sibley Lecture, March 1994)', 25 *Georgia Journal of International and Comparative Law* (1995/96), p. 38. For a more finely balanced position, see Akehurst, 'The Hierarchy of the Sources of International

cautious approach.[97] The view that denies the admissibility of persistent objection to a norm of *jus cogens* has also the backing of a statement from the bench. In a separate opinion attached to the International Court's judgment in the *North Sea Continental Shelf* cases, Judge Lachs wrote as follows:

> Nor can a general rule which is not of the nature of *jus cogens* prevent some States from adopting an attitude apart. They may have opposed the rule from its inception and may, unilaterally, or in agreement with others, decide upon different solutions of the problem involved.[98]

The inference from these words is that a State cannot be a persistent objector to a customary rule belonging to *jus cogens*. This is in line with a statement that Lachs had made a few years earlier, as a member of the International Law Commission, when during a debate on the draft articles of the Vienna Convention he had said that 'the very fact that a State was a member of the international community made it incumbent upon it to accept the rules of *jus cogens*'.[99]

Additional support for the proposition that the principle of the persistent objector does not apply to peremptory rules can be found in the first opinion rendered by the *ad hoc* Arbitration Commission on the former

Law', 47 *B.Y.I.L.* (1974/75), p. 285; Sztucki, 'Some Questions Arising from Reservations to the Vienna Convention on the Law of Treaties', 20 *G.Y.I.L.* (1977), pp. 294–5; Stein, 'The Approach of the Different Drummer', p. 481; Heiskanen, *International Legal Topics* (Helsinki, 1992), pp. 392–4. Many (if not most) writers from the former socialist States agree that the principle of the persistent objector does not apply to the norms of *jus cogens*. See Aleksidze, 'Legal Nature of *Jus Cogens* in Contemporary International Law', 172 Hague *Recueil* (1981, III), pp. 246 and 258; Bokor-Szegö, *New States and International Law* (Budapest, 1970), p. 70; Mullerson, 'Sources of International Law: New Tendencies in Soviet Thinking', 83 *A.J.I.L.* (1989), pp. 503–5; Niciu, *Dreptul international public*, i (Iasi, 1992), p. 15. See also the statements of Pechota and Lukashuk in Zacklin (ed.), *The Process of Change in International Law (Report of a Conference organized by the Carnegie Endowment for International Peace, Geneva, 1963)* (Geneva, 1965), pp. 16–17 and 20–1. The various positions among the former Soviet writers are discussed in Aleksidze, *Nekotorye voprosy*, pp. 200–6.

[97] See Charney, 'The Persistent Objector Rule', p. 3, note 9; p. 19, note 81; id., 'Universal International Law', 87 *A.J.I.L.* (1993), pp. 541–2; Chaumont, 'Cours général', pp. 370–7; Wolfke, '*Jus Cogens* in International Law (Regulations and Prospects)', 6 *P.Y.I.L.* (1974), p. 149; Magallona, 'The Concept of *Jus Cogens* in the Vienna Convention on the Law of Treaties', 51 *Philippine Law Journal* (1976), pp. 528–9; Shestakov, *Imperativnye normy*, pp. 36–43; Cassese, *International Law*, pp. 178–9; Danilenko, 'The Theory of International Customary Law', pp. 41–3; id., 'International *Jus Cogens*: Issues of Law-Making', 2 *European Journal of International Law* (1991, No. 1), pp. 48–57; Bernhardt, 'Customary International Law: New and Old Problems', 19 *Thesaurus Acroasium* (1992), pp. 219–20.

[98] I.C.J. Reports 1969, p. 229. References to the concept of *jus cogens* occur also in the judgment (p. 42, para. 72) and in the opinions of Judge Padilla Nervo (p. 97), Judge Tanaka (p. 182), and Judge Sörensen (p. 248). However, none of these touches upon the issue of the persistent objector.

[99] *Y.I.L.C.* (1966, I, Part 2), p. 69, para. 62 (853rd meeting). Indirect statements on the universal opposability of peremptory rules have been made during the work of codification of State responsibility. See *Y.I.L.C.* (1976, I), p. 248, para. 12 (Sir Francis Vallat) and p. 249, para. 20 (Quentin-Baxter).

Yugoslavia, which was set up in 1991 by the Foreign Ministers of the member States of the former European Community (now European Union).[100] This first opinion is being examined here for discussion purposes only, without entering into the question of its legal value.[101]

In its first opinion, the Arbitration Commission addressed the issue of whether the process then under way in the former Yugoslavia was one of dissolution (with the consequence that all constituent republics would have equal rights of succession) or, instead, of secession of some only of the constituent republics. Its conclusion was that the Yugoslav Federation was undergoing a process of dissolution, and the constituent republics should settle all problems of succession on the basis of international law, including respect for human rights and the rights of peoples and minorities. In this respect, the Arbitration Commission wrote that

> the peremptory norms of general international law and, in particular, respect for the fundamental rights of the individual and of the rights of peoples and minorities, are binding on all the parties to the succession.[102]

The reasoning of the Arbitration Commission in this passage is economical, and reflects the concise style of French judgments which the Arbitration Commission has adopted for its opinions.[103] Yet, despite the

[100] On the Arbitration Commission, see the present writer's 'Introductory Note to "Conference on Yugoslavia Arbitration Commission: Opinions on Questions Arising from the Dissolution of Yugoslavia"', 31 *I.L.M.* (1992), pp. 1488–90 (providing background information which is still of some use despite subsequent developments). See also Craven, 'The European Community Arbitration Commission on Yugoslavia', 66 *B.Y.I.L.* (1995), pp. 333–413; Pellet, 'Note sur la Commission d'arbitrage de la Conférence européenne pour la paix en Yougoslavie', 37 *A.F.D.I.* (1991), pp. 329–48; id., 'L'activité de la Commission d'arbitrage de la Conférence européenne pour la paix en Yougoslavie', 38 ibid. (1992), pp. 220–38; id., 'L'activité de la Commission d'arbitrage de la Conférence internationale pour l'ancienne Yougoslavie', 39 ibid. (1993), pp. 286–303. On the Arbitration Commission's references to *jus cogens*, see Degan, 'Mixed International Jurisdictions as the Last Instances in Enforcement of Human Rights in Successor States of Former Yugoslavia', 106 *Studi senesi* (1994), pp. 328–31.

[101] On the question of the legal value of the opinions rendered by the Arbitration Commission, compare the views expressed by the representatives of Yugoslavia (Serbia and Montenegro) and of Bosnia and Herzegovina in *Case Concerning the Application of the Convention on the Prevention and Punishment of the Crime of Genocide (Bosnia and Herzegovina v. Yugoslavia (Serbia and Montenegro))*, uncorrected Verbatim Record (respectively, CR 96/5, pp. 27–8 (Mr Mitic) and CR 96/8, p. 56 (Mr Pellet), these references being indicative only, and not exhaustive). (The writer is grateful to Dr Laurence Boisson de Chazournes, formerly Assistant Professor, Graduate Institute of International Studies, Geneva, for providing him with a copy of the uncorrected Verbatim Record.)

[102] Para. 1, point (e). The original French text reads as follows: 'les normes impératives du droit international général et, en particulier, le respect des droits fondamentaux de la personne humaine et des droits des peuples et des minorités, s'imposent à toutes les parties prenantes à la succession.' The English translation of the French original text of Opinion 1 can be found in 31 *I.L.M.* (1992), pp. 1494–7.

[103] This concise style is criticized by Sir Hersch Lauterpacht in *The Development of International Law*, p. 41, note 9. The issue is complex, and cannot be addressed here. For a discussion of different judicial styles, from an international and comparative perspective, see *La sentenza in Europa*, with contributions from representatives of different legal systems.

brevity of expression, three elements at least can be evinced from this passage. In it, the Arbitration Commission (a) invoked the concept of *jus cogens* outside the context of the validity of a treaty, (b) held that the fundamental human rights of the individual and the rights of peoples and minorities all belong to *jus cogens*, and (most importantly for the present purposes) (c) declared that peremptory norms are binding ('s'imposent') on all the parties to the succession: a categorical statement that does not seem to leave any room for even considering whether the operation of the principle of the persistent objector might not apply to the case in question.

To sum up, there is support for the view that the principle of the persistent objector is incompatible with the very concept of *jus cogens*. This is, at least, how the situation looks in principle. In practice, things are somewhat more complicated. When it is a question of the universal opposability of an undisputed example of *jus cogens* such as the prohibition of aggression or the protection from genocide, the issue of the persistent objector does not even arise. However, when it is a question of less evident examples of *jus cogens*, or concrete applications of the more general peremptory rules, claims of persistent objection cannot be dismissed so easily. Two practical examples illustrate this point.

At the Vienna Conference, France was the only country that voted against the adoption of the Vienna Convention on the Law of Treaties. It has still not ratified it. The main, if not only, reason for this attitude is clearly the dissatisfaction of this country with the provisions on *jus cogens* contained in the Vienna Convention.[104] France, though, does not seem to be opposed to the concept of *jus cogens* as such. The interventions of the French representatives at the Vienna Conference made it clear that France would have had no problems in subscribing to a concept of *jus cogens* restricted to certain basic human values shared by all States, but did have problems accepting an ill-defined concept of *jus cogens* that would jeopardize the stability of treaties and the sovereign rights of States.[105]

[104] A publication of the French Foreign Ministry, which was issued immediately after the adoption of the Vienna Convention, contains the following statement: 'Les dispositions les plus graves, les plus lourdes de conséquences de la Convention sont celles qui ont trait au "jus cogens".' ('La Convention de Vienne sur le droit des traités', *Notes et Etudes Documentaires* (25 Sep. 1969, No. 3622), p. 7.) Also, in response to a question from a French MP, the French Foreign Minister declared: 'La France n'est pas devenue partie à la convention de Vienne du 23 mai 1969 sur le droit des traités en raison . . . de la consécration par ce texte de la notion de "normes impératives du droit international" (*jus cogens*).' (*Journal Officiel, Assemblée Nationale* (23 Nov. 1992), p. 5288.) On the French critical attitude towards the provisions on *jus cogens* in the Vienna Convention, see Villiger, *Customary International Law*, pp. 310–11; Colard, 'Premières réflexions sur le "Traité des Traités": la Convention de Vienne du 23 mai 1969', 97 *J.D.I.* (1970), pp. 284–7. It appears that Articles 53 and 64 may be a contributing factor explaining why other States have refused to ratify the Vienna Convention on the Law of Treaties. For example, on the position of Brazil, see Rezek, *Direito internacional publico. Curso elementar*, 2nd edn. (Sao Paulo, 1991), p. 120.

[105] *U.N.C.L.T., Off. Recs., First Session*, pp. 309–10 (intervention of de Bresson);

These worries were not being voiced in a vacuum. The Vienna Convention was adopted six years after the adoption of a treaty on the partial ban of nuclear testing, to which France had not at the time (and has not so far) become a party. France was concerned by the possibility of a claim that, out of this treaty, a customary norm of *jus cogens* could emerge and become opposable to all States, including France.[106] Given this possibility, reliance on the principle of the persistent objector would be the last defence for a country such as France which, in the words of de Lacharrière (a former legal adviser to the French Foreign Ministry and Vice-President of the International Court), was willing to pursue a policy on defence and foreign affairs as an 'independent and solitary State, neither leader nor satellite'.[107] In a case such as that of atmospheric testing, the universal opposability of a norm of *jus cogens* raises not only a problem of effectiveness, but also the difficulty of explaining convincingly why persistent objectors should be bound by this norm.[108]

The second example is the position of South Africa, until recently, on the international prohibition of apartheid.[109] Despite the persistent objection of South Africa to the peremptory character of this prohibition (and indeed to this prohibition as such), the international community has consistently held that this prohibition exists and is also opposable to South Africa. The policy of apartheid affected basic human rights, and one would be inclined to accept without question the proposition that no persistent objection to this prohibition is admissible; yet articulating the reasons for this conclusion is not easy. For example Bernhardt, a judge of the European Court of Human

U.N.C.L.T., Off. Recs., Second Session, pp. 93–5 (intervention of Hubert). Similar considerations were developed by the French representative with respect to the Vienna Convention of 1986. See *United Nations Conference on the Law of Treaties Between States and International Organizations or Between International Organizations, Official Records* (New York, 1995), i, pp. 31–2 (intervention of Delon). Curiously, at the time of the League of Nations, the French representative, Cot, had criticized the concept of 'immoral treaties' for similar reasons (*L.N.O.J.* (Apr. 1933), p. 510).

[106] In his general course at the Hague Academy, Virally acknowledged that the main reason for the French opposition to Article 53 at the Vienna Conference was the French policy of nuclear defence ('Panorama', p. 177). See also de Lacharrière, 'Tendances contradictoires en matière de consentement des Etats', *L'élaboration du droit international public (Colloque de Toulouse)* (Paris, 1975), p. 187; Deleau, 'Les positions françaises', p. 16.

[107] 'Un Etat indépendante et solitaire, ni leader ni satellite.' ('Aspects du relativisme du droit international', Bos and Siblesz (eds.), *Realism: essays Riphagen*, p. 95.) French authors are especially sensitive to the issue of protecting the independence of a State from the will of the majority, or of the great Powers. See id., *La politique juridique extérieure* (Paris, 1983), pp. 23–7; Chaumont, 'Cours général', pp. 373–7; Ruzié, *Droit international public*, 12th edn. (Paris, 1996), p. 3. The expression of this concern is not a new phenomenon among French authors. See Dupuis, 'Règles générales du droit de la paix', 32 Hague *Recueil* (1930, II), pp. 72–4.

[108] On some aspects of the disputes relating to atmospheric testing in the South Pacific in the early seventies, see Chapters 9 and 10, below.

[109] See Chapter 7, below.

Rights and a leading international writer, has written, almost with disarming simplicity, as follows:

> South Africa has persistently objected, and it practices apartheid. Is South Africa therefore exempted from the norm? Certainly not, but how can this legally and theoretically be explained? I pose the question without giving an answer.[110]

VII. Conclusions

This chapter has confirmed the similarities between the concept of *jus cogens* and the concept of obligations *erga omnes* on account of several factors: (a) like obligations *erga omnes*, norms of *jus cogens* are meant to protect the common interests of States and basic moral values, (b) the classic examples of norms of *jus cogens* which emerged during the codification of the law of treaties largely coincide with the examples of obligations *erga omnes* given in the *Barcelona Traction* case, and (c) characteristic expressions attaching to the concept of *jus cogens* (such as the international community 'as a whole') occur also in the International Court's dictum on obligations *erga omnes*.

These similarities are not meant to gloss over the obscurities which still surround the concept of *jus cogens*. The tests provided in Article 53 of the Vienna Convention do not allow a precise definition of the content of *jus cogens* beyond the few examples which are universally admitted. In addition, these tests do not provide an entirely satisfactory answer to the question whether the principle of the persistent objector applies to *jus cogens*. The different approach reflected in the dictum on obligations *erga omnes* has allowed the International Court to avoid many, if not all, of these obscurities. In its dictum, the International Court has given four concrete examples of obligations *erga omnes* and has expressly written that obligations *erga omnes* are 'by their very nature' the concern of all States. In other words, the International Court has adopted what may be called a 'value-oriented' approach supported by practical examples, as opposed to the 'test-oriented' approach reflected in Article 53 of the Vienna Convention.

This chapter and the immediately preceding one have now cleared the decks for a closer examination of the concept of obligations *erga omnes*. In this examination, a convenient starting point is the four examples of obligations *erga omnes* given by the International Court. By definition, an example is a fact or thing which illustrates a general rule. Fowler has written that illustrative sentences are a necessary supplement to definition 'when a word has different senses between which the distinction is fine, or when a definition is obscure and unconvincing until exemplified'.[111] Both seem to be valid

[110] 'Custom and Treaty in the Law of the Sea', 205 Hague *Recueil* (1987, V), p. 269.

[111] *The Concise Oxford Dictionary of Current English*, 4th revised edn. McIntosh (Oxford, 1951), p. vi (Preface to the first edition of 1911).

reasons,[112] in the case of obligations *erga omnes*, for proceeding with a detailed examination of the four examples given in the dictum and of a few other candidates put forward in the international literature.

112 There are in fact 'different senses' in which the expression 'obligations *erga omnes*' is being used. (See section IV of Chapter 10, below.) In addition, it has been remarked that the International Court's dictum on obligations *erga omnes* 'is not a very clear one'. (Arangio-Ruiz, 'Human Rights and Non-Intervention in the Helsinki Final Act', 157 Hague *Recueil* (1977, IV), p. 240.)

4

The Examples of Obligations *Erga Omnes* Given by the International Court in its Dictum: (a) The Outlawing of Acts of Aggression

I. The International Prohibition of Aggression

The first example of obligation *erga omnes* given by the International Court in the *Barcelona Traction* case is the 'outlawing of acts of aggression'.

The term 'aggression' has a long history as a military, political and legal concept, and the quest for its definition has been the source of considerable confusion and controversy.[1] For present purposes, it is unnecessary to examine this history at any length, and the United Nations Charter may conveniently be taken as the starting point.[2]

Article 1, paragraph 1, of the Charter proclaims that the first purpose of the United Nations is to maintain international peace and security and, to this end, to take effective collective measures with a view to suppressing 'acts of aggression or other breaches of the peace'. The power to determine the existence of a 'threat to the peace, breach of the peace, or act of aggression' rests with the Security Council (Article 39). No direct reference to aggression appears in Article 2, paragraph 4, of the Charter, the key provision on the prohibition of the illegal use of force and, in Henkin's words,

[1] See Brownlie, *International Law and the Use of Force by States* (Oxford, 1963), pp. 351–8. See also Oppenheim, *International Law. A Treatise*, ii, 7th edn. Lauterpacht, H. (London, 1952), p. 189; Guggenheim, *Traité de Droit international public*, ii (Geneva, 1954), pp. 253–61; Stone, *Aggression and World Order. A Critique of United Nations Theories of Aggression* (London, 1958); Schwebel, 'Aggression, Intervention and Self-Defence in Modern International Law', 136 Hague *Recueil* (1972, II), pp. 411–98; Tunkin, *Theory*, pp. 49–57; Ferencz, *Defining International Aggression. The Search for World Peace* (New York, 1975); Rosenne, '"On Defining International Aggression. An Exercise in Futility". A book review of Benjamin B. Ferencz, "Defining International Aggression. The Search for World Peace"', 12 *Israel Law Review* (1977), pp. 401–5; Reuter, *Droit international public*, pp. 512–19; Kudriavtsev (ed.), *Kurs mezhdunarodnogo prava v semi tomakh*, ii. (Lukashuk ed.), (Moscow, 1989), ch. 4 (by Mullerson and Fedorov), pp. 73–5.

[2] The Charter was signed at San Francisco on 26 June 1945 and entered into force on 24 October 1945. One hundred and eighty-five States have become parties (*Multilateral Treaties Deposited with the Secretary-General. Status as at 31 December 1995*, p. 3). The text of the Charter is reproduced in Brownlie, *Basic Documents*, pp. 1–35. Among the commentaries, see Cot and Pellet (eds.), *La Charte des Nations Unies* (Paris, 1991); Simma (ed.), *The Charter of the United Nations. A Commentary* (Oxford, 1994).

'the distillation and embodiment of the primary value of the inter-state system'.[3] Article 2, paragraph 4, reads as follows:

All Members shall refrain in their international relations from the threat or use of force against the territorial integrity or political independence of any State, or in any other manner inconsistent with the Purposes of the United Nations.[4]

The omission of the term 'aggression' from Article 2, paragraph 4, suggests that not all forms of illegal use of force amount to aggression. Conversely, the international community has condemned as aggression certain acts that had not involved the use of force.[5] In other words, the concept of 'aggression' is close to, but not coextensive with, the threat to or breach of peace. In practice, the prevailing view is that the distinction is essentially one of degree, in the sense that aggression is 'the most serious and dangerous form of the illegal use of force'. These are in fact the words used in the Preamble of the 'Definition of Aggression', which the United Nations General Assembly adopted by consensus in 1974.[6] This resolution further provides, in Article 1, that

[a]ggression is the use of armed force by a State against the sovereignty, territorial integrity or political independence of another State, or in any other manner inconsistent with the Charter of the United Nations, as set out in this Definition.

The committee endowed with the task of preparing this resolution agreed unanimously that a definition of aggression (which was eventually

[3] *International Law*, p. 113. On Article 2, paragraph 4, of the Charter and on the prohibition of the illegal use of force there is a vast literature. For a useful starting point for further enquiries see the general courses at the Hague Academy, such as Sörensen, 'Principes', pp. 234–45; Waldock, 'General Course', pp. 230–46; Jiménez de Aréchaga, 'International Law', pp. 87–100; Lachs, 'The Development and General Trends', pp. 153–74; Virally, 'Panorama', pp. 99–107. Among the monographs, see Brownlie, *International Law and the Use of Force by States*. See also Waldock, 'The Regulation of the Use of Force by Individual States in International law', 81 Hague *Recueil* (1952, II), pp. 451–517; Kelsen, *International Law Studies. Collective Security under International Law* (Washington, 1957); Schachter, *International Law*, pp. 106–83; Cassese (ed.), *The Current Legal Regulation of the Use of Force* (Dordrecht, 1986); Butler (ed.), *The Non-Use of Force in International Law* (Dordrecht, 1989).

[4] This paragraph must be read in conjunction with Article 2, paragraph 3, which provides for the obligation of peaceful settlement of international disputes.

[5] Röling gives the examples of the 'Anschluss' of Austria by Germany and the annexation of Namibia by South Africa ('The 1974 U.N. Definition of Aggression', Cassese (ed.) *The Current Legal Regulation*, pp. 413–14).

[6] 'Resolution 3314 (XXIX) of the United Nations General Assembly on the Definition of Aggression (adopted on 14 Dec. 1974)', *Gen. Ass. Off. Recs., Twenty-ninth Session*, Supp. 31 (A/9631), pp. 142–4. For commentary, see Broms, 'The Definition of Aggression', 154 Hague *Recueil* (1977, I), pp. 299–400. (The author was the Chairman of the Special Committee for the 'Definition of Aggression'.) See also Zourek, 'Enfin une Définition de l'Agression', 20 *A.F.D.I.* (1974), pp. 9–30; Cassin, Debevoise, Kailes and Thompson, 'The Definition of Aggression', 16 *Harvard International Law Journal* (1975), pp. 589–613; Garvey, 'The U.N. Definition of "Aggression": Law and Illusion in the Context of Collective Security', 17 *Virginia Journal of International Law* (1977), pp. 177–99; Stone, 'Holes and Loopholes in the 1974 Definition of Aggression', 71 *A.J.I.L.* (1977), pp. 224–46.

embodied in Article 1) should be accompanied by a non-exclusive list of specific examples of acts of aggression. According to Article 3 of the resolution, the following acts amount to aggression:

(a) the invasion or attack by the armed forces of a State of the territory of another State, or any military occupation, however temporary, resulting from such invasion or attack, or any annexation by the use of force of the territory of another State or part thereof;
(b) bombardment by the armed forces of a State against the territory of another State or the use of any weapons by a State against the territory of another State;
(c) the blockade of the ports or coasts of a State by the armed forces of another State;
(d) an attack by the armed forces of a State on the land, sea or air forces, or marine and air fleets of another State;
(e) the use of armed forces of one State which are within the territory of another State with the agreement of the receiving State, in contravention of the conditions provided for in the agreement or any extension of their presence in such territory beyond the termination of the agreement;
(f) the action of a State in allowing its territory, which it has placed at the disposal of another State, to be used by that other State for perpetrating an act of aggression against a third State;
(g) the sending by or on behalf of a State of armed bands, groups, irregulars or mercenaries, which carry out acts of armed force against another State of such gravity as to amount to the acts listed above, or its substantial involvement therein.

Together with the emergence of an agreed definition of aggression, there is now a clearer perception of the position that the prohibition of aggression occupies in the hierarchy of international norms. By the time the United Nations Charter was adopted, an international customary rule prohibiting aggression and the illegal use of force had already emerged.[7] As to concrete instances of aggression, the International Court has expressly acknowledged that the prohibition of acts of aggression by irregular forces under Article 3, paragraph (g), of the 'Definition of Aggression' (which was the specific point of interest to the International Court in the *Nicaragua* case) 'may be taken to reflect customary international law'.[8]

Both before and after the adoption of the 'Definition of Aggression', aggression and the illegal use of force have been categorically and repeatedly condemned by the international community, as, for example, in the United Nations Declaration on friendly relations of 1970,[9] and more

[7] See Brownlie, *International Law and the Use of Force by States*, p. 110 ('. . . a customary rule had developed by 1939 if not before that time.').

[8] *Military and Paramilitary Activities in and against Nicaragua (Nicaragua* v. *United States of America)*, Merits, Judgment, I.C.J. Reports 1986, p. 103, para. 195.

[9] 'Declaration on Principles of International Law Concerning Friendly Relations and Co-Operation Among States in Accordance with the Charter of the United Nations' (Annex to Resolution 2625 adopted, without a vote, on 24 Oct. 1970), *Gen. Ass. Off. Recs. Twenty-fifth Session*, Supp. 28 (A/8028). The text is reproduced in Brownlie, *Basic Documents*, pp. 36–

recently in a United Nations Declaration on the use of force adopted in 1987.[10] Nor have the frequent episodes of violence among States affected the legal status of the prohibition. When breaching the international peace, States often claim that, in the particular instance, resort to force was justified, and never put into question the very existence of an international prohibition of aggression and the illegal use of force.[11] The International Court has rightly pointed out that this attitude ends up strengthening rather than weakening the prohibition.[12]

Today, there is widespread agreement that the international prohibition of aggression and the illegal use of force is binding on all States as a rule of *jus cogens*,[13] and that, if the category of 'crimes' is part of international law, then aggression is a crime that entails both individual[14] and State

45. For commentary, see Arangio-Ruiz, *The United Nations Declaration on Friendly Relations and the System of the Sources of International Law (with an Appendix on the Concept of International Law and the Theory of International Organisation)* (Alphen aan den Rijn and Germantown, 1979). See also the various contributions to Lowe and Warbrick (eds.), *The United Nations and the Principles of International Law. Essays in memory of Michael Akehurst* (London and New York, 1994).

[10] Declaration on the Enhancement of the Effectiveness of the Principle of Refraining from the Threat or Use of Force in International Relations, Annex to General Assembly resolution 42/22 of 18 November 1987. For commentary, see Treves, 'La Déclaration des Nations Unies sur le renforcement de l'efficacité du principe du non-recours à la force', 33 *A.F.D.I.* (1987), pp. 379–98.

[11] Resort to justifications and exceptions is not peculiar to breaches of the international prohibition of aggression and the illegal use of force. See Henkin, *How Nations Behave. Law and Foreign Policy*, 2nd edn. (New York, 1979), pp. 68–87; Meron, 'The Geneva Conventions as Customary Law', 81 *A.J.I.L.* (1987), p. 369.

[12] *Military and Paramilitary Activities in and against Nicaragua (Nicaragua* v. *United States of America)*, Merits, Judgment, I.C.J. Reports 1986, p. 98, para. 186. For a convincing argument that the prohibition of the illegal use of force has not been rendered obsolete by its repeated violations, see Schachter, *International Law*, pp. 130–1; id., 'In Defence of International Rules on the Use of Force', 53 *The University of Chicago Law Review* (1986), pp. 116–19.

[13] In his 'Addendum to the eighth report on State responsibility' (Doc.A/CN.4/318/ADD.5–7), the Special Rapporteur Ago wrote that, by the end of the Second World War, there had arisen 'an imperative rule imposing on all States the duty to refrain from all recourse to armed force in their reciprocal relations.' (*Y.I.L.C.* (1980, II, Part 1), p. 63, para. 108.) According to Sörensen, Article 2, paragraph 4, is an example 'd'une disposition conventionnelle qui produit des effets *erga omnes* car elle formule un principe qui correspond à une conviction juridique universelle' ('Principes', p. 236). According to Thierry, the international rule against aggression is 'incontestablement une norme du *jus cogens*' ('L'évolution du droit international', pp. 67–8). Nagendra Singh, a former President of the International Court, remarked in his separate opinion to the judgment on the merits in the *Nicaragua* case that this judgment had reaffirmed the peremptory character of the prohibition of the illegal use of force. (I.C.J. Reports 1986, p. 153). See also the reference to *jus cogens* contained in the judgment (ibid., pp. 100–1, para. 190). For commentary, see Christenson, 'The World Court and *Jus Cogens*', 81 *A.J.I.L.* (1987), pp. 93–101.

[14] See Article 2 of the draft Code of Offences Against the Peace and Security of Mankind, adopted by the International Law Commission at its sixth session (1954), according to which '[a]ny act of aggression' is an offence against the peace and security of mankind, and therefore a crime under international law (*Y.I.L.C.* (1954, II), paras. 49–54). As such, aggression entails individual responsibility (see Doc.A/CN.4/L.532).

responsibility.[15] Actually, the prohibition of aggression and the illegal use of force was the most often cited example of rules of *jus cogens* during the work of codification of the law of treaties.[16] One may wonder whether the peremptory character applies not only to the prohibition of aggression but also to the wider prohibition of the illegal use of force.[17] However, there is no need to address this question here because, in its dictum on obligations *erga omnes*, the International Court specifically referred to the prohibition of aggression (as opposed to the wider prohibition of the illegal use of force), a prohibition which belongs to *jus cogens* without any shade of doubt.

Given the overwhelming consensus against aggression and the illegal use of force, it is not surprising that, in its dictum in the *Barcelona Traction* case, the International Court should list the prohibition of aggression as the first example of obligation *erga omnes*.[18] On the other hand, the unanimous support for this prohibition may raise the question whether its character *erga omnes* is not largely irrelevant. In other words, the argument would be that, if all States agree that aggression is prohibited, and a breach of this prohibition affects all States, then to say that this prohibition is *erga omnes* would not add much to what is already known about it.

This simple line of reasoning may seem attractive but misses an important aspect of the concept of obligations *erga omnes*: the relevance of the concept lies not only in allowing the opposability to all States of that obliga-

[15] For bibliographical references to the concept of 'international crime', see section IV of Chapter 1, above.

[16] See, for example, the declarations of the representatives of States at the first session of the Vienna Conference, reproduced in *U.N.C.L.T., Off. Recs., First Session*, p. 294, para. 3 (former USSR); p. 296, para. 31 (Kenya); pp. 296–7, para. 34 (Cuba); p. 297, para. 43 (Lebanon); p. 300, para. 9 (Sierra Leone); p. 301, para. 15 (Ghana); p. 302, para. 35 (Poland); p. 303, para. 48 (Uruguay); p. 304, para. 59 (United Kingdom); p. 306, para. 69 (Cyprus); p. 307, para. 9 (former Byelorussian SSR); p. 311, para. 42 (Italy); p. 312, para. 55 (Romania); p. 318, para. 25 (former Czechoslovakia); p. 318, para. 31 (Federal Republic of Germany); p. 320, para. 42 (Ecuador); p. 322, para. 6 (former Ukrainian SSR); p. 323, para. 20 (Philippines); p. 323, para. 22 (Canada); pp. 323–4, para. 26 (Switzerland); p. 326, para. 51 (Malaysia). See also 'Draft Articles on the Law of Treaties with Commentaries, Adopted by the International Law Commission at its Eighteenth Session', Article 50, Commentary (3).

[17] See the considerations developed in Ago, 'Addendum to the eighth report on State responsibility' (Doc.A/CN.4/318/ADD.5–7), *Y.I.L.C.* (1980, II, Part 1), p. 44, para. 66. In the last edition of his *Principles*, Brownlie listed among the least controversial examples of *jus cogens* the 'prohibition of the use of force' (p. 513), while in the earlier editions of the same work he had referred instead to the 'prohibition of aggressive war'. (See, for example, 3rd edn. (Oxford, 1979), p. 513.)

[18] In his general course at the Hague Academy, Abi-Saab has referred to a plurality of obligations *erga omnes* deriving from the prohibition of aggression and the illegal use of force ('autres obligations *erga omnes* que l'acte même du recours à la force fait naître à la charge des tiers . . .', 'Cours général', p. 368). While sections II and IV of this chapter, and section II of Chapter 9, below, contain relevant elements for the discussion of some other candidates of such obligations, the purpose of the present work is not to examine exhaustively all possible candidates.

tion, but also in the consequences and analogies that can be drawn from the character *erga omnes* of a certain obligation. There is probably no better example than the prohibition of aggression to illustrate this point, as the remaining part of this chapter will try to show by referring to the work of codification on the law of State responsibility and to the International Court's judgments on the merits in the *Corfu Channel* case and the *Nicaragua* case.[19]

II. The Impact of the Concepts of *Jus Cogens* and *Erga Omnes* on Self-Defence and Other Circumstances Precluding Wrongfulness: Brief Considerations Based on the Codification of the Law of State Responsibility

Article 2, paragraph 4, of the Charter does not preclude all kinds of resort to force indiscriminately, but only those which are 'inconsistent with the Purposes of the United Nations'. The real concern of the Charter is not the prohibition of the use of force as such but rather the allocation of power in respect of the threat or use of force as a political instrument.[20] Hence there are circumstances in which the use of force is justified.[21] In its work of codification of the law of State responsibility, the International Law Commission has examined the so-called 'circumstances precluding wrongfulness'.[22] Although this category is wider than that of legal justifications for the use of force (in the sense that the use of force is only one of several acts that need justification lest they be regarded as unlawful), a brief reference to the International Law Commission's work is useful in the present context.

In 1981, the International Law Commission provisionally adopted several draft articles on the law of State responsibility. In particular, chapter V of

[19] These are the two classic cases in which a dispute involving the use of force was brought before the International Court. However, they are not the only ones. For a comprehensive list until 1987, see Schachter, 'Disputes Involving the Use of Force', Damrosch (ed.), *The International Court of Justice at a Crossroads* (New York, 1987), pp. 223–7. On the judicial function in cases involving forcible action, with particular regard to the *Corfu Channel* and *Hostages* cases, see Jennings, 'International Force and the International Court of Justice', Cassese (ed.), *The Current Legal Regulation*, pp. 322–35.

[20] Brownlie, 'The United Nations Charter and the Use of Force, 1945–1985', Cassese (ed.) *The Current Legal Regulation*, p. 496. The control of the use of force is essentially a problem of international organization (see Jennings, 'General Course', pp. 582–600).

[21] Legal justifications for the use of force are studied in Brownlie, *International Law and the Use of Force by States*, pp. 214–349.

[22] *Gen. Ass. Off. Recs. Thirty-Fifth Session*, Supp. 10 (A/35/10), chapter V, Articles 29–35. The Special Rapporteur preferred the expression 'circumstances precluding wrongfulness' to 'circumstances precluding responsibility' for the reasons explained in his 'Eighth report on State responsibility', (Doc.A/CN.4/318 and ADD.1–4), *Y.I.L.C.* (1979, II, Part 1), pp. 27–30, paras. 48–55.

the adopted draft lists a number of circumstances precluding wrongfulness, namely consent (draft Article 29), legitimate countermeasures (draft Article 30), force majeure (draft Article 31), distress (draft Article 32), state of necessity (draft Article 33) and self-defence (draft Article 34).[23] With respect to the first circumstance in the list, the Special Rapporteur Ago adopted, as a starting point, the international principle according to which consent is a circumstance precluding wrongfulness.[24] He then asked whether this principle is subject to any exceptions. On this question, evidence from State practice is rare. However, Ago concluded that consent does not preclude wrongfulness if, among other grounds, it conflicts with an international obligation deriving from a norm of *jus cogens*. The legal reasoning behind this statement is that consent is the element of an agreement between the territorial sovereign and the intervening State, and this agreement cannot depart from peremptory rules which, by definition, do not allow derogation between States.[25] Draft Article 29, as provisionally adopted by the International Law Commission in 1981, reads as follows:

1. The consent validly given by a State to the commission by another State of a specified act not in conformity with an obligation of the latter State towards the former State precludes the wrongfulness of the act in relation to that State to the extent that the act remains within the limits of that consent.
2. Paragraph 1 does not apply if the obligation arises out of a peremptory norm of general international law. For the purposes of the present draft, a peremptory norm of general international law is a norm accepted and recognized by the international community of States as a whole as a norm from which no derogation is permitted and which can be modified only by a subsequent norm of general international law having the same character.

Under paragraph 1, the effects of consent as a circumstance precluding wrongfulness are restricted to obligations of the consenting State towards another State, to the exclusion of those towards the international community as a whole. On the other hand, paragraph 2 explicitly excludes obligations deriving from norms of *jus cogens* from the operation of consent.

In both cases, the issue is not that of derogation from a rule, but of breach of an obligation. Hence, with respect to paragraph 2, it is legitimate to ask whether these obligations deriving from peremptory rules of general international law are not obligations *erga omnes*. If they are, the consequence would be that, while draft Article 29 does not expressly refer to the concept of oblig-

[23] Draft Article 35 reserves any question of compensation for damage caused by an act under draft Articles 29, 31, 32 or 33.

[24] 'Eighth report on State responsibility' p. 35, para. 68.

[25] Ibid., p. 38, paras. 75–6. On the incidence of *jus cogens* on consent as a circumstance precluding wrongfulness, see Ronzitti, *Rescuing Nationals Abroad Through Military Coercion and Intervention on Grounds of Humanity* (Dordrecht, 1985), pp. 84–6; id., 'Use of Force, Jus Cogens and State Consent', Cassese (ed.), *The Current Legal Regulation*, pp. 147–66.

ations *erga omnes*, it may be regarded as implicitly prohibiting consent to the commission of an act conflicting with an obligation *erga omnes*.

Similar considerations apply to a state of necessity, which is another circumstance precluding wrongfulness.[26] The difference from the case provided in draft Article 29 is that a State acting under necessity did not seek the consent of another State to commit a certain act or, if such consent was sought, it was not given. Draft Article 33, paragraph 1, as provisionally adopted by the International Law Commission in 1981, restricts the possibility that a State may invoke necessity as a ground for justifying an otherwise unlawful act to those cases when (a) there were no other means of safeguarding an essential interest of the State against a grave and imminent peril, and (b) an essential interest of the State towards which the obligation existed has not been seriously impaired. Pursuant to paragraph 2 of the same draft Article, a state of necessity may not be invoked as a ground for precluding wrongfulness if, among other reasons,

(a) . . . the international obligation with which the act of the State is not in conformity arises out of a peremptory norm of general international law . . .

This was the context in which the Special Rapporteur Ago remarked that aggression is the 'most typical and incontrovertible' example of an act prohibited by *jus cogens*, with the consequence that necessity cannot be invoked to justify an act of aggression.[27] Once again, even without an express reference to the concept in draft Article 33, it is legitimate to ask whether necessity cannot be invoked to preclude the wrongfulness of an act conflicting with an obligation *erga omnes*.

Another circumstance precluding wrongfulness which the International Law Commission listed in the draft articles on State responsibility is self-defence (draft Article 34).[28] Unlike necessity, self-defence presupposes

[26] On necessity, see *Dictionnaire de la Terminologie du Droit international, sub voce*, and (with extensive bibliographical references) Ago, 'Addendum to the eighth report on State responsibility', pp. 14–51, paras. 1–81. In the more recent literature, see Schachter, *International Law*, pp. 169–73; Barboza, 'Necessity (Revisited) in International Law', Makarczyk (ed.), *Essays in International Law in Honour of Judge Manfred Lachs* (The Hague, 1984), pp. 27–44; Salmon, 'Faut-il codifier l'état de nécessité en droit international?', ibid., pp. 235–70.

[27] 'Addendum to the eighth report on State responsibility', pp. 20–1 (para. 16) and pp. 37–9 (para. 55).

[28] On self-defence, see the statements made by the International Court in its judgment on the merits in the *Nicaragua* case (I.C.J. Reports 1986, especially paras. 195–9 and 211). In the literature, a classic monograph on the subject is Bowett, *Self-Defence in International Law* (Manchester, 1958). See also Brownlie, *International Law and the Use of Force by States*, pp. 231–80. Among the more recent works, see Dinstein, *War, Aggression and Self-Defence*, 2nd edn. (Cambridge, 1994); Schachter, *International Law*, pp. 135–83; *Oppenheim's International Law*, i, pp. 416–27. The customary requirements of necessity and proportionality, to which self-defence is subject, were thoroughly examined by diplomats when discussing measures to be taken in response to the Iraqi invasion of Kuwait (see Schachter, 'United Nations in the Gulf Conflict', 85 *A.J.I.L.* (1991), pp. 460–1).

the existence of a wrongful act (involving, as a rule, the use of force) against which a State protects itself, alone or with the assistance of other States. In his report on draft Article 34, the Special Rapporteur wrote that the prohibition of the illegal use of force and the right of self-defence are based on 'parallel and equally imperative' rules.[29]

Under Article 51 of the United Nations Charter, self-defence is an 'inherent' right of every member State. However, the content of this right, and the assessment of the various instances in which it has been invoked, are a matter of considerable controversy. It is therefore legitimate to inquire whether the concept of obligations *erga omnes* has had any impact on the discussions relating to the limits within which self-defence can be invoked. Too broad an inquiry would fall outside the scope of the present work. It therefore seems preferable to refer to two cases relating to the use of force which were brought before the International Court, namely the *Corfu Channel* case and the *Nicaragua* case. The focus of the analysis will be the international obligation to notify the existence of a minefield which, in the *Nicaragua* case, had a clear relevance to the question of self-defence invoked by the United States.

III. The Character *Erga Omnes* of the Obligation to Notify International Shipping of the Existence of a Minefield: (a) The *Corfu Channel* Case

In 1947, the United Kingdom instituted proceedings against Albania before the International Court. The dispute arose out of the explosion of mines in Albanian waters in 1946, which had caused loss of life and severe damage to British warships while passing through the Corfu Channel.[30]

In a first judgment on a preliminary objection raised by Albania, the International Court upheld its jurisdiction to hear the merits of the case.[31] Immediately after this first judgment, the United Kingdom and Albania concluded a Special Agreement by which they submitted to the International Court two questions for its decision. The first question was whether Albania was responsible for the explosions which had occurred in its territorial waters, and had a duty to pay compensation for the loss of life and the damage caused. The second question was whether the United Kingdom had violated Albanian sovereignty (and was therefore bound to give satisfaction) by sending warships into Albanian territorial waters in the first instance and then, immediately after the explosions, by undertaking a minesweeping operation in the Corfu Channel without Albania's consent.[32]

[29] 'Addendum to the eighth report on State responsibility', p. 63, para. 108.
[30] See Bernhardt, 'Corfu Channel Case', Heidelberg *Encycl.*, ii, pp. 61–4.
[31] *Corfu Channel*, Preliminary Objection, Judgment, 1948, I.C.J. Reports 1947–1948, p. 15.
[32] The text of the Special Agreement is reproduced in I.C.J. Reports 1949, p. 6.

The Special Agreement between the parties was the basis for the further proceedings. On 9 April 1949, the International Court delivered a judgment on the merits. On the first question, it found, by eleven votes to five, that Albania was responsible for the explosions and, by ten votes to six, reserved the assessment of the amount of compensation. On the second question, the International Court found, by fourteen votes to two, that the British passage through the Corfu Channel at the time of the explosions did not violate Albanian sovereignty, but found unanimously that the minesweeping operation was in breach of Albanian sovereignty.[33] In a third judgment, the International Court then assessed the amount of reparation that Albania owed to the United Kingdom.[34]

In its second judgment on the case (the one on the merits), the International Court was faced with several questions of fact: were the explosions caused by mines belonging to the minefield which the United Kingdom later discovered in its minesweeping operation? If so, had Albania laid the minefield, or at least acquiesced in the laying of the mines? Was Albania aware of the existence of a minefield in its territorial waters? To answer these questions, the International Court had to weigh the evidence produced by the parties and their experts. At the same time, the meticulous analysis of the relevant facts did not preclude the International Court from dwelling upon important legal issues.[35] Among these was the nature of the international obligations relating to minelaying in time of peace.

On this question, the starting point in the reasoning of the International Court was the obligations laid down in the Hague Convention No. VIII of 18 October 1907, headed 'Convention relative to the laying of automatic submarine contact mines',[36] which resulted from the efforts undertaken at the end of the nineteenth century to regulate the conduct of war.[37] As this

[33] *Corfu Channel*, Merits, Judgment, I.C.J. Reports 1949, p. 4.

[34] *Corfu Channel*, Assessment of Amount of Compensation, Judgment, I.C.J. Reports 1949, p. 244.

[35] According to Sir Hersch Lauterpacht, the decision on the merits of the *Corfu Channel* case is a classic example in which the examination of questions of fact prompted the International Court to lay down general rules of law (*The Development of International Law*, p. 35).

[36] The French original, and the English translation of this Convention, are reproduced in Scott (ed.), *The Hague Peace Conferences of 1899 and 1907. A Series of Lectures Delivered Before the Johns Hopkins University in the Year 1908*, ii (Baltimore, 1909), p. 429. For brief comments on the Convention, see Guggenheim, *Traité de Droit international public*, ii, p. 405.

[37] See Westlake, *International Law*, ii (2nd edn., Cambridge, 1913), pp. 56–63; Oppenheim, *International Law*, ii, 7th edn. Lauterpacht, H., pp. 226–36. The text of all the documents adopted at the Hague Peace Conferences of 1899 and 1907 is reproduced in Scott (ed.), *The Hague Peace Conferences*, ii. In 1959, the Polish Supreme Court stated that the Hague Convention No. IV of 18 October 1907 respecting the laws and customs of war on land 'constitutes *jus cogens*, *i.e.*, it contains rules the application of which does not depend on the free discretion of any State.' (*In re Koch*, 30 *I.L.R.* (1966), p. 503.)

Convention is only meant to apply in time of war,[38] the International Court could not apply it in this particular case. At the same time, there was no doubt that, if not the Hague Convention No. VIII itself, at least the basic principles it embodied would also apply in time of peace. On this point, the International Court and both parties shared the same view.

In its Memorial, the United Kingdom remarked that, while the rules adopted at the Hague Conference of 1907 were meant to apply in time of war, they constitute a 'minimum international standard binding at all times on civilised States.' Further, it wrote that minelaying unjustified by the necessity of war is an 'international delinquency' and that such an act is aggravated and becomes an 'offence against humanity' if the law-breaker fails also to satisfy the strict requirements on notification embodied in the Hague Convention No. VIII.[39] Likewise, Albania affirmed in its Duplique that, although it was not a party to the Hague Convention No. VIII, it considered itself to be bound by the rules embodied in it. In particular, had it known about the existence of a minefield in its waters, it would have certainly given notice of it. It then acknowledged that clandestine minelaying in time of peace is undoubtedly prohibited.[40]

Thus, the difference between the parties was not whether a State laying mines or conniving in the laying of mines in time of peace must notify international shipping (on this, both parties agreed that it must). Rather, the controversy was about the interpretation of the facts, namely whether Albania had taken part in, or at least was aware of, the laying of mines in its territorial waters. On this issue, the International Court concluded that Albania must have been aware that there was a minefield in its territorial waters. As it did not notify international shipping of the existence of the minefield, and the approaching British warships of the imminent danger to which they were exposed, Albania was in breach of its international obligation to notify. The International Court explained the grounds for its conclusion. It wrote that the international obligations relating to notification are based on certain 'general and well-recognized principles', namely

> elementary considerations of humanity, even more exacting in peace than in war; the principle of the freedom of maritime communication; and every State's obligation not to allow knowingly its territory to be used for acts contrary to the rights of other States.[41]

[38] In his dissenting opinion, Judge Azevedo added that the Hague Convention No. VIII deals only with 'direct' minelaying, and not with minelaying by a third party (I.C.J. Reports 1949, p. 84). However, as the International Court acknowledged in its judgment (ibid., p. 17), the authors of the minelaying in the Albanian territorial waters remained unknown.

[39] *I.C.J. Pleadings, Corfu Channel*, i, pp. 37–8, para. 64; p. 40, para. 72.

[40] Ibid., ii, pp. 324–5, para. 27.

[41] I.C.J. Reports 1949, p. 22. The French authoritative text reads as follows: 'des considérations élémentaires d'humanité, plus absolues encore en temps de paix qu'en temps de guerre, le principe de la liberté des communications maritimes et l'obligation, pour tout Etat, de ne pas laisser utiliser son territoire aux fins d'actes contraires aux droits d'autres Etats.'

The reference to the 'elementary considerations of humanity', which appears in this passage, has been the subject of extensive commentaries, but it seems unnecessary to discuss them here.[42] On the other hand, it is useful to explore why the International Court felt the need to resort to 'elementary considerations of humanity' beyond the two other grounds on which it relied. An easy explanation is that the International Court wanted to list exhaustively all possible grounds for the international obligation to notify. However, the International Court may also have had a stronger reason for referring to the 'elementary considerations of humanity', a reason which emerges from a comparison between the legal status of the 'elementary considerations of humanity' and the two other grounds on which the International Court relied in its judgment.

The first of these other grounds is the 'freedom of maritime communication', which is a general principle of international law.[43] The rights of the coastal States can qualify this general principle in various ways. For example, in the *Corfu Channel* case, Albania claimed that, in 'exceptional circumstances', a coastal State is entitled to regulate the passage of foreign warships through its territorial waters. According to Albania, 'exceptional circumstances' existed when the incidents occurred.[44] Similar considerations apply to the other ground mentioned in the judgment, namely the obligation incumbent on every State 'not to allow knowingly its territory to be used for acts contrary to the rights of other States'. This obligation is not absolute. As the International Court expressly stated in its decision on the merits in the *Corfu Channel* case, the mere fact of the control by a State over its territory does not imply the responsibility of such a State for every wrong occurring in its territory.[45]

The case of the 'elementary considerations of humanity' is different. In the words of the International Court, these considerations are 'even more exacting in peace than in war'. They are opposable to all States and their application does not vary depending on any particular circumstances. Unlike the principle of freedom of maritime communication and the obligation of a State not to allow its territory to be used for wrongful purposes, no 'exceptional circumstances' or conflicting rights can qualify the 'elementary considerations of humanity'. All this leads to the conclusion that the obligation to notify has an absolute value. The International Court did not employ the expression 'obligation *erga omnes*'. However, by referring to 'elementary considerations of humanity', which are binding on all States in

[42] See Brownlie, *Principles*, p. 28; Fitzmaurice, 'The Law and Procedure of the International Court of Justice: General Principles and Substantive Law', 27 *B.Y.I.L.* (1950), p. 4; Schwarzenberger, *International Law*, i, p. 51; Chung, *Legal Problems Involved in the Corfu Channel Incident* (Geneva, 1959), pp. 161–2.

[43] See Brownlie, *Principles*, pp. 233–7.

[44] I.C.J. Reports 1949, p. 12 (Nos. 2, 3 and 4).

[45] Ibid., p. 18. For commentary on this point, see Fitzmaurice, 'The Law and Procedure', 27 *B.Y.I.L.* (1950), p. 4, note 4; p. 5, note 1.

all circumstances, it relied on a concept which is functionally equivalent to the concept of obligations *erga omnes*. The ensuing analysis of some aspects of the judgment on the merits in the *Nicaragua* case will confirm this conclusion.

IV. The Character *Erga Omnes* of the Obligation to Notify International Shipping of the Existence of a Minefield: (b) The *Nicaragua* Case

The international obligation to notify international shipping of the existence of a minefield was also relevant to the judgment on the merits in the *Nicaragua* case. In 1984, Nicaragua instituted proceedings against the United States before the International Court in respect of a dispute concerning certain hostile activities in and against Nicaragua. In its Application, Nicaragua requested the International Court to declare that the United States was in breach of several conventional and customary rules of international law and that, in consideration of these breaches, the United States had a duty to desist immediately from all illegal activities and to pay reparation for damages.[46]

In 1986, less than two years after deciding that it had jurisdiction over the case and that the Application of Nicaragua was admissible,[47] the International Court delivered its judgment on the merits.[48] Subparagraphs (6) to (8) of the operative clause of the judgment deal with minelaying in Nicaraguan waters. By a majority of twelve votes to three (subparagraph (6)), the International Court held that, by laying mines in Nicaraguan waters, the United States had violated the international customary rules against the illegal use of force and intervention in the internal affairs of another State, and those which protect sovereignty and peaceful maritime commerce. By a majority of fourteen votes to one (subparagraph (7)), the International Court then held that, by laying the mines, the United States was also in breach of Article XIX of the 1956 Treaty of Friendship,

[46] Application of the Republic of Nicaragua, dated 11 April 1984, para. 26. After the International Court's decision on the merits, Nicaragua introduced a case for reparations, but it then renounced to pursue its claim. By an Order dated 26 September 1991, the President of the International Court recorded the discontinuance of the proceedings and directed the removal of the case from the Court's list. On this complex case, see Gill, *Litigation Strategy at the International Court. A Case Study of the Nicaragua* v. *United States Dispute* (Dordrecht, 1989). On the International Court's decision on the merits, see the various contributions under the heading 'Appraisals of the ICJ's Decision: Nicaragua v. United States (Merits)', 81 *A.J.I.L.* (1987), pp. 77–183.

[47] *Military and Paramilitary Activities in and against Nicaragua (Nicaragua* v. *United States of America)*, Jurisdiction and Admissibility, Judgment, I.C.J. Reports 1984, p. 392.

[48] *Military and Paramilitary Activities in and against Nicaragua (Nicaragua* v. *United States of America)*, Merits, Judgment, I.C.J. Reports 1986, p. 14.

Commerce and Navigation between the United States and Nicaragua, which provides for freedom of commerce and navigation between the two parties. Finally, by a majority of fourteen votes to one (subparagraph (8))—the only dissent coming from Judge Oda for reasons that will be explained later in this section—the International Court held that, by failing to notify international shipping of the existence and location of the mines in the Nicaraguan waters, the United States was in breach of the customary rule relating to the obligation to notify. While indicating in subparagraphs (6) and (7) that the United States had committed a breach against Nicaragua, in subparagraph (8) the International Court wrote that the United States had violated its obligations under customary international law, without specifying which State had suffered damage from this breach.

Before commenting on several passages from the judgment and some of the dissenting opinions, it is helpful to summarize a few relevant facts, which the International Court ascertained with difficulty because the United States did not participate in the proceedings on the merits.[49] (While the decision by the United States not to appear before the International Court could not affect the validity of the judgment, it certainly limited the extent to which the International Court could have knowledge of all the relevant facts: as noted in the judgment, 'the Court cannot by its own enquiries entirely make up for the absence of one of the parties'.)[50]

The facts, as summarized in the judgment, are the following.[51] In the first few months of 1984, fishing vessels registered in various countries were either destroyed or damaged by mines while navigating off the coasts of Nicaragua. The exact position of the mines was a matter of uncertainty (whether they were in the internal waters or instead in the territorial sea of Nicaragua), and equally unclear were their size and nature. According to press reports, United States officials acknowledged that the mines had been built with the support of the United States, but the United States Government does not appear to have warned the shipping community of the existence and the location of the mines. There was no direct evidence before the International Court of any diplomatic protests, even after some explosions involving fishing vessels of third States. Apparently, the United Kingdom deplored the mining 'as a matter of principle', independently of any actual damage suffered by a vessel flying the British flag.

The facts summarized so far indicate a major difference between the *Nicaragua* case and the *Corfu Channel* case. In the *Corfu Channel* case, the dispute was between the State whose warships had been damaged by the explosions (the United Kingdom) and the State that must have known about the existence of the minefield (Albania). On the other hand, in the

[49] See the letter dated 18 January 1985 from the Agent of the United States to the International Court, partly reproduced ibid., p. 17, para. 10.

[50] Ibid., p. 25, para. 30.

[51] Ibid., pp. 46–8, paras. 76–80.

Nicaragua case, the dispute was between the State in whose waters the mines had exploded (Nicaragua) and the State that the International Court found to be responsible for minelaying and for failing to notify international shipping of the existence and location of the mines (the United States). Despite this difference, the principles affirmed by the International Court in the two cases are essentially the same. In its judgment on the merits in the *Nicaragua* case, the International Court wrote that minelaying in the internal or territorial waters of another State in time of peace is unlawful. In addition, if the State responsible for the minelaying fails to give warning or notification of the existence of the minefield, it is in breach of the 'principles of humanitarian law'. According to the International Court, these principles are embodied in the Hague Convention No. VIII of 1907 and correspond to the 'elementary considerations of humanity' to which the International Court referred in the *Corfu Channel* case.[52]

Some of the dissenting opinions addressed very clearly the question of the absolute validity of the international obligation to notify, and its impact on the right of self-defence. Judge Oda expressed the only dissent from the International Court's finding, in subparagraph (8) of the operative clause, that the United States was in breach of a customary rule of international law for failing to notify the existence and location of the mines in the Nicaraguan waters. His dissent was based on procedural, rather than substantive, grounds.[53] Judge Oda voted against subparagraph (8) because he believed that the International Court had no jurisdiction over the case other than on the ground of the 1956 Treaty of Friendship, Commerce and Navigation between the United States and Nicaragua.[54] As he explained in his dissenting opinion, he could not vote in favour of subparagraph (8)

[52] I.C.J. Reports 1986, p. 112, para. 215. This paragraph was followed by an extensive analysis of the 'fundamental general principles of humanitarian law' embodied in the four Geneva Conventions signed on 12 August 1949. The International Court wrote that Article 3, which is common to all four Geneva Conventions, defines certain rules which today reflect the 'elementary considerations of humanity' referred to in the judgment on the merits in the *Corfu Channel* case. In his dissenting opinion, Judge Jennings took a more cautious approach to the customary nature of the principles embodied in the Geneva Conventions (ibid., p. 537). The issue of the customary nature of the Geneva Conventions, and especially of the fourth, was discussed in a case before the Supreme Court of Israel (H.C. 698/80, *Kawasme et al.* v. *Minister of Defence et al.* 35(1) *Piskei Din* 617), partly reproduced in Domb, 'Judicial Decisions of the Supreme Court of Israel Relating to the Administrated Territories', 11 *Israel Yearbook on Human Rights* (1981), pp. 349–54.

[53] The grounds for Judge Oda's dissenting opinion are briefly discussed in McWhinney, *Judge Shigeru Oda and the Progressive Development of International Law. Opinions (Declarations, Separate Opinions, Dissents) on the International Court of Justice, 1976–1992* (Dordrecht, 1993), pp. 47–8.

[54] See Judge Oda's dissenting opinion from the International Court's decision on jurisdiction and admissibility, I.C.J. Reports 1984, p. 471. An interesting question, which is beyond the scope of the present research, is the extent to which a judge's dissent on the issue of jurisdiction can and does affect his or her position on the merits of the case.

because such a decision by the Court concerning a breach of obligations *erga omnes* under customary international law is out of place in this Judgment.[55]

Thus, the most explicit statement on the character *erga omnes* of the obligation to notify came from the only judge who voted against subparagraph (8).

Two other dissenting opinions considered the impact of the international obligation to notify on the right of self-defence. Judge Schwebel, who wrote a forceful dissenting opinion and disagreed with the International Court on twelve out of the sixteen counts of the operative clause,[56] joined the majority in condemning the United States for the unannounced mining of the Nicaraguan ports. He wrote that the mining of the Nicaraguan ports, like other measures of pressure, was lawful against Nicaragua but was a violation of international law in light of the standards of necessity and proportionality which apply to self-defence. In Judge Schwebel's words, the mining of the Nicaraguan ports

could affect and did affect third States as against whom no rationale of self-defence could apply in these circumstances.[57]

This passage seems to indicate that the unannounced minelaying was inherently in conflict ('could affect and did affect') with the strict criteria that must be satisfied in order that an action taken in self-defence be justified.

A similar position was also taken by Judge Jennings. In his dissenting opinion, he agreed that the laying of mines by the United States in the Nicaraguan waters was unlawful. Judge Jennings then noted that a possible justification of this act by the United States, namely collective self-defence, was outside the jurisdiction of the International Court. This was his conclusion:

With the question of collective self-defence undecided, it is far from clear that the respondent State is answerable to Nicaragua for damaging, or impeding its shipping; and the third States whose shipping was involved are not before the Court. However, since the laying of unnotified mines is of itself an unlawful act, it seemed right nevertheless to vote for subparagraph (8).[58]

Two points in this passage are noteworthy for the present purposes. First of all, Judge Jennings considered the unnotified minelaying to be 'of itself' an unlawful act. One cannot fail to note the analogy between this expression and the words used by the International Court in the *Barcelona Traction* case, when it wrote that certain international obligations are 'by

[55] I.C.J. Reports 1986, p. 214, para. 2. For the same reason, Judge Oda wrote that he could vote in favour of subparagraph (7) of the operative clause, on which the International Court based its finding on the 1956 Treaty, but not subparagraph (6), on which the International Court based its finding on customary international law.

[56] Judge Schwebel voted in favour of subparagraphs (1), (8), (9) and (16).

[57] I.C.J. Reports 1986, p. 269, para. 8.

[58] Ibid., p. 537.

their very nature' *erga omnes*. In other words, the absolute value attaching to the prohibition of unnotified minelaying is grounded in the very essence of this prohibition and the values it protects.

Secondly, from the absolute value of the prohibition of unnotified minelaying, it follows that unnotified minelaying cannot ever be justified even if resorted to in self-defence. This confirms the impact of obligations *erga omnes* on the circumstances precluding wrongfulness, which were discussed earlier in this chapter within the limited context of the work of codification of State responsibility.

V. Conclusions

It is incontrovertible that the prohibition of aggression is valid *erga omnes*: it is opposable to all States without exception and affects the interests of all. At first sight, the unanimous support behind the universal opposability of the prohibition of aggression may lead one to believe that its character *erga omnes* is largely irrelevant. But this is not so, as is clear if one considers, for example, the contribution that the concept of obligations *erga omnes* is making to clarify the limits within which self-defence and other circumstances precluding wrongfulness can be invoked.

In the work of codification of the law of State responsibility, the influence of the concept of obligations *erga omnes* has been somewhat preempted (with respect at least to the draft articles on circumstances precluding wrongfulness) by the more familiar concept of *jus cogens*. However, there are also instances in which this contribution has been more visible, as in the case of the consequences attaching to the character *erga omnes* of the international obligation to notify the existence of a minefield.

A few passages on this latter obligation contained in the judgment on the merits in the *Corfu Channel* case and in some dissenting opinions appended to the decision on the merits in the *Nicaragua* case disclose another important aspect of the concept of obligations *erga omnes*. In his dissenting opinion to the judgment on the merits in the *Nicaragua* case, Judge Oda expressly stated that the prohibition of unnotified minelaying in time of peace is an obligation *erga omnes*. Other passages from the dissenting opinions of Judge Jennings and Judge Schwebel seem to endorse the same conclusion. Such a clear statement of the character *erga omnes* of the prohibition of unnotified minelaying was absent from either the judgment on the merits in the *Corfu Channel* case or the opinions appended to it. Yet, without using the expression 'obligations *erga omnes*', in the *Corfu Channel* case the International Court made use of a concept ('elementary considerations of humanity') which, by its absolute value, presents clear elements of analogy with the concept of obligations *erga omnes*.

Almost forty years after the *Corfu Channel* case, the broad criteria of public policy embodied in the 'elementary considerations of humanity' were now subsumed under the heading of obligation *erga omnes*. This shows how earlier pronouncements contribute to the formation of concepts utilized by the International Court in later cases. This point will emerge even more clearly from the analysis developed in the next chapter.

5

The Examples of Obligations *Erga Omnes* Given by the International Court in its Dictum: (b) The Outlawing of Genocide

I. The International Prohibition of Genocide

The second example of obligation *erga omnes* given by the International Court in its dictum is the 'prohibition of acts of genocide'.[1]

The origins of the international prohibition of genocide date back to the end of the Second World War, at the time of the adoption of the Charter of the International Military Tribunal at Nuremberg, and the prosecution of the Major War Criminals of the European Axis.[2] While not expressly referring to 'genocide', the Nuremberg Charter condemned as 'crimes against humanity' all

> murder, extermination, enslavement, deportation, and other inhumane acts committed against any civilian population, before or during the war, or persecutions on political, racial or religious grounds in execution of or in connection with any crime

[1] On genocide, see the two reports produced in 1978 and 1985 by the United Nations Sub-Commission on Prevention of Discrimination and Protection of Minorities, headed 'Study of the Question of the Prevention and Punishment of the Crime of Genocide' (prepared by Nicodèm Ruhashyankiki), Doc.E/CN.4/Sub.2/416, and 'Revised and Updated Report on the Question of the Prevention and Punishment of the Crime of Genocide' (prepared by Ben Whitaker), Doc.E/CN.4/Sub.2/1985/6. See also Kuper, *The Prevention of Genocide* (New Haven and London, 1985); id., *International Action against Genocide* (Minority Rights Group Report No. 53, London, 1982); Porter (ed.), *Genocide and Human Rights: A Global Anthology* (Washington, 1982); Shaw, 'Genocide and International Law', Dinstein (ed.), *International Law. Essays Rosenne*, pp. 797–820; Cassese, 'La communauté internationale et le génocide', *Le droit international. Mélanges Virally*, pp. 183–94; Thornberry, *International Law and the Rights of Minorities* (Oxford, 1991), pp. 57–109; Verhoven, 'Le crime de génocide. Originalité et ambiguïté', 24 *Revue belge de droit international* (1991), pp. 5–26; Andreopoulos (ed.), *Genocide: Conceptual and Historical Dimensions* (Philadelphia, 1994).

[2] The text of the Charter, annexed to the Agreement for the Prosecution and Punishment of the Major War Criminals of the European Axis, signed in London on 8 August 1945, and the text of the judgment, are reproduced in *Trial of the Major War Criminals before the International Military Tribunal. Nuremberg 14 November 1945—1 October 1946*, i (Nuremberg, 1947), pp. 10–16 and 171–367. For the documentary record of the negotiations which led to the adoption of the London Agreement, see *Report of Robert H. Jackson, United States Representative to the International Conference on Military Trials. London, 1945* (Washington, 1949). On the Nuremberg trials, see Taylor, 'The Nuremberg War Crimes Trials', 450 *International Conciliation* (1949), pp. 243–371; id. *The Anatomy of the Nuremberg Trials* (New York, 1992).

within the jurisdiction of the Tribunal, whether or not in violation of the domestic law of the country where perpetrated.[3]

Apparently, it was a Polish lawyer, Raphael Lemkin, who coined the term 'genocide' in 1944.[4] As to official documents, the word appeared for the first time in the indictment of 8 October 1945, in which the Major War Criminals of the European Axis were charged to have conducted

deliberate and systematic genocide, viz. the extermination of racial and national groups, against the civilian populations of certain occupied territories in order to destroy particular races and classes of people and national, racial or religious groups . . .[5]

The principles proclaimed at Nuremberg were then recognized as 'principles of international law' by Resolution 95, which was unanimously adopted at the first session of the General Assembly of the United Nations.[6] Then, Resolution 96 openly condemned genocide as a 'denial of the right of existence of entire human groups', and a 'crime under international law'.[7] This opened the way for the adoption by the General Assembly of a Convention for the Prevention and Punishment of the Crime of Genocide.[8]

[3] Article 6(c). On the concept of 'crime against humanity', see Clark, 'Crimes Against Humanity', Ginsburgs and Kudriavtsev (eds.), *The Nuremberg Trial and International Law* (Dordrecht, 1990), pp. 177–99; Reshetov, 'Development of Norms of International Law on Crimes Against Humanity', ibid., pp. 199–212; Decocq, 'Le droit et la notion de crime contre l'humanité', *Revue des Sciences morales et politiques* (1992), pp. 357–72.

[4] He defined the term as 'a coordinated plan of different actions aiming at the destruction of essential foundations of the life of national groups, with the aim of annihilating the groups themselves.' (*Axis Rule in Occupied Europe* (Washington, 1944), p. 79.) See also id., 'Genocide as a Crime under International Law', 41 *A.J.I.L.* (1947), p. 145.

[5] *Trial of the Major War Criminals before the International Military Tribunal*, i, pp. 43–4.

[6] 'Resolution 95(I) of the United Nations General Assembly on the Affirmation of the Principles of International Law recognized by the Charter of the Nuremberg Tribunal (adopted on 11 Dec. 1946)', *Resolutions adopted by the General Assembly during the Second Part of its First Session from 23 October to 15 December 1946*, p. 175.

[7] 'Resolution 96(I) of the United Nations General Assembly on the Crime of Genocide (adopted on 11 Dec. 1946)', ibid., pp. 175–6. The concept of genocide as a 'crime under international law' has been restated in the commentary to Article 1 of the draft Code of Offences against Peace and Security of Mankind. See 'Titles and texts of articles on the Draft Code of Crimes against the Peace and Security of Mankind adopted by the International Law Commission at its forty-eighth session (1996)' (Doc.A/CN.4/L.532), Article 17. The preparation of a draft Code of Offences against Peace and Security of Mankind was decided by General Assembly Resolution 177 (II) of 21 November 1947. This resolution asked the International Law Commission to formulate the principles of international law recognized in the Nuremberg Charter and in the judgment of the Nuremberg Tribunal.

[8] 'Resolution 260A (III) of the United Nations General Assembly on the Convention on the Prevention and Punishment of the Crime of Genocide (adopted on 9 Dec. 1948)', *Gen. Ass. Off. Recs., Third Session*, p. 174 (Doc.A/810). The Convention entered into force on 12 January 1951 and one hundred and twenty States have become parties (*Multilateral Treaties Deposited with the Secretary-General. Status as at 31 December 1995*, p. 87). The text is reproduced in Brownlie (ed.), *Basic Documents on Human Rights*, 3rd edn. (Oxford, 1992), pp. 31–4. A classic commentary is Robinson, *The Genocide Convention. A Commentary* (New York, 1960). Brief comments can be found in O'Connell, *International Law*, 2nd edn. (London, 1970), ii, pp. 745–6.

In Article I of this Convention, the contracting parties merely 'confirmed' that genocide was a 'crime under international law', which they undertook to prevent and punish. While the Genocide Convention avoids any explicit reference to the Nuremberg principles,[9] the preparatory works suggest that the language of Article I was carefully chosen to indicate that the prohibition of genocide was already an established principle of international law.[10] This latter point, however, is still controversial in the international literature.[11]

Another element of continuity with the Nuremberg trial is the definition of genocide in Article II of the Convention. According to this article,

> genocide means any of the following acts committed with intent to destroy, in whole or in part, a national, ethnical, racial or religious group, as such:
> (a) Killing members of the group;
> (b) Causing serious bodily or mental harm to members of the group;
> (c) Deliberately inflicting on the group conditions of life calculated to bring about its physical destruction in whole or in part;
> (d) Imposing measures intended to prevent births within the group;
> (e) Forcibly transferring children of the group to another group.

The strict correlation between this definition and the concept of 'crimes against humanity' in the Nuremberg Charter, and that of genocide in the indictment of the Major War Criminals, is apparent, except that the Convention provides a more detailed definition of genocide and applies not only in time of war (as was the case of 'crimes against humanity' under the Nuremberg Charter) but also in time of peace.

Today, there is wide support for the view that the customary rule against genocide, like the rule outlawing acts of aggression, belongs to *jus cogens*. During the codification of the law of treaties, the prohibition of genocide was in fact the most often cited example of peremptory rule in the field of international human rights.[12] However, serious problems remain, with

[9] To this effect, an amendment to the draft preamble of the Convention was submitted by Venezuela at the 109th meeting of the Sixth Committee of the General Assembly. This amendment was approved by a majority of States at the 110th meeting (*Gen. Ass. Off. Recs., Third Session, Part I, Legal Questions, Sixth Committee, Summary Records of Meetings 21 September—10 December 1948*, pp. 489–90 and 498–509).

[10] The word 'confirm' was introduced at the instance of France. See ibid., pp. 49–53 (68th meeting), and pp. 480–1 (108th meeting).

[11] A clear statement to the effect that the Genocide Convention is declaratory of customary law is contained in the decision of the District Court of Jerusalem in the *Eichmann* case (36 *I.L.R.* (1968), p. 26), and in the conclusions of the 'Judgment of the Permanent Peoples' Tribunal on the Genocide of the Armenians' (Paris, 13–16 April 1984), reproduced in Kuper, *The Prevention of Genocide*, pp. 247–53. For Cassese, it was only after 1948 that a customary rule on genocide emerged (*Human Rights in a Changing World* (Philadelphia, 1990), p. 78). See also *Polyukhovich* v. *Commonwealth of Australia and Another* (Australia, High Court, 14 Aug. 1991), 91 *I.L.R.* (1993), pp. 60–1 (*per* Brennan J (dissenting)).

[12] See, for example, the declarations of the representatives of States during the first session of the Vienna Conference, *U.N.C.L.T., Off. Recs., First Session*, p. 296, para. 31 (Kenya);

respect especially to the prevention and punishment of acts of genocide, and the identification of the obligations relating to genocide which may be regarded as obligations *erga omnes*.

One of the main issues relating to prevention and punishment is jurisdiction to punish. The question is whether all States, irrespective of any links with the territory in which the offence occurred, may punish an individual responsible for acts of genocide. In other words, is genocide, like piracy and slavery, subject to the principle of universal jurisdiction?[13] During the preparatory work of the Genocide Convention, one of the draft provisions stipulated that genocide was a crime subject to universal jurisdiction. However, this proposal was rejected.[14] The compromise solution embodied in the present text of Article VI of the Genocide Convention is that a person charged with genocide must be tried either before the competent tribunals of the State where the crime was committed, or before an international criminal court. While under the Convention there is no universal jurisdiction to punish, certain judgments delivered by courts of different States[15] provide some support for the proposition that universal jurisdiction to punish genocide 'is widely accepted as a principle of customary law'.[16] It has also been suggested that the concept of obligations *erga omnes* might play a role in expanding the area of universal jurisdiction.[17]

A related issue is the identification of the obligations relating to genocide which may be regarded as obligations *erga omnes*. The character *erga omnes* of the prohibition of acts of genocide is indisputable, and has been reaffirmed after the International Court's dictum in the *Barcelona Traction* case.[18] Does the character *erga omnes* attach only to this prohibition, or can

p. 297, para. 43 (Lebanon); p. 301, para. 15 (Ghana); p. 302, para. 35 (Poland); p. 303, para. 48 (Uruguay); p. 306, para. 69 (Cyprus); p. 318, para. 25 (former Czechoslovakia); p. 323, para. 20 (Philippines); p. 323, para. 22 (Canada).

13 On universal jurisdiction, see Brownlie, *International Law and the Use of Force by States*, p. 305; Henkin, *International Law*, p. 240.

14 Doc.E/447, pp. 8 and 38 (1947); Doc.E/794, pp. 32–3 (1948). See also *Gen. Ass. Off. Recs., Third Session, Part I, Legal Questions, Sixth Committee, Summary Records of Meetings 21 September–10 December 1948*, pp. 394–405 (100th meeting).

15 *Attorney General of Israel* v. *Eichmann*, 36 *I.L.R.* (1968), p. 277 (Supreme Court of Israel, 1962); *Matter of Demjanjuk*, 603 F.Supp. 1468 (N.D.Ohio), *affirmed*, 776 F.2d 571 (6th Cir. 1985), *certiorari denied*, 457 U.S. 1016, 106 S.Ct. 1198, 89 L.Ed.2d 312 (1986), *Matter of Barbie*, [1983] Gaz. Pal. Jur. 710 (Cass. Crim. Oct. 6, 1983).

16 *Restatement of the Law. The Foreign Relations Law of the United States (Third Restatement)*, Section 404, Reporter's Note (1).

17 See Schachter, *International Law*, p. 269; Higgins, R., *Problems and Process*, pp. 56–7. See also McDougal, Lasswell and Chen, *Human Rights and World Public Order. The Basic Policies of an International Law of Human Dignity* (New Haven and London, 1980) pp. 359–60.

18 See, for example, the Final Report of the Commission of Experts, attached to the 'Letter dated 24 May 1994 from the Secretary-General to the President of the Security Council' (Doc.S/1994/674), p. 24, para. 88: 'In view of the rights involved, the legal obligations to refrain from genocide are recognized as *erga omnes*.'

it be extended also to other obligations relating to genocide? Of the two instances in which the International Court has addressed questions arising under the Genocide Convention, the more recent one shows how controversial the answer to this question is, and how problematic the identification of obligations *erga omnes* may be, even in the area of genocide.

In the proceedings that the Republic of Bosnia-Herzegovina (as its official name then was) instituted before the International Court against the Federal Republic of Yugoslavia, both parties referred to the concept of obligations *erga omnes*.[19] The judgment delivered by the International Court on the preliminary objections raised by the Federal Republic of Yugoslavia contains a passage on obligations *erga omnes*. In it, the International Court wrote that

> the rights and obligations enshrined by the [Genocide] Convention are rights and obligations *erga omnes*. The Court notes that the obligation each State thus has to prevent and to punish the crime of genocide is not territorially limited by the Convention.[20]

Thus, the character *erga omnes* would not be restricted to the prohibition of genocide, but would attach in general to the 'rights and obligations enshrined by the Convention', an expression that would seem to include the obligations to prevent and punish acts of genocide.

The International Court made this statement in the course of its consideration of the fifth preliminary objection of the Federal Republic of Yugoslavia, relating to jurisdiction *ratione materiae*. This objection was rejected by eleven votes to four. Of the four dissenting members of the International Court (Judges Oda, Shi, Vereshchetin and Judge *ad hoc* Kreca), Judge Oda and Judge *ad hoc* Kreca referred to the concept of obligations *erga omnes* in their respective declaration and dissenting opinion.

In his declaration, Judge Oda recalled that, during the preparation of the Genocide Convention, some delegates had expressed their preference for the inclusion in the preamble, and not in the main text, of the general clause on the prevention and punishment of genocide, which is now in Article 1 of the Genocide Convention. In any event, assuming that this general clause is to be interpreted as binding on the parties to the Genocide Convention to prevent and punish acts of genocide, Judge Oda agreed that these obligations

[19] See *Case Concerning the Application of the Convention on the Prevention and Punishment of the Crime of Genocide (Bosnia and Herzegovina* v. *Yugoslavia (Serbia and Montenegro))*, uncorrected Verbatim Record, CR 96/9, pp. 53–4 (Franck); CR 96/10, p. 12 (Brownlie); CR 96/11, pp. 32–5 (Pellet) and 76 (Stern).

[20] *Application of the Convention on the Prevention and Punishment of the Crime of Genocide*, Preliminary Objections, I.C.J. Reports 1996 (mimeographed text), p. 23, para. 31. The French authoritative text reads as follows: 'les droits et obligations consacrés par la convention [sur le génocide] sont des droits et obligations *erga omnes*. La Cour constate que l'obligation qu'a ainsi chaque Etat de prévenir et de réprimer le crime de génocide n'est pas limitée territorialement par la convention.'

are borne in a general manner *erga omnes* by the Contracting Parties in their relations with all the other Contracting Parties to the [Genocide] Convention—or, even, with the international community as a whole – but are *not* obligations in relation to any specific and particular signatory Contracting Party.[21]

On this ground, Judge Oda disagreed with the idea that a State's failure to prevent and punish acts of genocide could be remedied by invoking State responsibility before the International Court.

Judge *ad hoc* Kreca took another approach. He acknowledged that the prohibition of genocide derives from a norm of *jus cogens* and 'establishes obligations of a State toward the international community as a whole, hence by its very nature it is the concern of all States.' However, while recognizing in this way the character *erga omnes* of the prohibition of genocide, Judge *ad hoc* Kreca restricted the scope of this universal character, when he wrote that

[a]s an absolutely binding norm prohibiting genocide, it binds all subjects of international law even without any conventional obligation. To that effect, and only to that effect, the concrete norm is of universal applicability (a norm *erga omnes*) . . . The position is different, however, when it comes to the implementation or enforcement of the norm of genocide prohibition.[22]

Neither the issue of jurisdiction to punish, nor that of the identification of obligations *erga omnes* relating to genocide, can be pursued here, as the analysis of these issues would require a major digression from the main line of inquiry developed in the present work. One particular aspect of the diverging views expressed in the case of the Republic of Bosnia-Herzegovina against the Federal Republic of Yugoslavia (and reproduced above) will be examined, though, later in this work.[23]

A more appropriate topic for consideration in the present chapter is the relationship between the concept of obligations *erga omnes* and the reasoning behind an advisory opinion that the International Court delivered in 1951 on a request relating to the Genocide Convention. There are at least two good reasons for concentrating on this advisory opinion. The first one is that the advisory opinion on the Genocide Convention is the only 'precedent' to which the International Court expressly referred in its dictum on obligations *erga omnes*. The second one is that, as the remaining part of this chapter will show, this advisory opinion anticipated some elements of the definition of obligations *erga omnes*, which the International Court fully developed twenty years later in the *Barcelona Traction* case.[24]

21 *I.C.J. Reports* 1996 (mimeographed text), p. 2, para. 4, of Judge Oda's declaration.

22 Ibid., pp. 84–5, para. 101, of Judge *ad hoc* Kreca's dissenting opinion.

23 See section III of Chapter 8, below.

24 'The Court thus recognized that genocide is supremely unlawful under both conventional and customary law, foreshadowing its later holdings on international obligations *erga omnes*.' (Schwebel, 'Human Rights in the World Court', 24 *Vanderbilt Journal of Transnational Law*

II. The Advisory Opinion on the Genocide Convention

In 1950, the General Assembly of the United Nations adopted a resolution by which it requested the International Court to give an advisory opinion on certain questions relating to reservations to the Genocide Convention.[25] The main issue before the International Court was whether a reserving State can be regarded as a party to the Convention if one or more parties have objected to that reservation.[26] The Genocide Convention is silent on reservations, and the member States of the United Nations had different views on the issue. After the adoption of the Genocide Convention, some States purported to make unilateral reservations, to which other countries objected. A practical question was therefore whether the reserving States counted towards the twenty ratifications or accessions needed before the Genocide Convention could enter into force.

Until the advisory opinion on the Genocide Convention, the traditional view was that a reserving State could become a party to a multilateral treaty only if all the other parties to that treaty had expressly or tacitly accepted the reservation. This view relied on two well-established principles. The first one is the principle of consent, on the basis of which a State cannot be bound by a conventional rule without its agreement, with the consequence that a reservation (regarded as a counter-offer) would not be opposable to an objecting State. The second principle is that a multilateral treaty is the result of free agreement among the contracting parties. From this it follows that a contracting party cannot frustrate the purpose of a convention by a unilateral decision. Accordingly, all contracting States must accept a reservation in order that the reserving State may become a party to the treaty concerned. This traditional view was not immune from practical difficulties.

(1991), p. 958.) In Ziccardi Capaldo (ed.), *Repertory of Decisions of the International Court of Justice (1947–1992)* (Dordrecht, 1995), i, pp. 69–70, an extract from the advisory opinion on the Genocide Convention is reproduced under the heading '*Erga omnes* obligations', immediately before the dictum from the *Barcelona Traction* case.

[25] General Assembly Resolution 478(V) of 16 November 1950, reproduced in I.C.J. Reports 1951, pp. 16–17. On the advisory jurisdiction of the International Court, see Brownlie, *Principles*, pp. 730–3. On the advisory opinion on the Genocide Convention, see Klein, 'Genocide Convention (Advisory Opinion)', Heidelberg *Encycl.*, ii, pp. 107–9, and, more extensively, Diez de Velasco, 'El sexto dictamen del Tribunal Internacional de Justicia: Las reservas a la Convencion sobre el Genocidio', 4 *Revista espanola de derecho internacional* (1951), pp. 1029–89.

[26] Neither resolution 478(V) nor the advisory opinion of the International Court defines the term 'reservation'. In the *Ambatielos* case, Judge Zoricic defined reservation as 'a provision agreed upon between the parties to a treaty with a view to restricting the application of one or more of its clauses or to clarifying their meaning' (I.C.J. Reports 1952, p. 76). Article 2, para. (d), of the Vienna Convention on the Law of Treaties gives a more complete definition: '"reservation" means a unilateral statement, however phrased or named, made by a State, when signing, ratifying, accepting, approving or acceding to a treaty, whereby it purports to exclude or to modify the legal effect of certain provisions of the treaty in their application to that State.'

A small minority of States (or even a single State), by objecting to a reservation, could prevent the reserving State from becoming a party to a convention, even if the reservation concerned a minor aspect of the convention in question and the great majority of the parties had no objection to it. This fact was becoming more and more intolerable, especially in the light of the adoption of an increasing number of multilateral treaties, such as the Genocide Convention, having a humanitarian purpose and aimed at attracting as many parties as possible.

In its advisory opinion on the Genocide Convention, the International Court acknowledged these concerns when it wrote that there was a 'new need for flexibility' in approaching the subject. On the main question submitted by the General Assembly, the International Court concluded, by a narrow majority of seven votes to five (with four judges attaching a joint dissenting opinion),[27] that a reserving State can be regarded as being a party to the Genocide Convention, provided that its reservation is compatible with the object and purpose of the Convention. The narrow margin in favour of the International Court's finding reflects the divergent views that emerged not only in the General Assembly, but also in the pleadings before the International Court.[28]

After rejecting the unanimity theory, which would require that a reservation be accepted by all other States for the reserving State to become a party to the convention in question, the International Court found itself on completely new ground. Its answer to the main question submitted by the General Assembly was that a reserving State can be regarded as being a party to the convention, provided that its reservation is compatible with the object and purpose of the convention. This conclusion represents—in the words used by Sir Hersh Lauterpacht—a classic example of 'judicial legislation'.[29] It is therefore not surprising that the advisory opinion on the Genocide Convention became the target of criticism. For example, Fitzmaurice regretted that the International Court was unable to produce anything but a subjective test (the criterion of 'compatibility' with the object and purpose of a convention) to distinguish between admissible and inadmissible reservations.[30] (While this criticism is well founded in theory, the

[27] Judges Guerrero, McNair, Read and Hsu Mo attached a joint dissenting opinion. Judge Alvarez attached a dissenting opinion. At the time of the League of Nations, McNair had co-authored (with Fromageot and Diena) a report on the progressive development of international law, which also considered the question of reservations (*L.N.O.J.* (1927), p. 880).

[28] See *I.C.J. Pleadings, Reservations to the Convention on the Prevention and Punishment of the Crime of Genocide*, pp. 42–4 (written statement of the U.S.A.); pp. 62–9 (written statement of the United Kingdom); pp. 202–3 (written statement of Israel); pp. 334–9 (statement by Rosenne (Israel)); pp. 378–93 (statement by Sir Hartley Shawcross (U.K.)); pp. 402–16 (statement by Fitzmaurice (U.K.)); pp. 426–9 (statement by Rousseau (France)).

[29] *The Development of International Law*, pp. 186–90 and 372–4.

[30] Fitzmaurice, 'Reservations to Multilateral Conventions', 2 *I.C.L.Q.* (1953), pp. 1–26; id., 'The Law and Procedure of the International Court of Justice 1951–4: Treaty Interpretation

flexible approach indicated by the International Court, which the Vienna Convention on the Law of Treaties later embodied in Article 19(c),[31] has worked fairly well in practice.)[32]

In any event, there is no need to discuss here the merits of the International Court's conclusion.[33] What is relevant is the reasoning developed by the International Court in reaching it. After making the point that the parties to the Genocide Convention can make reservations, but not all kinds of reservation indiscriminately, the International Court addressed the following question: how is it possible to distinguish between admissible and inadmissible reservations? To answer this question it examined the origin and purpose of the Convention, with a view to ascertaining the will of the General Assembly and of the parties to the Genocide Convention on this particular point. In this respect, the International Court remarked that, by Resolution 96, the General Assembly of the United Nations had condemned genocide not only as a wrongful act under international law, but also as a crime which is 'contrary to moral law and to the spirit and aims of the United Nations'. The International Court drew two main conclusions from this observation. The first one was that the Genocide Convention was meant to be universal in scope. The second one was that

> the principles underlying the Convention are principles which are recognized by civilized nations as binding on States, even without any conventional obligation.[34]

The International Court then examined the purpose for which the General Assembly had adopted the Genocide Convention. This was 'a purely humanitarian and civilizing purpose', aimed at protecting the life of human groups and confirming 'the most elementary principles of morality', so that

and Other Treaty Points', 33 *B.Y.I.L.* (1957), pp. 272–93; id., 'Judicial Innovation—Its Uses and its Perils—As exemplified in some of the Work of the International Court of Justice during Lord McNair's Period of Office', *Cambridge Essays in International law—Essays in Honour of Lord McNair* (London, 1965), pp. 31–5. Sir Gerald Fitzmaurice took part in the drafting of the Genocide Convention as a representative of the United Kingdom on the Sixth Committee of the United Nations General Assembly. He also appeared before the International Court, on behalf of the United Kingdom, in the proceedings relating to the advisory opinion on the Genocide Convention.

[31] Initially, in 1951, the International Law Commission opposed the 'compatibility' test as too subjective, but then, in 1962, it accepted it. Article 19(c) of the Vienna Convention provides that, if the treaty in question does not require otherwise, a State may formulate a reservation unless 'the reservation is incompatible with the object and purpose of the treaty'.

[32] See Brownlie, *Principles*, p. 611.

[33] On reservations, see McNair, *Law of Treaties*, pp. 158–77; Ruda, 'Reservations to Treaties', 146 Hague *Recueil* (1975, III), pp. 95–218; Bowett, 'Reservations to Non-Restricted Multilateral Treaties', 48 *B.Y.I.L.* (1976/77), pp. 67–92; Redgwell, 'Universality or Integrity? Some Reflections on Reservations to General Multilateral Treaties', 64 ibid. (1993), pp. 245–82. See also Pellet, 'Le droit et la pratique concernant les réserves aux traités' (Doc.A/CN.4/454).

[34] I.C.J. Reports 1951, p. 23. The French authoritative text reads as follows: 'les principes qui sont à la base de la Convention sont des principes reconnus par les nations civilisées comme obligeant les Etats même en dehors de tout lien conventionnel.'

the contracting States do not have any interests of their own; they merely have, one and all, a common interest, namely, the accomplishment of those high purposes which are the raison d'être of the convention.[35]

As the origin and purpose of the Genocide Convention indicate, it was the intention of the General Assembly that as many States as possible become parties to the Convention, including States making reservations. However, universal participation could not be achieved at all costs: the only admissible reservations are therefore those 'compatible' with the moral and humanitarian object of the Convention.

As was recalled earlier, the International Court reached its conclusions by a narrow majority. While disagreeing with the 'compatibility' test, the dissenting judges fully endorsed the International Court's considerations on the humanitarian and moral purpose of the Genocide Convention. In their joint dissenting opinion, Judges Guerrero, McNair, Read and Hsu Mo remarked that the paramount consideration behind the Genocide Convention is the 'acceptance of common obligations . . . in order to attain a high objective for all humanity'. From this observation they drew the opposite conclusion that the 'interests of the international community' require that a reserving State cannot become a party to the Genocide Convention against the objection of another party or other parties, which have undertaken to comply fully and unconditionally with the obligations of the Convention.[36] Likewise, in his dissenting opinion, Judge Alvarez remarked that treaties such as the Genocide Convention, which 'are not established for the benefit of private interests but for that of the general interest', constitute an indivisible whole and do not admit of reservations.[37]

To sum up, the majority of the International Court and the dissenting judges agreed on the essential characteristics of the prohibition of genocide, but disagreed on the balance between the opposite values of 'integrity' and 'universality' of the Genocide Convention, and ultimately on the consequences to be drawn with respect to the question of reservations.

III. Elements of Analogy between the Advisory Opinion on the Genocide Convention and the Dictum on Obligations *Erga Omnes*

The above-quoted passages from the advisory opinion on the Genocide Convention present certain elements of analogy with the dictum on obligations *erga omnes* in the *Barcelona Traction* case. These elements of analogy

[35] *I.C.J. Reports* 1951, p. 23. The French authoritative text reads as follows: 'les Etats contractants n'ont pas d'intérêts propres; ils ont seulement, tous et chacun, un intérêt commun, celui de préserver les fins supérieures qui sont la raison d'être de la convention.'

[36] Ibid., pp. 46–7.

[37] Ibid., pp. 51 and 53.

are all the more noticeable as they arose in different contexts. In the *Barcelona Traction* case, the International Court distinguished between two kinds of obligation while addressing the issue of legal standing, whereas in the advisory opinion on the Genocide Convention, the International Court was addressing an issue relating to the law of treaties.

The first element of analogy relates to the language used by the International Court. In the advisory opinion, the accent is on a 'common interest' of States outside any 'individual advantages' or 'perfect contractual balance between rights and duties'. Likewise, in the dictum on obligations *erga omnes* in the *Barcelona Traction* case, the accent is on international obligations owed towards the 'international community as a whole', which are 'by their very nature' the 'concern of all States'.

The second element of analogy is the content embodied in this language. In its advisory opinion, the International Court wrote that the Genocide Convention was adopted for a purely humanitarian purpose, with a view to confirming and endorsing the 'most elementary principles of morality'. This language is reminiscent of the words used in the decision on the merits in the *Corfu Channel* case, when the International Court referred to 'elementary considerations of humanity'.[38] Both expressions contain a common core of meta-juridical values protected and promoted by positive law. In the case of the advisory opinion on the Genocide Convention, the International Court remarked that the principles underlying the Convention are 'recognized by civilized nations as binding on States, even without any conventional obligation'.

Some writers have suggested that, by this reference, the International Court was expressing the view that the prohibition of genocide had already become part of customary international law.[39] This suggestion is plausible in consideration of the fact, which is widely acknowledged in the international literature, that a treaty can (a) restate a pre-existing custom, (b) crystallize an emerging rule, or (c) generate a practice of States that will eventually harden into an international custom.[40] Whether the process that led to a customary prohibition of genocide is one or other of the three that have just been listed is a matter of debate, but hardly anyone has any doubts today that such a process has been completed.[41]

[38] See section III of Chapter 4, above.

[39] See, for example, Rodley, 'Human Rights and Humanitarian Intervention: The Case Law of the World Court', 38 *I.C.L.Q.* (1989), p. 322.

[40] See Jiménez de Aréchaga, 'International Law in the Past Third of a Century', pp. 12–23; Shihata, 'The Treaty as a Law-Declaring and Custom-Making Instrument', 22 *Revue égyptienne de droit international* (1966), pp. 51–90; Baxter, 'Multilateral Treaties as Evidence of Customary International Law', 41 *B.Y.I.L.* (1965/66), pp. 275–300; id., 'Treaties and Custom', 129 Hague *Recueil* (1970, I), pp. 25–106.

[41] Some views in the opposite direction (see, for example, Starkman, 'Genocide and International Law: Is there a Cause of Action?', 8 *ASILS International Law Journal* (1984), pp. 13–18) were not convincing when they were expressed and are even less so now.

Other arguments, however, are not easily reconcilable with the identification of the principles underlying the Genocide Convention with principles of customary law. The main objection is based on the language used by the International Court. In its advisory opinion, the International Court referred to 'principles . . . recognized by civilized nations', an expression that, in the terms of the traditional sources of international law, is much closer to the 'general principles of law recognized by civilized nations' than custom.[42] An indirect argument supporting the view that the principles underlying the Genocide Convention would belong to the 'general principles of law recognized by civilized nations' is the role that this source of international law played in the writings of Basdevant, who was the President of the International Court at the time of the advisory opinion on the Genocide Convention.[43] Others, on the contrary, have resolutely excluded that the International Court meant to refer to the 'general principles of law recognized by civilized nations'.[44] However, an assessment of these views would require a detailed analysis (which is obviously outside the scope of this work) of this source of international law.

The different views on the identification of the formal source(s) of the principles to which the International Court referred in its advisory opinion need not be elaborated here. Irrespective of these differences, the important element of analogy with the dictum on obligations *erga omnes* is that the International Court derived the universal effect of the principles underlying the Genocide Convention from the conception that genocide is contrary to moral law and the spirit and aims of the United Nations, and on this premise it acknowledged that the legal prohibition of genocide is recognized as binding on all States alike, whether or not they are parties to the Genocide Convention. In other words, in its reasoning on the character *erga omnes* of the legal prohibition of genocide, the International Court did not

[42] See Article 38, paragraph 1, of the Statute of the International Court, reproduced in section III of Chapter 3, above.

[43] See, for example, his 'Règles générales du droit de la paix', pp. 497–504.

[44] See, for example, Mosler, *The International Society*, p. 70. The 'general principles of law recognized by civilized nations' remain, to a large extent, an 'enigmatic' source of international law (Jennings, 'What is International Law and How Do we Tell it When we See it?', 37 *Ann. suisse* (1981), pp. 71–3). A useful starting point for the analysis of this source is the debate that led to the adoption of Article 38 of the Statute of the Permanent Court of International Justice (*Cour Permanent de Justice International, Comité Consultatif de Juristes, Procès Verbaux des Séances du Comité 16 juin—24 juillet avec Annexes* (The Hague, 1920), pp. 293–7, 306–25, 332–8, 344–6, 351 and 730–1). In the literature, besides the general treatises on international law, see Cheng, *General Principles of Law*. See also Herczegh, *General Principles of Law and the International Legal Order* (Budapest, 1969); Lammers, 'General Principles of Law Recognized by Civilized Nations', Kalshoven, Kuyper and Lammers (eds.), *Essays on the Development of the International Legal Order in Memory of Haro F. Van Panhuys* (Aalphen aan den Rijn and Rockville, 1980), pp. 53–9; Battaglini, 'Il riconoscimento internazionale dei principi generali del diritto', *International Law. Essays Ago*, i, pp. 97–140; Degan, 'General Principles of Law (A Source of General International Law)', 3 *Finnish Yearbook of International Law* (1992), pp. 1–101.

only rely on the positive element of recognition by States, but also on the underlying moral considerations of this prohibition.[45] This introduces a strong element of analogy with the dictum in the *Barcelona Traction* case, in which the International Court drew the distinction between obligations towards an individual State and obligations *erga omnes* from the 'nature' of the obligations involved and the 'importance' of the corresponding rights of protection.

IV. Conclusions

The idea of the universal opposability of the prohibition of genocide in the International Court's advisory opinion on the Genocide Convention presents clear elements of analogy with the dictum on obligations *erga omnes* in the *Barcelona Traction* case, with respect to both its substance and terminology. The aspects of the International Court's legal reasoning discussed in this chapter suggest that, in this respect, the advisory opinion on the Genocide Convention may be regarded as a 'precedent' of the dictum on obligations *erga omnes*. The similarities contained in the two pronouncements of the International Court are significant not only in this conclusion, which relates specifically to the concept of obligations *erga omnes*, but also in one other respect. As Judge Oda once remarked, 'new developments in international law may well be crystallized through the jurisprudence of the Court'.[46] The analysis developed in this chapter has showed how the legal reasoning followed in earlier pronouncements can be an important component of the process by which later decisions of the International Court crystallize new legal developments.

[45] Tanaka has written that the spirit of the advisory opinion on the Genocide Convention can be extended to human rights in general, in the sense that '[t]he seat of human rights is not in any positive law, not in the public authorities, but in "the conscience of mankind" and "moral law". . .' ('Some Observations on Peace, Law, and Human Rights', Friedmann, Henkin and Lissitzyn (eds.), *Transnational Law in a Changing Society. Essays in Honor of Philip C. Jessup* (New York, 1972), p. 254.)

[46] *Legality of the Use by a State of Nuclear Weapons in Armed Conflicts*, Advisory Opinion, I.C.J. Reports 1996 (mimeographed text), p. 1, para. 3, of Judge Oda's separate opinion.

6

The Examples of Obligations *Erga Omnes* Given by the International Court in its Dictum: (c) Protection from Slavery

I. The International Protection from Slavery and the Slave Trade

Protection from slavery is the third example of obligation *erga omnes* given by the International Court in the *Barcelona Traction* case.[1]

The International Convention to Suppress Slave Trade and Slavery, adopted under the auspices of the League of Nations on 25 September 1926,[2] gives the following definition of slavery and the slave trade in Article 1:

(1) Slavery is the status or condition of a person over whom any or all of the powers attaching to the right of ownership are exercised.

(2) The slave trade includes all acts involved in the capture, acquisition or disposal of a person with intent to reduce him in slavery; all acts involved in the acquisition of a slave with a view to selling or exchanging him; all acts of disposal by sale or exchange of a slave acquired with a view to being sold or exchanged, and, in general, every act of trade or transport in slaves.

The same definition, with minor modifications, appears in Article 7 of a Supplementary Convention adopted in 1956,[3] which confirms the

[1] There is a wide literature on slavery. For an introductory treatment, with bibliographical references, see Finley, 'Slavery', Sills (ed.), *International Encyclopedia of the Social Sciences*, xiv (New York, 1968), pp. 307–13; Hellie, 'Slavery', *The New Encyclopaedia Britannica (Macropaedia)*, 15th edn. (Chicago, 1974; 1994), xxvii, pp. 288–300. On the slave trade, see a UNESCO publication headed *The African slave trade from the fifteenth to the nineteenth century* (Paris, 1979). On the emergence of an international rule against slavery and the slave trade, see McDougal, Lasswell and Chen, *Human Rights*, pp. 473–508. See also Lachs, 'Slavery: the past and the present', Delissen and Tanja (eds.), *Humanitarian Law, Essays Kalshoven*, pp. 613–25; Vitta, C., 'La défense internationale de la liberté et de la moralité individuelles' 45 Hague *Recueil* (1933, III), pp. 557–666.

[2] 60 *L.T.N.S.* 253. The text is reproduced in Brownlie (ed.), *Basic Documents on Human Rights*, pp. 52–7. The Convention entered into force on 9 March 1927. A Protocol Amending the Slavery Convention (212 *U.N.T.S.* 17) was approved by resolution 794 (VIII) of the United Nations General Assembly on 23 October 1953, and was opened for signature and entered into force on 7 December 1953. Fifty-seven States have become parties (*Multilateral Treaties Deposited with the Secretary-General. Status as at 31 December 1995*, p. 699).

[3] Supplementary Convention on the Abolition of Slavery, the Slave Trade, and Institutions and Practices Similar to Slavery, 266 *U.N.T.S.* 3. The text is reproduced in Brownlie (ed.),

condemnation of slavery and the slave trade and calls upon the contracting parties to bring about the complete abolition of practices similar to slavery, such as debt-bondage, serfdom, the sale of a woman into marriage and the traffic in children.

While the dictum on obligations *erga omnes* in the *Barcelona Traction* case refers only to slavery, it is reasonable to assume that the prohibition extends to the slave trade. History shows that there cannot be effective prohibition of the slave trade if slavery is a lawful practice, and it is obvious that there cannot be any trade of slaves if slavery is prohibited.

Until modern times, slavery was a commonly accepted institution throughout the world. For Aristotle, a slave was such 'by nature'.[4] Christianity, while primarily concerned with an interior attitude of brotherhood rather than the challenge of slavery as a social structure,[5] condemned slavery and the slave trade long before the modern age.[6] For Thomas

Basic Documents on Human Rights, pp. 58–63. This Convention was adopted on 7 September 1956, and entered into force on 30 April 1957. One hundred and fourteen States have become parties (*Multilateral Treaties Deposited with the Secretary-General. Status as at 31 December 1995*, p. 705).

[4] Aristotle, *The Complete Works (The Revised Oxford Translation)*, Barnes ed. (Princeton, 1988), 1253b15–1255b39 (Politics).

[5] This attitude clearly emerges from the letter of St. Paul to Philemon. For commentary, see Fitzmyer, 'The Letter to Philemon', Brown, Fitzmyer and Murphy (eds.), *The New Jerome Biblical Commentary* (Englewood Cliffs, N.J., 1990), pp. 869–70 (especially para. 6). Over the ages, this attitude has been witnessed by countless Christians, such as Peter Claver (on whom, see Valtierra, *Peter Claver. Saint of the Slaves*, English trans. Perry and Woodward (Westminster, Maryland, 1960)) or Pierre Toussaint (on whom, see Couve de Murville, *Slave from Haiti: A Saint for New York? The Life of Pierre Toussaint* (London, 1995)).

[6] For an early denunciation of slavery, see the 'epistula' of Pope John VIII headed *Unum est* of September 873. Slavery of the Indians of Latin America was condemned by Pope Paul III in the 'breve' headed *Pastorale officium* of 29 May 1537. For a later statement, see the harsh words against the slave trade pronounced by Pope Gregory XVI in the 'constitution' headed *In supremo apostolatus fastigio* of 3 December 1839. Extracts from all these documents are reproduced in Denzinger-Schönmetzer, *Enchiridion Symbolorum definitionum et declarationum de rebus fidei et morum*, 36th edn. (Freiburg, 1976), paras. 668, 1495 and 2745–6. In more recent times, see the forceful condemnation of slavery by John Paul II during his visit to Senegal ('From this African shrine of sorrow let us implore heaven's forgiveness', *L'Osservatore Romano* (Weekly Edition in English, 4 March 1992), p. 2). For background considerations, see Williams, C., 'Slavery (and the Church)', *New Catholic Encyclopedia*, xiii (New York, 1967), pp. 281–2, and (more extensively) Dutilleul, 'Esclavage', *Dictionnaire de Théologie Catholique*, v/1 (Paris, 1939), columns 457–520. These references are not meant to belittle the contribution of other Christian denominations, and other religions, to the abolition of slavery and to the present reflection on past practices. See, for example, the resolution on slavery adopted by the Southern Baptist Convention, the largest Protestant denomination in the United States, in June 1995 (Niebuhr, 'Baptist Group Votes to Repent Stand on Slaves', *New York Times*, 21 June 1995, p. A1). The position of the various religious denominations on slavery is part of the wider (and largely neglected) question of the relationship between religion and international law, on which, apart from the various contributions published over the years in the Hague *Recueil*, see Janis (ed.), *The Influence of Religion on the Development of International Law* (Dordrecht, 1991). Within the context of this relationship between law on the one hand, and religions and philosophical traditions on the other hand, Weeramantry, for example, has remarked that obligations *erga omnes* (along with other key concepts of international law) 'can be richly

Aquinas, the condition of being a slave was not brought about by nature.[7] This was a fundamental step in the process that eventually led to the recognition that slavery and the slave trade were unlawful under international law. Municipal courts have played a decisive role in this respect. In a classic decision of the Court of King's Bench, Lord Mansfield held that

> [t]he state of slavery is of such a nature, that it is incapable of being introduced on any reasons, moral or political; but only positive law . . . it's so odious, that nothing can be suffered to support it, but positive law.[8]

At first, it was the slave trade that came under attack as a breach of international law, and only later did the issue of legality extend to slavery. Slavery belonged to the sphere of exclusive jurisdiction of States, and States were (and still tend to be) very reluctant to renounce their exclusive jurisdiction. Denmark was apparently the first country in Europe to abolish the slave trade, at the end of the eighteenth century, followed by the United Kingdom. Later, the great Powers concluded treaties of co-operation for the suppression of the slave trade.[9] In the diplomatic correspondence of the time, the slave trade was declared to be 'a crime of the darkest character and an offence against our common humanity'.[10]

Yet other developments were needed before the slave trade, and even more so slavery, could be regarded as being prohibited under general international law.[11] The League of Nations gave a noticeable contribution to this

fertilized by the insights of Buddhism'. ('The International Court of Justice in the Age of Multiculturalism', 36 *Indian Journal of International Law* (1996, No. 2), p. 23.)

[7] Thomas Aquinas, *Summa Theologiae*, IIa IIae, q. 57, a. 3, *ad secundum*. Justinian's Institutes define slavery ('*servitus*') as 'constitutio iuris gentium, qua quis dominio alieno contra naturam subicitur' (Latin text edited by Krueger, reproduced in *Justinian's Institutes*, Birks and McLeod eds. (London, 1987), I.3.2). Similar language is also used in Isidorus, *Etymologiae*, Lindsay ed. (Oxford, 1911), Liber V, ch. 6.

[8] *Somerset against Stewart*, 98 E.R. 499 (K.B.1772), at p. 510. Buckland and McNair have remarked that the background to Lord Mansfield's holding, and to other English decisions on slavery, is 'the strong leaning in favour of liberty which has marked the common law from the very early times' (*Roman Law and Common Law*, p. 30).

[9] For reference, see *Oppenheim's International Law*, i, pp. 979–80. Truyol y Serra has underlined the contribution of general multilateral treaties to the establishment of an international prohibition of the slave trade. (*Los derechos humanos. Declaraciones y Co'venios internacionales*, 3rd edn. (Madrid, 1982) p. 19.

[10] Earl Russell to Earl Cowley (Paris), 28 February 1865, Draft of a Note to be presented to the French Government, reproduced in Bruns (ed.), *Fontes*, Series B, Section 1, Tomus 1, Pars 1, pp. 112–13, para. 388.

[11] For a long time, there was a 'dormant' obligation ('obligation latente') against slavery and the slave trade. See the intervention of Tammes at the 1368th Session of the International Law Commission, *Y.I.L.C.* (1976, I), p. 44, para. 37. Many leading treatises on international law of the last century denied that slavery or the slave trade were prohibited under customary law. See, for example, Wheaton, *Elements of International Law: with a Sketch of the History of the Science* (Philadelphia, 1836), pp. 114–18; Creasy, *First Platform of International Law* (London, 1876), pp. 259–77; *Kent's Commentary on International Law*, 2nd edn. Abdy (Cambridge and London, 1878). For a more cautious position, see Bluntschli, *Le Droit international codifié*, pp. 19–21 and 203–4; Phillimore, *Commentaries upon International Law*, 2nd

process. Under its auspices, various measures against slavery and the slave trade (in addition to the Slavery Convention of 1926) were adopted, especially in the context of the mandate system. Since the Second World War, the Universal Declaration of Human Rights (Article 4),[12] and all the major instruments for the protection of human rights such as the International Covenant on Civil and Political Rights (Article 8),[13] the European Convention on Human Rights (Article 4),[14] the American Convention on Human Rights (Article 6),[15] and the African Charter on Human and Peoples' Rights (Article 5),[16] have expressly condemned slavery and the slave trade.[17]

These instruments, together with State declarations and parallel developments under municipal law, support the conclusion that there is now a customary rule outlawing slavery and the slave trade, and that this rule applies universally as a rule of *jus cogens*.[18] Despite this universal support, the exact scope of the prohibition under general international law is still controversial.[19] Its effective implementation remains likewise problem-

edn. (London, 1873), i, pp. xxxiii–xxxiv and 342–74. Lorimer, a writer whose thought is 'strongly linked with theology' (Lachs, *The Teacher in International Law (Teachings and Teaching)* (The Hague, 1982), p. 76), speaks of a 'bad custom' (*The Institutes of the Law of Nations. A Treatise of the Jural Relations of Separate Political Communities*, i (Edinburgh and London, 1883), p. 32). As recently as 1942, Brierly wrote that '[a]part from convention slave-trading is not illegal by international law' (*The Law of Nations. An Introduction to the International Law of Peace*, 3rd edn. (Oxford, 1942), p. 193). A similar remark was made five years later in Oppenheim, *International Law. A Treatise*, i, 6th edn. Lauterpacht, H. (London, 1947), p. 664.

[12] 'Resolution 217(III) of the United Nations General Assembly (adopted on 10 Dec. 1948)', *Gen. Ass. Off. Recs., Third Session* (Doc.A/811), p. 71. The text is reproduced in Brownlie, *Basic Documents*, pp. 255–61; id. (ed.), *Basic Documents on Human Rights*, pp. 21–7.

[13] 'Annex to Resolution 2200(XXI) of the United Nations General Assembly (adopted on 16 Dec. 1966)', *Gen. Ass. Off. Recs., Twenty-first Session*, Supp. 16 (Doc.A/6316), p. 52. The text is reproduced in Brownlie, *Basic Documents*, pp. 276–97; id. (ed.), *Basic Documents on Human Rights*, pp. 125–43. The Covenant entered into force on 23 March 1976.

[14] 213 *U.N.T.S.* 221. The text is reproduced in Brownlie, *Basic Documents*, pp. 320–47; id. (ed.), *Basic Documents on Human Rights*, pp. 326–41. The European Convention was signed on 4 November 1950 and entered into force on 3 September 1953.

[15] *O.A.S. Official Records*, OEA/Ser.K/XVI/1.1 Doc. 65, Rev. 1, Corr. 1 (7 Jan. 1970). The text is reproduced in Brownlie (ed.), *Basic Documents on Human Rights*, pp. 495–520. The American Convention was signed on 22 November 1969 and entered into force on 18 July 1978.

[16] The text is reproduced in Brownlie (ed.), *Basic Documents on Human Rights*, pp. 551–66. The African Charter was adopted by the 18th Assembly of the Heads of State and Government of the Organization of African Unity, Nairobi, Kenya, on 17 June 1981. It entered into force on 21 October 1986.

[17] For a comprehensive list of international instruments, not limited to those relating to human rights, see Bassiouni, 'Enslavement as an International Crime', 23 *N.Y.U.J.I.L.P.* (1991), pp. 445–517.

[18] See *Third Restatement*, Section 702, Comment (e) and Reporter's Note (4). During the preparatory work that led to the adoption of the Vienna Convention on the Law of Treaties, the prohibition of slavery was one of the most frequently cited examples of norms of *jus cogens*.

[19] See *Oppenheim's International Law*, i, p. 982.

atic.[20] In this situation, one might ask whether the character *erga omnes* of the protection from slavery can contribute to the solution of these and other outstanding problems.

A case decided by an Italian court prompts a few considerations on this question. In 1985, a ten-year-old child was found wandering alone in Milan. From his appearance, it was clear that the child had been abused. Questioned by the public attorney, the child said that a man had kidnapped him in his native country, and that he now lived in a camp of nomads near Milan. His kidnapper forced him to steal, and beat him whenever he went back to the camp empty-handed. The experience of this child was not unique, but was part of a systematic exploitation of minors by adults who forced them to steal or beg. These children are the so-called 'argati', a word of Slavic origin which means 'workers', but in effect designates a relationship of absolute subjection. Their masters (the so-called 'gazda') are rarely their parents. Most often, these masters kidnap the children or buy them from their parents by a contract of sale. The children remain in this condition until they reach the age of majority. Then, the grown-up children 'train' the younger ones and the cycle continues. The system is highly profitable for the masters, particularly as under Italian law a child under fourteen cannot be guilty of any offence and therefore cannot be prosecuted.[21]

The main legal issue before the 'Corte d'Assise' of Milan was whether the slavery-like practice just described is prohibited under Article 600 of the Italian criminal code, which applies to slavery.[22] The answer to this question depends on whether the expressions 'slavery' and 'slavery-like condition' in Article 600 cover only those situations amounting to slavery as a practice accepted by law, or also to factual situations presenting the same character. Until a decision of the Italian Constitutional Court of 1981,[23] the prevailing interpretation of Article 600 was that it applied only to legal, as opposed to factual, slavery. Factual situations were punished under a different article of the code. However, this restrictive interpretation would make Article 600 redundant, because there is of course no legal slavery under Italian law.

In its judgment, the 'Corte d'Assise' of Milan concluded that Article 600 applies to legal and factual slavery alike.[24] Part of the argument developed by the Court in reaching this conclusion referred to the effects of the Slavery

[20] See *Slavery: Report prepared by Benjamin Whitaker, Special Rapporteur of the Sub-Commission on Prevention of Discrimination and Protection of Minorities, updating the 'Report on Slavery' submitted to the Sub-Commission in 1966* (Doc. E/CN.4/Sub.2/1982/20/ Rev.1 (1982)).

[21] See Article 97 of the Italian criminal code (R.D. 19 October 1930, No. 1398).

[22] Article 600 reads as follows: 'Whoever reduces a person to slavery, or to a slavery-like condition, shall be sentenced to imprisonment for a period of five to fifteen years.'

[23] Judgment dated 8 June 1981, *Foro italiano* (1986), Part One, column 1815.

[24] Judgment dated 18 May 1988, *Foro italiano* (1989), Part Two, column 121.

Convention of 1926 and the Supplementary Convention of 1956—both ratified by Italy[25]—on the interpretation of Article 600 of the Italian criminal code. In particular, the Court recalled that, among the slavery-like practices, the Supplementary Convention lists, in Article 1(d),

> any institution or practice whereby a child or young person under the age of eighteen years is delivered by either or both of his natural parents or by his guardian to another person, whether for reward or not, with a view to the exploitation of the child or young person or of his labour.

This provisions clearly covers factual conditions of slavery. The same is true of Article 600 of the Italian criminal code because, as the Court wrote in its judgment, the expressions 'slavery' and 'slavery-like practices' in Article 600 derive their meaning from the international treaties which Italy has ratified.

Would this conclusion have been the same if Italy had not been a party to either the Slavery Convention of 1926 or the Supplementary Convention of 1956? If the prohibition embodied in Article 1(d) of the Supplementary Convention belongs to customary law and is opposable *erga omnes*, would the character *erga omnes* of the international obligation against slavery exclude any restrictive interpretation, under municipal law, of slavery and slavery-like practices? Or could a State put forward arguments based on its municipal law, or on prescriptive rights, to evade the application of this prohibition to its fullest extent?

These questions show the practical consequences that may derive from the application of the concept of obligations *erga omnes*. At the same time, the search for an answer to each of these questions, within the specific context of the case brought before the 'Corte d'Assise' of Milan, would require a major digression on the relevant provisions of Italian criminal law, and on the reception of international law in the Italian legal system. While this line of inquiry cannot be followed here, some consideration of several cases on slavery and the slave trade which were decided in the nineteenth century may contribute to a better understanding of the long and controversial process by which the prohibition of slavery and the slave trade has emerged and acquired universal value.

The reference to cases which are more than one hundred and fifty years old should not be surprising. History is, according to Pearce Higgins, one of the perspectives from which light can be shed on any international legal issue.[26] Nor should the presence, among these old cases, of one decided by

[25] On 25 August 1928, and 12 February 1958, respectively.

[26] 'Il y a trois façons d'aborder la matière du droit international: la manière philosophique, la manière historique et la manière analytique; pour le dominer d'une façon complète, il est nécessaire d'avoir une nature d'esprit capable d'envisager le problème à tous ces points de vue différents.' (Higgins, A. P., 'La contribution de quatre grands juristes britanniques au droit international (Lorimer, Westlake, Hall et Holland)', 40 Hague *Recueil* (1932, II), p. 32.)

a municipal court be any more surprising, especially in view of the current interest, among international writers belonging to different legal traditions, in the role played by municipal courts in ascertaining and implementing international law.[27]

II. The Emergence of the Prohibition of Slavery and the Slave Trade: the *Enterprise* Case and the *Lawrence* Case

In 1853, Great Britain and the United States signed a convention which provided for the adjustment of certain claims by a mixed commission and, failing agreement between the commissioners, for a decision by an umpire appointed by the parties. Among the claims submitted to the commission, and then to the umpire, some related to the British action against American vessels engaged in the slave trade.

The *Enterprise* (or *Enterprize*, according to a different spelling also used in the case)[28] was an American brig which at the beginning of 1835—as will be seen later, the date was decisive for the decision—was sailing from the District of Columbia to South Carolina with a large number of slaves on board. After encountering heavy winds, and being short of water provisions because of the delay thus occasioned, the master of the *Enterprise* decided to enter a port in the Bermudas (then a British colony) for supplies. Before the brig could leave the harbour, the captain was served a writ of habeas corpus requiring his appearance before the court and the production of the slaves still remaining on board. The slaves were produced before the court, and the court declared that no law authorized their detention. Once they were told that they were free persons, most of the slaves chose to remain on shore, while a few preferred to return on board and continue their voyage.

The United States Government was now claiming compensation in respect of the loss suffered by the slaves' owners as a result of the slaves' release. The ground for this claim was that, in time of peace, a vessel on the high seas engaged on a lawful voyage is under the exclusive jurisdiction of the State to which it belongs. Exclusive jurisdiction continues to apply if the

[27] This interest is reflected, for example, in the general course that Conforti gave at the Hague Academy in 1988 (then revised, translated into English and published as a separate volume headed *International Law and the Role of Domestic Legal System*), and in Lukashuk's monograph on international law before municipal courts, headed *Mezhdunarodnoe pravo v sudakh gosudarstv* (Saint Petersburg, 1993).

[28] The umpire's decision is reproduced in Moore, *History and Digest of International Arbitrations to which the United States has been a Party*, iv (Washington, D.C., 1898), pp. 4349–73.

vessel is forced by unavoidable circumstances into the port of a foreign country.[29]

The British commissioner did not dispute that a vessel, forced by a stress of weather or other circumstances into a foreign port, is exempt from penalties under the local law. However, he denied, as a general proposition of law, that exemption from local jurisdiction is absolute and also, on the facts of the case, that the *Enterprise* was really compelled by necessity to enter into the port of the Bermudas. Moving from the assumption (shared by Lord Mansfield, as was seen earlier) that the only grounds for slavery are the laws of each individual State, the British commissioner remarked that, when a vessel with a cargo of slaves gets out of a territory where a law protecting slavery prevails, then the 'natural right' of the slaves to freedom revives. This would be true irrespective of whether or not the vessel was compelled to enter into a foreign port under unavoidable circumstances.

The umpire in this case (Mr Bates) rejected the arguments put forward by the British commissioner. He noted that the *Enterprise* had entered the port in the Bermudas in distress and therefore had an absolute right to protection (and exemption from local jurisdiction) under the 'law of nations' and the 'laws of hospitality'. Accordingly, the owners of the slaves on board of the *Enterprise* were entitled to compensation. The umpire added that different considerations would apply if, at the time of the transaction on which the American claim was founded, slavery could be regarded as being prohibited under international law. But, he added, it could not.

In a later case, developments occurred in the meantime led Mr Bates to a different conclusion on the question of compensation. The case is that of the *Lawrence*.[30] The *Lawrence* was an American brig on voyage from Cuba to Cabenda, in Africa, at the end of 1848, when it was forced into the port of Freetown in Sierra Leone to stop a leak. While the cargo on board of the *Lawrence* consisted only of supplies of low value, the vessel was seized in the vice-admiralty court, and the vessel and the cargo were then decreed forfeited to the Crown, because the *Lawrence* was well equipped for the slave trade and was therefore considered to be a slave trading vessel whenever the opportunity should arise. In deciding that the owners of the *Lawrence* had no valid claim, the umpire declared that, at the time of condemnation, the African slave trade 'was contrary to the law of nations' and prohibited 'by all civilized nations . . . and . . . by the laws of the United States'. Therefore, the changes in international law and the law of the United States which had occurred between 1835 (the date of the voyage of

[29] In his argument, the American commissioner relied on precedents and the authority of writers, particularly Vattel (who was also quoted in the opinion of the British commissioner). On the influence of Vattel in England and the United States, see Lapradelle's introduction to Vattel, *The Law of Nations*, pp. xxxiv–xxxviii.

[30] The umpire's decision is reproduced in Moore, *History and Digest of International Arbitrations*, iii (Washington, D.C., 1898), pp. 2824–5.

the *Enterprise*) and 1848 (the date of the voyage of the *Lawrence*) led the umpire, who decided both cases on the basis of the applicable law when the relevant events took place, to different solutions.

The reasoning followed by Mr Bates attracted the attention of the International Law Commission during its work of codification of the law of State responsibility. In his fifth report, the Special Rapporteur Ago raised the question whether an umpire of our times would decide a case like that of the *Enterprise* in the same way in which the case was decided by Mr Bates. The Special Rapporteur's answer to this question was that a contemporary case would not be decided in the same way because today slavery and the slave trade are prohibited not only by the law of 'civilized nations', but also by an international rule that the international community as a whole regards as peremptory (*jus cogens*).[31] From this it follows that a State (such as Great Britain in the *Lawrence* case) should not be held liable for an act which, while unlawful at the time it was committed, has since then become not only lawful but also required, in the sense that a State is bound, for example, to reject any possible claim to the property of human beings.[32] In other words, the Special Rapporteur applied to the issue before the International Law Commission considerations close to the concept of *jus cogens superveniens*,[33] and drew useful indications on the effect of time on the outcome of a case from a comparison between the reasoning developed by Mr Bates and the reasoning that a contemporary arbitrator would presumably apply in a similar case.

Another aspect worth noticing in the umpire's decision in the *Lawrence* case is directly relevant to the present examination of the prohibition of slavery and the slave trade as an obligation *erga omnes*. The ground for the umpire's decision was that not only the 'laws of nations' but also the 'laws of the United States' had changed in respect of the African slave trade. The following question arises: would Mr Bates's decision in the *Lawrence* case have been the same if the 'laws of nations' had changed, but not the 'laws of the United States'? In particular, would that change in international law have been opposable to the United States even if the United States had persistently objected to this change?

A case in point had been brought to the Supreme Court of the United States some thirty years before Mr Bates's decisions. This case is that of *The Antelope*.

[31] 'Fifth Report on State responsibility', *Y.I.L.C.* (1976, II, Part 1), pp. 18–19, para. 49.

[32] The consequences would be different if the act, while unlawful at the time it was committed, had then become a lawful, even if not a required, act (ibid., p. 20, para. 56). See the discussion on this point by the International Law Commission in *Y.I.L.C.* (1976, I), pp. 35–61 (Sessions 1367th to 1371st).

[33] See Article 64 of the Vienna Convention on the Law of Treaties, reproduced in section I of Chapter 3, above.

III. The Question of the Universal Opposability of the Prohibition of the Slave Trade: *The Antelope* Case

The Antelope was a Spanish vessel which in 1819, after many vicissitudes, was seized, while hovering off the coast of Florida with a cargo of African slaves, by an American revenue cutter. A number of parties claimed the vessel and the cargo on different grounds before the Circuit Court of Georgia. The Court ordered the assignment of a proportion of the African slaves to the United States and the division of the remainder between the Spanish and Portuguese Vice-Consuls (who had filed claims on the Africans on behalf of their nationals). The United States appealed against the decree which had ordered the restitution of a certain number of the Africans to Spain and Portugal, alleging that the Africans in question were not slaves but freemen. On appeal from the Circuit Court of Georgia, the case was heard by the Supreme Court of the United States.[34] The opinion of the Court was delivered by Chief Justice Marshall.[35] The key question for the Supreme Court was the following: is the slave trade prohibited under international law? This question was a thorny one, and no clear answer could be extracted from precedents.

Some early decisions like that in the *Amedie* case[36] held that there is no right to the restitution of slaves unless the claimant can prove title under municipal law. In other words, possession would raise no presumption of property in slaves, and the 'natural right' of all men to freedom would determine an inversion in the burden of proof. Another consequence is that the legality of the capture of a vessel engaged in the slave trade depends on the law of the country to which the vessel belongs. This approach seemed to open the way to far-reaching developments, and in particular the declaration in due course that the slave trade is contrary to international law. Indeed, the Circuit Court of the United States in Massachusetts, in the case of *La Jeune Eugenie*,[37] forcefully proclaimed in 1822 that the slave trade was prohibited by universal law, and that 'no practice whatsoever can obliterate

[34] 10 Wheat. 1825, pp. 66–133. For the historical background of *The Antelope* case, see Friedman, *A History of American Law*, 2nd edn. (New York, 1985), pp. 85–9 and 218–29. For a summary of the Supreme Court's decision, see Wiecek, 'Antelope, The', Hall, K. L. (ed.), *The Oxford Companion to the Supreme Court of the United States* (New York and Oxford, 1992), p. 34.

[35] For a portrait of the personality and judicial style of John Marshall, see White, *The American Judicial Tradition. Profiles of Leading American Judges*, expanded edn. (New York and Oxford, 1988), pp. 7–34. On the Supreme Court at the time of Marshall, see id., *The Marshall Court and Cultural Change 1815–1835*, abridged edn. (New York and Oxford, 1991), especially (on slavery and other human rights issues) pp. 674–740.

[36] 1 Acton's Rep. 240 (*per* Sir William Grant). See also the cases of the *Fortuna* and of the *Diana* (1 Dodson's Rep. 81 and 95, respectively).

[37] 26 Fed. Cas. 832.

the fundamental distinction between right and wrong'.[38] However, this view had not yet been generally accepted. A few years earlier, in 1817, in the case of *Le Louis*,[39] Sir William Scott had pronounced in equally explicit terms that the slave trade, though morally detestable, was neither piratical nor contrary to the law of nations.[40]

Therefore, when *The Antelope* case was brought before the Marshall Court,[41] precedents were divided as to whether or not the slave trade was prohibited under international law. In delivering the opinion of the Court, Chief Justice Marshall agreed that the slave trade is contrary to the 'law of nature'. However, he added that, from time immemorial, the 'usage of all' has consecrated slavery as a legitimate result of force.[42] Accordingly (the opinion continues), as the test of international law is the assent of all, slavery and the slave trade are not contrary to international law. Being sanctioned by the assent of all, each country has a right to engage in the slave trade, and the 'perfect equality' of States under international law entails that a State, while free to renounce its right, cannot compel the others to do the same. The Chief Justice declared that

> [a] right, then, which is vested in all by the consent of all, can be divested only by consent; and this trade, in which all have participated, must remain lawful to those who cannot be induced to relinquish it.[43]

The interpretation of this statement is controversial. On the one hand, the context in which it appears seems to suggest that Chief Justice Marshall was merely denying that a *statute* can bind non-parties, without any implication for custom or general principles.[44] Moreover, the real question before the Court was one of jurisdiction to enforce, namely whether the slave trade, like piracy, was subject to universal jurisdiction. On the other hand, the broad language of the passage, and the existence of similar statements in other judgments of the time,[45] make it plausible to interpret the above

[38] 26 Fed. Cas. 846.

[39] 2 Dodson's Rep. 238.

[40] There is no need here to discuss the consequence drawn from this finding by Sir William Scott, namely that no right of visit and search can be exercised on foreign vessels unless permitted by treaty. On the right of visit relating to vessels engaged in the slave trade, see Rousseau, *Droit international public*, iv, pp. 337–9. On the dispute between Great Britain and the United States on this matter, see Phillimore, *Commentaries*, iii, pp. 525–30.

[41] In using this expression, the present writer is aware of Chief Justice Rehnquist's remark that shorthand expressions such as 'Marshall Court' are convenient expressions, but of limited connotation (*The Supreme Court. How It Was, How It Is* (New York, 1987), p. 127).

[42] Even under Roman law, the capture of prisoners in foreign (but not civil) wars was one of the sources of slavery. See Thomas, *Textbook of Roman Law* (Amsterdam, 1976), p. 391.

[43] 10 Wheat. 1825, p. 122.

[44] In the following paragraph, the Chief Justice wrote that the slave trade, being consistent with international law, can be made piracy only by statute, 'and the obligation of the statute cannot transcend the legislative power of the state which may enact it' (ibid.).

[45] For example, in the case of *La Jeune Eugenie* (in which, as was mentioned earlier, it was held that the slave trade is illegal under international law), Circuit Justice Story remarked that, before a foreign tribunal can apply the penalty of confiscation to a French vessel engaged in

passage in wider terms than its specific context might otherwise require. For example, in his general course at the Hague Academy, Bishop quoted the passage as a classic statement of the principle of the persistent objector.[46]

To the extent that this latter interpretation of Chief Justice Marshall's words is admissible, it is possible to raise the question that the Special Rapporteur Ago formulated in respect of the decisions of Mr Bates: would a judge of our time agree with the statement of Chief Justice Marshall? The answer is probably not. Apart from any jurisprudential objection to the alleged validity of a practice which, though consecrated by the 'usage of all', is contrary to the 'law of nature', today slavery and the slave trade are prohibited by an international custom, and the obligations deriving from this rule of general international law are binding *erga omnes*. Therefore, no State would be entitled to engage in slavery or the slave trade on the ground that it had not renounced these practices and had persistently objected to the emergence of this prohibition.

IV. Conclusions

Slavery and the slave trade, once lawful practices in international society, have gradually become unlawful and are now prohibited *erga omnes*.

The study of some early cases shows that this development can be clearly distinguished from the emergence of other obligations *erga omnes* relating to practices, such as genocide, which have been for a long time outside the scope of international law and have never been regarded as accepted institutions. A major consequence deriving from this difference is that the development of an obligation *erga omnes* prohibiting an established practice will probably, even if not invariably,[47] take a longer period of time, and the evidence may be more difficult to establish.[48] At least, this seems to be the lesson that can be drawn from the controversies attaching to the emergence of the international prohibition of slavery and the slave trade.

Another indication from the foregoing discussion of early cases is the following. The rejection of slavery and the slave trade crystallized in the conviction of States when slavery assumed a racial connotation. Although traces of the medieval institution of 'villeinage' persisted up to this cen-

the slave trade, 'a prohibitory law of France should concur with the public law of nations' (26 Fed. Cas. 849).

[46] 'General Course of Public International Law', pp. 226–7.

[47] *A priori*, the possibility of an 'instant' obligation *erga omnes* against an established practice cannot be excluded.

[48] For a similar remark, relating to the emergence of the prohibition of slavery but without discussing its character *erga omnes*, see Mann, *Foreign Affairs in English Courts* (Oxford, 1986), p. 125.

tury,[49] and indentured servitude was an important element in the economic development of colonies,[50] in more recent times slavery has essentially been identified with that of African slaves, at least in Western societies. There is therefore a clear connection between slavery and racial discrimination,[51] and even more so between slavery and apartheid, the gravest form of racial discrimination and (in the words of the Whitaker Report)[52] a kind of 'collective slavery'. It is therefore not surprising that protection from racial discrimination should be another example of obligation *erga omnes* given in the *Barcelona Traction* case. This is the subject of the next chapter.

[49] This is a form of unfree tenure regulated in England after the Norman conquest. See Vinogradoff, *Villeinage in England: Essays in English Medieval History* (London, 1892; reprinted 1927).

[50] This is a form of temporary slavery. See Smith, A. E., *Colonists in Bondage. White Servitude and Convict Labor in America, 1607–1776* (Chapel Hill, N.C., 1947).

[51] See the statement of the representative of Ghana in *U.N.C.L.T., Off. Recs., First Session*, p. 301, para. 16.

[52] *Slavery*, para. 33.

7

The Examples of Obligations *Erga Omnes* Given by the International Court in its Dictum: (d) Protection from Racial Discrimination

I. The International Protection from Racial Discrimination: the Principle of Equality and Non-Discrimination

Protection from racial discrimination is the fourth example of obligation *erga omnes* given in the *Barcelona Traction* case.

A convenient starting point to examine this obligation is the principle that all human beings are equal. This principle was proclaimed in the solemn declarations that belong to the foundations of modern democracies.[1] In international law, a substantial body of conventions and practices of international organizations against discrimination has evolved over the years, especially after the Second World War.[2] The Charter of the United Nations and the Universal Declaration of Human Rights are the key instruments to understand later developments. Various provisions of the Charter refer to the protection of human rights and freedoms 'for all without distinction as to race, sex, language or religion'.[3] The Universal Declaration of Human

[1] For example, the American Declaration of Independence of 4 July 1776 proclaims that 'it is self-evident . . . that all men are equal'. The text is reproduced in Heffner, *A Documentary History of the United States*, 5th edn. (New York, 1991). The French Declaration of the Rights of Man and of the Citizen of 26 August 1789 proclaims in Article I that 'les hommes naissent et demeurent libres et égaux'. The text of the French Declaration (in its version of 1791), together with the various drafts that preceded its adoption, is reproduced in Rials, *La Déclaration des droits de l'homme et du citoyen* (Paris, 1988). While the provisions of the Declaration of 1789 bind the legislator like other constitutional norms, an individual cannot 's'en prévaloir, devant les tribunaux, autrement qu'à titre d'argument' (Carbonnier, *Droit civil. Introduction*, 24th edn. (Paris, 1996), p. 76.

[2] See Vierdag, *The Concept of Discrimination in International Law with Special Reference to Human Rights* (The Hague, 1973); McKean, *Equality and Discrimination under International Law* (Oxford, 1983); Thornberry, *International Law and the Rights of Minorities*, pp. 113–328. See also Greenberg, 'Race, Sex and Religious Discrimination in International Law', Meron (ed.), *Human Rights in International Law: Legal and Policy Issues* (Oxford, 1984), ii, pp. 307–43; Bernhardt, 'Völkerrechtliche Verbote der Diskriminierung von Individuen', Jekewitz, Klein, Kühne, Petersmann and Wolfrum (eds.), *Des Menschen Recht zwischen Freiheit und Verantwortung. Festschrift für Karl Josef Partsch zum 75. Geburtstag* (Berlin, 1989), pp. 97–102.

[3] See Articles 1(3), 13(1)(b), 55(c), 56, 59, and 76(c). See also Article 62(2), which refers to the promotion of human rights and freedoms 'for all'.

Rights may be regarded as the 'Magna Carta' of equality among human beings. In addition to Article 2, which proclaims in general terms that all rights and freedoms set forth in the Declaration belong to every person 'without distinction of any kind', other articles develop this principle in greater detail.[4]

Racial discrimination is universally rejected as an inadmissible derogation from this principle of equality.[5] General and regional treaties on the protection of human rights,[6] as well as international declarations,[7] contain specific provisions against racial discrimination. A decisive step in the emergence of a general prohibition of racial discrimination was taken in the sixties, with the adoption of a United Nations Declaration on the Elimination of All Forms of Racial Discrimination,[8] and then of an international Convention with the same heading.[9] Article 1, paragraph 1, of this Convention defines racial discrimination as follows:

[4] The Preamble proclaims the inherent dignity and equality of all human beings. See also Article 1 (all are equal in dignity and rights), Article 7 (all are equal before the law), Article 16 (all have an equal right to marry and found a family), Article 21 (all have a right of equal access to public services in their individual countries, and elections shall be held by universal and equal suffrage), Article 23 (all have a right to equal pay for equal work) and Article 26 (education shall promote racial tolerance and friendship). For commentary, see Eide, Alfredsson, Melander, Rehof and Rosas (eds.), *The Universal Declaration of Human Rights: A Commentary* (Oslo, 1992).

[5] On the prohibition of racial discrimination under international law, see McDougal, Lasswell and Chen, *Human Rights*, pp. 569–611 (with ample bibliography); Ténékidès, 'L'action des Nations Unies contre la discrimination raciale', 168 Hague *Recueil* (1980, III), pp. 269–487; Banton, *International Action Against Racial Discrimination* (Oxford, 1996). See also Henkin, 'National and International Perspectives in Racial Discrimination', 4 *Human Rights Journal* (1971), pp. 263–9; Schachter, 'How Effective are Measures against Racial Discrimination?', ibid., pp. 293–310.

[6] Among the general treaties see, for example, the International Covenant on Civil and Political Rights (in particular, the Preamble and Article 2); the International Covenant on Economic, Social, and Cultural Rights (in particular, Articles 2, 7 and 13). Among the regional instruments, see the African Charter on Peoples' and Human Rights (in particular, the Preamble and Articles 2, 3, 12, 13, 15, 19, 22 and 28); the American Convention on Human Rights (in particular, Articles 1, 8, 13, 17, 22, 23, 24 and 27); the European Convention on Human Rights (in particular, Article 14).

[7] See the Final Act of Helsinki (reproduced in 14 *I.L.M.* (1975), p. 1292), in which the signatory States undertook to respect human rights and fundamental freedoms 'for all without distinction as to race, sex, language or religion' (Article VII). (The political or legal nature of the Final Act does not need to be discussed here.) As a follow-up, see the condemnation of racial discrimination in the Charter of Paris for a New Europe, done at Paris on 21 November 1990 (reproduced in 30 *I.L.M.* (1991), p. 190). See also Annex 3 ('Declaration on Racism and Xenophobia') attached to the European Council Presidency Conclusions, done at Maastricht on 9 and 10 December 1991, in which the European Council stressed the 'undiminished validity' of the international obligations against discrimination and racism (reproduced in 31 *I.L.M.* (1992), p. 233).

[8] Resolution 1904 (adopted on 20 November 1963), *Gen. Ass. Off. Recs., Eighteenth Session, Supp. (No. 15) 35 (1963) (Doc.A/5515)*.

[9] 'International Convention on the Elimination of All Forms of Racial Discrimination', 660 *U.N.T.S.* 195. The text is reproduced in Brownlie, *Basic Documents*, pp. 310–27; id. (ed.), *Basic Documents on Human Rights*, pp. 148–61. The Convention was adopted by Resolution 2106 A on 21 December 1965 (*Gen. Ass. Off. Recs., Twentieth Session, Supp. 14* (Doc.A/6014), p. 47), and

any distinction, exclusion, restriction or preference based on race, colour, descent, or nationality or ethnic origin which has the purpose or effect of nullifying or impairing the recognition, enjoyment or exercise, on an equal footing, of human rights and fundamental freedoms in the political, economic, social, cultural or any other field of public life.

This picture would be incomplete without recalling the contribution of the International Court to the condemnation of racial discrimination. Apart from the dissenting opinions to the judgment on the merits in the *South West Africa* cases (on which more will be written later in this chapter), the International Court's advisory opinion on Namibia affirmed that South Africa, as the former mandatory for South West Africa, was bound to respect human rights and fundamental freedoms for all without racial discrimination, any contrary policy being a 'flagrant violation of the purposes and principles of the Charter'.[10]

Today, there is overwhelming support for the view that the prohibition of racial discrimination is the subject of an international custom,[11] and that this international custom belongs to *jus cogens*.[12] Thus, it shares the same peremptory character as the rules giving rise to the other obligations *erga*

entered into force on 4 January 1969. One hundred and forty-six States have become parties to it (*Multilateral Treaties Deposited with the Secretary-General. Status as at 31 December 1995*, p. 95). For commentary, see Schwelb, 'The International Convention on the Elimination of All Forms of Racial Discrimination', 15 *I.C.L.Q.* (1966), pp. 996–1059; Lerner, *The U.N. Convention on the Elimination of All Forms of Racial Discrimination*, 2nd edn. (Alphen aan den Rijn and Rockville, 1980); Meron, 'The Meaning and Reach of the International Convention on the Elimination of All Forms of Racial Discrimination', 79 *A.J.I.L.* (1985), pp. 283–318. See also Reisman, 'Responses to Crimes of Discrimination and Genocide: An Appraisal of the Convention on the Elimination of Racial Discrimination', 1 *Denver Journal of International Law and Policy* (1971), pp. 29–64.

[10] *Legal Consequences for States of the Continued Presence of South Africa in Namibia (South West Africa) notwithstanding Security Council Resolution 276 (1970)*, Advisory Opinion, I.C.J. Reports 1971, p. 57, para. 131. On this advisory opinion, see section II of Chapter 9, below.

[11] See Brownlie, *Principles*, pp. 598–601. The *Third Restatement* restricts the customary nature of the rule to racial discrimination which is 'systematic', such as apartheid (Section 702, Comment (i) and Reporter's Note (7)).

[12] See, for example, the statement of the Italian representative at a World Conference to Combat Racism and Racial Discrimination, partly reproduced in Ramcharan, 'Equality and Nondiscrimination', Henkin (ed.), *The International Bill of Rights: The Covenant on Civil and Political Rights* (New York, 1981), pp. 464–5, note 10. In the literature, see Brownlie, *Principles*, p. 513 and pp. 600–1; Mullerson and Tunkin (eds.), *International Law* (Moscow, 1990), p. 21. See also Gros Espiell, 'No discriminacion y libre determinacion como normas imperativas de derecho internacional, con especial referencia a los efectos de su denegacion sobre la legitimidad de los estados que violan o desconocen esas normas imperativas', 6 *Anuario hispano-luso-americano de derecho internacional* (1981), pp. 33–81. With respect to 'systematic' racial discrimination, see the *Third Restatement*, Section 702, Comment (n). During the preparatory work that led to the adoption of the Vienna Convention on the Law of Treaties, the prohibition of racial discrimination was one of the most frequently cited examples of norms of *jus cogens*.

omnes listed by the International Court in its judgment in the *Barcelona Traction* case.[13]

II. Qualifications to the Principle of Equality and Non-Discrimination

The principle of equality must not be interpreted as requiring absolute identity of treatment among human beings. This would go against the diverse qualities which distinguish one person from another and the different conditions in which people operate. In other words, the principle is qualified by a certain measure of proportionality. This idea, summarized in the need that equals be treated equally, and unequals be treated unequally in proportion to the inequality, can be traced back to classic philosophy.[14]

Likewise, the principle of non-discrimination, which complements equality by prohibiting unjust inequalities, is not to be interpreted in a dogmatic way, as if all differences were to be prohibited. Time and again, courts have endorsed a more flexible approach. For example, in the advisory opinion on *Minority Schools in Albania*, delivered in 1935, the Permanent Court of International Justice distinguished between 'equality in law' and 'equality in fact' and concluded that equality in fact may require different treatment to achieve an equilibrium between different situations.[15] Another classic statement is contained in the judgment on the merits rendered by the European Court of Human Rights in the *Belgian linguistic* case. In this case, the European Court remarked that equality (which is expressly protected under Article 14 of the European Convention on Human Rights) is violated if the distinction has no 'objective' and 'reasonable' justification in light of the aim and effects of the measure under consideration.[16] To sum up, it is

[13] The conclusions of Chapter 6, above, pointed out the links between slavery and racial discrimination. Likewise, Richard Goldstone, as chief prosecutor at the International Criminal Tribunal for Yugoslavia, indicated that one of the learning experiences of his position was that 'discrimination of any kind, anywhere, contains the seeds of genocide.' (Drozdiak, 'Noted Jurist Says Bias Contains "Seeds of Genocide"', *The Washington Post*, 2 July 1995, p. A24.)

[14] Aristotle, *The Complete Works*, 1131a10–1131a24 (Nicomachean Ethics).

[15] *P.C.I.J., Series A/B, No. 64*, p. 19. For comment, see Lauterpacht, H., *The Development of International Law*, pp. 257–62.

[16] *Case relating to Certain Aspects of the Laws on the Use of Languages in Education in Belgium* (Judgment on the merits of 23 July 1968, ser. A, No. 6), 11 *Yearbook of the European Convention on Human Rights* (1968), p. 832. The English text of the judgment is reproduced in 45 *I.L.R.* (1972), pp. 114–231. The President of the European Court at that time was the French jurist René Cassin, a distinguished supporter of human rights. Among the other members, some were leading international lawyers, such as Verdross, Ross, Balladore Pallieri, Mosler, Favre, and Waldock. Sörensen and Guggenheim, both prominent international lawyers and authors of writings on the principle of equality and non-discrimination, appeared before the European Court on behalf, respectively, of the European Commission of Human Rights and the Belgian Government. On the principle of non-discrimination in the decisions of the European Court, see Merrills, *The Development of International Law by the European*

generally accepted that certain forms of differentiation are admissible, provided that they have an objective justification.[17]

The real issue is to determine the criteria according to which one can distinguish legal from illegal differentiation. In particular, can race be such a criterion?[18] Today, scientists agree that all human beings belong to the same species and descend from a common stock.[19] Race is not a valid criterion of differentiation, except for circumstances that require special protection of certain groups. While admissible, these protective measures command a heavy burden of proof and are subject to restrictions. For example, Article 1, paragraph 4, of the International Convention on the Elimination of All Forms of Racial Discrimination provides that special measures for the advancement of racial groups can be taken only if 'necessary' and must be discontinued as soon as their objective has been achieved. Moreover, such measures cannot maintain separate rights for different racial groups. This issue of separate development of racial groups has been a thorny issue for a long time, as evidenced by the controversies that led to the landmark decisions of the United States Supreme Court on school segregation,[20] which rejected the 'separate but equal' doctrine in the field of public education.

Court of Human Rights (Manchester, 1988), pp. 152–9; Partsch, 'Discrimination', Macdonald, Matscher and Petzold (eds.), *The European System for the Protection of Human Rights* (Dordrecht, 1993), pp. 571–92.

[17] See Jaenicke, 'Diskriminierung', Strupp and Schlochauer (eds.), *Wörterbuch*, i, pp. 387–92; Guggenheim, 'Quelques remarques au sujet de l'article 14 de la Convention européenne des droits de l'homme', *René Cassin Amicorum Discipulorumque Liber I. Problèmes de protection internationale des droits de l'homme* (Paris, 1969), pp. 95–100; McKean, 'The Meaning of Discrimination in International and Municipal Law', 44 *B.Y.I.L.* (1970), pp. 177–92; Tomuschat, 'Equality and non-discrimination under the International Covenant on Civil and Political Rights', *Staatsrecht-Völkerrecht-Europarecht, Festschrift für Hans-Jurgen Schlochauer* (Berlin, 1981), pp. 712–16; Gubin, *Rasovaya diskriminatsiya: reaktsionnaya sushchnost' i mezhdunarodnaya protivopravnost'* (Moscow, 1979), pp. 9–28.

[18] On the concept of race, see Harris, 'Race', Sills (ed.), *International Encyclopedia*, xiii (New York, 1968), pp. 263–9.

[19] See *Declaration on Race and Racial Prejudice adopted by the General Conference of UNESCO at its twentieth session, Paris, 27 November 1978* (Paris, 1979). Among the various works on this subject published under the auspices of UNESCO, see Dunn, *Race and Biology* (Paris, 1958), and *Racism, science and pseudo-science. Proceedings of the symposium to examine pseudo-scientific theories invoked to justify racism and racial discrimination, Athens, 30 March to 3 April 1981* (Paris, 1983) (in particular, the article of the Senegalese anthropologist Diop headed 'The unity of the origin of the human species', pp. 133–7). Among recent scientific works, see Cavalli-Sforza, Menozzi and Piazza, *The History and Geography of Human Genes*, abridged paperback edition (Princeton, 1994), p. 19: 'The classification into races has proved to be a futile exercise . . . there is no doubt that there is only one human species . . .'.

[20] See, in particular, *Brown et al.* v. *Board of Education of Topeka, Shawnee County, Kan., et al.*, 347 U.S. 483 (1959). For a summary of this case, see Hutchinson, D. J., 'Brown v. Board of Education', Hall, K. L. (ed.), *The Oxford Companion to the Supreme Court*, pp. 93–6. For a much more extensive treatment, see Kluger, *Simple Justice* (New York, 1977). On the concept of segregation, see Kuper, 'Segregation', Sills (ed.), *International Encyclopedia*, xiv (New York, 1968), pp. 144–50.

An extreme form of racial segregation is apartheid, i.e. the systematic policy of racial discrimination (accompanied by elements of slavery and physical deprivation) established in South Africa in 1948,[21] and then extended over the territory of the former South West Africa to maintain white domination.[22] After repeated condemnation by the international community,[23] culminating in the adoption of an International Convention on the Suppression and Punishment of the Crime of Apartheid,[24] apartheid has now been cancelled from the statute book of South West Africa (now the sovereign State of Namibia) and of South Africa itself.[25]

Despite these developments, the controversies on apartheid, and especially some of the arguments that were submitted before the International Court in the *South West Africa* cases, still provide useful elements for the analysis of

[21] For a survey of the elements of continuity and innovation from the earlier policy of segregation to the new policy of apartheid after 1948, see Cowen, *The Foundations of Freedom with Special reference to Southern Africa* (Cape Town, 1961), pp. 23–30. On apartheid (with ample bibliography), see McDougal, Lasswell and Chen, *Human Rights*, pp. 521–60. A key measure of apartheid, the Bantu Education Act, 1953, is reproduced in Brownlie (ed.), *Basic Documents on African Affairs* (Oxford, 1971), pp. 415–25.

[22] See *Special Study of Racial Discrimination in the Political, Economic, Social and Cultural Spheres (Report submitted by the Special Rapporteur, Mr. Hernan Santa Cruz), United Nations Economic and Social Council, Commission on Human Rights, Sub-Commission on Prevention of Discrimination and Protection of Minorities, Twenty-third Session*, para. 857 (Doc.E/CN.4/Sub 2/307/Add.3).

[23] See *The United Nations and Apartheid 1948–1994* (New York, 1994). See also the references to apartheid in all the Reports of the Secretary-General of the United Nations in the period from 1982 to 1991 (Pérez de Cuéllar, *Anarchy or Order. Annual reports 1982–1991* (New York, 1991), pp. 8, 31, 63, 93–4, 119–20, 143–4, 177, 240, 268 and 340). Dugard has remarked that the General Assembly of the United Nations has condemned apartheid 'in the most extravagant language' (*Recognition and the United Nations* (Cambridge, 1987), p. 106, note 121). In 1979, Crawford, while acknowledging the 'considerable support' for the peremptory character of the principle of racial equality and non-discrimination, wrote on apartheid as follows: '*Apartheid* as such, a particular institution adopted in one country, is probably not illegal as a matter of customary international law, but it provides a clear case of a policy predicated on a fundamental denial of equality on the grounds of race or ethnic origin' (*The Creation of States in International Law* (Oxford, 1979), pp. 226–7, footnotes omitted). Apartheid was regarded as a breach of *jus cogens* in the 'Declaration of the Seminar on the Legal Status of the *Apartheid* Régime held at Lagos, Nigeria, from 13 to 16 August 1984' (Doc.A/39/423–5/16709 and Corr. 1, p. 10).

[24] Adopted on 30 November 1973 by General Assembly resolution 3068, *Gen. Ass. Off. Recs., Twenty eighth Session, Supp. 30* (Doc.A/9030). The text is reproduced in Brownlie (ed.), *Basic Documents on Human Rights*, pp. 162–8. The Convention entered into force on 18 July 1976. Ninety-nine States have become parties (*Multilateral Treaties Deposited with the Secretary-General. Status as at 31 December 1995*, p. 164).

[25] On the independence process in Namibia, see the various articles published in 15 *South African Yearbook of International Law* (1989–90) (Namibian Independence Edition), and 1 *African Yearbook of International Law* (1993) (Special Theme: Namibia: The Independence Process). See also Kamto, 'L'accession de la Namibie à l'indépendance', 94 *R.G.D.I.P.* (1990), pp. 577–634. On constitutional developments in South Africa, see Dugard, *International Law. A South African Perspective* (Kenwyn, South Africa, 1994), p. 339. On the protection of human rights under the 1993 Constitution, see id., 'International Human Rights', van Wyk, Dugard, de Villiers and Davis (eds.), *Rights and Constitutionalism. The New South African Legal Order* (Kenwyn, South Africa, 1994), pp. 191–5.

the concept of obligations *erga omnes*. For this reason, the remaining part of this chapter will focus on some of the arguments developed by the parties in these cases. The present study will only cover a minimal part of the massive record of the written pleadings and oral arguments in the *South West Africa* cases.[26] The only question that will be addressed (and this too with a considerable degree of selectivity in choosing the relevant passages) is the dispute between the parties as to whether an international prohibition of non-discrimination or non-separation could be said, at that time, to be opposable to South Africa as the mandatory for South West Africa.

III. The Question of the Opposability *Erga Omnes* of the Protection from Racial Discrimination and the Prohibition of Apartheid in the *South West Africa* Cases

In 1960, Ethiopia and Liberia instituted proceedings against South Africa before the International Court. The subject of the dispute was the mandate for South West Africa.[27] This was the fourth time that the International Court was requested to pronounce on the mandate for South West Africa, and the first time that the issue was raised in contentious proceedings.[28]

In their Memorial, the applicant States alleged that South Africa, by practising apartheid in South West Africa, had breached the obligations incumbent upon it, as a mandatory, under Article 22, paragraph 1, of the Covenant of the League of Nations and Article 2, paragraph 2, of the mandate.[29] Article 22, paragraph 1, of the Covenant embodied the guiding principle of all mandates, namely that the well-being and development of the people living in a territory under a mandate formed a 'sacred trust of civi-

[26] The pleadings amount to over 3700 pages, while the hearings lasted for nearly 100 days.

[27] For a short and effective treatment of the political and legal issues attaching to the mandate for South West Africa, see *Oppenheim's International Law*, i, pp. 300–7. For a longer presentation, see Slonim, *South West Africa and the United Nations: An International Mandate in Dispute* (Baltimore and London, 1973); Zacklin, 'The Problem of Namibia in International Law', 171 Hague *Recueil* (1981, II), pp. 225–340. On the mandates system, see Diena, 'Les mandats internationaux', 5 Hague *Recueil* (1924, IV), pp. 211–65; Rolin, 'La pratique des mandats internationaux', 19 Hague *Recueil* (1927, IV), pp. 493–628.

[28] On each of the three previous occasions, the International Court had received a request from the General Assembly of the United Nations for an advisory opinion. See *International Status of South West Africa,* Advisory Opinion, I.C.J. Reports 1950, p. 128; *Voting Procedure on Questions relating to Reports and Petitions concerning the Territory of South West Africa,* Advisory Opinion, I.C.J. Reports 1955, p. 67; *Admissibility of Hearings of Petitioners by the Committee on South West Africa,* Advisory Opinion, I.C.J. Reports 1956, p. 23. For a summary of the International Court's four advisory opinions and two judgments relating to the mandate for South West Africa, see Rosenne, *The World Court. What it is and how it works,* 5th revised edn. (Dordrecht, 1995), pp. 168–75.

[29] *I.C.J. Pleadings, South West Africa*, i, pp. 104–66 (the Submissions are at pp. 197–8). The English text of the relevant provisions from the Covenant and the mandate are reproduced ibid., pp. 200–2.

lization'. In fulfilment of this principle, Article 2, paragraph 2, of the mandate for South West Africa provided that the mandatory 'would promote to the utmost the material and moral well-being and the social progress' of the peoples of South West Africa.[30]

On which grounds could it be proved that the policy of apartheid was incompatible with the obligations of the mandatory? From the very beginning of the case, the applicant States were confronted with the need to indicate legal criteria that would enable the International Court to adjudge the merits. One of the arguments put forward by the applicant States was that the mandatory, in its administration of South West Africa, was bound to respect an international customary norm of 'non-discrimination' or 'non-separation'.[31] In their Reply, Ethiopia and Liberia defined 'non-discrimination' and 'non-separation' as follows:

> stated negatively, the terms refer to the absence of governmental policies or actions which allot status, rights, duties, privileges or burdens on the basis of membership in a group, class or race rather than on the basis of individual merit, capacity or potential; stated affirmatively, the terms refer to governmental policies and actions the objective of which is to protect equality of opportunity and equal protection of the laws to individual persons as such.[32]

The applicant States added that, by the time the dispute was brought before the International Court, an international custom of 'non-discrimination' or 'non-separation' had emerged and was universally accepted.

South Africa had a different view. In its Rejoinder, it wrote that no international custom of non-discrimination had yet emerged, or at least not one like the one defined by the applicant States.[33] South Africa did not deny that a rule against discrimination existed, in the sense that measures prejudicially affecting certain groups would be precluded. Its point was rather that no international norm would prohibit racial separation as such,

[30] At the hearings, Judge Fitzmaurice drew the attention of the parties to certain discrepancies between the English and French texts of Article 2 of the mandate (ibid., viii, p. 32). For the present purposes, this issue may be left aside.

[31] The present discussion is not concerned with the applicant States' contention that the prohibition of apartheid had evolved not only as a legal norm, but also as a 'standard' applicable to the mandate (see *I.C.J. Pleadings, South West Africa*, ix, pp. 309–42, in particular, and the dissenting opinion of Judge Jessup from the final judgment of the International Court, I.C.J. Reports 1966, pp. 429–42). On the concept of 'standard', see Pound, *An Introduction to the Philosophy of Law*, 2nd edn. (New Haven and London, 1954), pp. 57–9; Dillard, 'Some Aspects of Law and Diplomacy', 91 Hague *Recueil* (1957, I), pp. 477–8. On the development of standards in the mandates system, see Wright, *Mandates under the League of Nations* (Chicago, 1930), p. 219, see also section IV of Chapter 8, below.

[32] *I.C.J. Pleadings, South West Africa*, iv, p. 493.

[33] Ibid., v, pp. 140–1. There is no need, in the present context, to discuss the South African contention that the International Court had no jurisdiction to consider an argument based on an international norm of non-discrimination.

irrespective of any evidence that this policy had a discriminatory intent or effect. In other words, a policy of separate development of races would not be, of itself, inadmissible. As a further step, South Africa argued that, even assuming that a norm like that defined by the applicant States existed in international customary law, such a norm would not be opposable to South Africa, because South Africa had 'openly and consistently' objected to this norm from the very beginning of its formation.[34] In practice, South Africa claimed that it was a persistent objector to the alleged customary rule indicated by the applicant States.

At the hearings, the applicant States maintained that a norm of 'non-discrimination' or 'non-separation' was opposable to all States, irrespective of any claim of persistent objection. The key passage that summarizes the applicants' position reads as follows:

> . . . the norm of non-discrimination and non-separation involves the promotion of common interests and collective interests of States, and of the organized international community taken as a whole. These are, moreover, common interests which rest upon a widely shared and deeply felt and often eloquently expressed humanitarian conviction. In this respect apartheid corresponds to genocide, and the nature of the law-creating process in response to both has been remarkably similar: one in which the collective will of the international community has been shocked into virtual unanimity, and in which the moral basis of law is most visible. It is precisely because there is an offender that there has been a drive to create a norm. If the offender is allowed to avoid the legal condemnation of his action by stating a protest, then international law is rendered impotent in the face of a grave challenge to the values underlying the international social order.[35]

In summary, the applicant States relied on three grounds to show that South Africa, as the mandatory for South West Africa,[36] was bound by the norm of 'non-discrimination' or 'non-separation' despite its persistent objection. The three grounds are (a) the 'moral basis' and the promotion of the 'common interests of States, and of the organized international community taken as a whole', embodied in the norm, (b) the 'virtual unanimity' of the international community in support of this norm, and (c) the negative consequences that would follow from allowing South Africa to evade this norm. These grounds will now be examined in reverse order.

First of all, the applicants submitted that, if South Africa could legally

[34] In addition to the pages cited in the previous footnote, see *I.C.J. Pleadings, South West Africa*, viii, p. 676, and x, pp. 9–11 and 28–41. (For a better understanding of the pages just cited, it is advisable to read the whole text at pp. 3–53.)

[35] Ibid., ix, p. 351.

[36] Apartheid in South Africa was not in issue. However, the Agent for the applicant States acknowledged, in a pronouncement made outside the proceedings of the *South West Africa* cases, that one of the applicant States' objectives was to put on trial the whole system of apartheid, wherever applied by the Government of South Africa. See Gross, '*The South West Africa Cases*: On the Threshold of Decision', 3 *C.J.T.L.* (1964), pp. 19–25.

evade the application of the norm of 'non-discrimination' or 'non-separation', then the object of the mandate would be defeated. This argument was criticized by South Africa as being 'purely legislative',[37] in the sense that the norm in question would bind South Africa only because it would be 'desirable' that it should do so. Upon a literal interpretation of the applicants' argument, this criticism contains some element of truth. However, the applicants' argument can also be interpreted as meaning that, if South Africa could validly claim to be a persistent objector to the norm of 'non-discrimination' or 'non-separation', the obligation to administer the mandate 'in accordance with international law' would effectively be destroyed.[38] In other words, this argument would ultimately derive from the special character of the mandate.

Secondly, the applicant States argued that the international community had given rise, by international consensus—i.e. an 'overwhelming . . . convergence of international opinion' expressed in 'formal acts' of international organizations—to a norm binding on all States.[39] Thus, the norm of 'non-discrimination' or 'non-separation' would be the product of a norm-creating process endowed with 'quasi-legislative' effects. This point in the applicants' argument is not entirely convincing. One certainly cannot deny the role played by resolutions in the emergence of the international prohibition of racial discrimination, and more generally in the international protection of human rights.[40] However, expressions such as the 'organized international community taken as a whole' or the 'collective will of the international community' do not appear to correspond to the present reality of international relations, let alone to that existing in the sixties, when the *South West Africa* cases took place. Arguably, the applicant States overstated their point for strategic reasons,[41] with a view to emphasizing the

[37] *I.C.J. Pleadings, South West Africa*, x, p. 30. [38] Ibid., ix, p. 349.

[39] Ibid., p. 345. There is a wide literature on 'consensus'. See, for example, Jenks, 'Unanimity, The Veto, Weighted Voting, Special and Simple Majorities and Consensus as Modes of Decision in International Organisations', *Cambridge Essays McNair*, pp. 48–63; Charpentier, 'La procédure de non objection (A propos d'une crise constitutionnelle de l'O.N.U.)', 70 *R.G.D.I.P.* (1966), pp. 862–77; de Lacharrière, 'Consensus et Nations Unies', 14 *A.F.D.I.* (1968), pp. 9–14; D'Amato, 'On Consensus', 8 *Canadian Yearbook of International Law* (1970), pp. 104–22; Jessup, 'Silence Gives Consent', 3 *Georgia Journal of International Law* (1973), pp. 46–54; Bastid, 'Observations sur la pratique du consensus', Tittel (ed.), *Multitudo Legum Ius Unum. Festschrift für Wilhelm Wengler zu seinem 65. Geburtstag* (Berlin, 1973), i, pp. 11–25; Cassese, 'Consensus and Some of its Pitfalls', 58 *Riv. dir. int.* (1975), pp. 754–61; Kas'ian, *Konsensus v sovremennykh mezhdunarodnykh otnosheniyakh (mezhdunarodno-pravovye voprosy)* (Moscow, 1983).

[40] See the Preliminary Exposé, Provisional Report, Definitive Report and Draft Resolution relating to 'Resolutions of the General Assembly of the United Nations' presented by Krzysztof Skubiszewski to the Institute of International Law at the Helsinki Session of 1985, 61 *Ann. Institut* (1985), i, pp. 29–334. (See also the 'Observations of the Members of the Thirteenth Commission on the Provisional Report', pp. 335–8.)

[41] In general, strategic issues are crucial for interpreting the arguments put forward by the parties. For example, counsel for the applicants expressly acknowledged that the issue of

special role of international institutions in controlling the exercise of the mandate for South West Africa. At any rate, even a milder statement of the applicants' argument would not have dissipated all doubts. It may be argued that the dissent by South Africa from the resolutions on apartheid did not deprive those resolutions of their evidentiary force in interpreting the provisions of the United Nations Charter which are binding on all States, such as those contained in Articles 55 and 56. However, those resolutions, supported by almost all States, have at most a 'high degree of persuasive force',[42] without being either legally binding or opposable to those States that have voted against them.

Finally, the third argument put forward by the applicant States embodies a value judgment on the prohibition of racial discrimination. The passage from the applicants' oral reply reported above contains some characteristic expressions, such as 'common interests and collective interests of States', 'humanitarian conviction', 'moral basis of the law', 'values underlying the international social order'. During the proceedings, the applicant States repeatedly affirmed that the dictum of the International Court in the *Fisheries* case[43] did not constitute a relevant precedent for the proposition that South Africa could validly escape from a norm to which it had persistently objected from its inception. According to the applicants, the customary norm in question in the *Fisheries* case aimed at 'adjusting directly competing or conflicting interests', whereas the norm of 'non-discrimination' to which they were referring in the present case involved 'world community standards'.[44] The applicants did not fully develop this point. From the pleadings, it may even appear that they were ready to concede that the doctrine of the persistent objector, while irrelevant to the case of South West Africa, would be a plausible argument had the litigation been about apartheid in South Africa.[45]

Likewise, the applicants referred to, but did not fully explore, certain elements of similarity between the international prohibition of genocide and the protection from racial discrimination. As was mentioned earlier, in its advisory opinion on the Genocide Convention the International Court examined the object of the Genocide Convention and the intention of States in condemning genocide. It wrote that the member States of the United Nations, by adopting resolution 96, had intended to condemn genocide as a 'crime' against 'moral law and . . . the spirit and aims of the United

justiciability, raised in the joint dissenting opinion of Judges Fitzmaurice and Spender at the jurisdictional phase (I.C.J. Reports 1962, pp. 466–7), had made an impact on the litigation strategy adopted by the applicants (Falk, *The Status of Law in International Society* (Princeton, 1970), pp. 383–4, note 16). At the hearings, Judge Fitzmaurice asked the applicants to clarify the 'purely juridical basis' on which they founded their case (*I.C.J. Pleadings, South West Africa*, viii, p. 30).

[42] Schachter, *International Law*, p. 91.

[43] See section V of Chapter 3, above.

[44] *I.C.J. Pleadings, South West Africa*, ix, pp. 351–2.

[45] See ibid., pp. 348–9.

Nations'. It then added that the Genocide Convention had been adopted for a 'purely humanitarian and civilizing purpose' in the 'common interest' of States. From this, the International Court concluded that the principles underlying the Genocide Convention were binding on all States without exception.[46]

The analogies with the protection from racial discrimination are evident. In the preamble to the International Convention on the Elimination of All Forms of Racial Discrimination, the contracting States declared that any doctrine of racial superiority is 'morally condemnable', and the existence of racial barriers is 'repugnant to the ideals of any human society'. For the same reasons, a few years later, the contracting States of the International Convention on the Suppression and Punishment of the Crime of Apartheid defined apartheid, in Article 1, as a 'crime against humanity'. This clear contradiction with moral law and the shared values of the international community explains why such a short period of time was needed for the conclusion, and then the entry into force, of the international instruments condemning genocide, racial discrimination, and apartheid.

The International Court did not pronounce on these elements of analogy between the prohibition of genocide and the protection from racial discrimination, and on the question of the opposability *erga omnes* (including any persistent objector) of a norm of 'non-discrimination' in the sense indicated by the applicant States. In fact, the International Court did not pronounce at all on the merits of the dispute because it found, on the casting vote of its President,[47] that the applicant States lacked standing. However, some of the judges, over the objection of the President, declared that they were entitled, if not judicially bound, to examine the merits of the issues raised by the parties in the course of the proceedings.[48] In his dissenting opinion, Judge Tanaka discussed in great detail the prohibition of racial discrimination. The starting point in his reasoning was that human rights derive from the concept of the human being as a person. States do not create human rights, but only confirm their existence. Thus, human rights exist independently of the will of States. In support of his argument, Judge Tanaka referred to the passage from the advisory opinion on the Genocide

[46] See section II of Chapter 5, above.

[47] Article 55, paragraph 2, of the Statute of the International Court provides as follows: 'In the event of an equality of votes, the President or the judge who acts in his place shall have a casting vote.'

[48] In a declaration appended to the judgment, the President of the International Court, Sir Percy Spender, wrote that 'opinions should not purport to deal with matters that fall entirely outside the range of the Court's decision, or of the decision's motivation' (I.C.J. Reports 1966, pp. 51–7). Judge Tanaka disagreed and wrote that 'the majority opinion cannot be conceived to establish any limits to the separate opinions of individual judges' (ibid., p. 262). In his dissenting opinion, Judge Jessup considered it to be his 'judicial duty to examine the legal issues in this case which has been before the Court for six years' (ibid., p. 325). On individual opinions, see Lauterpacht, H., *The Development of International Law*, pp. 66–70.

Convention in which the International Court had affirmed that the principles underlying the Convention were binding on States 'even without any conventional obligation'.[49] From this argument, Judge Tanaka drew the conclusion that

> States which do not recognize this principle [i.e. the protection of human rights] or even deny its existence are nevertheless subject to its rule.[50]

Upon this ground, he concluded that the prohibition of racial discrimination, which is 'in itself' contrary to the principle of equality among human beings, is subject to a prohibition opposable to all States.[51]

The reasoning developed by Judge Tanaka in his dissenting opinion can be fully appreciated only in its entirety and in light of the views on international law and the general theory of law held by this judge.[52] Any consideration of these views would obviously fall outside the scope of the present analysis. At the same time, the specific point made by Judge Tanaka on the opposability *erga omnes* of the prohibition of racial discrimination may be summarized as follows: the binding effect *erga omnes* of the prohibition of racial discrimination derives from the underlying moral and social values that the prohibition is meant to protect, as reflected in the recognition by States of this prohibition.[53]

IV. Conclusions

One of the main questions which arose in the pleadings of the *South West Africa* cases was whether an international norm of 'non-discrimination', comprising also a prohibition of the policy of apartheid, would be opposable *erga omnes*, including South Africa as the mandatory for South West Africa. South Africa did not object to the general prohibition of racial discrimination, but rejected an interpretation of this prohibition that would include its policy of apartheid.

[49] See section II of Chapter 5, above.

[50] *I.C.J. Reports* 1966, p. 298. The part of Judge Tanaka's dissenting opinion dealing with the concept of equality is reproduced in Brownlie (ed.), *Basic Documents on Human Rights*, pp. 567–98.

[51] *I.C.J. Reports* 1966, pp. 313–16.

[52] See, for example, Tanaka, 'Du droit international au droit mondial', *Etudes juridiques offertes à Léon Julliot de la Morandière* (Paris, 1964), especially pp. 563–7 (on the sources of international law and, in particular, the 'general principles of law recognized by civilized nations'). On Tanaka's principle of equality, and philosophical background, see Saito, 'Judge Tanaka, natural law and the principle of equality', Alfredsson and Macalister-Smith (eds.), *The Living Law of Nations: essays on refugees, minorities, indigenous peoples and the human rights of other vulnerable groups in memory of Alte Grahl-Madsen* (Kehl, 1996)

[53] An argument in some ways similar to that of Judge Tanaka had been developed, more than thirty years earlier, by Judge Gardiner, a South African appellate judge, in his dissenting opinion in the case of *Minister of Posts and Telegraphs* v. *Rasool*, The South Africa Law Report 1934, Appellate Division, p. 167, at pp. 183–93.

Unlike the cases discussed for the three other examples of obligations *erga omnes* listed in the judgment in the *Barcelona Traction* case, the *South West Africa* cases have shown some unique features, namely that (a) there was an actual dispute about the opposability of an international obligation to a persistent objector, and (b) this dispute was not about the universal opposability of a general obligation (i.e. the prohibition of racial discrimination), but was about the universal opposability of the specific prohibition of a discriminatory policy (i.e. apartheid). This latter point makes it possible to appreciate fully how accurate was the terminology chosen by the International Court in its dictum in the *Barcelona Traction* case: the obligation *erga omnes* against racial discrimination (and slavery) is meant not only to *outlaw* racial discrimination (and slavery) in general, but also to *protect* human beings from specific policies in contradiction with this obligation.[54]

Although the International Court did not pronounce on the merits of the *South West Africa* cases, certain arguments developed by the applicant States in their pleadings, and by Judge Tanaka in his dissenting opinion, present elements of analogy with the reasoning of the International Court in its advisory opinion on the Genocide Convention, to the effect that the moral basis of an international obligation, and the support by a substantial proportion of the international community, would justify the opposability *erga omnes* of the international obligation in question.

This concludes the analysis of the four examples of obligations *erga omnes* given by the International Court in its classic dictum. Section I of the next chapter will summarize the main findings of this analysis.

[54] The link between prohibition and protection has been underlined, in a different context, by Nincic. In classifying the provisions contained in the Declaration of Principles that is part of the Final Act of Helsinki, he identified a category of 'normes prohibitives', which are 'destinées à protéger les valeurs fondamentales, c'est-à-dire à empêcher qu'il soit leur porté atteinte' ('Les implications générales juridiques et historiques de la Déclaration d'Helsinki', 154 Hague *Recueil* (1977, I), p. 79).

8

Selected Candidates of Obligations *Erga Omnes* Proposed in the International Literature

I. Introduction

The findings of Chapters 4 to 7, which have examined the examples of obligations *erga omnes* given in the *Barcelona Traction* case, may be summarized as follows:

(a) for certain obligations, such as the outlawing of acts of aggression, the specific contribution of the concept lies not so much in rendering the obligation opposable to all States irrespective of consent (no State, for example, objects to the outlawing of aggression) as in clarifying the corollaries attaching to the obligation in question (in the case of the outlawing of aggression, the limits within which circumstances precluding wrongfulness can be invoked);
(b) while it was the dictum in the *Barcelona Traction* case that put the concept of obligations *erga omnes* on the international agenda, elements of legal reasoning relevant to the concept were already present in earlier pronouncements of the International Court, notably the advisory opinion on the Genocide Convention;
(c) while three out of the four obligations *erga omnes* indicated by the International Court prohibit practices which were formerly beyond the reach of international law, one of the four examples, namely the protection from slavery, is that of an international obligation prohibiting what had been for centuries an accepted institution; and
(d) whereas all four examples relate to obligations that do not aim at any particular situation, for one at least of these four examples, namely the protection from racial discrimination, there are arguments in support also of a prohibition *erga omnes* of the policy of racial segregation.

After examining the four examples separately, it is useful to compare them with one another and try to highlight any elements that they may have in common. The analysis developed in Chapters 4 to 7 reveals the existence of at least five common elements, as follows:

(1) all four examples relate to narrowly defined obligations (outlawing of

aggression rather than, more broadly, the illegal use of force; outlawing of genocide rather than, more broadly, crimes against humanity; protection from slavery rather than, more broadly, all kinds of unlawful restrictions on freedom; protection from racial discrimination rather than, more broadly, all kinds of discrimination);

(2) while two out of the four examples are expressed in terms of the 'outlawing' of certain practices, and the two others in terms of the 'protection from' certain other practices, all four examples are essentially those of negative obligations (or prohibitions),[1] rather than positive obligations;[2]

(3) all four examples are those of 'obligations', or 'duties',[3] in the strict sense (i.e. what 'one ought or ought not to do'),[4] to the exclusion of other fundamental legal conceptions;[5]

(4) all four examples are those of obligations deriving from rules of general international law belonging to *jus cogens* and codified by international treaties to which a high number of States have become parties; and

(5) all four examples are those of obligations instrumental to the main

[1] For some thought-provoking considerations on the legal conception of 'prohibition', see Kelsen, *General Theory of Norms*, pp. 92–3.

[2] In Austin's words, a party bound by a positive obligation 'is commanded to do or perform', while a party bound by a negative obligation 'is commanded to forbear or abstain'. (*Lectures on Jurisprudence*, p. 346.) Instead of 'positive obligations', some writers use the expression 'affirmative duties'. (See, for example, Brilmayer, *Justifying International Acts* (Ithaca, N.Y., and London, 1989), pp. 118–38.)

[3] At common law, the expressions 'obligations' and 'duties' are 'roughly synonymous'. (Hart, *The Concept of Law*, p. 284.) The situation does not seem to be any different in international law, although in its advisory opinion on the International Status of South West Africa the International Court used the term 'obligation' when referring to a legal concept, and the term 'duty' when referring to a political or moral concept (I.C.J. Reports 1950, p. 140; see also the dissenting opinion of Judge Alvarez, ibid., p. 177). In his dissenting opinion in the *East Timor* case, Judge Weeramantry used indifferently the expressions '*erga omnes* obligation' and '*erga omnes* duty' (I.C.J. Reports 1995, p. 215). For a comparison between the two concepts, from a philosophical perspective, see Brandt, 'The Concepts of Obligation and Duty', 73 *Mind* (1964), pp. 374–93.

[4] *Lake Shore & M. S. R. Co.* v. *Kurtz*, (1894) 10 Ind. App., 60; 37 N.E., 303, 304.

[5] See Hohfeld, *Fundamental Legal Conceptions*, pp. 23–114 (to which reference is made here for mere reasons of convenience). Hohfeld's terminology and legal analysis are current in English jurisprudence (see Hart, *Essays on Bentham. Studies in Jurisprudence and Political Theory* (Oxford, 1982), p. 162), and have also been found helpful by some international lawyers (see, for example, Mendelson, 'State Acts and Omissions as Explicit or Implicit Claims', *Le droit international. Mélanges Virally*, pp. 373–82), and at least one member of the International Court (see Weeramantry's dissenting opinion in the *East Timor* case, I.C.J. Reports 1995, p. 209). On the Hohfeldian analysis of fundamental legal conceptions, see Kocourek, 'The Hohfeld System of Fundamental Legal Concepts', 15 *Illinois Law Review* (1920), pp. 24–39; Campbell, 'International Law and the Student of Jurisprudence', 35 *Transactions of the Grotius Society* (1935), pp. 122–3; Hart, 'Definition and Theory in Jurisprudence', 70 *Law Quarterly Review* (1954), p. 49, note 15; Dias, *Jurisprudence*, 3rd edn. (Oxford, 1970), pp. 269–72; *Salmond on Jurisprudence*, p. 225, note (*m*); Finnis, *Natural Law and Natural Rights* (Oxford, 1980), pp. 199–205; Raz, *The Concept of a Legal System*, 2nd edn. (Oxford, 1980), pp. 179–81; Halpin, 'Hohfeld's Conceptions: from Eight to Two', 44 *Cambridge Law Journal* (1985), pp. 435–57.

political objectives of the present time, namely the preservation of peace and the promotion of fundamental human rights,[6] which in turn reflect basic goods (or moral values),[7] first and foremost life and human dignity.

These five common elements are merely descriptive. In listing them here, there is no presumption that they should be regarded as prescriptive criteria that an international obligation must satisfy to be an obligation *erga omnes*. These elements have been inferred from the comparison among the four obligations *erga omnes* that the International Court indicated in its dictum by way of a non-exhaustive list of examples. Therefore, the fact that these elements are common to the four examples mentioned by the International Court does not mean that they must invariably apply to all obligations *erga omnes*.

These five common elements may provide, though, a useful framework for the analysis of a few selected candidates of obligations *erga omnes* put forward in the literature and before the International Court,[8] which will be examined in this chapter and in Chapter 9. The purpose is not to evaluate whether these selected candidates are credible examples of obligations *erga omnes*, but to dig further into the concept of obligations *erga omnes*.

While there have been attempts to provide lists of norms of *jus cogens*,[9] nobody has tried as yet to compile an inventory of existing or emerging obligations *erga omnes* (not, at least, to the writer's knowledge). Since this is still virgin ground, any selection of candidates is bound to be discretionary. In order that this exercise of discretion be not perceived as merely arbitrary, it is appropriate to indicate the reasons for choosing certain candidates instead of others.

[6] Pursuant to the two opening paragraphs of the Charter, the 'Peoples of the United Nations' are determined 'to save succeeding generations from the scourge of war', and 'to reaffirm faith in fundamental human rights'.

[7] Throughout this work, the terms 'good' and 'value' are used as synonyms, denoting something that is intrinsically worthy. On the philosophical history of these two terms, see Abbagnano, *Dizionario di filosofia*, 2nd edn. (Turin, 1971), pp. 100–2 (on 'good') and pp. 908–11 (on 'value'). In using the term 'value', the present writer is aware that '[c]ette expression ne signifie pas grand-chose parce qu'elle englobe finalement trop de choses.' However, he is also convinced, with the author of this remark, that '[e]lle renvoie . . . à un niveau très important de la réalité humaine: la morale.' (Lustiger, 'La personne devant le Cardinal Archevêque de Paris', *Recueil Dalloz Sirey* (1995, No. 2), p. 7.)

[8] One can hardly agree with de Hoogh's proposition that, from the International Court's examples, 'one cannot determine any criterion on which to base the *erga omnes* character of an obligation' (*Obligations 'Erga Omnes' and International Crimes*, p. 55). In making his remark, de Hoogh ascribes excessive importance to the circumstance that the examples given by the International Court belong to different areas of international law. While criticizing de Hoogh's remark, the present writer is aware that de Hoogh's study does not really focus on the concept of obligations *erga omnes* (and hence on their criteria of identification), but on international crimes and questions of State responsibility. (See ibid., pp. xvii and 4.)

[9] See, for example, Whiteman, '*Jus Cogens* in International Law, with a Projected List', 7 *Georgia Journal of International and Comparative Law* (1977), pp. 609–26; Haimbaugh, 'Jus Cogens: Root & Branch (an Inventory)', 3 *Touro Law Review* (1987), pp. 203–27; Hannikainen, *Peremptory Norms*, pp. 716–23.

The candidates that will be discussed in this chapter belong to the areas of (a) human rights, (b) development law, and (c) environmental law. Human rights are probably the leading idea of the present time and the only one that, together with peace, has attracted universal and unconditional support in the international community.[10] Three out of the four examples of obligations *erga omnes* given by the International Court relate to human rights. This shows that, while it is true that the concept of obligations *erga omnes* can and does contribute to the protection and promotion of human rights, it is equally true (as clearly indicated, for example, by Carillo Salcedo)[11] that human rights are instrumental to the consolidation of such concepts as obligations *erga omnes*. Hence one may confidently assume that this area of the law, which is constantly expanding through new 'generations' of rights and refined mechanisms for their protection, will continue to be a privileged domain for the evolution of the concept of obligations *erga omnes*. It is therefore relatively easy to justify further enquiry into this area.

Confining the concept of obligations *erga omnes* to human rights would be unduly restrictive. One of the four examples given by the International Court (the outlawing of acts of aggression) is not that of the protection of a human right, and this chapter and Chapter 9 will show how candidates of obligations *erga omnes* are emerging in other areas as well. The reason for concentrating on development law and environmental law is eminently practical: today the promotion of development and the preservation of the environment are key chapters of the international agenda, and their connection with peace and human rights is indisputable.[12] The same pragmatic approach justifies the selection of other candidates, to be examined in Chapter 9, which were discussed before the International Court a few years after the judgment in the *Barcelona Traction* case.

II. Candidates Protecting Human Rights other than those Listed by the International Court in its Dictum on Obligations *Erga Omnes*

In giving the examples of the outlawing of genocide and the protection from slavery and racial discrimination, the International Court wrote that

[10] See Henkin, *The Age of Rights* (New York, 1990), p. ix.

[11] *Soberania de los estados y derechos humanos en derecho internacional contemporaneo* (Madrid, 1995), pp. 106–11.

[12] On this connection, see, for example, the statement by Douglas Hurd, former Foreign Secretary of the United Kingdom and President of the Council of the European Communities, to the United Nations General Assembly on 22 September 1992 (reproduced in *Bulletin of the European Communities* (No. 9, Sep. 1992), pp. 97–100). In the literature, see Henkin, *International Law*, pp. 288–95; Giuliano, Scovazzi and Treves, *Diritto internazionale. Parte generale*, pp. 51–78.

obligations *erga omnes* may derive, in general, from the 'principles and rules concerning the basic rights of the human person'.[13] This language calls for comment.

The International Court referred to 'principles and rules'. Dillard, a former member of the International Court, once remarked that in the international literature the two terms of 'rule' and 'principle' are often used interchangeably.[14] His observation is correct. The word 'principle' tends to be used as a synonym of 'rule'.

In theory, one may still distinguish between the two terms. Different writers have based this distinction on different criteria, depending on their different jurisprudential premises.[15] For example, in the words of Fitzmaurice, a principle is something 'which underlies a rule, and explains or provides the reason for it'.[16] By equating a principle with an authoritative starting point for legal reasoning, this definition essentially translates into legal terms the Aristotelian definition of 'principle' or 'origin'.[17] Mosler, while accepting Fitzmaurice's definition as one of the possible meanings of 'principle', suggests an additional difference between the two terms: 'principles' have a 'wider meaning' and give rise to a 'wider variety of means of application and execution', whereas 'rules' define rights and obligations 'in a clearer way'.[18]

These definitions are not mutually exclusive, and there is no need to dwell upon them. By referring in its dictum to both terms, the International Court has clearly indicated that obligations *erga omnes* may derive from principles and rules alike. It has done so in a passage that specifically refers to the protection of human rights. Does this mean that the International Court's remark applies to human rights alone? Nothing in the dictum seems to require this conclusion. Moreover, the proposition that obligations *erga omnes* may derive in general not only from rules but also from principles introduces an element of analogy with *jus cogens*. During the work of codification that led to the adoption of the Vienna Convention, the proposed

[13] I.C.J. Reports 1970, p. 32, para. 34.

[14] 'Some Aspects of Law and Diplomacy', pp. 477–81. Likewise, on the International Court's practice, Mendelson has written that it 'tends to treat the two terms as synonymous' ('The International Court of Justice and the sources of international law', Lowe and Fitzmaurice, M. (eds.), *Fifty Years. Essays Jennings*, p. 80).

[15] In the general theory of law, see the definitions of 'principle' and 'rule' given in Pound, 'Hierarchy of Sources and Forms in Different Systems of Law', 7 *Tulane Law Review* (1933), pp. 482–4 (some extracts are reproduced in Dillard, 'Some Aspects of Law and Diplomacy', p. 477, note 3), and Paton, *Jurisprudence*, pp. 236–7. See also the extract from the *Gentini* case quoted in Cheng, *General Principles of Law*, p. 24.

[16] 'The General Principles', p. 7. On this definition, see the considerations developed in Scobbie, 'Towards the Elimination of International Law: Some Radical Scepticism about Sceptical Radicalism', 61 *B.Y.I.L.* (1990), p. 358, note 88.

[17] Aristotle, *The Complete Works*, 1012b34–1013a23 (Metaphysics).

[18] *The International Society*, p. 73.

examples of *jus cogens* included both principles and rules.[19] Indeed, it has been remarked that the very nature of *jus cogens*, which places it at the level of the fundamental principles of the international system, makes it more likely that principles rather than rules have a peremptory character.[20]

The issue becomes more complex if one tries to analyse the practical consequences, if any, that would attach to the proposition that obligations *erga omnes* derive from 'principles and rules'. In his dissenting opinion to the judgment of the International Court in the *East Timor* case,[21] Judge Weeramantry developed some thought-provoking considerations which are relevant to this point.

In 1991, Portugal instituted proceedings against Australia concerning certain Australian activities with respect to East Timor. Among other requests, Portugal asked the International Court to adjudge and declare that, by negotiating, concluding, and implementing the Timor Gap Cooperation Treaty of 1989 with Indonesia,[22] Australia was in breach of its obligation to respect the powers of Portugal as the administering Power of East Timor, and was infringing the right of the people of East Timor to self-determination and permanent sovereignty over natural resources.[23] As Australia raised preliminary questions of jurisdiction and admissibility,[24] the Agents of the parties agreed with the President of the International Court that these questions should be determined when the merits of the dispute were considered.[25] By a judgment delivered on 30 June 1995, the International Court concluded that, to decide the claims of Portugal, it

[19] See, for example, the International Law Commission's 'Draft Articles on the Law of Treaties', pp. 67–8, para. 3. This paragraph lists the *principle* of self-determination as one of the suggested examples of peremptory *rules*.

[20] Ziccardi, 'Règles d'organisation et règles de conduite en droit international. (Le droit commun et les ordres juridiques)', 152 Hague *Recueil* (1976, IV), p. 327: 'Le *jus cogens* s'exprime tant en forme de principes que de normes, selon qu'il énonce des fins et des résultats comme obligatoires et prééminents, ou qu'il dérive au contraire des types de comportement absolument obligatoires ou interdits . . . Que le *jus cogens* comprenne des principes plutôt que des normes, ressort de sa nature même, qui le place sur le plan des principes fondamentaux du système, considéré dans son unité globale, au point que son individualisation est celui de l'interprétation systématique.'

[21] *East Timor (Portugal* v. *Australia)*, Judgment, I.C.J. Reports 1995, pp. 139–223. (The writer is grateful to Mr Eduardo Valencia-Ospina, Registrar of the International Court, for providing him with a copy of the mimeographed text of the Portuguese Memorial and the Australian Counter-Memorial.)

[22] 'Treaty between Australia and Indonesia on the Zone of Cooperation in an Area between the Indonesian Province of East Timor and Northern Australia, done over the Zone of Cooperation, December 11, 1989', 29 *I.L.M.* (1990), pp. 469–537.

[23] See the bibliographical references to these rights in section III of this chapter.

[24] The final submissions of the parties are reproduced in para. 10 of the International Court's judgment.

[25] Pursuant to Art. 31 of the revised Rules of Court, '[i]n every case submitted to the Court, the President shall ascertain the views of the parties with regard to questions of procedure. For this purpose, he shall summon the agents of the parties to meet him as soon as possible after their appointment, and whenever necessary thereafter.'

would have to rule on the conduct of a third State (Indonesia) without this State's consent. Therefore, by fourteen votes to two, the International Court found that it could not exercise its jurisdiction to adjudicate on the dispute.

Judge Weeramantry was one of the two members of the International Court who dissented from this decision.[26] In his dissenting opinion, he wrote that self-determination is 'a right assertible *erga omnes*'.[27] This statement reflected a point made by Portugal in its Memorial,[28] which Australia did not contest—at least as a general proposition independently of its application to the case at hand[29]—and the International Court acknowledged in its judgment.[30] A more controversial part of the dissenting opinion is Judge Weeramantry's definition of the obligation correlative to the right of self-determination. According to Judge Weeramantry, the obligations to respect the right of self-determination and its 'basic constituent', namely the right to permanent sovereignty over natural resources,

> extend far further than mere compliance with specific rules or directions and the avoidance of prohibited conduct.[31]

On this basis, Judge Weeramantry rejected the argument put forward by Australia that this country had respected the right of self-determination, in the sense that it had not contravened either express directions from the United Nations or prohibitions under international law, with respect to East Timor. In other words, according to Judge Weeramantry, the test of the performance of an international obligation (and specifically the obligation *erga omnes* to respect self-determination) would be the compliance not only with the particular directions or prohibitions that it may contain, but also with its 'underlying norms and principles'.[32]

There is no need to discuss here the merits of these considerations and the conclusions derived by Judge Weeramantry with respect to the dispute between Portugal and Australia. The important point for the present analysis is that, by appealing to the 'underlying norms and principles', Judge Weeramantry drew from the obligation *erga omnes* to respect self-determination much wider consequences than those that Australia was ready to concede on the basis of a strict interpretation of the directions and

[26] The other judge who voted against the International Court's decision was Judge *ad hoc* Skubiszewski.

[27] *I.C.J. Reports* 1995, p. 202.

[28] Memorial Submitted by the Government of the Republic of Portugal, 18 November 1991, para. 4.71 (mimeographed text).

[29] Counter-Memorial of the Government of Australia, 1 June 1992, para. 194 (mimeographed text).

[30] *I.C.J. Reports* 1995, p. 102, para 29. In the literature, the character *erga omnes* of the obligation to respect self-determination is discussed in Guarino, *Autodeterminazione dei popoli e diritto internazionale* (Naples, 1984), especially pp. 189–207 and 223–32.

[31] *I.C.J. Reports* 1995, p. 210.

[32] Ibid., p. 211.

prohibitions embodied in this obligation.[33] Hence, irrespective of any theoretical disquisition on whether or not rules (or norms) differ from principles, in practice there may be different consequences depending on whether the origins of an obligation *erga omnes* are traced back to a broad principle or to a narrow rule.

The other expression used by the International Court in its dictum, which will now be examined, is 'basic rights of the human person'. This expression raises the difficulty (which goes beyond the context of obligations *erga omnes*) of defining which human rights may be regarded as 'basic' or 'fundamental'.[34] This dichotomy is not always easy to define, even in those legal systems that recognize a separate category of fundamental rights.[35] In international law, the two expressions are sometimes used interchangeably, both in official documents and in the literature.[36] A typical example is the passage in which Fawcett wrote that '[h]uman rights are sometimes called fundamental rights or basic rights or natural rights',[37] without any apparent distinction among these expressions.

Lately, there has been a revival of this terminological discussion, perhaps under the inspiration also of the express reference by the International Court, in its dictum, to 'basic' human rights.[38] For example, the issue was raised during the preparation of a resolution on extradition, which the

[33] On the distinction between the general 'principle' and the specific 'rules' relating to self-determination, see also Cassese, *Self-determination of peoples. A legal reappraisal* (Cambridge, 1995), pp. 126–33.

[34] Historically, the concept has been linked to natural law theories (Perrott, 'The Logic of Fundamental Rights', Bridge, Lasok, Perrott and Plender (eds.), *Fundamental Rights. A volume of essays to commemorate the 50th anniversary of the founding of the Law School in Exeter. 1923–1973* (London, 1973), pp. 1–17), although some writers have tried to justify it on other grounds (see, for example, Smith, J. C., *Legal Obligation* (London, 1976), p. 234).

[35] See, for example, with respect to Spanish law, Perez Luno, *Los derechos fundamentales*, 2nd edn. (Madrid, 1986) and, with respect to French law, Champeil-Desplats, 'La notion de droit "fondamental" et le droit constitutionnel français', *Recueil Dalloz Sirey* (1995, No. 42), pp. 323–9. See also, with respect to the European Convention on Human Rights, Sudre, 'Droits intangibles et/ou droits fondamentaux: y a-t-il des droits prééminents dans la Convention européenne des droits de l'homme?', *Liber Amicorum Marc-André Eissen* (Brussels and Paris, 1995), pp. 381–98.

[36] The wording of international conventions and other official documents is examined in Meron, 'On a Hierarchy of International Human Rights', 80 *A.J.I.L.* (1986), pp. 1–23.

[37] *The Law of Nations*, 2nd edn. (Harmondsworth, 1971), p. 159.

[38] The suggestion that behind the revival there may be the dictum on obligations *erga omnes* is advanced in Simma (ed.), *The Charter*, p. 779 (Partsch's commentary on Art. 55(c)). The influence of the dictum can also be seen, for example, in the International Law Commission's document headed 'State responsibility - Draft Commentaries to articles 13 and 14 of Part Two of the draft articles' (Doc.A/CN.4/L.521). In para. 27 of this document, one reads that, in drafting sub-paragraph (d) of Article 14, '[t]he Commission preferred the phrase "basic human rights", chosen by the International Court of Justice in its judgment in the Barcelona Traction case, to the phrase "fundamental human rights" which appears in Article 1, paragraph 3 of the United Nations Charter . . .'. (Footnote omitted.)

Institute of International Law adopted at its Cambridge session in 1983.[39] The final text of Article IV provides that extradition may be refused if there is a well-founded fear of violation of the 'fundamental human rights' of the accused in the territory of the requesting State.[40] The original draft prepared by Doehring, the rapporteur for the resolution, referred to the protection of the 'human rights', not 'fundamental human rights', of the accused.[41] The amendment to the original draft was the result of an exchange of views on the distinction between the two expressions that took place among the members of the committee working on the resolution.[42]

To sum up, the fact that the two expressions of 'human rights' and 'fundamental human rights' are sometimes used as synonyms (as a result also of a trend against 'atomizing human rights')[43] does not exclude the possibility that, at least for certain purposes, the distinction between the two may be important. In the case of obligations *erga omnes*, the issue behind this distinction may be formulated as follows: do all the international obligations for the protection of human rights constitute obligations *erga omnes*?

In its dictum, the International Court restricted its list of examples of obligations *erga omnes* in the area of human rights to three examples only, namely the prohibition of genocide and the protection from slavery and racial discrimination. Moreover, by confining its dictum to the 'basic rights of the human person', it seemed to convey the clear message that the character *erga omnes* does not apply indiscriminately to all principles and rules protecting human rights.[44] Likewise, the last Restatement on foreign relations law adopted by the American Law Institute, in listing human rights that would now be protected by international customs and entail the responsibility of a law-breaker to all other States (*erga omnes*), mentions only a few other obligations than those listed by the International Court in its dictum. The additional obligations are 'the murder or causing the dis-

[39] The text of this resolution (headed 'New problems of extradition') is now reproduced in Institut de Droit International (under the auspices of), *Tableau des Resolutions adoptées (1957–1991)* (Paris, 1992), pp. 161–5.

[40] For comments, see Schachter, *International Law*, p. 344.

[41] 60 *Ann. Institut* (1983, II), p. 214.

[42] Ibid., pp. 234–5 (Mosler); p. 239 (Salmon); p. 241 (Yankov); pp. 258–60 (in particular, the proposal by Schwebel).

[43] See Mbaye, 'Introduction (Human Rights and Rights of Peoples)', Bedjaoui (ed.), *International Law*, p. 1056, para. 65.

[44] This interpretation of the dictum is supported by some writers (for example, Kooijmans, 'In the shadowland between civil war and civil strife: some reflections on the standard-setting process', Delissen and Tanja (eds.), *Humanitarian Law. Essays Kalshoven*, p. 235) but rejected by others (for example, Provost, 'Reciprocity', p. 430, note 174). In the present writer's opinion, the restriction of the character *erga omnes* to the obligations protecting 'basic' human rights is supported not only by the dictum on obligations *erga omnes*, but also by another passage in the *Barcelona Traction* judgment (reproduced in section VI of Chapter 10, below), in which the International Court, while addressing the issue of protection against denial of justice (which is not binding *erga omnes*), correctly used the expression 'human rights' rather than 'basic human rights'.

appearance of individuals', 'torture or other cruel, inhuman, or degrading treatment or punishment', 'prolonged arbitrary detention', and 'a consistent pattern of gross violations of internationally recognized human rights'.[45]

The reason for referring to the Restatement is not to consider whether there are convincing arguments for concluding that each of the additional human rights listed in the Restatement is indeed protected by an obligation *erga omnes*. Nor is it to discuss whether international customs in the area of human rights give rise invariably to obligations *erga omnes*, as the Restatement seems to imply.[46] The important point here is a different one, namely the fact that the Restatement, almost twenty years after the International Court's dictum, took the same cautious approach and restricted the character *erga omnes* to only a few obligations in the area of human rights.[47]

A different approach was taken by the Institute of International Law, when it adopted a resolution on human rights and non-intervention at its session in Santiago de Compostela in 1989.[48] In it, the Institute put forward the proposition that the very obligation of States to ensure the protection of human rights is an obligation *erga omnes*. Article 1 of the resolution reads as follows:

Human rights are a direct expression of the dignity of the human person. The obligation of States to ensure their observance derives from the recognition of this dignity as proclaimed in the Charter of the United Nations and in the Universal Declaration of Human Rights.

This international obligation, as expressed by the International Court of Justice, is *erga omnes*; it is incumbent upon every State in relation to the international community as a whole, and every State has a legal interest in the protection of human

[45] *Third Restatement*, Section 702.

[46] A note of caution is necessary because Henkin (the Restatement's Chief Reporter) has on another occasion and in a different role made the following remark: 'I would be disposed to relate the idea of fundamental human rights to those that have become principles of customary law, whether or not they are also of *jus cogens*' (63 *Ann. Institut* (1989, I), p. 415). If customary rules protecting human rights and rules of *jus cogens* protecting human rights do not necessarily overlap, could not the same be said of the relationship between obligations deriving from customary rules protecting human rights and obligations *erga omnes* in the area of human rights?

[47] A similar approach was also taken in a document headed 'The Responsibility of the Government of Chile under International Law' (Doc.A/34/583/Add.1), p. 96, para. 190.

[48] The text of this resolution (headed 'The protection of human rights and the principle of non-intervention in internal affairs of states') is now reproduced in Institut de Droit International (under the auspices of), *Tableau des Resolutions adoptées (1957–1991)*, pp. 207–13. On this resolution, see Rucz, 'Les mesures unilatérales de protection des droits de l'homme devant l'Institut de droit international', 38 *A.F.D.I.* (1992), pp. 579–628. See also the considerations developed in Dupuy, R. J., 'L'action humanitaire', Delissen and Tanja (eds.), *Humanitarian Law. Essays Kalshoven*, pp. 74–5; Weil, 'Le droit international', pp. 343–4; Valticos, 'Des parallèles qui devraient se rejoindre: les méthodes de contrôle international concernant les conventions sur les droits de l'homme', Beyerlin, Bothe, Hofmann and Petersmann (eds.), *Recht. Festschrift Bernhardt*, p. 648.

rights. The obligation further implies a duty of solidarity among all States to ensure as rapidly as possible the effective protection of human rights throughout the world.[49]

The reasoning behind this text develops from the fundamental moral value of the 'dignity of the human person',[50] then to human rights as a 'direct expression'[51] of this value, and finally to the character *erga omnes* of the international obligation to observe such rights. The moral foundation of the concept of obligations *erga omnes* could not be expressed more clearly. However, for present purposes, the main aspect to consider is that, pursuant to Article 1 of the resolution, the character *erga omnes* would not attach to a specific obligation, but to the general obligation to ensure respect for human rights.[52]

[49] The French original of Article 1 reads as follows: 'Les droits de l'homme sont l'expression directe de la dignité de la personne humaine. L'obligation pour les Etats d'en assurer le respect découle de la reconnaissance même de cette dignité que proclament déjà la Charte des Nations Unies et la Déclaration universelle des droits de l'homme. Cette obligation internationale est, selon une formule utilisée par la Cour internationale de Justice, une obligation *erga omnes*; elle incombe à tout Etat vis-à-vis de la communauté internationale dans son ensemble, et tout Etat a un intérêt juridique à la protection des droits de l'homme. Cette obligation implique au surplus un devoir de solidarité entre tous les Etats en vue d'assurer le plus rapidement possible une protection universelle et efficace des droits de l'homme.'

[50] In the preparatory work of the resolution, Jean-Flavien Lalive criticized the use of the expression 'human person' (instead of 'man') as a 'nouveau jargon à la mode' that means nothing unless one were ready to accept that there are 'inhuman' or 'non-human' persons (63 *Ann. Institut* (1989, I), p. 428). This criticism is justified if it means that, on earth, *all* human beings, from conception to natural death, and *only* human beings are natural persons. (For a critical assessment of certain views expressed against this truth, see the editorial headed '"Chi" è persona? Persona umana e bioetica', 143 *La Civiltà cattolica* (1992, No. 3420), pp. 547–59; on the inherent dignity of every human life, in all stages of its development, see also Amerasinghe, *Studies in International Law* (Colombo, 1969), especially pp. 144–7 and 160–1.) In other respects, however, an outright rejection of the expression 'human person' is not entirely justified. The expression is used both in the United Nations Charter and the Universal Declaration of Human Rights, and so can hardly be regarded as a 'nouveau jargon à la mode'. In addition, 'person', as a philosophical concept, did not originate and develop as an exclusive attribute of human beings. In the sixth century, Boetius gave his classic definition of 'person' ('*naturae rationalis individua substantia*') in a treatise on the two natures (divine and human) in the one 'person' of Christ ('Liber de persona et duabus naturis contra Eutychen et Nestorium, ad Joannem Diaconum Ecclesiae Romanae', in *Manlii Severini Boetii Opera Omnia*, ii (Paris, 1847), column 1343c). Seven centuries later, Thomas Aquinas examined the name 'person' as an attribute of God (*Summa Theologiae*, I, q. 29, a. 3) which, like other names, applies by analogy to God and the human being (ibid., I, q. 13, a. 5). In this sense, the term 'person' is not an exclusive attribute of human beings.

[51] In earlier drafts of the resolution, it was written that human rights are 'strictly linked' ('étroitement liés') with human dignity. Then, Sahovic proposed to write instead that human rights are a 'direct expression', in the sense of being one of the constitutive elements, of human dignity. See 63 *Ann. Institut* (1989, I), p. 421.

[52] The English version of Article 1 provides that '[t]his international obligation [i.e. the obligation to ensure respect for human rights], as expressed by the International Court of Justice, is *erga omnes*'. This language is somewhat ambiguous, in that the parenthetical 'as expressed by the International Court' might either refer to the term '*erga omnes*' or instead qualify the international obligation *erga omnes*, in the sense that it would restrict the character *erga omnes* to the three examples of human rights listed by the International Court in its

An examination of the preparatory work of the resolution reveals that the prominent position of Article 1 in the final text, and its content, were the result of subsequent revisions. Initially, draft Article 1 dealt with the principle of non-intervention, while the obligation of States to respect human rights followed later, in draft Article 6. Yet it was fairly soon acknowledged that the principle of the respect for human rights should come first,[53] and therefore in all later drafts the opening article of the resolution proclaimed this principle.

The first draft reflected also the position that, while all human rights relate to the inherent dignity of the human person, only some of these rights are fundamental. Although this distinction had initially received unanimous support[54] within the committee that was responsible for drafting the resolution,[55] various considerations led to its rejection. First of all, there was the usual difficulty of identifying those human rights that may be regarded as fundamental. Henkin and Dinstein (who were not original members of the committee but joined it later) very convincingly criticized the underlying assumption of the initial draft, namely that fundamental human rights would coincide with non-derogable rights in a public emergency.[56] Secondly, already at the beginning of the committee's work, the rapporteur had been reluctant to overestimate the distinction between fundamental and all other human rights. The reason was that all human rights, whether fundamental or not, relate to the inherent dignity of every person, and the distinction would have no place in a resolution on the principle of non-intervention in the internal affairs of States. A State that has undertaken an international obligation to respect human rights (whether fundamental or not) cannot resort to the exception of domestic jurisdiction and

dictum. However, the French original of Article 1 ('Cette obligation internationale est, selon une formule utilisée par la Cour internationale de Justice, une obligation *erga omnes*') clearly indicates that the parenthetical phrase refers to the terminology introduced by the International Court and is not meant to restrict the character *erga omnes* to the three obligations protecting basic human rights listed by the International Court.

[53] See 63 *Ann. Institut* (1989, I), p. 314.

[54] See ibid. and also Paul De Visscher's and Ténékidès's views reproduced at pp. 361 and 365–6, respectively.

[55] The rapporteur for the resolution was Giuseppe Sperduti, whose contribution to the adoption of the resolution, and to its reference to obligations *erga omnes*, has been highlighted in Frowein, 'Reactions', p. 410. The other original members of the committee were Boutros-Ghali, Castaneda, R. J. Dupuy, J. F. Lalive, Marek, do Nascimento e Silva, Pescatore, Sahovic, Ténékidès, Truyol y Serra, Tunkin and P. De Visscher.

[56] See Dinstein's letter to the rapporteur dated 11 March 1986, and Henkin's letter to the rapporteur dated 25 March 1986, reproduced in 63 *Ann. Institut* (1989, I), pp. 412–13 and 414–16. On non-derogable rights in states of emergencies, see Cancado-Trindade, 'Co-existence and Co-ordination of Mechanisms of International Protection of Human Rights (at Global and Regional Levels)', 202 Hague *Recueil* (1987, II), pp. 75–90, and (more extensively) Oraa, *Human Rights in States of Emergency in International Law* (Oxford, 1992).

non-intervention in its internal affairs,[57] whenever questions arise with respect to the interpretation or application of its international engagements.[58] These considerations led the Institute of International Law to endorse the idea that the general obligation to respect human rights is itself an obligation *erga omnes*.

The interaction between the concept of obligations *erga omnes* and the exception of domestic jurisdiction has already been explored in the international literature.[59] Moreover, without relying on the concept of obligations *erga omnes*, in a special report submitted to the Institute of International Law in 1973, Fitzmaurice referred to a 'general duty of respect for human rights', which had already entered into the body of customary international law.[60] Within these limits, the idea embodied in Article 1 of the Institute's resolution is wholly acceptable.

A more troublesome interpretation is the one that has led Dinstein, for example, to suggest that Article 1 of the Institute's resolution means that every right recognized in the Universal Declaration of Human Rights creates an obligation *erga omnes*.[61] In the same vein, Meron has written that the distinction proposed by the International Court between basic and other human rights is no longer acceptable (at least with respect to the character *erga omnes*), because 'international practice and scholarly opinion seem to have moved well beyond the *erga omnes* dictum of *Barcelona Traction*'.[62] While these views may or may not be agreeable as statements of desirable developments in the area of human rights, one may legitimately doubt whether they accurately reflect the present reality of obligations *erga omnes*. Moreover, these views are based on ideas which, while entirely respectable, are open to question, such as the idea that an obligation to respect a certain human right may well be *erga omnes* without necessarily belonging to *jus cogens*.[63]

[57] On domestic jurisdiction, see Brownlie, *Principles*, pp. 291–7 and 553–4. Among the various monographs on the subject, there is one written by the rapporteur for the resolution, namely Sperduti, *Il dominio riservato* (Milan, 1970).

[58] See the rapporteur's letter to Paul De Visscher dated 30 September 1983, reproduced in 63 *Ann. Institut* (1989, I), p. 316, and the arguments developed ibid., at pp. 381–8.

[59] See Henkin, 'Human Rights and "Domestic Jurisdiction"', Buergenthal (ed.), *Human Rights, International Law and the Helsinki Accord* (Montclair, N.J., 1977), pp. 21–40 (especially pp. 27–8). See also Oellers-Frahm, 'Comment: The erga omnes Applicability of Human Rights', 30 *Archiv des Völkerrechts* (1992), pp. 28–37 (especially pp. 29–30); Bedjaoui and Thierry, 'Future of International Law', Bedjaoui (ed.), *International Law*, p. 1243, para. 36; Schwebel, 'Human Rights', p. 965; Simma (ed.), *The Charter*, pp. 152–3 (Ermacora's commentary on Art. 2(7)).

[60] 'The Future of Public International Law and of the International Legal System in the Circumstances of Today', Institut de Droit International (under the auspices of), *Livre du Centenaire 1873–1973. Evolution et perspectives du droit international* (Basel, 1973), p. 323, para. 111(c).

[61] 'The erga omnes Applicability of Human Rights', 30 *Archiv des Völkerrechts* (1992), p. 17.

[62] *Human Rights and Humanitarian Norms as Customary Law* (Oxford, 1989), p. 199.

[63] See Dinstein, 'The erga omnes Applicability', p. 17. The same view is shared by Meron (*Human Rights and Humanitarian Norms*, p. 194), who makes extensive use of arguments

To sum up, the search for a deeper understanding of the consequences deriving from the concept of obligations *erga omnes* for the protection of all human rights has led some writers to conclude that the character *erga omnes* would inhere in all obligations deriving from international customary rules that protect human rights. However, the International Court, by restricting its reference to *basic* human rights and listing a few specific examples, seems to have implicitly rejected this conclusion. While certain effects deriving from the concept of obligations *erga omnes* (such as its influence on the scope of the exception of domestic jurisdiction) may strengthen the protection of human rights generally, the fact remains that each obligation should be assessed on its own merits, with a view to ascertaining whether or not it is an obligation *erga omnes*.

III. Candidates in the Area of Development Law

Since the end of the Second World War, and particularly since the end of the colonial era in the early sixties, the international community has become aware that development is a key factor in the promotion of its common interests, in the sense that peace and human rights risk becoming empty words if individuals and entire populations remain in the grip of hunger, malnutrition and exploitation. By its origin, development is not primarily a legal concept. Questions of economics and ethics are crucial: no legal right to development, however clearly articulated, can achieve its purpose without being backed by adequate resources and, above all, by a change of moral behaviour in developed and developing countries.[64]

The United Nations Charter states, in its Preamble, that the achievement of 'social progress and better standards of life' is one of the four aims of the United Nations (together with peace, human rights and justice), and in Article 55 it expressly refers to development. When the Charter was adopted, the concept of a legal right to development had not yet entered into international legal parlance, but this was no obstacle to its growing

derived from the so-called 'self-existent obligations' (on which, see section IV of Chapter 10, below) in support of his views on obligations *erga omnes* (ibid., pp. 197–8).

[64] The need for a changed moral attitude in support of all rights reflecting fundamental values is emphasized in the 'Yamoussoukro Declaration on Peace in the Minds of Men', adopted at an international congress held in Yamoussoukro, Ivory Coast, from 26 June to 1 July 1989 on the initiative of UNESCO (and attended, among other authorities, by José Maria Ruda, then President of the International Court). The text of the Yamoussoukro Declaration is reproduced in 3 *International Law: News and Information from Asia and the Pacific* (June 1989), p. 18. Likewise, Weeramantry has written that, while development may well include 'the increased availability of consumer goods and a heightened level of industry', the 'core of the concept . . . centres around the dignity of every human being.' ('The Teaching of Human Rights', 1 *Sri Lanka Journal of International Law* (1989), p. 89.)

influence. Drawing a general conclusion from the early history of the right to development, Brownlie has remarked that '[i]deas may have currency and influence without having any connection with law'.[65]

The general idea of a 'law of development' surfaced in the francophone literature of the sixties.[66] But the credit for formulating for the first time, in the early seventies, the idea of a 'right to development' is usually ascribed to Keba Mbaye, a former Vice-President of the International Court.[67] With the passage of time, the concept acquired greater significance, when it was repeatedly proclaimed in a series of international agreements and United Nations resolutions.

These instruments belong to different traditions, which reflect the composite origins of the right to development. There is the tradition of human rights (both individual and collective, including the right to self-determination),[68] represented by such agreements as the International Covenant on Economic, Social and Cultural Rights,[69] the African Charter on Human and Peoples' Rights,[70] and the United Nations Convention on the Rights of the Child.[71] Then there is a series of resolutions adopted by the General Assembly and its subsidiary organs, which aim at promoting a new order based on considerations of international social justice and co-operation among States, such as the Declaration on the Establishment of a New International Economic Order and the Charter of Economic Rights

65 *The Human Right to Development* (London, 1989), p. 14.

66 According to Virally ('Vers un droit international du développement', 11 *A.F.D.I.* (1965), p. 420, note 1), it was André Philip who coined the expression 'international law of development' ('droit international du développement').

67 See his article headed 'Le droit au développement comme un droit de l'homme', 5 *Revue des droits de l'homme* (1972), pp. 503–34. R. J. Dupuy ('Thème et variations sur le droit au développement', *Mélanges offerts à Ch. Chaumont: Le droit des peuples à disposer d'eux-mêmes. Méthodes d'analyse du international* (Paris, 1984), p. 264) has also recalled, among the earliest references to the concept, a 1969 message of Cardinal Duval, then archbishop of Algiers.

68 On 'collective' rights, see Crawford (ed.), *The Rights of Peoples* (Oxford, 1988); *Les droits de l'homme, droits collectifs ou individuels. Acts du Colloque de Strasbourg des 13 et 14 mars 1979* (Paris, 1980). On the principle of self-determination, see Brownlie, *Principles*, pp. 595–8.

69 Adopted and opened for signature, ratification and accession by General Assembly Resolution 2200 A(XXI) of 16 December 1966, *Gen. Ass. Off. Recs., Twenty-first Session, Supp. 16*, p. 49 (Doc.A/6319). The text of the Resolution and the annexed International Covenant on Economic, Social and Cultural Rights is reproduced in Brownlie, *Basic Documents*, pp. 263–75; id. (ed.), *Basic Documents on Human Rights*, pp. 114–24. The Covenant entered into force on 3 January 1976. One hundred and thirty-three States have become parties (*Multilateral Treaties Deposited with the Secretary-General. Status as at 31 December 1995*, p. 111).

70 For references see section I of Chapter 6, above.

71 Adopted without a vote by General Assembly Resolution 44/25 of 20 November 1989. The text of the Convention is reproduced in Brownlie (ed.), *Basic Documents on Human Rights*, pp. 182–202. The Convention entered into force on 2 September 1990. One hundred and eighty-five States have become parties (*Multilateral Treaties Deposited with the Secretary-General. Status as at 31 December 1995*, p. 198).

and Duties of States adopted in 1974.[72] Finally, there are two important declarations which contain elements of both traditions, namely the Declaration on Social Progress and Development adopted in 1969,[73] and the Declaration on the Right to Development adopted in 1986.[74]

The present work cannot summarize the many controversies that still attach to the right to development, above all its status and content under customary international law.[75] Rather, it is advisable to concentrate briefly

[72] The Declaration was adopted by General Assembly Resolution 3201(S-VI) of 1 May 1974, and is reproduced in 13 *I.L.M.* (1974), p. 715. The Charter was adopted by Resolution 3281 (XXIX) on 12 December 1974, and is reproduced in Brownlie, *Basic Documents*, pp. 240–54. On the concept of a new international economic order, see Brownlie, 'Legal Status of Natural Resources', pp. 255–71; Bedjaoui, *Towards a new international economic order* (Paris, New York and London, 1979); Makarczyk, *Principles of a New International Economic Order* (Dordrecht, 1988); Dupuy, R. J. (ed.), *The New International Economic Order. Commercial, Technological and Cultural Aspects* (Workshop organized by the Hague Academy of International Law and the United Nations University, held at The Hague on 23–25 Oct. 1980) (The Hague, 1981). On the Charter, see Brownlie, *Principles*, pp. 541–3 (with extensive bibliography); Seidl-Hohenveldern, 'The Charter of Economic Rights and Duties of States', *Studi in onore di Giorgio Balladore Pallieri* (Milan, 1978), ii, pp. 550–6.

[73] Adopted by Resolution 2542 (XXIV) of 11 December 1969. The text of the Declaration is reproduced in *United Nations Juridical Yearbook 1969*, pp. 55–63. On the same day, the General Assembly adopted Resolution 2543 (XXIV) on the application of the Declaration.

[74] Adopted by General Assembly Resolution 41/128 of 4 December 1986, by one hundred and forty-six votes with eight abstentions and one against (the United States). On the same day, the General Assembly adopted Resolution 41/133 on certain measures required to achieve the right to development. (This resolution was supported by one hundred and thirty-three States, and many of the developed States that had voted in favour of the Declaration decided to abstain or vote against this resolution.) The text of the Declaration (except for the Preamble), and a thorough discussion of it, can be found in Brownlie, *The Human Right to Development*. See also Kenig-Witkowska, 'The UN Declaration on the right to development in the light of its travaux préparatoires', de Waart, Peters and Denters (eds.), *International Law and Development* (Dordrecht, 1988), pp. 381–8; Petersmann, 'The Right to Development in the United Nations: An Opportunity for Strengthening Popular Participation in Development. Programs and Prospects', Jekewitz, Klein, Kühne, Petersmann and Wolfrum (eds.), *Des Menschen Recht. Festschrift Partsch*, pp. 125–40.

[75] Over the last twenty years, many works have been published on the right to development and more generally on the law of development. See, for example, Gros Espiell, *Derecho internacional del desarrollo* (Valladolid, 1975); Schachter, 'The Evolving International Law of Development' 15 *C.J.T.L.* (1976), pp. 1–16; Flory, *Droit international du développement* (Paris, 1977); Dupuy, R. J. (ed.), *The Right to Development at the International Level—Workshop, The Hague, 16–18 October 1979* (Alphen aan den Rijn, 1980); Tomuschat, 'Das Recht auf Entwicklung', 25 *G.Y.I.L.* (1982), pp. 85–112 (in German, with English summary); Virally, 'Panorama', pp. 317–32; Flory, Mahiou and Henry (eds.), *La formation des normes en droit international du développement—Table Ronde franco-magrébine Aix-en-Provence, 7 et 8 octobre 1982* (Paris and Algiers, 1984); Uribe Vargas, 'La troisième génération des droits de l'homme', 184 Hague *Recueil* (1984, I), pp. 355–76 (especially pp. 367–76); Pellet, *Le droit international du développement*, 2nd edn. (Paris, 1987); Snyder and Slinn (eds.), *International Law of Development: Comparative Perspectives* (Abingdon, 1987); Cassese, *International Law*, pp. 351–75; Alston, 'Some Notes on the Concept of the Right to Development', Prémont (ed.), *Essays on the Concept of a 'Right to Live' in Memory of Yougindra Khushalani* (Brussels, 1988), pp. 74–84; Abi-Saab, 'Le droit au développement', 44 *Ann. suisse* (1988), pp. 9–24; Bedjaoui, 'The Right to Development', Bedjaoui (ed.), *International Law*, pp. 1177–1203; Carty (ed.), *Law and Development* (Aldershot, 1992), pp. 167–330; Schachter, 'Human Rights and Economic Development', Bello and Ajibola (eds.), *Essays in honour of Judge Taslim Olawale*

on certain suggestions relating to the opposability *erga omnes* of the right to development and its correlative obligation. A useful starting point is provided by the two General Assembly declarations of 1969 and 1986, which have just been mentioned. Article 1 of the Declaration on Social Progress and Development reads as follows:

All peoples and all human beings, without distinction as to race, colour, sex, language, religion, nationality, ethnic origin, family or social status, or political or other conviction, shall have the right to live in dignity and freedom and to enjoy the fruits of social progress and should, on their part, contribute to it.

This text expressly relates social progress to human dignity, a basic value which underlies the human rights listed by the International Court as examples of obligations *erga omnes*. The Declaration on the Right to Development contains other important elements. Article 1 of this declaration reads as follows:

1. The right to development is an inalienable human right by virtue of which every human person and all peoples are entitled to participate in, contribute to and enjoy economic, social, cultural and political development, in which all human rights and fundamental freedoms can be fully realised.
2. The human right to development also implies the full realisation of the right of peoples to self-determination, which includes, subject to relevant provisions of both International Covenants on Human Rights, the exercise of their inalienable right to full sovereignty over all their natural wealth and resources.

This article defines the right to development as an 'inalienable' right inhering in every person (as an individual right) and in all peoples (as a collective right). It also establishes a link between this right and the peoples' rights to self-determination and to the sovereignty over their natural resources, i.e. two rights deriving from rules which, according to some writers, probably belong to *jus cogens*.[76]

Elias (Dordrecht, 1992), i, pp. 389–98; Chowdhury, Denters and de Waart (eds.), *The Right to Development in International Law* (Dordrecht, 1992); Bulajic, *Principles of International Development Law. Progressive Development of the Principles of International Law Relating to the New International Economic Order*, 2nd edn. (Dordrecht, 1993); Cancado Trindade, 'Environment and Development: Formulation and Implementation of the Right to Development as a Human Right', 3 *Asian Yearbook of International Law* (1993), pp. 15–45; Steiner and Alston (eds.), *International Human Rights in Context. Law, Politics, Morals. Texts and Materials* (Oxford, 1996), pp. 1110–46. In the award rendered on 14 February 1985 for the delimitation of the maritime boundary between Guinea and Guinea-Bissau, the *ad hoc* arbitral tribunal (composed by Manfred Lachs (President), Keba Mbaye and Mohammed Bedjaoui) wrote in para. 123 that it could not 'contest the right of the peoples concerned to a level of economic and social development which fully preserves their dignity' (25 *I.L.M.* (1986), p. 302).

[76] See, for example, Brownlie, *Principles*, p. 513. (Brownlie had used a more tentative language in the earlier editions of his *Principles*. While Jennings, at p. 564 of his general course at the Hague Academy, criticized Brownlie's reference to self-determination and permanent sovereignty in the context of *jus cogens*, Lachs, at p. 340, note 794, of his general course at the Hague Academy, acknowledged that Brownlie was merely referring to 'candidate rules'.) See

Apart from these elements, the two declarations do not expressly state that the right to development is opposable *erga omnes*. Nor do more precise indications emerge from the practice of States, particularly as certain broad statements on development in the context of the promotion of international justice have dubious evidentiary value for a legal right to development. For example, the head of the delegation of the Holy See to the United Nations Conference on Environment and Development (the Rio Conference)[77] spoke of an 'inalienable right and duty of all peoples to development'.[78] However, no hasty conclusion should be drawn from this statement, because the main (although not exclusive) inspiration of the Holy See at the Rio Conference, as on other occasions, was to voice religious and moral concerns rather than articulate detailed legal rights and obligations.[79]

In the international literature, a forceful argument in support of the character *erga omnes* of the right to development was made by Bedjaoui in an article in which he developed, under a self-explanatory heading, some 'unorthodox' reflections.[80] Though unorthodox, Bedjaoui's considerations deserve to be examined in some detail.

According to Bedjaoui, the right to development is based on the right to life, the right to self-determination and international solidarity, which Bedjaoui defines as the 'realization of the interdependence of nations'.[81] Bedjaoui believes that the rights to life and self-determination derive from rules of *jus cogens*, with the consequence that the right to development, based on these rights, would likewise have a peremptory character. In Bedjaoui's view, it would be contradictory to say on the one hand that the prohibition of genocide, which aims at protecting the elementary right to life, derives from a rule of *jus cogens*, but on the other hand that the right to development, which aims at protecting the same right to life, does not also derive from a rule of *jus cogens*. In other words, the ground for Bedjaoui's conclusion on the peremptory character of the right to development is essentially an argument based on analogy.

also Gros Espiell, 'Self-Determination and *Jus Cogens*', Cassese (ed.), *U.N. Law Fundamental Rights. Two Topics in International Law* (Alphen aan den Rijn, 1979), pp. 167–73. A classic statement on the peremptory character of the right to self-determination is in Judge Ammoun's separate opinion to the judgment on the merits in the *Barcelona Traction* case (I.C.J. Reports 1970, p. 304, para. 11). On the peremptory character of the principle of permanent sovereignty over natural resources, see the considerations developed later in this section.

[77] On the Rio Conference, see section IV, below.

[78] 'All human needs must be respected (Intervention of Archbishop Martino at the UN Conference on Environment and Development)', *L'Osservatore Romano* (Weekly Edition in English) (17 June 1992), p. 13.

[79] See ibid., and also 'Holy See and the "Earth Summit"—Memorandum on the Holy See's position on environment and development', *L'Osservatore Romano* (Weekly Edition in English) (10 June 1992), p. 6.

[80] 'Some Unorthodox Reflections on the "Right to Development"', Snyder and Slinn (eds.), *International Law of Development*, pp. 87–116.

[81] Ibid., pp. 93–101.

Bedjaoui's argument has the obvious merit of underlining the link between the right to development and other basic rights such as the right to life and to self-determination. However, to become a rule of *jus cogens*, an international rule must satisfy certain specific criteria, including acceptance and recognition as a rule of *jus cogens* by the international community of States as a whole.[82] An argument based on analogy will not, as a rule, do away with the need to prove that these criteria are satisfied. This point was clearly made in an award on the delimitation of the maritime boundary between Senegal and Guinea-Bissau, in which the international Arbitration Tribunal (of which Bedjaoui was a member) rejected for lack of evidence an argument put forward by Guinea-Bissau that the principle of permanent sovereignty over natural resources was a corollary of the principle of self-determination, and thus partook of its peremptory character.[83]

An additional difficulty attaching to Bedjaoui's argument is the definition of the precise content of the right to development and its corresponding obligation. Bedjaoui identifies two components in this right.[84] The first one is the right of each State to be, in Bedjaoui's words, the 'master in its own house'. This aspect would be an essential requirement for the effective protection of State sovereignty, in the sense that sovereignty would be fictitious for those States that have not reached an adequate level of economic development. One practical consequence is that every State would have an inalienable right of permanent sovereignty over its natural resources.[85] In other words, the character *erga omnes* of the right to development would

[82] See section III of Chapter 3, above.

[83] *Arbitration Tribunal for the Determination of the Maritime Boundary (Guinea-Bissau* v. *Senegal)*, 83 *I.L.R.* (1990), p. 26, para. 43. The Arbitration Tribunal, composed of Barberis (President), Bedjaoui and Gros (Arbitrators), rendered the arbitral award on 31 July 1989. On 24 August 1989, Guinea-Bissau challenged the arbitral award before the International Court, which, by a judgment dated 12 November 1991, confirmed the validity of the award. In the English translation from the French original, the relevant passage from para. 43 of the arbitral award reads as follows: 'the relation between these two propositions is not that of a corollary in which the soundness of one proposition can be inferred from that of the other by a simple operation of formal logic. Guinea-Bissau has not put forward any evidence or any demonstration to show that the logical relation existing between the two rules is that of a corollary. The mere assertion that there is a certain logical relationship between two propositions is not sufficient. The rule invoked by Guinea-Bissau has a content which cannot be inferred from the right of peoples to self-determination. It constitutes a legal norm independent of the principle of self-determination and one which is connected more with the principle of effectiveness and the rules governing the formation of States in the international sphere.'

[84] 'Some Unorthodox Reflections', pp. 101–11.

[85] See the United Nations General Assembly resolution 1803 (XVII), adopted in 1962 by eighty-seven votes to two, with two abstentions, reproduced in Brownlie, *Basic Documents*, pp. 235–9. On the concept of permanent sovereignty over natural resources, see id., *Principles*, pp. 539–41. On the wider issue of access to, and sharing of, natural resources, see id., *Loaves and Fishes: Access to Natural Resources and International Law (An Inaugural Lecture)* (London, 1978); Schachter, *Sharing the World's Resources* (New York, 1977); id., 'Principles of International Social Justice', *Jus et Societas. Essays in Tribute to Wolfgang Friedmann* (The Hague, 1979), pp. 249–77.

entail the universal opposability of the principle of permanent sovereignty over natural resources, a proposition which was controversial when Bedjaoui wrote his article and remains controversial today.[86]

The second component of the right to development, as identified by Bedjaoui, is largely programmatic and embodies considerations of international social justice, such as fair prices for raw materials and an equitable share of the goods which are part of the common heritage of mankind. This component implies a positive obligation, i.e. an obligation not only to abstain from doing certain acts but also to do certain other acts. This is precisely the point where Bedjaoui's argument is most problematic, at least for the purposes of the present analysis. As was mentioned in section I, above, one of the common elements emerging from the examples of obligations *erga omnes* given by the International Court is that these examples are essentially those of negative obligations. With respect to the wider concept of international public policy, Schwarzenberger has written that all rules of public policy 'are merely disabling', in the sense that they can do no more than prohibit 'anything contrary to the supreme interests of international society'.[87] Some writers have made similar considerations on peremptory rules,[88] while others are against restricting *jus cogens* to prohibitory norms.[89] As in the case of international public policy and *jus cogens*, in the case also of obligations *erga omnes* it is legitimate to ask whether they must invariably have a prohibitory content, in the sense of prohibiting (or protecting from) the commission of certain acts.

[86] Compare, for example, the arbitral award rendered on 19 January 1977 in *Texaco Overseas Petroleum Company/California Asiatic Oil Company* v. *Libyan Arab Republic* (R. J. Dupuy, Sole Arbitrator), 17 *I.L.M.* (1978), pp. 25–6, paras. 74–8, with the arbitral award rendered on 24 March 1982 in *Government of Kuwait* v. *American Independent Oil Company Aminoil* (Reuter, President; Sultan and Fitzmaurice, Members), 66 *I.L.R.* (1984), pp. 587–8. In the literature, compare Jiménez de Aréchaga, 'International Law in the Past Third of a Century', pp. 297–8, with Seidl-Hohenveldern, *International Economic Law*, 2nd edn. (Dordrecht, 1992), pp. 102–3. See also Chowdhury, 'Permanent sovereignty and its impact on stabilization clauses, standards of compensation and patterns of development co-operation', Hossain and Chowdhury (eds.), *Permanent Sovereignty Over Natural Resources in International Law. Principle and Practice* (New York, 1984), pp. 51–2 and 57; Peters, Schrijver and de Waart, 'Responsibility of States in Respect of the Exercise of Permanent Sovereignty over Natural Resources; An Analysis of Some Principles of the Seoul Declaration (1986) by the International Law Association', 36 *Netherlands International Law Review* (1989), pp. 292–4.

[87] 'International Jus Cogens?', p. 469.

[88] For example, Simma, in writing on fundamental human rights belonging to *jus cogens*, has remarked that '[l]ike most, if not all, rules of *jus cogens*, these human rights obligations will be obligations on States to abstain from certain inhuman actions...' ('International Human Rights and General International Law: A Comparative Analysis', 4 *Collected Courses of the Academy of European Law* (1993, II), p. 226.)

[89] See, for example, Picone, 'Diritto internazionale dell'economia e costituzione economica dell'ordinamento internazionale', Picone and Sacerdoti (eds.), *Diritto internazionale dell'economia. Raccolta sistematica dei principali atti normativi internazionali ed interni con testi introduttivi e note* (Milan, 1982), p. 59, note 58 (where the author touches upon the question of the positive or negative content of peremptory rules in the broader context of his considerations on the possibility that States may be called to act, *uti universi*, on behalf of the international community).

In principle, prohibitions have the virtue of binding in absolute terms, irrespective of the particular circumstances. On the contrary, the implementation of positive prescriptions depends on the particular circumstances, which may or may not allow a positive prescription to achieve its stated aim. Thus, it should not be surprising that the International Court, in its dictum, restricted the list of obligations *erga omnes* to a few negative obligations. However, after the dictum, the proposition that obligations *erga omnes* may also include positive obligations has been advanced in the international literature, and reflected in at least one pronouncement of the International Court and several opinions of its members.

In the literature, apart from general statements,[90] the example provided by Bedjaoui is not an isolated candidate of a positive obligation *erga omnes*. Another example comes from international humanitarian law.[91] Article 1 of each of the four Geneva Conventions of 1949 provides that the contracting States to each Convention undertake not only to respect but also to 'ensure respect' for the Convention 'in all circumstances'.[92] According to the prevailing interpretation, this obligation comprises the duty of each contracting State (a) to take all necessary measures in order that its contractual obligations be respected, and (b) to act in order that another contracting party failing to respect its obligations be brought back to compliance.[93] In the opinion of many writers, the rules giving rise to the conventional obligations covered by Article 1 have become rules of customary international law, and the obligation 'to respect and to ensure respect' has become an obligation *erga omnes*.[94]

[90] For example, Nastase has written that obligations *erga omnes* 'can be obligations *in non faciendo* or *in faciendo*.' ('The Right to Peace', Bedjaoui (ed.), *International Law*, p. 1225.)

[91] The expression 'humanitarian law' is used here in its traditional sense, as synonymous with 'law of armed conflicts'. The expression 'humanitarian law' was apparently introduced by Pictet (see Pictet, *Development and Principles of International Humanitarian Law* (Dordrecht, 1985), p. 1).

[92] See Convention (I) for the Amelioration of the Condition of the Wounded and Sick in Armed Forces in the Field; Convention (II) for the Amelioration of the Condition of Wounded, Sick and Shipwrecked Members of Armed Forces at Sea; Convention (III) Relative to the Treatment of Prisoners of War; Convention (IV) Relative to the Protection of Civilian Persons in Time of War. All four Conventions were signed at Geneva on 12 August 1949. Their text is reproduced in Roberts and Guelff (eds.), *Documents on the Laws of War*, 2nd edn. (Oxford, 1989), pp. 169–337.

[93] See, for example, Pictet (ed.), *Commentary. III Geneva Convention Relative to the Treatment of Prisoners of War* (Geneva, 1960), pp. 17–18 (commentary on Article 1).

[94] Condorelli and Boisson de Chazournes, 'Quelques remarques à propos de l'obligation des Etats de "respecter et faire respecter" le droit international humanitaire "en toutes circonstances"', Swinarski (ed.), *Studies and essays on international humanitarian law and Red Cross principles in honour of Jean Pictet* (Geneva and The Hague, 1984), pp. 17–35. See also Abi-Saab, 'The specificities of humanitarian law', ibid., p. 270; Barile, '*Obligationes erga omnes* e individui nel diritto internazionale umanitario', 68 *Riv. dir. int.* (1985), pp. 5–31; Post, 'Some Curiosities in the Sources of the Law of Armed Conflict Conceived in a General International

Two cases brought before the International Court, which have been examined earlier in this work, provide the opportunity for additional thoughts on this issue.[95] In Chapter 4, some evidence was examined in support of the proposition that the prohibition of unnotified mining is valid *erga omnes*. If this is the case, then a State would comply with this prohibition by notifying international shipping of the existence of a minefield. Hence the international prohibition *erga omnes* relating to minelaying would comprise a positive obligation to perform a certain act, i.e. notification.

Similar considerations may be made with respect to the international obligations relating to genocide. As was mentioned in Chapter 5 of this work, the judgment on preliminary objections in the case brought by the Republic of Bosnia-Herzegovina against the Federal Republic of Yugoslavia contains a passage (endorsed with some qualifications by Judge Oda, and criticized by Judge *ad hoc* Kreca) that extends the character *erga omnes* to the obligations to prevent and punish acts of genocide. Hence the international obligations *erga omnes* relating to genocide would comprise positive obligations to perform certain acts, i.e. the prevention and punishment of genocide.

These two examples of positive obligations *erga omnes* have an element in common, namely the fact that they are incidental to negative obligations: in the case of the obligation to notify the existence of a minefield, the negative obligation is (at least indirectly) the prohibition of the illegal use of force, while in the case of the obligation to prevent and punish acts of genocide, the negative obligation is (evidently) the prohibition of genocide.

Despite this common element, which might reflect a restrictive view of positive obligations *erga omnes*, the configuration of such obligations remains problematic. In theory, it is difficult to see how an obligation that is meant to be binding irrespective of any particular circumstances may be a positive prescription. Irrespective of this theoretical difficulty, the identification and enforcement of positive obligations *erga omnes* would require, in practice, a high degree of cohesion within the international community. For both reasons, much caution needs to the exercised when weighing the evidence in support of positive obligations *erga omnes*.

Legal Perspective', 25 *Netherlands Yearbook of International Law* (1994), pp. 109–13; Schindler, 'Die erga omnes-Wirkung des humanitären Völkerrechts', Beyerlin, Bothe, Hofmann and Petersmann (eds.), *Recht. Festschrift Bernhardt*, pp. 199–211; Paust, 'The Complex Nature, Sources and Evidences of Customary Human Rights', 25 *Georgia Journal of International and Comparative Law* (1995/96), pp. 152–3.

[95] Apart from these cases, it should be recalled that, in his declaration attached to the International Court's advisory opinion on the *Legality of the Threat or Use of Nuclear Weapons*, President Bedjaoui wrote that the 'double *obligation générale* . . . de négocier de bonne foi et de parvenir au résultat recherché' is opposable *erga omnes*. (I.C.J. Reports 1996 (mimeographed text), p. 5, para. 23, of President Bedjaoui's declaration.)

IV. Candidates in the Area of Environmental Law

Like development law, environmental law represents a fairly recent development in international relations.[96] While international conventions for the protection of nature and wildlife,[97] as well as arbitral awards and international decisions articulating fundamental principles of environmental law,[98] date back some decades, the turning point for the emergence of an international law of the environment was the United Nations Conference on the Human Environment, which took place in Stockholm in 1972.[99] It was after this Conference that the expression 'international environmental law' entered into widespread use, and that treaties, resolutions and writings relating to the environment started accumulating.[100]

The Stockholm Conference consecrated the ideas, among others, that (a) the environment is a global entity to be protected in its entirety (although this does not diminish the importance of particular rules applicable to different sources of pollution and to different components of the environment), and (b) environmental protection is a necessary condition for

[96] See Kiss and Shelton, *International Environmental Law* (New York and London, 1991), pp. 33–54. In municipal law too, a systematic regulation for the protection of the environment represents a fairly recent development. However, environmental pollution is an old problem and early attempts to limit it date back, in England, to the reign of Edward I (Markesinis and Deakin, *Tort Law*, 3rd edn., (Oxford, 1994), pp. 455–6, note 18).

[97] See, for example, the Convention Relative to the Preservation of Fauna and Flora in their Natural State, done in London on 8 November 1933 (172 *L.N.T.S.* 241), and the Convention on Nature Protection and Wildlife Preservation in the Western Hemisphere, done in Washington on 12 October 1940 (161 *U.N.T.S.* 193).

[98] The three classic cases are, in chronological order, the *Trail Smelter* case (II arbitral award, 11 Mar. 1941), R.I.A.A., iii, p. 1905; the *Corfu Channel* case (judgment on the merits), I.C.J. Reports (1949), p. 4; the *Lake Lanoux* case (*France* v. *Spain*) (19 Nov. 1956), R.I.A.A., xii, p. 281.

[99] By Resolution 2398 (XXIII) of 3 December 1968, the United Nations General Assembly proposed to convene an international environmental conference. This conference took place in Stockholm from 5 to 16 June 1972 and brought together about 6,000 participants from 113 States and various international organizations, and observers from over 400 non-governmental organizations.

[100] Among the collections of documents, see Birnie and Boyle (eds.), *Basic Documents on International Law and The Environment* (Oxford, 1995). In the literature, see Brownlie, 'A Survey of International Customary Rules of Environmental Protection', Teclaff and Utton (eds.), *International Environmental Law* (New York, 1974), pp. 1–11; Wolfke, 'Some Reflections on International Environmental Law-Making and Enforcement', 8 *P.Y.I.L.* (1976), pp. 33–53; Kiss, 'The International Protection of The Environment', Macdonald and Johnston (eds.), *The Structure and Process*, pp. 1069–93; Schachter, 'The Greening of International Law', *Humanité. Mélanges René-Jean Dupuy*, pp. 271–7; Dupuy, R. J. (ed.), *The Future of the International Law of the Environment. Workshop The Hague, 12–14 November 1984* (Dordrecht, 1985); 'Symposium. Earth Rights and Responsibilities: Human Rights and Environmental Protection', 18 *Yale Journal of International Law* (1993), pp. 213–411; Fitzmaurice, M. A., 'International Environmental Law as a Special Field', 25 *Netherlands Yearbook of International Law* (1994), pp. 181–226.

the promotion of peace, human rights and development. After overcoming several objections,[101] these ideas are now generally accepted.

That the environment is one and interdependent has now been proclaimed in various documents on environmental protection, such as the Declaration on the Human Environment adopted by acclamation at the Stockholm Conference,[102] the World Charter for Nature approved by the United Nations General Assembly ten years after the Stockholm Declaration,[103] and the Rio Declaration on Environment and Development adopted by a United Nations Conference convened in Rio de Janeiro to mark the twentieth anniversary of the Stockholm Conference.[104] These documents also show how the protection of the environment is closely related to the promotion of the other basic values of the international community, first and foremost development but also peace and human rights. For example, the Stockholm Declaration proclaimed in Principle 8 that development is an essential component of an environment conducive to a better quality of life. The Rio Conference reaffirmed and further developed this principle when, in the final declaration, it articulated a concept of 'sustainable development', the essence of which is that peace, development, and the protection of the environment 'are interdependent and indivisible'.[105]

[101] See the observations on this point developed in Schachter, *International Law*, p. 362.

[102] Doc.A/Conf.48/14/Rev.1. The text is reproduced in 11 *I.L.M.* (1972), p. 1416.

[103] Resolution 37/7 of 28 Oct. 1982 (Doc.A/37/51) (1982), *Gen. Ass. Off. Recs., Thirty-Seventh Session, Supp. 51*). For comment, see European Council for Environmental Law (under the auspices of), *The World Charter for Nature* (Berlin, 1986).

[104] Doc.A/Conf.151/5/Rev.1 (13 June 1992). The United Nations Conference on Environment and Development was held in Rio de Janeiro from 3 to 14 June 1992. More than 170 States were represented. Some of the documents approved at the Rio Conference (including the Rio Declaration on Environment and Development) are reproduced in 31 *I.L.M.* (1992), p. 814. For the complete annotated documents of the Rio Conference, see Johnson, *The Earth Summit. The United Nations Conference on Environment and Development (UNCED)* (Dordrecht, 1993). See also 'United Nations: General Assembly Second Committee (Economic and Financial) Report containing the Recommended Resolutions in Follow-up to the United Nations Conference on Environment and Development', Doc.A/47/719, dated 18 December 1992, reproduced in 32 *I.L.M.* (1993), p. 236. On issues and trends after Rio, see Ferrari Bravo, 'Considérations sur la méthode de rêcherche des principes généraux du droit international de l'environnement', 7 *Hague Yearbook of International Law* (1994), pp. 3–10. See also Beyerlin, 'Rio-Konferenz: Beginn einer neuen globalen Umweltrechtsordnung?' 54 *Z.a.ö.R.V.* (1994), pp. 124–49 (in German, with English summary); Kiss, 'La contribution de la Conférence de Rio de Janiero au développement du droit international coutumier', Al-Nauimi and Meese (eds.), *International Legal Issues Arising under the United Nations Decade of International Law* (The Hague, 1995), pp. 1079–92.

[105] See Principle 25 of the Rio Declaration on Environment and Development. The concept of 'sustainable development' was introduced by a 1987 report of the World Commission on Environment and Development, an independent body established by the United Nations General Assembly in 1983 and known (from the name of the former Norwegian Prime Minister who chaired the Commission) as the 'Brundtland Commission'. The report was published under the title *Our Common Future* (Oxford, 1987). On 'sustainable development', a concept which is not devoid of contradictions, see also Singh, N., 'Right to Environment and Sustainable Development as a Principle of International Law', Bello and Ajibola (eds.), *Essays Elias*, i, pp. 181–95; Sands, 'International Law in the Field of Sustainable Development', 65

The very nature of the human environment as a holistic entity, and the relationship between its protection and the enhancement of the basic values of the international community, make environmental law an obvious area to explore, however briefly, in a study on the concept of obligations *erga omnes*. In this respect, René-Jean Dupuy has written that the concept of obligations *erga omnes* is especially concerned with respect for human rights 'and the environment'.[106] On several occasions, the concept of obligations *erga omnes* has indeed been referred to, sometimes explicitly sometimes implicitly, in the context of environmental protection. Such references can be found, for example, in the context of proceedings before the International Court,[107] in the work of codification of the International Law Commission on State responsibility,[108] and in the international literature.[109] An examination of these references would go beyond the scope of this work.

B.Y.I.L. (1994), pp. 303–81; Cancado Trindade, 'Relations Between Sustainable Development and Economic, Social and Cultural Rights: Recent Developments', Al-Nauimi and Meese (eds.), *International Legal Issues*, pp. 1051–77; McGoldrick, 'Sustainable Development and Human Rights: An Integrated Conception', 45 *I.C.L.Q.* (1996), pp. 796–818. On the relationship between the protection of the environment and the promotion of development the literature is constantly growing. For an overview see Handl, 'Environmental Protection and Development in Third World Countries: Common Destiny—Common Responsibility', 20 *N.Y.U.J.I.L.P.* (1988), pp. 603–27.

106 'Humanity and the Environment', 2 *Colorado Journal of International Environmental Law and Policy* (1991), p. 202.

107 See Judge Weeramantry's dissenting opinion attached to the International Court's advisory opinion on the *Legality of the Use by a State of Nuclear Weapons in Armed Conflict*, I.C.J. Reports 1996 (mimeographed text), pp. 28–30. Among the pleadings and oral arguments, see those relating to this advisory opinion, and to the International Court's advisory opinion on the *Legality of the Threat or Use of Nuclear Weapons* (which have been cited in section IV of Chapter 1, above), and those relating to the *Nuclear Tests* cases (some aspects of which will be examined in Chapters 9 and 10, below).

108 Article 19(3)(d) of the draft Articles on State Responsibility (reproduced in section IV of Chapter 1, above) lists among international crimes serious breaches of international obligations 'of essential importance for the safeguarding and preservation of the human environment, such as those prohibiting massive pollution of the atmosphere or of the seas.' In 1995, in para. 14 of his 'Draft Report of the International Law Commission on the Work of its Forty-Seventh Session. Chapter VII—Other Decisions and Recommendations of the Commission' (Doc.A/CN.4/L.518), the Rapporteur Villagran Kramer wrote that the International Law Commission 'intends to focus more on the field of duties *erga omnes* where the real complainant of deterioration of the environment is the international community at large rather than individual States, and thus the study would include the topic of "Global commons" as well.'

109 Besides Picone's article, discussed later in this paragraph, see, for example, *Third Restatement*, Part VI ('The Law of the Environment'), in particular Section 601, and Comment (a) on Section 604; Gonzalez Campos, Sanchez Rodriguez and Andres Saenz de Santa Maria, *Curso*, p. 717; Schachter, *International Law*, pp. 381–3; Henkin, *International Law*, pp. 93–4; Birnie and Boyle, *International Law and the Environment* (Oxford, 1993), pp. 154–7; Cancado Trindade, *Direitos humanos e meio-ambiente: paralelo dos sistemas de protecao internacional* (Porto Alegre, 1993), pp. 45–51, 145–50, 213–19, and 276–81 ('Report of the I Meeting of the UNEP Group of the Legal Experts to Examine the Implications of the "*Common Concern of Mankind*" Concept on Global Environmental Issues'); Guruswamy, Palmer and Weston, *International Environment Law and World Order. A Problem-Oriented Coursebook* (St. Paul, Minn., 1994), pp. 344–6. See also Yamada, 'Droits et obligations des Etats en matière de

However, it is appropriate to consider some aspects of the role that the concept of obligations *erga omnes* may play in promoting environmental protection.

In an article published a couple of years after the Stockholm Declaration, Brownlie remarked that pollution of the atmosphere and the high seas is such a dispersed and gradual process that a traditional approach based on liability can hardly lead to positive results because of the difficulties, for example, of identifying the tortfeasor and establishing the evidence of causation. Brownlie suggested that a possible solution to these problems would be a 'liberal approach' to *locus standi*, by analogy with standard-setting treaties.[110] In this way, all States would have standing to react when pollution affects the common environment.[111] The persistent importance of the problems identified by Brownlie finds indirect confirmation in an article written twenty years later, in which Valencia-Ospina made the point that the current problems of international environmental law clearly show the 'need for a departure from traditional rules of standing'.[112]

An important point raised by Brownlie in his article is that, while relaxation of standing among the parties to a treaty would only require that environmental obligations or standards[113] be binding on those parties, a 'liberal

protection de l'environnement', Doc.A/CN.4/454, para. 2(c). Weiss has suggested that an emerging 'fiduciary obligation to future generations' would encompass, among other duties and disabilities, an obligation *erga omnes* to conserve the natural and cultural heritage ('The Planetary Trust: Conservation and Intergenerational Equity', 11 *Ecology Law Quarterly* (1984), pp. 540–4). On the concept of 'fiduciary obligation to future generations' see ea., *In Fairness to Future Generations: International Law, Common Patrimony and Intergenerational Equity* (Tokyo and Dobbs Ferry, 1989), and the contributions of D'Amato, Weiss and Gundling published under the heading 'Agora: What Obligation Does Our Generation Owe to the Next? An Approach to Global Environmental Responsibility', 84 *A.J.I.L.* (1990), pp. 190–212. On the concept of 'intergenerational rights', see Judge Weeramantry's dissenting opinion in *Request for an Examination of the Situtation in Accordance with Paragraph 63 of the Court's Judgment of 20 December 1974 in the Nuclear Tests (New Zealand* v. *France) Case*, Order of 22 September 1995, I.C.J. Reports 1995, pp. 341–2.

110 Brownlie, 'A Survey of International Customary Rules of Environmental Protection', pp. 4–5.

111 There is no need here to examine the various forms that this reaction may take.

112 'The International Court of Justice and International Environmental Law', 2 *Asian Yearbook of International Law* (1994), p. 3. On the same problems, see also the considerations developed in Singh, G., 'The Greenhouse Effect—Need for Legal Control', Pathak and Dhokalia (eds.), *International Law in Transition. Essays in Memory of Judge Nagendra Singh* (Dordrecht, 1992), p. 153; Murase, 'Perspectives from International Economic Law on Transnational Environmental Issues', 253 Hague *Recueil* (1995), pp. 311–12; Sands, *Principles of international environmental law I. Frameworks, standards and implementation* (Manchester, 1995), pp. 150–4.

113 Standards may be defined as 'vaguely expressed prescriptions of desired social conduct' (Dillard, 'Some Aspects of Law and Diplomacy', p. 478). The concept of 'standard', and the distinction between 'standards' and 'norms', were thoroughly debated in the pleadings of the *South West Africa* cases. See, for example, *I.C.J. Pleadings, South West Africa*, viii (pp. 258–9; 680–5), ix (pp. 76–7; 261; 342). In the literature, see Riedel, 'Standards and Sources. Farewell to the Exclusivity of the Sources Triad in International Law?', 2 *European Journal of International Law* (1991, No. 2), pp. 58–84. See also section III of Chapter 7, above.

approach' to *locus standi* under general international law would require that obligations or standards of environmental conservation be opposable *erga omnes*. The key question is therefore the following: are there, in present international law, environmental standards and obligations binding on all States without exception? The importance of this issue is further emphasized by the fact that certain protection and conservation measures promoted by international fishery organizations have been frustrated by the action of third States.[114]

While a comprehensive study of environmental obligations *erga omnes* has still to be made, Picone has analysed in great detail whether obligations and standards opposable *erga omnes* already exist, or at least are emerging, against the pollution of the marine environment.[115] The expression 'pollution of the marine environment' is defined in Article 1, paragraph 1(4), of the United Nations Convention on the Law of the Sea,[116] as follows:

> the introduction by man, directly or indirectly, of substances or energy into the marine environment, including estuaries, which results or is likely to result in such deleterious effects as harm to living resources and marine life, hazards to human health, hindrance to marine activities, including fishing and other legitimate uses of the sea, impairment of quality for use of sea water and reduction of amenities.

By virtue of the interdependence of waters, the prejudicial effects of the most serious forms of marine pollution are often felt many miles away from where pollution occurred, and are potentially the concern of all States.

In his article, Picone discussed the concept of obligations *erga omnes* and its concrete applications to the environmental protection of the territorial sea, the exclusive economic zone and the high seas.[117] As to the territorial sea, the traditional view is that (a) a coastal State has no obligation *erga omnes* to protect its marine environment as such, and (b) if a State commits an environmental breach against the territorial sea of another State, only

[114] See Wolfrum, 'Purposes and Principles of International Environmental Law', 33 *G.Y.I.L.* (1990), p. 325.

[115] 'Obblighi reciproci ed obblighi *erga omnes*', pp. 94–135. Picone based his analysis on the draft text adopted at the tenth session of the United Nations Conference on the Law of the Sea in 1981. The differences between that draft and the final version are irrelevant, and therefore throughout this paragraph references will be made to the text of the United Nations Convention on the Law of the Sea, as finally adopted in 1982.

[116] Doc.A/Conf.62/122 and Corr. 1 to 11. The Convention was opened for signature on 10 December 1982 and entered into force on 16 November 1994, one year after Guyana deposited the 60th instrument of acceptance. Eighty-two States have become parties (*Multilateral Treaties Deposited with the Secretary-General. Status as at 31 December 1995*, p. 798). Parts I–IX of the Convention are reproduced in Brownlie, *Basic Documents*, pp. 129–208. For an early article on marine pollution, see Schachter and Serwer, 'Marine Pollution Problems and Remedies', 65 *A.J.I.L.* (1971), pp. 84–111.

[117] Picone assumed that no other sea areas (such as the contiguous zone or the continental shelf) need to be treated separately in a study on the protection of the marine environment. See 'Obblighi reciproci ed obblighi *erga omnes*', p. 103, note 190 (incorrectly indicated in the article as note 109).

the coastal State that has suffered damage can react against that breach. This traditional view is gradually being eroded. First of all, there now seems to be a general obligation of States to protect and preserve the marine environment as such, including the protection and preservation of the territorial sea. This obligation, which has been codified in Articles 192 and 193 of the United Nations Convention on the Law of the Sea,[118] prescinds from considerations of reciprocity and is regarded by Picone as being an obligation *erga omnes*. When trying to describe the concrete applications of this general obligation, Picone gave the example of the international obligation of a coastal State not to dispose of radioactive and nuclear wastes in its own territorial sea, at least when such disposal is likely to produce a high level of marine pollution.[119] One consequence of the character *erga omnes* of this obligation would be that, for the most serious breaches, the coastal State would be liable towards the whole international community.

While not examined by Picone, a particular aspect of the alleged character *erga omnes* of this prohibition deserves to be considered here, because it bears on the general concept of obligations *erga omnes*. This particular aspect is that the prohibition of nuclear and radioactive disposal would not be *erga omnes* in the strict sense of being opposable to all States of the international community. Rather, this prohibition would be opposable only to coastal States.[120] The consequence is that, within the general category of obligations *erga omnes*, there would be a sub-group of obligations opposable to all those States that satisfy certain geographical conditions for the operation of such obligations. Unlike self-existent obligations (in French, 'obligations solidaires') based on a treaty, this sub-category of obligations *erga omnes* would be opposable to all coastal States, without requiring an expression of consent from each individual State belonging to that group. On the other hand, unlike obligations deriving from the so-called 'regional *jus cogens*', this sub-category of obligations *erga omnes* would be opposable worldwide to *all* States which meet the necessary requisites for their application. Their opposability would not be restricted to States belonging to a certain region.[121] In this sense, this sub-group of obligations *erga omnes* would be universally opposable, and there would not seem to be a conflict between the general concept of obligations *erga omnes* and the

[118] Article 193, unlike Article 192, uses the term 'duty' instead of 'obligation'. As was mentioned in section I of this chapter, the two terms may be regarded as equivalent, at least for present purposes.

[119] 'Obblighi reciproci ed obblighi *erga omnes*', p. 114 (including note 207, where Picone discusses, quite independently from the alleged character *erga omnes* of the obligation in question, some difficulties attaching to the proposition that a customary international norm to this effect exists).

[120] Of course, all States may become coastal States by operation of the various modes of territorial acquisition.

[121] On self-existent obligations and regional *jus cogens*, see sections III and IV, respectively, of Chapter 10, below.

configuration of a sub-group of obligations *erga omnes* binding on States presenting certain geographical features. Whether such a sub-group already exists, and if so which obligations are part of it, is a question that goes beyond the scope of the present inquiry.[122]

Another candidate of obligation *erga omnes* relating to the environmental protection of the territorial sea is the obligation of a coastal State to notify other States immediately of the imminent danger of damage to their marine environment,[123] at least when the likely damage is serious or substantial. Besides Picone's article,[124] support for the character *erga omnes* of this obligation can be found in Section 601 of the last Restatement on foreign relations law adopted by the American Law Institute.[125] Once again, it is unnecessary here to try to assess whether or not the obligation to notify with respect to the imminent danger of a serious damage to the environment is a convincing candidate of obligation *erga omnes*. This would not be the only example of an obligation to notify opposable *erga omnes*. As was written in Chapter 4, above, there is also support for the proposition that the obligation to notify the international shipping community of the existence of a minefield is an obligation *erga omnes*.

The existence of obligations *erga omnes* relating to the exclusive economic zone is more problematic, because of the special nature of States' rights over this area. Reflecting international customary law, Article 56 of the United Nations Convention on the Law of the Sea provides that, in the exclusive economic zone, a coastal State has sovereign rights, duties and jurisdiction for certain limited purposes. Unlike the situation in the territorial sea, in the exclusive economic zone the coastal State does not have full sovereignty. On the other hand, unlike the situation on the continental shelf, where the coastal State has rights by operation of law,[126] in the exclusive economic zone the rights of the coastal State are optional, in the sense that they exist only if the coastal State has actually claimed an exclusive economic zone. Indeed, several States have so far abstained from claiming an exclusive economic zone.[127]

Article 56 does not refer only to rights, but also to jurisdiction and duties. A question therefore arises: are such jurisdiction and duties mere accessories

[122] Another question, which cannot be addressed here, is whether the process of formation of this sub-group would differ in any way from that of obligations *erga omnes* generally.

[123] See Article 198 of the United Nations Convention of the Law of the Sea.

[124] 'Obblighi reciproci ed obblighi *erga omnes*', pp. 115–16.

[125] Section 601, paras. (1)(a) and (2)(a), Comment (e) and Reporter's Note (4) relating to the same section.

[126] See Article 77, paragraph 3, of the United Nations Convention on the Law of the Sea.

[127] On this point, and more generally on the exclusive economic zone, see Brownlie, *Principles*, pp. 209–13. On the drafting of Article 56, see *The Law of the Sea. Exclusive Economic Zone. Legislative History of Articles 56, 58 and 59 of the United Nations Convention on the Law of the Sea* (Division for Ocean Affairs and the Law of the Sea, Office of Legal Affairs) (New York, 1992).

to the sovereign rights of the coastal State? A positive answer to this question would make it difficult to apply the concept of obligations *erga omnes* to the exclusive economic zone: if the jurisdiction and duties for the protection of this area were only accessories to optional rights, then they too would be optional, with the consequence that this optional character would conflict with the idea of obligations *erga omnes*, which by their very nature are not optional but opposable to all States irrespective of consent.

The optional character of the exclusive economic zone has not hindered the proposal of candidates of obligations *erga omnes* relating to this area. For example, Picone has written that possible examples of emerging obligations *erga omnes* would be the obligations of a coastal State in the exclusive economic zone to prevent, reduce and control pollution of the marine environment from sea-bed activities (codified by Article 208 of the United Nations Convention on the Law of the Sea), pollution by dumping (codified by Article 210 of the same Convention), and pollution from vessels (codified by Article 211).[128]

Another obligation which the last Restatement considers to be an obligation *erga omnes* is the obligation codified by Article 61, paragraph 2, of the United Nations Convention on the Law of the Sea, according to which a coastal State must ensure that the maintenance of the living resources in the exclusive economic zone is not endangered by over-exploitation. In fulfilling this obligation, a coastal State has to take positive actions, namely determine the allowable catch of the living resources in its exclusive economic zone, its own capacity to harvest these resources and the conditions under which other States will be allowed to catch the surplus.[129]

This idea put forward in the last Restatement shows the difficulties attaching to the alleged character *erga omnes* of obligations relating to the exclusive economic zone. The obligation of a coastal State to ensure the proper conservation and management of the living resources in the exclusive economic zone presupposes that the coastal State has actually claimed an exclusive economic zone. In other words, this obligation (which, moreover, would go beyond the mere prohibition of certain activities)[130] depends on the coastal State's proclamation of an exclusive economic zone, and might be regarded as being *erga omnes* only in the limited sense that, once a coastal State has claimed an exclusive economic zone, then (and only then) the coastal State would have an obligation towards all other States to take adequate measures for conservation and management of the living resources in its exclusive economic zone.

[128] 'Obblighi reciproci ed obblighi *erga omnes*', pp. 116–25.

[129] *Third Restatement*, Section 514, Comment (f).

[130] On the negative or positive content of obligations *erga omnes*, see section III of this Chapter.

The last marine area to consider is the high seas. As a global common over which no State has jurisdiction or control, the high seas should in principle be the main area to explore when considering the existence of obligations *erga omnes* relating to the protection of the marine environment. Indeed, certain trends in the procedural and substantive law of the sea confirm this assumption.[131]

By analogy with what was written earlier with respect to the territorial sea and the exclusive economic zone, a candidate of obligation *erga omnes* put forward in Picone's article is the prohibition to dispose of nuclear and radioactive wastes in the high seas. Other elements indicating a trend towards the emergence of obligations *erga omnes* in this area may be drawn from the enforcement mechanisms contained in the United Nations Convention on the Law of the Sea. For example, Article 218 of this Convention provides that, when a vessel is voluntarily within a port or at an off-shore terminal of a State, that State may undertake investigations and eventually institute proceedings in respect of any unlawful discharge from that vessel which occurred outside its own jurisdiction. The same article further provides that the port State must comply, as far as practicable, with a flag State's request for investigation of a discharge in breach of international rules and standards, 'irrespective of where the violation occurred'.

In other words, under Article 218, port States are entitled to enforce international rules and standards for the environmental protection of the high seas to the benefit of the common interests of States, irrespective of any damage to their own individual rights. Whether a customary rule embodying a similar provision, and giving rise to an obligation *erga omnes*, already exists is an issue that falls outside the scope of the present inquiry.

V. Conclusions

This chapter has examined a few suggested candidates of obligations *erga omnes*. In doing so, the aim was not to assess on the basis of the available evidence whether these are credible candidates, but to take advantage of them and concentrate on some of the common elements which emerged from the analysis of the obligations *erga omnes* identified in the *Barcelona Traction* case. These common elements (listed in section I, above) indicate that the dictum has given examples of obligations in the strict sense, with a narrowly defined and prohibitory content. The International Court has provided a concept of obligations *erga omnes* that is selective and is meant to apply to a limited number of international obligations.

[131] See Picone, 'Obblighi reciproci ed obblighi *erga omnes*', pp. 125–35.

This cautious approach followed by the International Court has not precluded the emergence of candidates that go much beyond the original idea contained in the dictum. For example, the candidates examined in this chapter would expand the concept of obligations *erga omnes* in such a way as to include not only particular rules but also general principles (as discussed with respect to human rights), not only prohibitions but also positive obligations (as discussed with respect to development law), and not only obligations in the strict sense but also obligations attaching to optional rights (as discussed with respect to environmental law). The justification of this expanded concept has relied either on a literal interpretation of the International Court's dictum (for example, its reference not only to 'rules' but also to 'principles') or, on the contrary, on the denial of any relevance at all of certain aspects of the dictum (for example, the distinction between 'basic' and other human rights).

All this shows the vitality of the concept of obligations *erga omnes*: far from being only a subject for academic inquiry, the concept is becoming more and more influential in different areas of international law, and lawyers resort to it in an effort to find viable answers to practical questions. At the same time, however, there is an evident risk of proliferation of candidates beyond the limits indicated by the International Court. This risk is all the more dangerous as the concept of obligations *erga omnes* affects, by its very nature, the freedom of consent and sovereign rights of States.

Hence the importance of examining, in Chapter 9, the two other common elements identified in section I, above, namely the moral content of obligations *erga omnes* and their required degree of support by the international community. Once again, these common elements will be discussed in a pragmatic way, by reference to actual cases brought before the International Court.

9

Other Selected Candidates in Light of the Advisory Opinion on Namibia and the *Nuclear Tests* Cases

I. Introduction

The last two common elements identified in section I of Chapter 8, namely the required degree of support and the moral content of obligations *erga omnes*, are the subject to be examined in this chapter. These two common elements will be considered in light of various references to the concept of obligations *erga omnes* contained in the advisory opinion on Namibia, and the pleadings relating to this advisory opinion and the *Nuclear Tests* cases.

Both instances have identified additional candidates of obligations *erga omnes*. While being the closest in time to the International Court's dictum of 1970, these have not been the only such instances since the *Barcelona Traction* case. In his dissenting opinion to the judgment in the *East Timor* case, Judge Weeramantry listed the following cases as those in which the International Court was confronted with the question of obligations *erga omnes* in addition to the *Barcelona Traction* case: *Northern Cameroons, South West Africa, Nuclear Tests, Hostages* and *Border and Transborder (Nicaragua* v. *Honduras)*.[1] In the present work, relevant aspects of all these cases have already been or will be examined, with the exception of the *Northern Cameroons* and the *Border and Transborder (Nicaragua* v. *Honduras)* cases. In fact, while important for a study on remedies, these cases do not appear to be directly relevant to a study on the concept of obligations *erga omnes*. As usual, the advisory opinion and cases discussed below will be examined selectively, to the limited extent that they shed light on the particular subject of this chapter.

II. References to the Concept of Obligations *Erga Omnes* in the Advisory Opinion and the Pleadings Relating to Namibia

The previous chapters have already referred to the mandate for South West Africa—or Namibia, as the territory was renamed by General Assembly

[1] *I.C.J. Reports* 1995, p. 214. Of the two cases discussed in this chapter, Judge Weeramantry included in his list the *Nuclear Tests* cases, but not the advisory opinion on Namibia.

resolution 2372 (XXII)—and to the fact that the International Court has delivered four advisory opinions and two judgments on several questions relating to the mandate.[2] The present section will consider the last of these pronouncements, namely the advisory opinion on Namibia of 1971.[3] It is not the whole text of this advisory opinion that needs to be examined here, but only the passage in which the International Court used the expression '*erga omnes*', a little more than a year after its judgment in the *Barcelona Traction* case. Before considering this passage, it may be useful to outline the background of this advisory opinion.

Shortly after the International Court concluded, in the *South West Africa* cases, that the applicant States had no legal standing to bring a claim against South Africa, the General Assembly of the United Nations terminated the mandate for South West Africa and decided that South Africa had no other right to administer the territory.[4] The question of South West Africa was then brought to the attention of the Security Council, which endorsed the General Assembly's revocation of the mandate.[5] In resolution 276 of 1970,[6] the Security Council declared that the continued presence of South Africa in Namibia was illegal and that all acts taken by South Africa on behalf of or concerning Namibia after the termination of the mandate were illegal and invalid. It also called upon all States to refrain from any dealings with the Government of South Africa that would be inconsistent with this declaration. In the same resolution, the Security Council set up an *ad hoc* sub-committee to study the means to implement effectively the Security Council's resolutions on Namibia. Upon the sub-committee's recommendation, the Security Council, by resolution 284, asked the International Court for an advisory opinion.[7] This resolution, originally

[2] See in particular section III of Chapter 7, above, for bibliographical references which are also relevant to the present discussion of the International Court's advisory opinion on Namibia.

[3] *Legal Consequences for States of the Continued Presence of South Africa in Namibia (South West Africa) notwithstanding Security Council Resolution 276 (1970)*, Advisory Opinion, I.C.J. Reports 1971, p. 16. For comment, besides the general works on the South West Africa question cited in section III of Chapter 7, above, see Mani, 'The Advisory Opinion in Namibia Case: A Critique', 11 *Indian Journal of International Law* (1971), pp. 467–80; Dugard, 'Namibia (South West Africa): The Court's Opinion, South Africa's Response, and Prospects for the Future', 11 *C.J.T.L.* (1972), pp. 14–49; Lissitzyn, 'International Law and the Advisory Opinion on Namibia', ibid., pp. 50–73; Rovine, 'The World Court Opinion on Namibia', ibid., pp. 203–39.

[4] Resolution 2145, by which the General Assembly terminated the mandate, was adopted on 27 October 1966. This resolution has been criticized on practical and legal grounds, as summarized in *Oppenheim's International Law*, i, p. 303, note 17.

[5] See resolutions 245 and 246 of 1968, 264 and 269 of 1969, and 276 and 283 of 1970.

[6] The text of resolution 276 is reproduced in 24 *Yearbook of the United Nations* (1970), pp. 752–3.

[7] The full text of resolution 284 is reproduced in para. 1 of the International Court's advisory opinion. (The Security Council based its request on Article 96 of the United Nations Charter, which provides for the power of the General Assembly and the Security Council to request the International Court for an advisory opinion on any legal question.)

proposed by Finland, was adopted on 29 July 1970 by twelve votes to none, with three abstentions.[8] It asked the International Court to determine the legal consequences deriving from the continued presence of South Africa in Namibia, notwithstanding Security Council resolution 276.

In the course of the proceedings before the International Court, written statements were submitted by the Secretary-General of the United Nations, the Government of South Africa, and the Governments of eleven other States.[9] These were followed by oral statements made by representatives of the Secretary-General of the United Nations, the Organization of African Unity,[10] the Government of South Africa, and the governments of seven other States.[11] In compliance with the Security Council's request for a response to its question at an early date, the International Court delivered its advisory opinion on 21 June 1971, less than a year after the adoption of resolution 284.

In the operative clause of its advisory opinion, the International Court considered the legal consequences that the continued presence of South Africa in Namibia had for South Africa, the member States of the United Nations, and all other States. By thirteen votes to two, the International Court concluded that the continued presence of South Africa in Namibia was illegal, and South Africa was bound to withdraw its administration from Namibia immediately. By eleven votes to four, the International Court then decided that (a) member States of the United Nations were bound to

[8] The former Soviet Union, Poland and the United Kingdom abstained. In their declarations of vote, the Soviet representative 'felt [that the resolution] would merely delay settlement of the question by creating the illusion that legal measures could replace political action'; the Polish representative 'questioned the effectiveness of measures limited to Namibia and held that the realization of United Nations objectives with respect to Namibia depended on effective measures taken against South Africa—the occupier of the territory'; and the United Kingdom representative 'believed that the proposed submission to the International Court of Justice was based on certain assumptions which should themselves be examined by the Court' (24 *Yearbook of the United Nations* (1970), p. 740).

[9] These States were the former Czechoslovakia, Finland, France, Hungary, India, The Netherlands, Nigeria, Pakistan, Poland, the United States and the former Yugoslavia.

[10] Although the International Court rarely allows international organizations other than the one that has asked for the advisory opinion to participate in the proceedings, on 29 January 1971 the International Court decided that it was prepared to hear an oral statement from the Organization of African Unity. Likewise, in the proceedings relating to the advisory opinion on the Genocide Convention (see Chapter 5, above), the President of the International Court had allowed the International Labour Organization and the Organization of American States to submit written statements.

[11] These States were Finland, India, The Netherlands, Nigeria, Pakistan, the Republic of Vietnam and the United States. They were all members of the United Nations, except for the Republic of Vietnam. (The Socialist Republic of Vietnam, a single State composed of the former Democratic Republic of Vietnam and the Republic of Vietnam, became a member of the United Nations in 1977.) The Republic of Vietnam could submit an oral statement because the President of the International Court had decided, on 21 August 1970, that non-member States 'entitled to appear before the Court' (see Article 66 of the Statute of the International Court) could furnish information on the question submitted to the International Court.

recognize such illegality and not to take any actions that would imply otherwise, and (b) non-member States should assist the United Nations, within the scope of paragraph (a) above, in its action with regard to Namibia.[12] The General Assembly and the Security Council accepted the International Court's advice.[13]

For present purposes, the crucial passage from the advisory opinion is the one where the International Court, while examining the legal consequences for non-member States of the United Nations, wrote that

> the termination of the Mandate and the declaration of the illegality of South Africa's presence in Namibia are opposable to all States in the sense of barring *erga omnes* the legality of a situation which is maintained in violation of international law: in particular, no State which enters into relations with South Africa concerning Namibia may expect the United Nations or its Members to recognize the validity or effects of such relationship, or of the consequences thereof. The Mandate having been terminated by decision of the international organization in which the supervisory authority over its administration was vested, and South Africa's continued presence in Namibia having been declared illegal, it is for non-member States to act in accordance with those decisions.[14]

The wording used by the International Court makes it reasonable to assume that this passage is relevant to the concept of obligations *erga omnes*. Yet doubts have been raised in this respect for at least two reasons. First of all, in the advisory opinion on Namibia, the International Court referred to 'effects *erga omnes*' instead of 'obligations *erga omnes*'. This difference, however, appears to be inconsequential. It is entirely legitimate to rephrase the language used by the International Court, without altering its meaning, in terms of a negative duty opposable universally, as follows: States have an international obligation *erga omnes* not to recognize the legality of South Africa's continued presence in Namibia, a situation maintained in violation of international law. Mann has even suggested that it would have been preferable if, in the operative clause, the International Court had expressly referred to a negative duty along these lines.[15]

Secondly, some writers[16] have expressed doubts on the relevance of the advisory opinion on Namibia to the concept of obligations *erga omnes*

[12] I.C.J. Reports 1971, p. 58, para. 133.

[13] See General Assembly's resolution 2871 (XXVI) and Security Council's resolution 301 (1971). They are both reproduced in 25 *Yearbook of the United Nations* (1971), pp. 560–4. See also the discussion that accompanied the adoption of Security Council's resolution 301, summarized ibid., pp. 548–51.

[14] I.C.J. Reports 1971, p. 56, para. 126.

[15] 'The Doctrine of Jus Cogens', p. 414, note 55. The issues of (a) the implications of this duty of non-recognition, and (b) the nature of the measures indicated by the International Court in its advisory opinion ('legal consequences' or 'enforcement measures'?) are extensively debated in the separate and dissenting opinions attached to the advisory opinion on Namibia.

[16] See Combacau and Sur, *Droit international public*, p. 107.

because, after declaring the illegality *erga omnes* of South Africa's presence in Namibia, the International Court added that as a result of this declaration no State entering into relations with South Africa should expect that the United Nations would recognize the validity of these relations. If this were the only consequence (these writers note), then non-member States would not be affected by an obligation *erga omnes*, but rather by the denial of a mere expectation of right. At first sight, this criticism seems to have some merit. However, a closer look at the language used by the International Court reveals that the denial of the expectation of right was envisaged as a 'particular' consequence of the declaration of illegality *erga omnes*, but not necessarily the only one. Hence the aforesaid criticism is not conclusive.

To sum up, there are no decisive reasons to exclude the passage from the advisory opinion quoted above from being relevant to the concept of obligations *erga omnes*. Nor should it be surprising that the character *erga omnes* would attach to an obligation relating to recognition.[17] Twenty years before the advisory opinion on Namibia, Fitzmaurice had written that the obligation to recognize a new State or government (if this obligation could be said to exist in international law) would be an example of 'obligations without the beneficiary of the rights relating to these obligations being known'.[18] This idea had originally been put forward by Judge Alvarez,[19] and may be regarded as another prefiguration of the concept of obligations *erga omnes*, at least in the sense that this category of obligations reflects (like obligations *erga omnes*) a common interest of States.[20]

Once it is established that there is no difficulty in thinking of an obligation *erga omnes* in the area of non-recognition, the key question to examine is the basis upon which the International Court reached its conclusion that the illegal presence of South Africa in Namibia was opposable *erga omnes*. It is true that the revocation of the mandate was decided by the international organization vested with supervisory authority over the mandate. However, this can only explain why the illegality should be opposable

[17] The terms 'recognition' and 'non-recognition' are used here according to the ordinary meaning attributed to them in the international literature. Their use here does not imply that they should be regarded as terms of art. See Brownlie, 'Recognition in Theory and Practice', 53 *B.Y.I.L.* (1982), pp. 197–9.

[18] 'The Law and Procedure of the International Court of Justice: General Principles and Substantive Law', 27 *B.Y.I.L.* (1950), pp. 14–15.

[19] See Judge Alvarez's dissenting opinion in *International Status of South West Africa*, Advisory Opinion, I.C.J. Reports 1950, p. 177: 'Because the new international law is based on social interdependence, many cases may be found in which States are under obligations without the beneficiary of the rights relating to these obligations being known. The beneficiary is the international community.'

[20] This was not the only innovative concept introduced by Alvarez. For an assessment of Alvarez's contribution to international law, written many years before Alvarez was elected to the International Court, see Le Fur, 'Règles générales du droit de la paix', 54 Hague *Recueil* (1935, IV), pp. 124–46.

to the member-States of the United Nations, but not why it should be opposable *erga omnes*. In other words, there is a real difficulty here, which has attracted several attempts to indicate a solution.

For example, in a separate opinion to the International Court's advisory opinion, Judge Ammoun suggested that the revocation of the mandate was effective *erga omnes* 'in view of the mandate's objective institutional character'.[21] This explanation is reminiscent of the notions of objective regime and international status, discussed in Chapter 2, above. It therefore attracts the same doubts attaching to them. In another separate opinion, Judge De Castro wrote that the revocation of the mandate should be respected like that of an owner 'who withdraws the mandate given by him to administer his property'.[22] In other words, the character *erga omnes* of the illegality of South Africa's presence in Namibia would depend on a general principle derived from municipal law. While this suggestion is ingenious, the extent to which the regulation of an international mandate may be based on analogies with municipal law is open to question,[23] and in any event it is even more doubtful whether any general principle exists to the effect that a third party dealing with a mandatory commits an illegal act only because the mandate has been withdrawn.[24]

Another possible explanation of the international obligation *erga omnes* not to recognize the legality of South Africa's continued presence in Namibia is related to the concept of *jus cogens*. The argument would run as follows. It is generally admitted that an act which is contrary to international law cannot be the source of legal rights for the wrongdoer (*ex injuria non oritur jus*).[25] But recognition, while not doing away with the illegality of the act, can validate its consequences. To avoid this, States have from time to time followed a policy of non-recognition of illegal situations or have recognized new States subject to the condition that these new entities abandon certain repugnant practices, such as the slave trade.[26]

A particular technique, which acquired greater impetus after the Stimson Note of 1932 relating to Manchuria, is the practice of collective non-recognition, which may result, for example, from the resolutions of

[21] I.C.J. Reports 1971, p. 73, para. 4

[22] Ibid., p. 219, para. VII.D.

[23] See the remarks of Le Tai Trien (Republic of Vietnam) in his oral statement to the International Court, *I.C.J. Pleadings, Legal Consequences for States of the Continued Presence of South Africa in Namibia (South West Africa) notwithstanding Security Council Resolution 276 (1970)*, ii, p. 283.

[24] For a similar observation, see Mann, 'The Doctrine of Jus Cogens', p. 415.

[25] On this principle, see Lauterpacht, H., *Recognition in International Law* (Cambridge, 1947), pp. 420–6; Fitzmaurice, 'The General Principles of International Law', pp. 117–28; Jennings, 'Nullity and Effectiveness in International Law', *Cambridge Essays McNair*, pp. 72–4; Brownlie, *Principles*, pp. 511–12. Kelsen regards this principle as a 'problematic presumption' (*Principles of International Law*, p. 415; see also pp. 420–33).

[26] See Smith, H. A. (ed.), *Great Britain*, i, pp. 127–31 (letter dated 10 October 1822, from Cunning to Hervey, relating to the recognition of Mexico) and 185–7 (dispatch dated 15 February 1823, from Cunning to Chamberlain, relating to the recognition of Brazil).

international organizations.[27] This technique has played a decisive role in the emergence of an international obligation of non-recognition under customary law.[28] Initially, this was an obligation, in Brownlie's words, 'not to recognize situations resulting from the illegal use of force'.[29] Subsequently, its scope has widened and today a duty of non-recognition exists, in Crawford's words, '[w]hen the illegality invoked is substantial, and in particular when it involves a norm of *jus cogens*'.[30]

Thus, there is now support for the view that all States are bound not to recognize a situation brought about in breach of an international rule of *jus cogens*.[31] The additional step would be to regard South Africa's presence in Namibia as being illegal *erga omnes* for the very reason that it was in breach of an international rule of *jus cogens*. In the pleadings relating the advisory opinion on Namibia, there were arguments in favour and arguments against the view that *jus cogens* was relevant to the case at hand.[32] These opposite views need not be examined here. One may readily accept the suggestion that, in this advisory opinion, the International Court acknowledged that the United Nations has a reservoir of necessary powers resulting in legal obligations opposable to all States when rules of *jus cogens* are involved.[33]

[27] On the 'Stimson doctrine' (derived from the Stimson Note), see McNair, 'The Stimson Doctrine of Non-Recognition', 14 *B.Y.I.L.* (1933), pp. 65–74. On collective non-recognition, see Brownlie, *Principles*, p. 98; Verhoeven, *La Réconnaissance internationale dans la pratique contemporaine* (Paris, 1975), pp. 525–33; Dugard, *Recognition*, pp. 24–40.

[28] On the obligation of non-recognition, see Brownlie, *International Law and the Use of Force by States*, pp. 410–23; Crawford, *The Creation of States*, pp. 120–8. See also Guggenheim, *Traité*, i, pp. 199–202; O'Connell, *International Law*, i, pp. 140–8; *Oppenheim's International Law*, i, pp. 183–203; Nguyen Quoc Dinh, Dailler and Pellet, *Droit international public*, pp. 536–8 (para. 371). The practice of States that led to the emergence of an obligation of non-recognition is analysed in Sharp, *Nonrecognition as a Legal Obligation 1775–1934* (Liège, 1934).

[29] Brownlie, *International Law and the Use of Force by States*, p. 423.

[30] Crawford, *The Creation of States*, p. 123.

[31] Besides Crawford's work, see the extensive treatment of the subject in Dugard, *Recognition*, pp. 123–63 (where the writer correctly remarks, at pp. 145–6, that Cheng had anticipated in 1951 the later developments on the relevance of *jus cogens* for international recognition). For a critical view, see Mann, 'The Doctrine of Jus Cogens', pp. 412–18. See also the dissenting opinion of Judge *ad hoc* Skubiszewski from the International Court's judgment in the *East Timor* case, in which Judge *ad hoc* Skubiszewski wrote that the hypothesis of a peremptory character attaching to non-recognition 'is a future development which is uncertain and has still to happen'. (I.C.J. Reports 1995, p. 262, para. 125.) Finally, pursuant to draft Article 6 in the 'Third Report on the content, forms and degrees of international responsibility (Part 2 of the draft articles on State responsibility)' (Doc.A/CN.4/354 and Add.1 and 2), submitted by the Special Rapporteur Riphagen to the International Law Commission in 1982, an international obligation of non-recognition is described as one of the consequences attaching to the commission of an international crime (*Y.I.L.C.*, II, Part 1), pp. 48–50.

[32] Compare the oral statement by Castrén (Finland) with the oral statements by Riphagen (The Netherlands) and Pirzada (Pakistan), *I.C.J. Pleadings, Legal Consequences*, ii, pp. 82, 123 and 142.

[33] Brownlie, 'The United Nations as a Form of Government', Fawcett and Higgins, R. (eds.), *International Organization: Law in Movement. Essays in Honour of John McMahon* (London, 1974), p. 34.

For the present purposes, the important point is not this, but that the International Court did not refer to *jus cogens* at all but referred instead to the concept of *erga omnes* and, in doing so, did not articulate the specific reasons that would account for the opposability *erga omnes* of the obligation not to recognize the legality of South Africa's continued presence in Namibia. In this latter respect, there is an element of continuity with the dictum in the *Barcelona Traction* case, despite the sixteen months that separate the two pronouncements and the changes in the composition of the International Court.[34] This element of continuity is the declaratory nature of the concept. In the *Barcelona Traction* case, the International Court had essentially relied on legal reasoning to identify a separate category of international obligations *erga omnes*. Likewise, in the advisory opinion on Namibia, the opposability *erga omnes* of the illegal presence of South Africa was regarded as a corollary of the particular facts and legal principles involved in the case.

A more intricate picture emerges from the explicit references to the concept of *erga omnes* that can be found in the pleadings.[35] In its written statement, the Government of Hungary wrote that the obligation of South Africa to withdraw from Namibia was owed *erga omnes*. The key passage from the Hungarian statement reads as follows:

> The continued presence of the Republic of South Africa in Namibia notwithstanding the termination of the Mandate, establishes its responsibility vis-à-vis all States. Its obligation to withdraw is an obligation *erga omnes*. The interests of the international community as a whole are violated by the illegal presence of South Africa in Namibia and from this fact States can draw the appropriate conclusions individually and collectively. States are especially entitled to appeal to the Security Council and request that it should adopt decisions of a mandatory character on various ways of bringing political, economic and military pressure to bear on the Republic of South Africa.[36]

Whether the obligation to which this passage refers is an obligation *erga omnes* is questionable. Perhaps it would be more appropriate to define the

[34] On 6 February 1970, the day after the International Court's judgment in the *Barcelona Traction* case, five new judges entered upon their term of office.

[35] There were also implicit references to the concept, such as those contained in the written statement of The Netherlands ('the rules of present-day general international law impose on the government of every State the legal duty to respect and promote the exercise of the right of self-determination of peoples in so far as this is within its effective power . . . This nowadays is a universal duty . . .', *I.C.J. Pleadings, Legal Consequences*, i, p. 352, para. 7), and in the oral statement by Chagla on behalf of India ('the inalienable right of the colonial people to self-determination and independence, the non-acquisition of territory by threat or use of force or any other form of aggression, the non-recognition of fruits of aggression or illegal occupation of territory, and the duty to fulfil international obligations in good faith, are in fact the foundations of international legal order. They are, therefore, of interest to the international community of States as a whole', ibid., ii, p. 119).

[36] Ibid., i, pp. 359–60.

obligation binding South Africa in terms of a special obligation deriving from its role as the mandatory for South West Africa and engendering responsibility towards all States alike in case of breach. In any event, assuming that the obligation to which Hungary refers is *erga omnes*,[37] then Hungary (like the International Court) did not think it necessary to provide any evidence in support of the character *erga omnes* of the obligation in question.

A similar approach was followed by the Secretary-General of the United Nations. In his written statement, he emphasized that States were bound to comply with all their obligations in relation to Namibia, including those concerning human rights and fundamental freedoms. Compliance was due even when the obligations in question did not derive from any of the classic sources of international law, namely customs, treaties and the general principles of law. In support of the idea of legal norms not deriving from these sources, the Secretary-General referred to the passage from the advisory opinion on the Genocide Convention relating to principles binding on States even without any conventional obligations,[38] and to the dictum on obligations *erga omnes* in the *Barcelona Traction* case.

In the oral proceedings, South Africa objected to this view. It argued that, in its dictum on obligations *erga omnes* in the *Barcelona Traction* case, the International Court had meant to refer to principles and rules 'derived from normally accepted sources of obligation in international law'. South Africa added that principles and rules concerning human rights and freedoms should not be regarded as binding on all States 'independently of a treaty basis or of general acceptance as rules of law'.[39] In other words, South Africa argued that obligations *erga omnes* derive from the classic sources of international law, and that whoever alleges the character *erga omnes* of an international obligation must prove it.

The issue of the evidence to be provided in support of the character *erga omnes* of an international obligation surfaced again, at least implicitly, a few years later in contentious cases brought before the International Court by

[37] Without referring to the written statement of Hungary, Thirlway has written that one possible interpretation of the passage contained in para. 126 of the advisory opinion on Namibia, in which the International Court used the expression *erga omnes*, 'is that South Africa was under an obligation *erga omnes*, of the kind contemplated in the *Barcelona Traction* judgment, to withdraw from Namibia, such that any State could seek the enforcement of that obligation, without being required to show an individual legal interest in the matter.' ('The Law and Procedure of the International Court of Justice', 60 *B.Y.I.L.* (1989), p. 99.) The present writer would suggest that the best reference for this alleged obligation *erga omnes* is not para. 126 of the advisory opinion, but the written statement of Hungary and, in the advisory opinion, para. 118, where the International Court specifically addressed the legal consequences for South Africa (including 'obligations and responsibilities under international law towards other States').

[38] This passage is discussed in sections II and III of Chapter 5, above.

[39] *I.C.J. Pleadings, Legal Consequences*, ii, p. 572.

Australia and New Zealand. It is therefore appropriate to examine the relevant aspects of these cases.

III. References to the Concept of Obligations *Erga Omnes* in the Pleadings Relating to the *Nuclear Tests* Cases

In 1973, Australia and New Zealand instituted separate proceedings against France before the International Court.[40] The subject of the disputes was the atmospheric nuclear tests conducted by France in the South Pacific.[41] In their applications,[42] Australia and New Zealand wrote that from July 1966 to July 1972 France had conducted almost thirty atmospheric tests of nuclear weapons in French Polynesia, against which Australia and New Zealand had repeatedly protested.[43] Despite these protests, and prolonged negotiations with the governments of both countries, France refused to change its programme of nuclear testing in the South Pacific, alleging that such testing was necessary to reach a stage allowing France to renounce atmospheric testing and rely exclusively on underground activities.[44] As a new series of nuclear tests was scheduled to start in 1973, Australia and New Zealand decided to bring their respective disputes with France before the International Court. France considered

[40] See Berg, 'Nuclear Tests Cases (Australia v. France; New Zealand v. France)', Heidelberg *Encycl.*, ii, pp. 216–19.

[41] On the legality of nuclear testing under international law (and, in particular, of nuclear testing in the atmosphere), see Margolis, 'The Hydrogen Bomb Experiments and International Law', 64 *Yale Law Journal* (1954–55), pp. 629–47; McDougal and Schlei, 'The Hydrogen Bomb in Perspective: Lawful Measures for Security', ibid., pp. 648–710; Furet, *Expérimentation des armes nucléaires et droit international public* (Paris, 1966); Tiewul, 'International Law and Nuclear Test Explosions on the High Seas', 8 *Cornell International Law Journal* (1974), pp. 45–70; Grief, 'Nuclear Tests and International Law', Pogany (ed.), *Nuclear Weapons and International Law* (New York, 1987), pp. 217–44; Miatello, *L'arme nucléaire en droit international* (Berne, 1987), pp. 458–513; Sarin, 'The Protection of the Human Environment in a Divided World and International Law', Bello and Ajibola (eds.), *Essays Elias*, i, pp. 240–3.

[42] The text of the application of Australia is reproduced in *I.C.J. Pleadings, Nuclear Tests*, i, p. 3; the text of the application of New Zealand is reproduced ibid., ii, p. 3.

[43] The intense opposition to the French nuclear testing in the seventies is regarded as one of the factors that subsequently led Australia, New Zealand and other States to sign the South Pacific Nuclear-Free Zone Treaty in 1985. The text of this treaty is reproduced in 24 *I.L.M.* (1985), p. 1440. For commentary, see Fischer, 'La zone dénuclearisée du Pacifique Sud', 31 *A.F.D.I.* (1985), pp. 23–57; Freestone and Davidson, 'Nuclear weapon-free zones', Pogany (ed.), *Nuclear Weapons and International Law*, pp. 195–201.

[44] See the French Note dated 7 February 1973, reproduced in *I.C.J. Pleadings, Nuclear Tests*, i, pp. 28–31, and the French statements reproduced in the judgments in the *Nuclear Tests* cases. See also Touscoz, *Droit international* (Paris, 1993), p. 357. On the French policy on nuclear testing in the fifties and sixties, see Kohl, *French Nuclear Diplomacy* (Princeton, 1971), pp. 164–8 and 245–51. For a recent restatement of the French doctrine of defence, see the *Livre blanc sur la défense 1994* (Paris, 1994) (extracts of this white paper were published in *Le Monde*, 25 February 1994, pp. 6–7).

that the International Court had no jurisdiction to try the cases and refused to take part in the proceedings.[45]

The International Court did not pronounce on either jurisdiction or the merits of the cases. In two separate judgments dated 20 December 1974,[46] it concluded that the real object of the applicant States was not a declaration that the nuclear tests were illegal under international law, but the termination of the French nuclear tests in the South Pacific. In this respect, it held that certain statements of the President of France and members of the French Government, which were not made before the International Court but were in the public domain,[47] constituted a unilateral undertaking *erga omnes* by France not to conduct further atmospheric tests.[48] On this ground, the International Court concluded that there were no longer any disputes between the parties and therefore there was nothing on which it should give a judgment.[49] This was the conclusion reached by the majority

[45] See the letter dated 16 May 1973, handed to the Registrar of the International Court by the French Ambassador to The Netherlands, reproduced (with the Annex) in *I.C.J. Pleadings, Nuclear Tests*, ii, pp. 347–57.

[46] *Nuclear Tests (Australia* v. *France)*, Judgment, I.C.J. Reports 1974, p. 99, and *Nuclear Tests (New Zealand* v. *France)*, Judgment, I.C.J. Reports 1974, p. 457. These two judgments were preceded by two orders on interim protection dated 22 June 1973 (I.C.J. Reports 1973, pp. 99 and 135). The International Court also issued four orders on the application of Fiji for permission to intervene (I.C.J. Reports 1973, pp. 320 and 324, and I.C.J. Reports 1974, pp. 530 and 535).

[47] Was the fact that the applicant States were not afforded an opportunity to comment on these statements a breach of the principle expressed in the maxim *audi alteram partem*? The International Court held that it was not. See I.C.J. Reports 1974, pp. 263–5 (paras. 32–33) and 468–9 (paras. 33–34). But see also the argument of Senator Murphy (Counsel for the Government of Australia), *I.C.J. Pleadings, Nuclear Tests*, i, p. 183. The issue is that of the weight carried by statements, which are relevant to a dispute before the International Court, when they are made by a non-appearing party outside the International Court, and the possibility for the party which participates in the proceedings to respond to these statements.

[48] Relevant passages from these statements are reported in the two judgments, I.C.J. Reports 1974, pp. 265–7 (paras. 34–40) and 469–71 (paras. 35–43). In the oral proceedings, both applicant States commented briefly on the Presidential statement (*I.C.J. Pleadings, Nuclear Tests*, i, pp. 389–90 (Argument of Senator Murphy) and 491–3 (Question by the President and Argument of Mr Lauterpacht); ibid., pp. 259–60 (Argument of Dr Finlay)). On the legal effects of unilateral acts of States, see Brownlie, *Principles*, pp. 637–40; *Oppenheim's International Law*, i, pp. 1187–96; Rousseau, *Droit international public*, i, pp. 416–32; Nguyen Quoc Dinh, Daillier and Pellet, *Droit international public*, pp. 353–9 (paras. 240–5); Giuliano, Scovazzi and Treves, *Diritto internazionale. Parte generale*, pp. 243–9. See also Rubin, 'The International Legal Effects of Unilateral Declarations', 71 *A.J.I.L.* (1977), pp. 1–30.

[49] Brownlie has remarked that 'the decision in the *Nuclear Tests* case was disappointing, and some observers regarded the case as an example of running for cover' ('Introduction: International Law in the Second Half of the Twentieth Century', Bello and Ajibola (eds.), *Essays Elias*, i, p. 11); Franck has written that the International Court 'decided not to decide' ('Word Made Law: The Decision of the ICJ in the Nuclear Tests Cases', 69 *A.J.I.L.* (1975), p. 613, and note 4 with some qualifications to this statement). According to Thirlway, the reason behind the International Court's conclusion 'was, apparently, the problem of jurisdiction' ('Reflections on the Articulation of International Judicial Decisions and the Problem of "Mootness"', Macdonald (ed.), *Essays in Honour of Wang Tieya* (Dordrecht, 1993), p. 804). See also Scobbie, 'Discontinuance in the International Court of Justice: the Enigma of the *Nuclear Tests* cases', 41 *I.C.L.Q.* (1992), p. 808.

of the International Court, from which four members (Judges Onyeama, Dillard, Jiménez de Aréchaga and Sir Humphrey Waldock), among the six who voted against the two judgments, expressed their forceful dissent in a joint opinion. Against the majority view, these four judges wrote that the object of the applicant States was to obtain a declaratory judgment.[50]

The International Court's reference, in its judgments,[51] to the concept and effects of unilateral statements made publicly and *erga omnes* raises several important issues. Thirlway has indicated one such issue by asking whether a unilateral declaration *erga omnes* necessarily produces an obligation *erga omnes*.[52] The assumption behind this question is that an obligation would be *erga omnes* not only if binding on all States alike, but also if opposable to one State alone (by way of a unilateral undertaking) and giving rise to correlative rights of protection vested in each other State. Though important, the question raised by Thirlway concerns a derivative application of the concept of *erga omnes*, which need not be discussed in the context of this work.

For the present purposes, elements of greater interest are to be found not in the judgments, but in the pleadings. Australia and New Zealand relied on the concept of obligations *erga omnes* when explaining their positions on the legality of nuclear testing in the atmosphere and justifying their legal standing to bring their disputes with France before the International Court. The two countries argued that the French nuclear tests violated several rights. In its Request, New Zealand asked for protection of its sovereign rights and stated that some of these rights (namely the right to be free from nuclear tests giving rise to radioactive fall-out, and the right to the preservation of the environment from unjustified artificial radioactive contamination) belonged to 'all members of the international community', including New Zealand.[53] Australia took, at least initially, a different approach. In its Request, it asked for protection of its sovereign rights—namely the right to be free from atmospheric nuclear tests, the right of territorial sovereignty, the right to determine the acts that could take place within its territory, the right to enjoy the freedom of the high seas, and certain rights based on the General Act for the Pacific Settlement of International Disputes to which

[50] I.C.J. Reports 1974, pp. 312 and 494. The joint dissenting opinion is partly reproduced in Brownlie, *System of the Law of Nations: State Responsibility. Part I* (Oxford, 1983), pp. 200–8. On declaratory judgments, see Brownlie, *Principles*, pp. 459–60.

[51] I.C.J. Reports 1974, p. 269 (para. 50) and 474 (para. 52).

[52] 'The Law and Procedure', 60 *B.Y.I.L.* (1989), pp. 11–12 and 18–20.

[53] 'Request for the Indication of Interim Measures of Protection submitted by the Government of New Zealand', *I.C.J. Pleadings, Nuclear Tests*, ii, p. 49, para. 2. See also 'Application Instituting Proceedings submitted by the Government of New Zealand', ibid., ii, p. 8, para. 28; 'Memorial on Jurisdiction and Admissibility submitted by the Government of New Zealand', ibid., ii, pp. 203–4, para. 190. On the argument put forward by New Zealand with respect to the protection of the environment, see Elkind, *Interim Protection. A Functional Approach* (The Hague, 1981), pp. 220–4.

Australia and France were parties—without articulating any of its claims in terms of rights held in common with other States.[54]

Despite this different approach, which counsel for New Zealand expressly acknowledged during the oral proceedings,[55] the arguments put forward by Australia and New Zealand presented strong similarities. Both States claimed that their right to be free from atmospheric nuclear testing did not depend on the actual proof of radioactive fall-out.[56] Likewise, both States relied in their pleadings on an international prohibition of nuclear testing in the atmosphere.

In support of this latter view, Australia and New Zealand referred, in the first place, to the Treaty Banning Nuclear Weapon Tests in the Atmosphere, in Outer Space and Under Water (the so-called 'Moscow Treaty'), which had been signed in Moscow ten years earlier.[57] Article I(1) of this treaty provides, in part, as follows:

> Each of the parties to this treaty undertakes to prohibit, to prevent, and not to carry out any nuclear weapon test explosion, or any other nuclear explosion, at any place under its jurisdiction or control:
> (a) in the atmosphere; beyond its limits, including outer space; or under water, including territorial waters or high seas; or
> (b) in any other environment if such explosion causes radioactive debris to be present outside the territorial limits of the State under whose jurisdiction or control such explosion is conducted . . .

[54] 'Request for the Indication of Interim Measures of Protection submitted by the Government of Australia', *I.C.J. Pleadings, Nuclear Tests*, i, p. 43, para. 3. See also 'Application Instituting Proceedings submitted by the Government of Australia', ibid., i, p. 14, para. 49; Argument of Senator Murphy, ibid., i, p. 167.

[55] Ibid., ii, p. 254. On the different approach followed by Australia and New Zealand, see Kos, 'Interim relief in the International Court: New Zealand and the Nuclear Test cases', 14 *Victoria University of Wellington Law Review* (1984), pp. 370–5 (referred to in Judge *ad hoc* Sir Geoffrey Palmer's dissenting opinion to *Request for an Examination of the Situation in Accordance with Paragraph 63 of the Court's Judgment of 20 December 1974 in the Nuclear Tests (New Zealand* v. *France) Case*, Order of 22 September 1995, I.C.J. Reports 1995, pp. 414–16, paras. 98–102).

[56] Although the language used in its Request may raise some doubts on this point, the oral proceedings clearly show that New Zealand too considered that atmospheric nuclear testing is prohibited as such, irrespective of the proof of damage. See, for example, the Argument of Dr Finlay, *I.C.J. Pleadings, Nuclear Tests*, ii, p. 100.

[57] The Moscow Treaty was done on 5 August 1963 and entered into force on 10 October 1963. The text is at 480 *U.N.T.S.* 43. For comment, see Furet, *Le Désarmement nucléaire* (Paris, 1973), pp. 86–111; Shaker, 'The Moscow Test Ban Treaty', 27 *Revue égyptienne de droit international* (1971), pp. 41–58. On the diplomatic negotiations that led to the adoption of the Moscow Treaty, see Jönsson, *The Soviet Union and the Test Ban. A Study in Soviet Negotiating Behavior* (Lund, 1975), pp. 77–176. On 10 September 1996, the United Nations General Assembly adopted a Comprehensive Nuclear-Test-Ban Treaty. The text of this Treaty (DOC.A/50/1027) is reproduced in 35 *I.L.M.* (1996), p. 1439. For background information on the negotiations that led to its adoption, see Schmalberger, *In Pursuit of a Nuclear Test Ban Treaty: A Guide to the Debate in the Conference on Disarmament* (New York, 1991); Schrag, *Global Action: Nuclear Test Ban Diplomacy at the End of the Cold War* (Boulder, 1992).

While this article would be relevant indeed, on account of its content, to the cases brought before the International Court, the problem is that, like all international agreements, the Moscow Treaty is binding only on the contracting parties.[58] This excludes from the reach of its prohibitions two major nuclear Powers, France and the People's Republic of China, which were not parties to the Moscow Treaty at the time of the *Nuclear Tests* cases, nor have since become parties to it.[59] Hence Australia and New Zealand were confronted with the question how the prohibition of nuclear testing in the atmosphere could be regarded as being opposable to France. While the pleadings contain a timid suggestion that Article I(1) of the Moscow Treaty would be opposable as such to third States,[60] the core of the argument developed by Australia and New Zealand was the opposability *erga omnes* of an international custom against atmospheric testing.

The two applicant States followed a two-step approach aimed at showing (a) the emergence of an international customary rule prohibiting nuclear testing in the atmosphere, and (b) the character *erga omnes* of the prohibition embodied in this rule. With respect to the first prong of the demonstration, Australia and New Zealand put forward the argument that a customary rule had gradually emerged as a result of the wide acceptance of the Moscow Treaty over a relatively short period of time,[61] and the reiterated protests of the international community to nuclear testing, especially if conducted in the atmosphere.[62] The process was similar to that described in

[58] On the principle of the relative effects of treaties, see section V of Chapter 2, above.

[59] France and China have not become parties to the Moscow Treaty. With respect to underground nuclear testing, on 8 April 1992 the French Government announced that it was suspending its programme for the rest of the year 'as a contribution to stop nuclear proliferation' (38 *Keesing's* (Apr. 1992), p. 38890). France then agreed to extend this moratorium on 4 July 1993 (39 *Keesing's* (July 1993), p. 39580). On 5 May 1994, the French President declared: 'Il n'y aura pas d'autres essais avant mai 1995. C'est ma décision. Tant que j'occuperai mes fonctions, il en sera ainsi . . .' ('M. Mitterand se dit persuadé que son successeur respectera le moratoire sur les essais nucléaires', *Le Monde*, 7 May 1994, p. 14). Upon his election as Mitterand's successor, Chirac ordered a final series of underground tests in the South Pacific, a decision that unleashed strong protests around the world. (As a result of this change of French policy, on 21 August 1995, New Zealand submitted to the International Court a 'Request for an Examination of the Situation' in accordance with para. 63 of the International Court's judgment in the *Nuclear Test* cases.) Before this final series, the People's Republic of China had been the only Power that had not observed a voluntary moratorium on underground testing, while declaring its commitment to a complete ban on nuclear testing in the context of effective nuclear disarmament. France and China have now signed the Comprehensive Nuclear-Test-Ban Treaty.

[60] See the Argument of Mr Byers, *I.C.J. Pleadings, Nuclear Tests*, i, p. 503.

[61] In a little more than ten years, by the time of the commencement of the proceedings before the International Court, 104 States had become parties to the Moscow Treaty (ibid., i, p. 510).

[62] For the arguments of Australia on the gradual emergence of an international custom against atmospheric tests of nuclear weapons, see ibid., i, especially pp. 182–6; 332–4, paras. 437–46; 502–4; 510. For those of New Zealand, see ibid., ii, especially pp. 50; 203, para. 189. This gradual process had been parallel to the evolving views of Australia and New Zealand on the legality of atmospheric testing. See the 'Australian Government's Aide-Memoire of 9

the International Court's judgment in the *North Sea Continental Shelf* cases, and the dissenting opinion of Judge Lachs (who had become the President of the International Court by the time of the *Nuclear Tests* cases), according to which a norm-creating provision contained in a treaty may acquire the status of a general rule of international law.[63] In other words, to establish the emergence of a customary rule prohibiting atmospheric testing, Australia and New Zealand adopted a line of argument which was already backed by authoritative pronouncements at the time of the pleadings.

Such an approach was unavailable for the second prong of the argument, because there was no 'traditional' path which Australia and New Zealand could follow to show that the international prohibition of atmospheric testing was opposable *erga omnes*. The judgment in the *Barcelona Traction* case, and the advisory opinion and the pleadings relating to Namibia, were certainly useful precedents for relying on the concept of obligations *erga omnes*, but did not contain any indication on how an argument based on this concept should be submitted to the International Court.

In its Memorial, Australia wrote that the various expressions and confirmations of the international custom against atmospheric tests

> are couched in terms of an *erga omnes* obligation and not in terms of an obligation owed to particular States. The duty to refrain from atmospheric nuclear testing is stated in absolute terms, rather than in terms relative to the incidence of the effect of nuclear testing upon particular States. The duty is thus owed to the international community; it is a duty of every State towards every other State.[64]

Similarly, New Zealand wrote in its Memorial that its right that no nuclear tests giving rise to radioactive fall-out be conducted, and its right to the preservation from unjustified artificial radioactive contamination of the environment,

> are shared in the sense that their violation in relation to any one nation will necessarily involve a violation of the same rights vested in other members of the international community. The degree of attention which individual countries are prepared to give to the protection of these rights and the degree of anxiety displayed in the event of their violation may, and obviously does, vary. Yet the rights are the same for all. They reflect a community interest in the protection of the security, life and health of all peoples and in the preservation of the global environment. The rights are held in common and the corresponding obligation imposed on France (and on any other nuclear power) is owed in equal measure to New Zealand and to every other member of the international community. It is an obligation *erga omnes*.[65]

September 1963', ibid., i, p. 19; 'Letter from New Zealand Prime Minister to French Ambassador, 19 December 1972', ibid., ii, p. 31.

[63] See *North Sea Continental Shelf*, Judgment, I.C.J. Reports 1969, p. 41, para. 71; p. 225 (Judge Lachs).

[64] *I.C.J. Pleadings, Nuclear Tests*, i, pp. 334–5, para. 448. (See also ibid., i, p. 331, para. 431.)

[65] Ibid., ii, p. 204, para. 191. (See also New Zealand's Request, ibid., ii, p. 52, para. 14.)

There are evident analogies between these definitions of an alleged obligation *erga omnes* against nuclear tests in the atmosphere and the International Court's concept of obligations *erga omnes* embodied in its dictum in the *Barcelona Traction* case. From the arguments developed by Australia and New Zealand, it is possible to infer that the obligation against nuclear tests in the atmosphere, as an obligation *erga omnes*,

(a) is stated in 'absolute' terms (the dictum refers to 'absolute' and 'unqualified' obligations);
(b) reflects a 'community interest' (the dictum refers to the 'concern of all States');
(c) protects fundamental goods, namely 'the security, life and health of all peoples' and 'the global environment' (security, life, and health are also some of the basic goods protected by the four examples of obligations *erga omnes* given in the dictum);
(d) has a prohibitory content (like the four examples given in the dictum);
(e) is not owed to particular States, but to the 'international community' (the dictum refers to the 'international community as a whole'); and
(f) its correlative rights of protection 'are held in common' (the dictum provides that 'all States can be held to have a legal interest' in the protection of obligations *erga omnes*).

The only major difference from the examples given in the International Court's dictum is that the alleged prohibition of nuclear testing in the atmosphere would not be opposable to all States, but only to nuclear Powers. However, as was mentioned earlier for another candidate,[66] this should be no obstacle to the configuration of an obligation *erga omnes*. After all, the fact that not all States are nuclear Powers does not affect the opposability of the alleged prohibition to all those States that are or will become nuclear Powers.

In justifying its contention that the prohibition of atmospheric testing was *erga omnes*, Australia relied in its oral arguments on the 'importance of the obligation' in question, which concerned the 'general rights of humanity' and involved 'questions of a moral order'. It also compared the first and second paragraphs of Article I(1) of the Moscow Treaty with one another, and concluded that the prohibition of atmospheric testing (unlike the prohibition of testing in other environments) is absolute because this activity 'by its very nature' leads to a fall-out that is potentially harmful to all States, with the consequence that each State has an interest in stopping it.[67]

[66] See section IV of Chapter 8, above.

[67] *I.C.J. Pleadings, Nuclear Tests*, i, pp. 411 (Argument of Senator Murphy), 502 and 504 (Argument of Mr Byers).

Likewise, New Zealand emphasized in its Memorial and oral arguments the similarities between the four examples of obligations *erga omnes* given by the International Court and the prohibition of atmospheric testing. With respect to the first category of rights that New Zealand claimed to hold in common with other States, namely the right to be free from nuclear tests giving rise to radioactive fall-out, New Zealand argued that the absolute prohibition of atmospheric testing 'has its roots in a universal concern for, and community interest in, the preservation of the security, life and health of the individual human being'. Hence the character *erga omnes* of the prohibition derives from the 'very essence' of the law on atmospheric testing. With respect to the second category of rights shared with other States, namely the right to the preservation of the environment, New Zealand insisted on its 'fundamental character' (partaken by the obligations *erga omnes* identified by the International Court), in the sense that their violation may be regarded as an 'affront to the conscience of mankind'.[68]

There is no need to discuss here whether the contention put forward by the applicant States is convincing. Though not participating in the proceedings, France voiced its objections to the view that an international custom prohibiting atmospheric tests had emerged and that this custom would be opposable to France.[69] Among the judges who appended separate opinions to the International Court's judgments in the *Nuclear Tests* cases, four addressed the issue of a customary prohibition of nuclear testing in the atmosphere. Two judges resolutely denied that such a custom had emerged,[70] one expressed doubts about it,[71] and one (the judge *ad hoc* chosen by the applicant States) acknowledged that the issue was controversial.[72] Opinions also vary in the international literature.[73] Moreover, it

[68] *I.C.J. Pleadings, Nuclear Tests*, ii, pp. 207–8, paras. 199–200, and pp. 210–11, paras. 208–10 (Memorial), and pp. 264–5 (Argument of Dr Finlay).

[69] On some aspects of the French position, see section V of Chapter 10, below.

[70] I.C.J. Reports 1974, pp. 286–8, paras. 15–20 (Judge Gros); pp. 305–6 and 489–90 (Judge Petrén).

[71] Ibid., p. 388, note 1 (Judge De Castro).

[72] Ibid., pp. 434–6 (Judge Barwick). Article 31, paragraph 2, of the Statute of the International Court of Justice provides that '[i]f the Court includes upon the Bench a judge of the nationality of one of the parties any other party may choose a person to sit as judge . . .' When Australia and New Zealand instituted proceedings against France, the International Court included among its members a judge of French nationality (Judge Gros) but no national of either Australia or New Zealand. Both countries chose the same person (Sir Garfield Barwick) to sit as judge *ad hoc* in their respective cases.

[73] Compare, for example, D'Amato, 'Legal Aspects of the French Nuclear Tests', 61 *A.J.I.L.* (1967), pp. 76–7, with Dupuy, P. M., 'L'affaire des essais nucléaires français et le contentieux de la responsabilité internationale publique', 20 *G.Y.I.L.* (1977), p. 398. See also Bianchi, 'Il Trattato di non proliferazione nucleare vent'anni dopo: prospettive di efficacia *ultra partes*', 100 *Studi senesi* (1988), pp. 314–15; Thierry, 'L'évolution du droit international', pp. 154–5. The question of the existence of a specific international custom prohibiting atmospheric testing does not pre-empt the question whether atmospheric tests may violate other customary

has been observed that the other nuclear Powers gave little support to the applicant States,[74] for fear that a ruling by the International Court against atmospheric testing might encroach upon their national defence strategies. While it is questionable whether this timid support should lead to the conclusion that no customary prohibition existed at that time, this element should certainly be taken into account when debating the possible character *erga omnes* of the outlawing of nuclear testing in the atmosphere.

Irrespective of the strengths and weaknesses of the argument put forward by the applicant States, the point to retain here from the foregoing discussion is that both Australia and New Zealand relied on elements of analogy with the obligations listed in the International Court's dictum to show that the prohibition of nuclear testing in the atmosphere was opposable *erga omnes*. While the International Court's decision not to address the merits of the cases precluded the applicant States from fully exploring the character *erga omnes* of the customary obligation against atmospheric testing,[75] the pleadings reveal without any shadow of doubt that Australia and New Zealand linked this character *erga omnes* to the content of this prohibition and the values it protects. On the other hand, neither State referred to any external test, such as the acceptance and recognition of the character *erga omnes* by the international community of States 'as a whole', as required for norms of *jus cogens*.[76] Even when the concept of *jus cogens* appears in the pleadings—for example, the reference to Waldock's suggestion ten years earlier that the rule prohibiting atmospheric testing was fast acquiring the status of a peremptory rule[77]—it does so to strengthen the argument that a customary prohibition of atmospheric testing had already emerged, without implying that the tests of *jus cogens* should also apply to obligations *erga omnes*.

rules of international law. See, for example, O'Connell, *Law of the Sea*, pp. 810–13; Barile, 'Sulle misure cautelari nell'affare degli esperimenti nucleari', 57 *Riv. dir. int.* (1974), pp. 23–4.

[74] See Reisman, 'Chinese Fallout', *The Nation*, 8 January 1977, as reproduced in McDougal and Reisman, *International Law*, pp. 44–6.

[75] For example, the Australian Memorial indicated that all the elements in support of the existence of a customary rule reflecting the prohibition embodied in the Moscow Treaty would be provided at the merits stage (*I.C.J. Pleadings, Nuclear Tests*, i, p. 333).

[76] See section III of Chapter 3, above.

[77] *I.C.J. Pleadings, Nuclear Tests*, i, p. 502. Australia was referring to Waldock's statement appearing in *Y.I.L.C.* (1964, I), p. 78, para. 47. Twenty years after Waldock's statement, Reuter was still rejecting the view that the Moscow Treaty 'was now the expression of a customary rule of *jus cogens*, binding on all States' (*Y.I.L.C.* (1984, I), p. 280, para. 20).

IV. Brief Considerations on the Required Degree of Evidence and Moral Content of Obligations *Erga Omnes*

The foregoing analysis of the advisory opinion on Namibia, and of the pleadings relating to it and the *Nuclear Tests* cases, calls for brief considerations on the required degree of evidence and moral content of obligations *erga omnes.*

All the four examples of obligations *erga omnes* given by the International Court in its dictum are those of obligations enjoying widespread support within the international community and, indeed, they all derive from norms of *jus cogens.* Whether obligations *erga omnes* and obligations deriving from peremptory rules coincide is a question that will be addressed, at least in part, in Chapter 10, below. In terms of legal argument, the analysis developed earlier in this work has shown that proof of the peremptory character of a rule is not a necessary pre-condition for inferring the character *erga omnes* of the ensuing obligation. In other words, the character *erga omnes* of an international obligation does not require proof that the norm giving rise to this obligation has been accepted and recognized as a norm of *jus cogens* by the international community of States as a whole. Thus, the distinguishing feature of obligations *erga omnes* must be sought elsewhere.

In its dictum, the International Court wrote that certain obligations are the concern of all States (i.e. are *erga omnes*) '[b]y their very nature'. Therefore, the International Court required that the 'nature' of a particular obligation, i.e. its 'essential qualities or properties', be examined to ascertain whether the obligation in question is *erga omnes.*[78] Instead of moving from the 'pessimistic' observation of the differences within the international community and providing for a safeguard such as the requirement of recognition and acceptance by the community 'as a whole',[79] the International Court took as a starting point the realistic acknowledgement that every obligation has a 'nature' that can be known and studied.[80] In doing so, the International Court was expressing, in theoretical terms, the approach that it had adopted in its advisory opinion on the Genocide Convention, when it considered the origin and purpose of the Genocide Convention and con-

[78] *Oxford English Dictionary*, x, under 'nature'. For Aristotle, '. . . the nature of a thing is its end. For what each thing is when fully developed, we call its nature . . .' (*The Complete Works*, 1252b (Politics).)

[79] This 'pessimistic' perspective that inspired the drafting of Article 53 of the Vienna Convention was clearly indicated by Ago, the Chairman of the Vienna Conference, in 'The Concept of "International Community as a Whole": A Guarantee to the Notion of State Crimes', Weiler, Cassese and Spinedi (eds.), *International Crimes*, pp. 252–3.

[80] In highlighting the different approach taken by the International Court and the Vienna Conference, the present writer is aware that part at least of this different approach can be explained in light of (a) the different process of decision-making followed by a judicial body and a diplomatic conference, and (b) the specific problems attaching to the nullity of treaties (i.e. the context in which the Vienna Conference addressed the issue of *jus cogens*).

cluded that the principles underlying this convention were binding on all States, irrespective of any conventional obligation.[81]

Thus, from the words and examples used by the International Court, it is clear that the rationale for the universal opposability of obligations *erga omnes* is not to be found in an extrinsic principle, such as the presumed or effective predominance of the will of the majority of States over a dissenting minority, but in the recognition of the universal validity of the basic moral values that these obligations are meant to protect. Each of the four obligations *erga omnes* listed by the International Court reflects an exceptionless moral norm (or moral absolute)[82] prohibiting an act which, in moral terms, is intrinsically evil (*malum in se*).[83] No State can elude the binding force of these obligations, not only because States recognize that it must be so, but also (and more fundamentally) because nobody can claim special exemptions from moral absolutes. This reasoning seems to the present writer to be entirely convincing, unless one is willing to take a 'short-sighted' view of rigid separation between law and morals,[84] or adheres to an 'archaic creed

[81] See section II of Chapter 5, above.

[82] On moral absolutes, see Finnis, *Moral Absolutes. Tradition, Revision, and Truth* (Washington, D.C., 1991). See also Rescher, *Moral Absolutes. An Essay on the Nature and Rationale of Morality* (New York, 1989); Tettamanzi, *Verità e libertà. Temi e prospettive di morale cristiana* (Casale Monferrato, 1993), pp. 367–416; May, W. E., *An Introduction to Moral Theology* (Huntington, Indiana, 1994), pp. 107–53.

[83] The distinction between *malum in se* and *malum prohibitum* dates back, at least implicitly, to Aristotle (*The Complete Works*, 1134b (Nicomachean Ethics)). On the history of this distinction, see Pinckaers, *Ce qu'on ne peut jamais faire. La question des actes intrinsèquement mauvais. Histoire et discussion*, 2nd edn. (Fribourg and Paris, 1995), especially pp. 20–66. The distinction is accepted, for example, in Blackstone, *Commentaries on the Laws of England* (A Facsimile of the First Edition of 1765–1769) (Chicago and London, 1979), i, pp. 57–8 (Introduction, Section II), but rejected, for example, in Kelsen, *General Theory of Law and State*, English trans. Wedberg (Cambridge, Mass., 1949), pp. 51–3 (Part One, Chapter III.A). Quoting a passage of the Pastoral Constitution on the Church in the Modern World *Gaudium et Spes* (of 7 December 1965), para. 80 of the Encyclical Letter *Veritatis Splendor* (of 6 August 1993) gives the following examples of intrinsic evils: '[w]hatever is hostile to life itself, such as any kind of homicide, genocide, abortion, euthanasia and voluntary suicide; whatever violates the integrity of the human person, such as mutilation, physical and mental torture and attempts to coerce the spirit; whatever is offensive to human dignity, such as subhuman living conditions, arbitrary imprisonment, deportation, slavery, prostitution and trafficking in women and children; degrading conditions of work which treat labourers as mere instruments of profit, and not as free responsible persons . . .' The three goods to which this list refers, namely life, physical and mental integrity, and human dignity, are essentially those protected by the four examples of obligations *erga omnes* given in the *Barcelona Traction* case. As to the specific evils cited by the International Court in its dictum, *Gaudium et Spes* had condemned genocide and slavery in para. 27, racial discrimination in para. 29, and war in para. 82. (For an English translation of *Gaudium et Spes*, see Abbott and Gallagher (eds.), *The Documents of Vatican II* (London, 1967), pp. 199–308.)

[84] Nguyen Quoc Dinh, Daillier and Pellet write of 'positivisme juridique à courte vue' (*Droit international public*, p. 206, para. 132). Among the innumerable international writings addressing (directly or indirectly) the relationship between law and morals, it will perhaps be sufficient to recall here the clear position expressed, with similar words, by Brierly and Baron Descamps. According to the former, while legal science 'tends necessarily to insist on the distinction between law and morality . . . the connexion between law and morals is really much more

of legal positivism' (increasingly difficult to support, if it was ever otherwise) such as that which was a contributory factor to the preservation of the system of apartheid.[85]

And in fact, the International Court was not reluctant to explore the 'very nature' of a category of international obligations, which it classified as obligations *erga omnes*. In doing so, it remained faithful to its role as a 'court of law'[86] without, however, confining itself to an 'ivory tower'.[87] In other words, in its dictum on obligations *erga omnes*, the International

fundamental than their distinction' ('The Basis of Obligation in International Law', Lauterpacht, H. and Waldock (eds.), *The Basis of Obligation in International Law and Other Papers by the Late James Leslie Brierly* (Oxford, 1958), p. 65). According to the latter, '[a]utant la distinction entre le droit et la morale est précise, naturelle, justifiée, et donne respectivement à chacune de ces sciences une physionomie propre, autant leur séparation serait arbitraire, pernicieuse et contre nature. . .' ('Le droit international nouveau. L'influence de la condamnation de la guerre sur l'évolution juridique internationale', 31 Hague *Recueil* (1930, I), pp. 421–2.) A clear understanding of the interaction between law and morals is all the more important for the study of contemporary international law, which seems to be more receptive to ethical considerations than was traditionally the case. (See Carrillo Salcedo, *El Derecho internacional en perspectiva historica* (Madrid, 1991), pp. 179–80.) On the current state of the debate on the interaction between law and morals, see George (ed.), *The Autonomy of Law. Essays on Legal Positivism* (Oxford, 1996).

85 Dugard, *Human Rights and the South African Legal Order* (Princeton, 1978), pp. 391–402. The present writer disagrees, however, with Dugard's 'new relativist approach'. If legal values were to be based on a relativist theory of ethics, how could one avoid the conclusion that the moral criteria of good and evil depend on the will of the majority or of the stronger, with the consequence that law may have whatever content the majority, or the stronger, decides? Against all forms of moral relativism, the following warning of O'Connell is as valuable today as when it was written: 'When a variety of contradictory moral attitudes are clamorously presented for our endorsement, one cannot be satisfied to regard them as equally moral; for a choice between them involves plumbing the depths of moral philosophy – something today people are distressingly reluctant to do.' ('The Law of Nature and the Law of Nations: Where does the Church Stand To-day?', 48/49 *Law and Justice* (1975), p. 52.)

86 In its judgment in the *South West Africa* cases (Second Phase), the International Court wrote that '[i]t is a court of law, and can take account of moral principles only in so far as these are given a sufficient expression in legal form.' (I.C.J. Reports 1966, p. 34, para. 49.) For some critical and thought-provoking remarks on this passage, see De Visscher, P., 'Cours général', p. 23, including note 33.

87 More generally, and quite independently from the concept of obligations *erga omnes*, Nagendra Singh articulated in a lucid way the concept that the International Court is not sitting in an 'ivory tower', as follows: 'Where should humanity look for guidance at such times of deep crisis if not to the spiritual leaders of whom you are one? "In the darkest hours of your existence, seek the wisdom and shelter of the sages" is what is ordained by my scriptures, and Your Holiness is indeed a sage of our times. We Members of the Court, sitting upon this bench, are appointed solely to deal with concrete problems or to advise on specific questions. But we try to do so in the light of general principles of justice and equity, hoping on each occasion to clarify and advance the application of a law acceptable to all nations. To that extent our work represents a moral, if not a spiritual, endeavour.' ('Address of welcome delivered by the President of the International Court of Justice, Judge Nagendra Singh, to His Holiness Pope John Paul II on the occasion of the latter's visit to the Court on 13 May 1985', *The International Court of Justice*, 3rd edn. (The Hague, 1986), p. 140.) The special significance of this passage has been highlighted by Weeramantry, in whose opinion it 'sums up the philosophy' of Judge Singh. ('An appreciation of Judge Nagendra Singh', Pathak and Dhokalia (eds.), *International Law. Essays Singh*, preliminary essay (vi).)

Court was free from what Merrills has called, in another context, the 'naive sophistication' that refrains from any mention of politics (and, one may add here, ethics) for fear that this might be seen as going beyond legal argument.[88]

A more troublesome question is the degree of evidence needed to show that the 'nature' of a particular obligation is such that the obligation is *erga omnes*.

In practice, the weight of evidence offered in support of the conclusion that an obligation is *erga omnes* varies depending on the particular circumstances of a case. Different factors are relevant, such as whether the question of the character *erga omnes* of an obligation arises before the International Court and, if so, whether it arises in a contentious case or in an advisory opinion, even if it would be wrong to assume that advisory opinions require a lesser degree of evidence, as they would invariably be a more propitious setting than judgments in contentious cases for the declaration of the character *erga omnes* of an international obligation. (The previous analysis has shown how several concurrent references to the concept of *erga omnes* appeared in the *Nicaragua* case[89] while, on the other hand, how problematic were the different views on the concept exposed in the pleadings relating to the advisory opinion on Namibia.)[90] As to the pleadings of the parties, the decision on how much evidence to produce in support of the proposition that an obligation is *erga omnes* becomes part of the wider strategy for the proceedings, which in turn depends on several other factors such as, for example, whether both parties or the applicant State alone appear before the International Court.

In all these respects, the International Court's judgments and advisory opinions discussed earlier in this work are instructive. For example, the International Court's finding that the prohibition of genocide is binding on States irrespective of any conventional obligation was merely declaratory, genocide being undoubtedly an intrinsic evil condemned by all States.[91] On the other hand, the proof that, in the early seventies, atmospheric testing was prohibited *erga omnes* presented greater difficulties for the applicant States. Behind the disputes leading to the *Nuclear Tests* cases, there was a clash of values and political priorities, namely respect for the environment on the one hand and respect for the sovereign right to national defence on the other, both abstractly worthy of protection. This explains at least in part why, in their pleadings before the International Court, Australia and New Zealand submitted very articulate arguments in support of the opposability *erga omnes* of the prohibition of atmospheric testing.[92] Perhaps, an inter-

[88] 'On Teaching International Law', 10 *The Journal of the Society of Public Teachers of Law* (New Series, 1968–69), p. 173.

[89] See section IV of Chapter 4, above.

[90] See section II, above.

[91] See section II of Chapter 5, above.

[92] See section III, above.

mediate case is provided in the *South West Africa* cases, where the applicant States had the problem of showing with respect to the mandate for South West Africa that not only the general outlawing of racial discrimination, but also the particular policy of apartheid, was prohibited *erga omnes*.[93] To sum up, there is no hard and fast rule to identify the required degree of evidence for an obligation *erga omnes*. Each case will have to be examined on its own merits.

Irrespective of any degree of evidence, is it not reasonable to fear the proliferation of obligations *erga omnes*, or conversely question the very possibility that such obligations may at all be identified, in the pluralistic society of States? The two components of this question should be clearly distinguished. On the one hand, in the International Court's dictum itself, the concept of *erga omnes* was restricted to only a few selected examples of international obligations supported by a widespread consensus within the international community, and protecting basic moral values. As repeatedly stated throughout the present work, the obligations *erga omnes* listed in the judgment in the *Barcelona Traction* case are no more than examples. However, the very concept embodied in the International Court's dictum allows the inference that additional candidates should not be multiplied freely, but identified rigorously.

On the other hand, the difficulties in identifying obligations *erga omnes* should not be exaggerated. Similar difficulties had to be confronted by the representatives of different human traditions who were called to contribute to the elaboration of the Universal Declaration of Human Rights. Despite their differences, these representatives succeeded in agreeing on the final text of the Universal Declaration. As one of them, the French philosopher Jacques Maritain, has remarked, this agreement on common principles of action was possible because it was not subject to a concurrent agreement on their underlying premises.[94] Likewise, sixteen judges representing the 'main forms of civilization' and the 'principal legal systems of the world'[95] succeeded in agreeing on the concept of obligations *erga omnes*,[96] thus showing that the pluralistic society of States can accommodate the recognition of international obligations which protect basic moral values and are binding on every State without exception. On this point, the present writer would go even farther, and submit that this recognition is (today more than

[93] See section III of Chapter 7, above.

[94] 'Autour de la nouvelle déclaration universelle des droits de l'homme (Introduction aux textes réunis par l'Unesco, juillet-août 1948)', reproduced in Maritain, *Les droits de l'homme*, Mougel ed. (Paris, 1989), pp. 125–37. In making this remark, Maritain was not denying, of course, the importance of searching and finding the truth about the underlying premises.

[95] See Article 9 of the Statute of the International Court

[96] As was mentioned in section III of Chapter 1, above, the only dissenting judge in the *Barcelona Traction* case, Judge *ad hoc* Riphagen, did not object to the concept of obligations *erga omnes*.

ever before) a pre-condition of any meaningful dialogue among the different components of international society.[97]

The sixteen members of the International Court agreed not only on the concept of obligations *erga omnes*, but also on four concrete examples which, to the present writer's knowledge, nobody has ever contested. These four examples may serve as the starting point when considering the character *erga omnes* of other candidates. This is indeed what happened in the *Nuclear Tests* cases, when New Zealand referred to the underlying values of the obligations identified by the International Court in support of its argument that the prohibition of atmospheric testing shared the same character.[98]

Apart from reasons of convenience, the reference to the four examples given by the International Court is important in another respect. In his general course at the Hague Academy, Lachs wrote that 'there is no way back' from norms of *jus cogens*.[99] The particular circumstance for this remark was the analysis of the concept of *jus cogens superveniens* and the idea that, in terms of legal technique, a peremptory rule may only be changed by a subsequent, equally peremptory, rule. By shifting the attention from legal technique to the underlying values, and by extending Lachs's remark from *jus cogens* to obligations *erga omnes*, it is legitimate to suggest that 'there is no way back' from obligations *erga omnes* either. It is difficult to imagine not only how the outlawing of aggression or the prohibition of genocide may cease to be obligations *erga omnes*, but also how an international obligation may be regarded as being *erga omnes*, if it is in conflict with any one of the four examples given by the International Court or is incompatible with the underlying values that these examples are meant to protect and promote.

V. Conclusions

The candidates of obligations *erga omnes* discussed in this chapter are those of prohibitions protecting values other than those underlying the examples given by the International Court in the *Barcelona Traction* case. In the advisory opinion on Namibia, it was an obligation of non-recognition; in the pleadings relating to the *Nuclear Tests* cases, it was an obligation in the area of environmental law. This confirms the vitality of the concept, which was also one of the findings of Chapter 8, above.

[97] In his speech at the Louvre in May 1961, King Baudouin of Belgium said that there cannot be dialogue, in any human society, without the common recognition of certain supreme truths: 'Nul dialogue n'est valable entre les hommes si ceux-ci ne communient pas à quelque vérité souveraine et reconnue par tous.' (The Louvre speech is partially reproduced in 'Baudouin Ier', *Le Soir*, Supp. of 2 August 1993, p. 16.) These words are all the more significant, as they were pronounced by a Head of State whose faithfulness to one such supreme truth was severely put to the test. (See Suenens, *Le Roi Baudouin. Une vie qui nous parle* (Ertvelde, 1995), pp. 126–8.)

[98] See section III, above.

[99] 'The Development and General Trends', p. 209.

However, the main conclusion from the foregoing analysis is not this, but the confirmation that obligations *erga omnes* reflect basic moral values, and, as such, must be identified regorously. The degree of evidence needed to prove the character *erga omnes* of an international obligation varies depending on the circumstances. A too rigid approach to this issue does not seem to correspond to the indications emerging from practice.

A final remark relates to the process followed so far in examining the concept of obligations *erga omnes*. The starting point was the separate analysis of each of the four examples given by the International Court. The four examples were then compared with one another. This comparison led to five common elements, which were in turn tested in light of selected candidates of obligations *erga omnes*. A better understanding of the concept of obligations *erga omnes* now requires an additional step in this process. This additional step is the comparison between the concept of obligations *erga omnes* and the concepts of *jus cogens* and *actio popularis*. This is the subject of the next chapter.

10

Particular Aspects of the Relationship Between the Concept of Obligations *Erga Omnes* and the Concepts of *Jus Cogens* and *Actio Popularis*

I. Introduction

Before examining the relationship between the concept of obligations *erga omnes*, on the one hand, and the concepts of *jus cogens* and *actio popularis*, on the other, it is appropriate to explain briefly why and within which limits the concept of obligations *erga omnes* is being compared with these notions.

With respect to *jus cogens*, the answer to the first question is implicitly contained in the analysis developed throughout this work. In particular, Chapter 3, above, showed that the concept of *jus cogens* was consecrated in the Vienna Convention on the Law of Treaties just a few months before the International Court's dictum on obligations *erga omnes*. The decisive contribution to the emergence of both concepts came from two organs of the United Nations, namely the International Court in the case of obligations *erga omnes* and the International Law Commission in the case of *jus cogens*.

The two concepts, however, have much more in common than the timing of their emergence and their derivation from the work of organs of the United Nations. In essence, both peremptory rules and obligations *erga omnes* are meant to protect basic moral values, and they both require significant support within the international community (in the case of *jus cogens*, the acceptance and recognition by the international community of States 'as a whole').

These similarities have led several writers to compare the two concepts with one another.[1] In the present context, it would be inappropriate to

[1] See, for example, Gaja, 'Obligations *Erga Omnes*, International Crimes and *Jus Cogens*: A Tentative Analysis of Three Related Concepts', Weiler, Cassese and Spinedi (eds.), *International Crimes*, pp. 151–60; de Hoogh, 'The Relationship between *Jus Cogens*, Obligations *Erga Omnes* and International Crimes: Peremptory Norms in Perspective', 42 *Austrian Journal of Public and International Law* (1991), pp. 183–214; Acosta Estévez, 'Normas de *ius cogens*, efecto *erga omnes*, crimen internacional y la teoria de los circulos concéntricos', 11 *Anuario de derecho internacional* (1995), pp. 3–22; Picone, 'Recensione: Lauri Hannikainen, *Peremptory Norms* (jus cogens) *in International Law. Historical Developments. Criteria, Present Status*, Helsinki, Finnish Lawyers' Publishing Company, 1988, pp. XXXII–781', *73 Riv.dir.int.* (1990), pp. 791–5; Macdonald, 'Fundamental Norms in Contemporary International Law', 25

develop a comprehensive comparison between the two concepts, especially because this work has discussed the concept of *jus cogens* within the limits of what is strictly necessary to obtain a clearer understanding of obligations *erga omnes*. Thus, there would be an obvious risk of drawing hasty conclusions from an incomplete analysis. At the same time, however, it is entirely legitimate to consider particular aspects of the relationship between the two concepts. Once again, the limited perspective will be that of elucidating the concept of obligations *erga omnes*.

As to *actio popularis*, its relevance here derives from the fact that, according to the International Court's dictum in the *Barcelona Traction* case, 'all States can be held to have a legal interest' in the protection of obligations *erga omnes*. As a subsequent section of this chapter will show, *actio popularis* has increasingly attracted the interest of international writers since the time of the dictum on obligations *erga omnes*, although much of the study on this subject remains to be done. Once again, the purpose here is neither to add to the general literature on *actio popularis*, nor to examine whether the admissibility of *actio popularis* is desirable for the protection of obligations *erga omnes*. Both questions would find their proper setting in a monograph on *actio popularis*. What belongs instead to a monograph on the concept of obligations *erga omnes* (such as the present one) is the more limited question whether the concept of obligations *erga omnes* necessarily implies the admissibility of *actio popularis*.

The fact that the greater proportion of the space here is dedicated to *jus cogens* rather than to *actio popularis* reflects the inchoate stage in the study of *actio popularis* and, more generally, of the correlative rights of obligations *erga omnes* and the available remedies in case of their breach.

II. Obligations *Erga Omnes* and Norms of *Jus Cogens*: (a) Preliminary Considerations

The starting point in comparing the concept of obligations *erga omnes* with the concept of *jus cogens* is an obvious consideration, so obvious that it runs the risk of being overlooked: when referring to *jus cogens*, one invariably refers to norms, whereas, when referring to *erga omnes*, one invariably refers to obligations. A peremptory rule, like other international norms, gives rise not only to obligations, but also to other legal relations. For example, according to the definition of *jus cogens* in Article 53 of the Vienna Convention, an important element is the disability, or absence of power, of States to contract out of a norm of *jus cogens*.[2]

Canadian Yearbook of International Law (1987), pp. 136–9; Strozzi, 'I "principi" dell'ordinamento internazionale', 47 *La Comunità internazionale* (1992), pp. 178–83.

[2] See section IV of Chapter 3, above.

Occasionally, international writers have used the expression '*erga omnes*' for rules instead of obligations. For example, in a loose sense, all customary rules may be said to apply *erga omnes* in the sense that custom, unlike international conventions, has a general sphere of efficacy.[3] However, this proposition must be qualified in several ways. First of all, a State may evade the application of a customary rule by operation of the principle of the persistent objector.[4] Secondly, unless an international custom belongs to the category of *jus cogens*, two or more States can derogate by treaty from the operation of that custom. Thirdly, even assuming that it is binding on all States because no State has objected to it or has derogated from it, an international custom will normally give rise to a series of separate, bilateral relations between States and not to relations between a State on the one hand, and the whole international community on the other. To sum up, speaking of all customs alike as being *erga omnes* is possible, but not in the technical sense in which the International Court referred to the concept of obligations *erga omnes* in its dictum.

Conversely, there have been instances where the adjective 'imperative' (which, in its common use, is synonymous with 'peremptory') has been predicated of obligations instead of rules. This happened, for example, in the International Court's judgment in the *Hostages* case.[5] In the late seventies, the United States brought a case against Iran before the International Court, alleging violation by Iran of certain customary and treaty rules in the area of diplomatic and consular protection. Some passages from the International Court's order on a request for provisional measures, and from the judgment on the merits, have given rise to different views in the international literature on whether the International Court meant to refer to the concepts of *jus cogens* and obligations *erga omnes*, even without expressly using these terms.[6]

In its order on provisional measures, the International Court mentioned certain 'imperative obligations' inherent in diplomatic and consular relations.[7] Then, in its judgment on the merits, it wrote that the tense

[3] See Ago in *Y.I.L.C.* (1976, I), p. 75.

[4] See section V of Chapter 3, above.

[5] See Oellers Frahm, 'United States Diplomatic and Consular Staff in Tehran Case', Heidelberg *Encycl.*, ii, pp. 282–6. For a critical evaluation of the International Court's contribution to the resolution of the hostages dispute, see Janis, 'The International Court', Janis (ed.), *International Courts for the Twenty-First Century* (Dordrecht, 1992), pp. 25–7.

[6] See, for example, Zoller, 'L'affaire du personnel diplomatique et consulaire des Etats-Unis à Teheran', 84 *R.G.D.I.P.* (1980), p. 1024; Bretton, 'L'affaire des "otages" américains devant la Cour Internationale de Justice', 108 *J.D.I.* (1980), p. 820; Morelli, 'Norme c.d. fondamentali e norme cogenti', 64 *Riv. dir. int.* (1981), pp. 509–10; Frowein, 'Jus Cogens', p. 329; Gaja, '*Jus Cogens* Beyond the Vienna Convention', p. 286; Lattanzi, *Garanzie dei diritti dell'uomo nel diritto internazionale generale* (Milan, 1983), p. 134, note 116; Gutiérrez Espada, *Derecho internacional publico. 1: Introduccion y fuentes*, 4th edn. (Barcelona, 1993), p. 83.

[7] *United States Diplomatic and Consular Staff in Tehran*, Provisional Measures, Order of 15 December 1979, I.C.J. Reports 1979, p. 20, para. 41. The English text, which is authoritative, uses the adjective 'imperative' instead of 'peremptory', which is the usual term that defines *jus*

diplomatic relations between Iran and the United States did not affect the 'imperative character' of the legal obligations incumbent on Iran, and drew the attention of the 'entire international community' to the 'irreparable harm' caused by events such as the taking of the United States hostages in Iran.[8] This is the language on which some writers have relied to conclude that the International Court meant to refer to obligations *erga omnes* deriving from norms of *jus cogens*.

However, other passages seem to support a different view. The International Court's order on provisional measures recalled that a State is under no obligation to maintain diplomatic relations with another and that, when two States enter into diplomatic relations with one another, the obligations thus assumed are 'reciprocal'.[9] From this, one may infer that, in the International Court's view, these obligations would be owed on an exclusively reciprocal basis, by one State to another, and not to the international community as a whole. This is not meant to deny that all States have an interest in that every State should comply with these obligations, because their breach poses a serious threat to peaceful relations at large.[10] (In the case of the United States hostages in Tehran, the international community took action in support of the efforts of the United States to obtain the release of the hostages.)[11] In this sense, the obligations relating to diplomatic protection may be regarded as being 'imperative'. They are, in the words used by Judge Lachs in a separate opinion attached to the judgment on the merits, the 'common property of the international community'.[12] As

cogens. On the other hand, the French translation of the judgment uses the expression 'obligations impératives', which closely resembles the expression 'normes impératives' used in the French text of Article 53 of the Vienna Convention on the Law of Treaties.

[8] *United States Diplomatic and Consular Staff in Tehran*, Judgment, I.C.J. Reports 1980, p. 41, para. 88; p. 42, para. 92.

[9] I.C.J. Reports 1979, p. 19, para. 38.

[10] In a statement dated 29 November 1979, the United States Secretary of State of the time, Cyrus Vance, declared before the United Nations Security Council that, by its action, Iran had placed itself 'in conflict with the structure of international law' (*I.C.J. Pleadings, United States Diplomatic and Consular Staff in Tehran*, p. 227). Likewise, in response to a request from the Diet, the Director-General of the Treaties Bureau of the Japanese Ministry of Foreign Affairs observed that the taking of the hostages in Tehran was 'not simply a bilateral issue between the United States and Iran but a problem for the international community as a whole' ('Minutes of the Committee for Foreign Affairs, House of Representatives, 91st Session of the Diet, No. 14 (April 9, 1980)', p. 3, partially reproduced, in English, in 29 *Japanese Annual of International Law* (1986), pp. 92–4). See also the debate in the House of Commons of the United Kingdom, reproduced in 982 *Parliamentary Debates—Commons* (1979–80), 5th Series, March 31 to April 18, pp. 790–6.

[11] See the reference contained in Arangio-Ruiz, 'Fourth Report on State Responsibility' (Doc.A/CN.4/444), para. 38. In the literature, see de Guttry, *Le rappresaglie non comportanti la coercizione militare nel diritto internazionale* (Milan, 1985), pp. 106–9.

[12] I.C.J. Reports 1980, pp. 48–9. Judge Lachs insisted that the principles and rules on diplomatic protection have been accepted, from time immemorial, by all the components of the international community. This passage in Judge Lachs's separate opinion may be considered to be an indirect response to the statement by the Iranian Revolution Council spokesman

such, they derive from the restricted number of international principles and rules which are essential for the orderly development of relations between States. However, these principles and rules do not all necessarily belong to *jus cogens* or give rise to obligations *erga omnes*.[13] In addition, one might have expected that the International Court, under the Presidency of Sir Humphrey Waldock (who had been a major player in the drafting of Article 53 of the Vienna Convention, as Special Rapporteur on the law of treaties), would have expressly referred to *jus cogens* if this was what it meant.

For present purposes, it is unnecessary to opt for one or the other of these different views on the relevance of the concepts of *jus cogens* and obligations *erga omnes* to the *Hostages* case. The relevant point is that these different views have been articulated in the traditional terms of rules of *jus cogens* and obligations *erga omnes*. In other words, the expression 'imperative obligations', as used by the International Court, is not a new term of art that would contradict the obvious consideration, made at the beginning of this section, that the concept of *jus cogens* refers to rules, while the concept of *erga omnes* refers to obligations. If it is so, then it is useless to compare in the abstract the two concepts with one another. One can compare entities or concepts belonging to the same category, such as a rule with another rule or an obligation with another obligation, but not a rule with an obligation.

Therefore, moving from the premise that an obligation, together with its correlative right(s), is one of the fundamental legal relations that a rule can produce, the relationship between *jus cogens* and obligations *erga omnes* can be better understood in terms of the following questions: do norms of *jus cogens* invariably give rise to obligations *erga omnes*? Conversely, do obligations *erga omnes* invariably derive from norms of *jus cogens*? The next two sections will address some aspects of these questions.

(Gotbzadeh), who declared on 19 November 1979 that the laws on diplomatic immunity 'have been made to guarantee the crimes that the representatives of the big powers have committed in the small countries.' This statement is reproduced in *I.C.J. Pleadings, United States Diplomatic and Consular Staff in Tehran*, p. 96.

[13] According to Jaenicke, the category of the international principles and rules which are the fundamental basis of the international legal system (which he calls 'international public order') is wider than the category of *jus cogens*. These fundamental rules and principles 'may possibly, though not necessarily' give rise to obligations *erga omnes* ('International Public Order', pp. 314–18). Among international writers, some think that the inviolability of diplomatic agents probably belongs to *jus cogens* (see, for example, von Glahn, *Law Among Nations. An Introduction to Public International Law*, 7th edn. (Boston, 1996), p. 482), while others hold the opposite view (see, for example, Tanzi, *L'immunità dalla giurisdizione degli agenti diplomatici* (Padua, 1991), pp. 176–81).

III. Obligations *Erga Omnes* and Norms of *Jus Cogens*: (b) Do Norms of *Jus Cogens* Invariably Give Rise to Obligations *Erga Omnes*? (Some Considerations in Light of the Concept of 'Regional' *Jus Cogens*)

Each of the four examples of obligations *erga omnes* given by the International Court in the *Barcelona Traction* case derives from a norm of *jus cogens*. This fact is significant, and confirms the close analogies between the two concepts. However, the list of examples provided by the International Court is not enough, by itself, to allow the inference that all peremptory rules give rise invariably to obligations *erga omnes*. As was indicated in the previous chapter, the proof of the character *erga omnes* of an international obligation does not require that this obligation satisfy the tests of norms of *jus cogens*.[14] Thus, while the peremptory character of a norm may make it easier to prove that the ensuing obligation is *erga omnes* (and *vice versa*), different kinds of supporting argument will separately apply to prove the peremptory character of the norm and, respectively, the character *erga omnes* of the obligation.

Moreover, as will be discussed in section V, below, certain legal relations resulting from a peremptory rule (such as those pertaining to the invocation of the invalidity of a treaty) do not operate *erga omnes*, but only with respect to the parties to the treaty derogating from the peremptory rule in question. From this it follows that the complex relationship that always exists between a rule and the obligation(s) deriving from it requires great caution in indicating precisely which legal relations deriving from a norm of *jus cogens* are *erga omnes*, and which are not.

A difficulty of a different kind arises when, instead of peremptory rules of general international law, one is confronted with norms belonging to the so-called 'regional' *jus cogens*. It is a fact of international life that groups of States establish institutions of regional co-operation, as well as treaty and customary rules that have a limited sphere of application. These closer links within groups of States vary with the changes of alliance among States, and the different levels of political and economic integration among them. In this respect, one may recall, for example, the controversies relating to the existence of a special system of international law among the States of the American continent,[15] or the principles of proletarian internationalism

[14] See section IV of Chapter 9, above.

[15] For a brief but very helpful analysis of the problem, see Oppenheim, *International Law*, i, 8th edn. Lauterpacht, H., pp. 52–3. The main views on the subject (and especially those of Alvarez on the one hand, and Sa Vianna on the other) are summarized and examined in various works, such as Urrutia, 'La codification du droit international en Amérique', 22 Hague *Recueil* (1928, II), pp. 170–3; Yepes, 'La contribution de l'Amérique latine au développement du droit international public et privé', 32 ibid. (1930, II), pp. 776–92; id., 'Les problèmes fondamentaux du droit des gens en Amérique', 47 ibid. (1934, I), pp. 5–16. For a more

among the countries of the former socialist bloc (if not a fully developed system of 'socialist' international law, as some have suggested).[16] Irrespective of these controversies, it is widely accepted that the existence of normative sub-systems does not affect the fundamental unity of international law,[17] and that regional treaties cannot derogate anyway from peremptory rules of general international law.[18]

Subject to this latter prohibition, can a group of States go one step further than the rest of the international community and create norms of 'regional' *jus cogens* that would be binding only on the States belonging to that group?[19] The Vienna Convention does not provide any indications on this issue, as it defines general *jus cogens* and is silent on 'regional' *jus cogens*. In principle, there does not seem to be any objection to the possibility of 'regional' *jus cogens*, provided (as was already mentioned above) that this is not in conflict with peremptory rules of general international law. After all, if States can establish regional systems of public order by treaty (such as the European Convention on Human Rights), there is no reason why they should not be allowed to establish a regional system of public order based on regional customs having a peremptory character.

In practice, however, 'regional' *jus cogens* differs in many essential ways from general *jus cogens*. First and foremost, the requirement of acceptance

recent evaluation, see Barberis, 'Les règles spécifiques du droit international en Amérique latine', 235 ibid. (1992, V), pp. 94–6. The references to an American legal system, in this footnote, and to a socialist legal system, in the next one, are not meant to neglect the debate about other regional systems. For example, on the existence of an Islamic legal system, see the considerations developed in Bedjaoui, 'La vision de las culturas no occidentales sobre la legitimidad del derecho internacional contemporaneo', 11 *Anuario de derecho internacional* (1995), pp. 54–62.

[16] See Tunkin, *Theory*, pp. 427–47. A comprehensive work on the subject is Schweisfurth, *Sozialistisches Völkerrecht? Darstellung—Analyse—Wertung der sowjetmarxistischen Theorie vom Völkerrecht 'neuen Typs'* (Berlin, 1979). Of interest is also a series of articles which appeared in the *American Journal of International Law* in the early seventies (the time when, in consideration of political events, the interest in the subject reached its peak). See Hazard, 'Renewed Emphasis upon a Socialist International Law', 65 *A.J.I.L.* (1971), pp. 142–8; Butler, '"Socialist International Law" or "Socialist Principles of International Relations"?', ibid., pp. 796–800; Osakwe, 'Socialist International Law Revisited', 66 ibid. (1972), pp. 596–600. The present writer examined this topic in 'Consuetudine internazionale, principi generali e norme di *jus cogens* nella dottrina sovietica (anche in rapporto all'Atto di Helsinki)' (Thesis for the J.D. degree (Laurea in Giurisprudenza), University of Ferrara, Faculty of Law, academic year 1983/84), pp. 171–5.

[17] See Arangio-Ruiz, *The United Nations Declaration on Friendly Relations*, pp. 157–60.

[18] Very explicit on this point is Tunkin, *Theory*, p. 444.

[19] On 'regional' *jus cogens*, see, for example, Virally, 'Réflexions sur le "*jus cogens*"', p. 14; *Conference on International law, Lagonissi (Greece)*, p. 71 (Suy), p. 107 (Boutros-Ghali); Sztucki, *Jus Cogens*, pp. 107–8; *L'élaboration du droit international public. Colloque de Toulouse*, p. 212 (Ténékidès); Thierry, Combacau, Sur and Vallée, *Droit international public*, 3rd edn. (Paris, 1981), pp. 77–8; Gaja, '*Jus Cogens* Beyond the Vienna Convention', p. 284. See also de Quadros, 'La Convention Européenne des Droits de l'Homme: un cas de ius cogens régional?', Beyerlin, Bothe, Hofmann and Petersmann (eds.), *Recht. Festschrift Bernhardt*, pp. 555–62.

and recognition by the 'international community of States as a whole' would not apply to 'regional' *jus cogens*, for at least two reasons. The first one is that behind 'regional' norms of *jus cogens* there is, by definition, a limited community of States (however large), and not the almost universal community of States which must support peremptory rules of general international law. The second reason is that a 'regional' norm of *jus cogens*, as a local custom, is not automatically opposable to all members of a particular community, but only to those that have accepted to be bound by the norm in question. In other words, a particular community cannot bring about a norm of 'regional' *jus cogens* that would automatically be applicable to every State in that region, irrespective of an expression of consent by each individual member of that community. Thus, 'regional' *jus cogens* differs from general *jus cogens* not only in its content, but also in its very concept.

For similar reasons, there is evidently no place for obligations *erga omnes* within the context of 'regional' *jus cogens*. First of all, peremptory rules which apply to a restricted community of States are inherently unable to produce international obligations binding on all States alike. Secondly, even within that restricted community, an obligation could not be *erga omnes* in the sense of binding a State irrespective of its consent. Despite this contrast, one cannot exclude the possibility that the concept of obligations *erga omnes* may be instrumental to the development of norms of 'regional' *jus cogens*. Evidence of this can be found in the resolution of the Inter-American Commission on Human Rights in the case of *Roach and Pinkerton*.[20] It is useful to consider this case briefly, starting from a summary of its facts.

Two United States nationals, James Roach and Jay Pinkerton had been found guilty, respectively in South Carolina and in Texas, for crimes they had committed when they were aged seventeen. For these crimes, they were both sentenced to death and executed.[21] By a petition brought on their

[20] Resolution No. 3/87 (Case No. 9647, United States), approved by the Commission at its 925th session held on 27 March 1987 (OEA/Ser.L/V/II.69—Doc. 17). Brief references to this decision, and a discussion on the broader issue whether an international prohibition of the death penalty is emerging in international law, can be found in Schabas, *The Abolition of the Death Penalty in International Law* (Cambridge, 1993); Schreuer, 'Capital Punishment and Human Rights', Beyerlin, Bothe, Hofmann and Petersmann (eds.) *Recht. Festschrift Bernhardt*, pp. 563–77; Orlin, 'The Prohibition of the Death Penalty: An Emerging International Norm?', Rosas, Helgesen and Gomien (eds.), *Human Rights in a Changing East–West Perspective* (London and New York, 1990), pp. 136–73.

[21] Imposition of capital punishment on juveniles continues to be a controversial issue in the United States. On 26 June 1989, the United States Supreme Court held, by five votes to four, that the execution of persons for murders committed at sixteen or seventeen years of age is not a cruel and unusual punishment in violation of the Eighth Amendment of the United States Constitution. See *Stanford* v. *Kentucky*, 492 U.S. 361 (1989). For a summary of this decision, see Lasser, 'Stanford v. Kentucky', Hall, K. L. (ed.), *The Oxford Companion to the Supreme Court*, p. 821. The decision is criticized in Fitzpatrick, 'The Relevance of Customary

behalf before the Inter-American Commission on Human Rights (an organ of the Organization of the American States),[22] the petitioners asked the Commission to find that the United States, by executing Roach and Pinkerton, had breached the American Declaration of the Rights and Duties of Man,[23] as interpreted in the light of an alleged international custom prohibiting the execution of persons for crimes committed when they were under the age of eighteen.[24]

In response to this latter contention, the United States Government disagreed with the petitioners' interpretation of the American Declaration. However, this point (like other important issues addressed by the parties before the Commission)[25] is not directly relevant here. The United States Government then rejected the idea that an international custom prohibited the execution of persons for crimes committed when they were under eighteen. In any event, this customary rule would not be binding on the United States, because that country had persistently objected to it. In support of this allegation, the United States Government recalled that it had opposed the provisions on the minimum age contained in the International Covenant on Civil and Political Rights and in the American Convention on Human Rights, and that the United States President's proposal to the Senate to ratify the American Convention on Human Rights expressly reserved the rights of the United States in this respect.

The dispute between the parties on the existence of the customary rule in question was directly relevant to the resolution of the case, because the American Convention on Human Rights, which expressly prohibits in Article 4, paragraph 5, the execution of juveniles for crimes committed when they were under eighteen, is not opposable as such to the United States, which is not a party to it. For this reason, in their argument before the Inter-American Commission, the petitioners submitted that a rule having the same content of Article 4, paragraph 5, had emerged in customary international law. In its resolution, the Inter-American Commission concluded that a customary rule on the minimum age of eighteen years was emerging, but had not yet emerged.[26] On this point, the Commission

International Norms to the Death Penalty in the United States', *25 Georgia Journal of International and Comparative Law* (1995/96), pp. 165–80.

[22] On the inter-American system for the protection of human rights, see Robertson and Merrills, *Human Rights in the World. An introduction to the study of the international protection of human rights*, 3rd edn. (Manchester and New York, 1989, reprinted with minor revisions 1992), pp. 161–95.

[23] The text is reproduced in Brownlie (ed.), *Basic Documents on Human Rights*, pp. 488–94.

[24] The petitioners also requested the Commission to recommend a moratorium on the execution of other juveniles in the United States, but there is no such recommendation in the Commission's conclusions.

[25] Another important issue was the extent to which the provisions of the Vienna Convention on the Law of Treaties (or, better, the customary rules that they reflect) apply to instruments like the American Declaration, which is not an international treaty.

[26] Resolution No. 3/87, para. 60.

substantially accepted the argument put forward by the United States, including the contention that this norm would not be binding on the United States anyway, because of its persistent objection. However, the Commission qualified its conclusion on this latter point in an important way: it wrote that the principle of the persistent objector applies to international customs generally, but not to rules of *jus cogens*.

Although neither the petitioners nor the United States Government had raised the question of *jus cogens* in their submissions, the Commission decided that the concept was relevant to the case in hand.[27] Having remarked that the major distinctive characteristic of *jus cogens* is its 'relative indelibility',[28] the Commission emphasized the humanitarian and moral content of peremptory rules by quoting extensively from the International Court's advisory opinion on the Genocide Convention,[29] and the dictum on obligations *erga omnes* in the *Barcelona Traction* case. It then concluded that

> in the member States of the OAS there is recognized a norm of *jus cogens* which prohibits the State execution of children. This norm is accepted by all States of the inter-American system, including the United States.[30]

Why did the Commission resort to the concept of 'regional' *jus cogens*, applicable within the inter-American system? The Commission denied the existence of an international custom establishing a minimum age for the imposition of the death penalty, but acknowledged that all the member States of the inter-American system (including the United States) agreed that an international custom prohibits the imposition of the death penalty on children. In other words, there was a general consensus against sentencing juveniles to death, but not all States agreed that juveniles, for this purpose, were those under the age of eighteen. For example, under the legal system of the United States, the individual States are free to determine the minimum age at which a juvenile offender may be transferred to an adult criminal court, and the death penalty can be imposed also on juveniles between the age of sixteen and eighteen.[31]

[27] 'The Commission . . . is not a judicial body and is not limited to considering only the submissions presented by the parties to a dispute.' (Ibid., para. 54.)

[28] In this observation, the Commission was expressly relying on Brownlie, *Principles of Public International Law*, 3rd edn. (Oxford, 1979), p. 513 (at the same page in the 4th edn.).

[29] See section II of Chapter 5, above.

[30] Resolution No. 3/87, para. 56. The two concepts of 'execution of children' and 'imposition of the death penalty on children' can be used interchangeably (as the Commission did in its resolution) because the time necessary for the proceedings makes it practically impossible that all remedies will be exhausted when the offender is still under the age of eighteen.

[31] This is the reason why the Committee of Foreign Relations of the United States Senate, while reporting favourably on the International Covenant on Civil and Political Rights, proposed that the United States, when ratifying the Convention, attach a reservation to Article 6 of the Convention that prohibits the imposition of the death penalty for crimes committed under the age of eighteen. See 'United States: Senate Committee on Foreign Relations Report on the International Covenant on Civil and Political Rights', 31 *I.L.M.* (1992), p. 645,

Accordingly, the main issue before the Commission was whether the United States Government, by leaving each member State of the United States the freedom to determine the minimum age for the imposition of the death penalty, was in breach of the human rights standards applicable within the inter-American system.[32] It is exactly on this point that the peremptory character of the prohibition for the member States of the Organization of American States to impose the death penalty on children acquired its full meaning. The practice within the United States is extremely varied. Some States have abolished the death penalty altogether, while others allow that a juvenile may be tried and sentenced in an adult criminal court. A sixteen-year-old offender may be sentenced to death in Virginia but not in the District of Columbia, if the same crime is committed across the Memorial Bridge. Thus, the imposition of the death penalty ends up depending on such a 'fortuitous' element as the place where the crime is committed. For these reasons, by a majority of five votes to one,[33] the Commission concluded that, in executing Roach and Pinkerton, the United States had violated Articles I and II of the American Declaration, which protect the right to life and the right to equality before the law.[34]

To sum up, without disposing of the case before the Inter-American Commission, the concept of obligations *erga omnes* was instrumental to the Commission's conclusions on the existence of a peremptory rule applicable within the inter-American system and on some of the consequences that may be drawn from that finding. It was not instrumental in the sense that the norm of 'regional' *jus cogens* found by the Inter-American Commission would be opposable to the United States even without its consent. As was mentioned earlier, this is not the effect of 'regional' systems of *jus cogens*, which are entirely based on consent. (In the particular instance, the Commission remarked that the prohibition of the execution of children was opposable to the United States because that country accepted this prohibition.) Rather, the concept of obligations *erga omnes* was instrumental to the Commission's conclusions in the sense that, by resorting to the dictum in the *Barcelona Traction* case, the Inter-American Commission singled out certain fundamental values that it found to be also at the basis of the prohibition of the execution of children applicable within the inter-American system. Thus, the concept of obligations *erga omnes*, while not dispositive of the case, was an important element in the reasoning of the Commission in reaching its conclusions on the contents and characters of the inter-American system of public order.

especially paras. VI.2, VII.2 and IX(2). In ratifying the Covenant in 1992, the United States reserved the right to impose capital punishment 'for crimes committed by persons below eighteen years of age.' (*Multilateral Treaties Deposited with the Secretary-General. Status as at 31 December 1995*, p. 130.)

32 Resolution No. 3/87, para. 43.

33 There is no explanation, in the resolution, of the reasons behind the one dissent.

34 Resolution No. 3/87, paras. 64 and 65.

IV. Obligations *Erga Omnes* and Norms of *Jus Cogens*: (c) Do Obligations *Erga Omnes* Invariably Derive from Norms of *Jus Cogens*? (Some Considerations in Light of the Concept of 'Self-Existent' Obligations)

Similar considerations to those developed at the beginning of section III may be repeated at the outset of this section. On the one hand, the particular content of obligations *erga omnes*, and their requirement for a high degree of support within the international community, make it reasonable to assume that the rules from which they derive will, as a rule, meet the tests of *jus cogens*. On the other hand, the separate degree of evidence of obligations *erga omnes* precludes the possibility of asserting that this must invariably be so. In practice, the main issue connected with the question raised in this paragraph is whether obligations *erga omnes* may be blurred into the wider category of the so-called 'self-existent' obligations. The issue may be summarized as follows.

Usually, a multilateral treaty gives rise to separate bilateral relations between each pair of the States parties to it. As Riphagen (a former Special Rapporteur on the law of State responsibility) has correctly pointed out, these legal relations remain bilateral even when they have uniform content for all States that are parties to that treaty.[35] A different situation exists in the case of obligations created by law-making or standard-setting treaties. In his second report on the law of treaties, Fitzmaurice distinguished between treaties that grant reciprocal benefits and those that require absolute or integral performance. Treaties belonging to this latter category give rise to what Fitzmaurice called 'self-existent' obligations, which exclude any considerations of reciprocity and are binding, as treaty rules, 'towards all the world rather than towards particular parties'.[36]

Among the traditional examples of treaties establishing 'self-existent' obligations, there are the international conventions protecting human rights. A written statement submitted by the United Kingdom to the International Court with respect to the question of reservations to the Genocide Convention sheds light on the essential characteristics of these obligations. The United Kingdom observed that certain treaties are 'contractual' not only in form but also in their operation, because they give rise

[35] See 'Preliminary Report on the content, forms and degrees of international responsibility (Part 2 of the draft articles on State responsibility)' (Doc.A/CN.4/330), *Y.I.L.C.* (1980, II, Part 1), p. 120, para. 65; 'Sixth Report on (1) the content, form and degrees of State responsibility, and (2) the "implementation" (mise en œuvre) of international responsibility and the settlement of disputes (Parts two and three of the draft articles)' (Doc.A/CN.4/389), *Y.I.L.C.* (1985, II, Part I), p. 7, para. 14.

[36] Fitzmaurice, 'Second Report on the Law of Treaties' (Doc.A/CN.4/107), *Y.I.L.C.* (1957, II), p. 54, para. 126.

to mutual rights and obligations between each party to the treaty in question and each other party. However (the British argument continued), the Genocide Convention does not belong to this category of treaties. Once a State has become a party to the Genocide Convention, it is bound to carry out obligations that are 'indivisible' and 'absolute' in the sense that, with respect to a party to the treaty, they are 'assumed for all and towards all'. In other words,

[i]t is only the method of their assumption which is contractual. Their *operation* is not dependent on the existence of a contractual tie with other States.[37]

These elements of indivisibility of the obligation and solidarity among the addressees of the corresponding right of protection present an evident element of analogy with obligations *erga omnes*. Therefore, it is not suprising that, besides the expressions 'self-existent obligations', 'obligations solidaires',[38] and 'obligations intégrales',[39] writers have also denoted this class of obligations by expressions such as 'obligations *erga omnes partes*',[40] and 'obligations *erga omnes contractantes*'.[41] These expressions are entirely legitimate, provided that they do not confuse the essential distinction between, on the one hand, obligations *erga omnes* in the sense indicated by the International Court in its dictum, i.e. obligations opposable to all States alike irrespective of consent, and, on the other hand, obligations that do not operate on a traditional basis of reciprocity but remain nevertheless contractual as to their origin.[42]

That the distinction between these two categories of obligations is not a purely terminological question is illustrated by the work of codification of the law of State responsibility, and the wider consequences of its debates. In his fourth report on this subject, Arangio-Ruiz remarked that

the concept of *erga omnes* obligation is not characterized by the importance of the interest protected by the norm—this aspect being typical of *jus cogens*—but rather by the 'legal indivisibility' of the content of the obligation, namely by the fact that the rule in question provides for obligations which bind simultaneously each and every addressee State with respect to all the others. This legal structure is typical not

[37] *I.C.J. Pleadings, Reservations to the Convention on the Prevention and Punishment of the Crime of Genocide*, p. 64 (and, to follow the development of the whole argument, pp. 62–9).

[38] Sperduti, 'Les obligations solidaires en droit international', Makarczyk (ed.), *Essays Lachs*, pp. 271–5.

[39] Reuter, *Droit international public*, p. 152.

[40] Hutchinson, D. N., 'Solidarity and Breaches of Multilateral Treaties', 59 *B.Y.I.L.* (1988), pp. 155–6.

[41] Cassese, 'Remarks on the Present Legal Regulation of Crimes of States', p. 57.

[42] The use of the expression 'obligations *erga omnes*' (without any additional qualifications such as those indicated in the text) to identify not only the obligations indicated by the International Court in its dictum, but also 'self-existent' obligations, would be a case of 'polysémie interne', which Cornu defines as the situation in which the same term has two or more different meanings. (*Linguistique juridique* (Paris, 1990), pp. 89–90.)

only of peremptory norms, but also of other norms of general international law and of a number of multilateral treaty rules (*erga omnes partes* obligations).[43]

This remark may be acceptable within its limited context. In fact, the same report clarifies that in the area of State responsibility the question concerning obligations *erga omnes* is not to identify their content, but to determine the consequences deriving from the relationship between obligations *erga omnes* and their correlative rights *omnium*.[44] In other words, it is understandable that the codification of the law of State responsibility should concentrate above all on the consequences attaching to the breach of international obligations. However, it would be wholly unacceptable to suggest in general terms, as it has been suggested,[45] that the defining characteristic of obligations *erga omnes* is that their breach affects all States (or, in the case of obligations *erga omnes partes*, all its addressees). This proposition, by reversing the order of priority between cause and effect, is unduly restrictive: it reduces the fundamental problem of the content of obligations *erga omnes* and the values they protect to issues of legal technique which, while important, certainly do not exhaust the definition of obligations *erga omnes*. Contrary to this proposition, it is useful to recall what Ago, one of Arangio-Ruiz's predecessors as Special Rapporteur of the International Law Commission on the law of State responsibility, wrote on the International Court's distinction, in the *Barcelona Traction* case, between obligations *erga omnes* and other obligations:

> . . . it seems unquestionable that, by making such affirmations, the Court sought to draw a fundamental distinction with regard to international obligations and hence with regard to acts committed in breach of those obligations. In addition, it implicitly recognized that that distinction should influence the determination of subjects entitled to invoke State responsibility. In the Court's view, there are in fact a number, albeit limited, of international obligations which, by reason of their importance to the international community as a whole, are—unlike the others—obligations in respect of which all States have a legal interest. It follows, the Court held, that the responsibility flowing from the breach of those obligations is entailed not only with regard to the State that has been the direct victim of the breach (e.g., a State which has suffered an act of aggression in its territory); it is also entailed with regard to all the other members of the international community . . .[46]

[43] 'Fourth Report on State Responsibility—*Addendum*' (Doc.A/CN.4/444/Add.1), para. 92. While this paragraph refers to 'obligations' *erga omnes*, the following paragraph refers to 'rules' *erga omnes*. Are these expressions meant to refer to one and the same concept? The context of both paragraphs would seem to suggest a positive answer to this question.

[44] 'Fourth Report on State Responsibility—*Addendum*' (Doc.A/CN.4/444/Add.2), para. 133.

[45] See, for example, Gaja, 'Obligations *Erga Omnes*, International Crimes and *Jus Cogens*', pp. 151–3, para. 1; Lattanzi, *Garanzie dei diritti dell'uomo*, pp. 124–39.

[46] 'Fifth Report on State responsibility' (Doc.A/CN.4/291 and Add.1 and 2), *Y.I.L.C.* (1976, II, Part 1), p. 29, para. 89.

This passage clarifies three important points for the analysis of the present section, namely:

(a) the obligations identified by the International Court in the *Barcelona Traction* case are *erga omnes* primarily because of the intrinsic value of their content, and only secondarily because of their legal structure;
(b) the reason why special rights and remedies attach to these obligations is that these obligations are *erga omnes*, and not the other way around; and
(c) obligations *erga omnes* are few in number, unlike 'self-existent' obligations, which are as many as the international treaties giving rise to them.

To sum up, despite the similarities in legal structure, there are fundamental differences between obligations *erga omnes* and 'self-existent' obligations. To merge both categories for all purposes under the same heading would be misleading, and prejudice at one time the ability to see the irreconcilable differences between them, and to examine critically their similarities without just assuming them.[47]

V. Obligations *Erga Omnes* and Norms of *Jus Cogens*: (d) Brief Considerations on the Respective Functions of the Two Concepts

So far, the relationship between *jus cogens* and obligations *erga omnes* has been examined in terms of the relationship between norm and obligation. Another useful perspective for the purpose of comparison is to consider the respective functions of the two concepts. More particularly, the question to be addressed here is the following: in which circumstances does a State resort to the concept of obligations *erga omnes* instead of *jus cogens*? The immediate answer that one might be tempted to give to this question is that resort to the concept of *jus cogens* is restricted to those instances where the question is about the nullity of a treaty This answer, however, would be simplistic and would not take proper account of the expansion of the concept of *jus cogens* well beyond the law of treaties.[48] At the same time, the distinction of a situation that involves the nullity of a treaty from one that

[47] Picone has appropriately written that the tendency to assimilate the operation of obligations *erga omnes* to that of 'self-existent' obligations 'is justified to the limited extent that the operation of the two categories of rules in analysed from a purely *structural* perspective . . . [b]ut it is methodologically more questionable if it extends to *all* the characteristic features of their respective legal regimes . . .' ('Recensione: Claudia Annacker, *Die Durchsetzung von erga omnes Verpflichtungen vor dem Internationalen Gerichtshof*, Hamburg, 1994, Verlag Dr. Kovac, pp. XXII–146', 77 *Riv. dir. int.* (1994), p. 1120).

[48] See section I of Chapter 3, above.

does not can still serve as a useful framework of analysis in this section. Thus, the first situation to be examined is one involving the nullity of a treaty.

Pursuant to the definition embodied in Article 53 of the Vienna Convention, a treaty in conflict with a norm of *jus cogens* is void. Which is the kind of nullity that attaches to such a treaty? In particular, who can invoke the nullity of a treaty allegedly in conflict with a norm of *jus cogens*? Only the prejudiced party to the treaty in question? All the parties to the treaty concerned? All the parties to the Vienna Convention on the Law of Treaties? All States without exception?[49] In his general course at the Hague Academy, Jiménez de Aréchaga distinguished, by analogy with municipal law, between absolute and relative nullity. Part of the distinction between the two types of nullity is that, while relative nullity may be invoked only by the State that has suffered the prejudice, absolute nullity operates *erga omnes* in the sense that any 'interested State' may invoke it or a court may declare it on its own initiative. From these premisses, Jiménez de Aréchaga concluded that the very concept of *jus cogens* suggests that the nullity attaching to derogation from a peremptory rule is absolute. However, he acknowledged that the letter of the Vienna Convention leaves the door open to a different conclusion.[50]

There are certainly grounds for arguing in favour of, or against, allowing all States to request that a treaty in conflict with a peremptory rule be declared void. Commenting on one of Sir Hersch Lauterpacht's early drafts on the law of treaties, Yepes (a former member of the International Law Commission) put forward a forceful argument in favour of allowing all States to request a declaration of nullity. He wrote as follows:

> It often happens that a weak State is obliged to sign an unlawful treaty under pressure from a more powerful State. For this reason it is necessary to provide for a kind of international *actio popularis*, and endow any State, even if it has no direct interest in the matter, with the power to apply for the annulment of a treaty with an unlawful object concluded by other States. This is the only effective way to obtain the annulment of certain treaties . . .[51]

[49] For a very useful discussion of these questions, see Rosenne, 'Bilateralism and Community Interest in the Codified Law of Treaties', Friedmann, Henkin and Lissitzyn (eds.), *Transnational Law. Essays Jessup*, pp. 202–27. See also Rozakis, *The Concept of Jus Cogens*, pp. 115–18; Ronzitti, 'La disciplina dello jus cogens', pp. 272–3.

[50] 'International Law in the Past Third of a Century', pp. 68–9 and 318, note 118.

[51] 'Mémoire presenté par M. J. M. Yepes' (Doc.A/CN.4/L.46), *Y.I.L.C.* (1953, II), pp. 163–6, at p. 166. The French original reads as follows: 'Il arrive bien souvent qu'un Etat faible soit obligé de signer un traité illicite sous la pression qu'exerce sur lui un autre Etat plus puissant. C'est pourquoi il faut établir une sorte d'action populaire internationale pour autoriser tout Etat, meme s'il n'a aucun intérêt direct, à demander l'annulation d'un traité à objet illicite conclu par d'autres Etats. C'est là le seul moyen efficace d'obtenir l'annulation de certains traités . . .' The English translation given in the text is a slightly revised version of the translation appearing in Rosenne, 'Bilateralism and Community Interest', p. 213.

Therefore, Yepes emphasized that the question of who can invoke the nullity of a treaty allegedly in conflict with a norm of *jus cogens* has a very practical aspect, because it may be extremely difficult for the weaker party to an unlawful treaty to request a declaration of nullity. However, opposite considerations have also been put forward. In its comment on Waldock's draft Article 37 (Article 53 in the final text of the Vienna Convention), the Luxembourg Government remarked that it was unclear from the draft

who would be entitled to invoke the ground of nullity dealt with in the article, the parties or third States. If the former, the Luxembourg Government says that this would mean that a party, which had itself contributed to the conclusion and entry into force of a treaty, would contradict its own act; in short, that it would be a case of *venire contra factum proprium*. On the other hand, if a third State were to be considered entitled to invoke the nullity of the treaty, the Luxembourg Government says this would be inconsistent with the principle of relativity which, in the absence of any supranational authority, continues still to dominate the whole subject of treaties.[52]

Between these opposite views, the Vienna Convention reflects a compromise solution. This solution is embodied in Article 65, which is the key provision (as the International Law Commission pointed out in its commentary on the draft articles)[53] on the application of the articles of the Vienna Convention relating to the invalidity, termination, or suspension of treaties, including Article 53.[54] The first paragraph of Article 65 reads in part as follows:

A party which, under the provisions of the present Convention, invokes either a defect in its consent to be bound by a treaty or a ground for impeaching the validity of a treaty, terminating it, withdrawing from it or suspending its operation, must notify the other parties of its claim.

The language is clear: it is only a 'party' to the treaty allegedly in conflict with a norm of *jus cogens* that can invoke its nullity.[55] Such a 'party' may be any party whatsoever to this treaty, and not only the party that has been prejudiced. On the other hand, the ability to invoke the invalidity is restricted to the parties to the treaty concerned, and therefore a general

[52] *Y.I.L.C.* (1966, II), pp. 20–1. At the Vienna Conference, some representatives of States discussed the issue of who can apply for a declaration of nullity. See *U.N.C.L.T., Off. Recs., First Session*, p. 299, para. 61 (Chile); p. 310, para. 38 (Israel); p. 314, para. 77 (Ethiopia); pp. 323–4, para. 26 (Switzerland); p. 325, para. 40 (Norway).

[53] 'Draft Articles on the Law of Treaties', p. 81, para. (1) (commentary on draft Article 62).

[54] The examination of the preparatory works of the Vienna Convention confirms that Article 65 covers all cases of invalidity. See Rozakis, *The Concept of Jus Cogens*, pp. 116–17.

[55] Under Article 2 of the Vienna Convention, 'party' means 'a State which has consented to be bound by the treaty and for which the treaty is in force', while 'treaty' means any 'international agreement concluded between States in written form and governed by international law . . .'. Therefore, there is no doubt that the term 'party' in Article 65 refers to a party to the treaty in question, and not to a party to the Vienna Convention.

interest is not a sufficient ground, under the Vienna Convention, for a third State to request a declaration of nullity. As Rosenne has noticed,[56] this reflects the general approach that emerged at the Vienna Conference, where States were reluctant to give full recognition to the community interest in regard of the procedures for the declaration of invalidity of a treaty as well as in other respects.

What are the practical consequences deriving from the impossibility for a third State to invoke the nullity of a treaty allegedly in conflict with a norm of *jus cogens*?[57] As was mentioned by Yepes, a weak State may find it impracticable to invoke the nullity of a treaty. Moreover, irrespective of the strength or weakness of each party, all parties could be willing to carry out a treaty allegedly in conflict with *jus cogens*. In similar circumstances, the concept of obligations *erga omnes* may have a very practical impact. Even without a formal declaration of nullity, the implementation of a treaty conflicting with a peremptory rule would be likely to be in breach of an obligation *erga omnes*, and therefore be the concern of all States.[58] Third States may react to this breach by requesting that the parties to the treaty concerned acknowledge that the treaty is void.[59] In this way, the measures taken outside the mechanism provided under the Vienna Convention would achieve a similar result to the one excluded by the Vienna Convention, namely the possibility for a third State to invoke the nullity of a treaty. To sum up, the concept of obligations *erga omnes* strengthens the protection of the fundamental values embodied in the norms of *jus cogens*, by allowing third States to put pressure on the parties to a treaty conflicting with *jus cogens*, with a view to making them desist from carrying it out.

As was mentioned at the beginning of this section, the relationship between the concept of obligations *erga omnes* and the concept of *jus cogens* may also be examined in situations that do not involve the nullity of a treaty. A practical instance of this case is offered by the disputes on nuclear testing in the South Pacific between France on the one hand, and Australia and New Zealand on the other. Chapter 9, above, examined at some length several arguments put forward by Australia and New Zealand in support of the proposition that an international obligation *erga omnes* prohibited nuclear tests in the atmosphere.

France rejected the idea that an international custom prohibiting atmospheric testing had emerged and added that, in any event, an international custom to that effect would not be opposable to it. France did not participate in the proceedings, and therefore could not submit to the International Court

[56] 'Bilateralism and Community Interest', pp. 221–2.

[57] See the brief discussion of this point by Mendelson, in Cassese and Weiler (eds.), *Change and Stability*, p. 98.

[58] See, on this point, Barile, 'La structure de l'ordre juridique international. Règles générales et règles conventionnelles', 161 Hague *Recueil* (1978, III), p. 90.

[59] See Ronzitti, 'Lo jus cogens nella Convenzione di Vienna', p. 273, note 56.

any arguments in support of its position. However, the French Government addressed the scientific and legal aspects of nuclear testing in the South Pacific in a white paper that was published immediately after the commencement of the proceedings before the International Court. In this white paper, it referred explicitly to the arguments submitted by Australia and New Zealand in their Requests,[60] thus making it possible to compare the opposite views on nuclear testing developed by the parties to the disputes.

The French Government articulated several arguments against the court proceedings initiated by Australia and New Zealand. In particular, it alleged that (a) the applicant States were discriminating against France by comparison with the other nuclear Powers, (b) the French nuclear tests in the South Pacific were neither in breach of the applicant States' sovereignty nor in violation of the international law of the environment, and (c) the International Court had no jurisdiction over the cases.[61] Besides raising these issues, the French Government also addressed the question of the legality of nuclear testing in the atmosphere.[62] On this point, the white paper reflects the view that the atmospheric tests conducted by France in the South Pacific were not in conflict with any new norm of *jus cogens* that would be opposable to all States. In support of this position, the French Government raised the general issue whether the concept of *jus cogens*, as embodied in an international agreement (the Vienna Convention of 1969) which at that time had not yet entered into force, could be regarded at all as being generally accepted. It further argued that, in any event, the alleged norm against atmospheric tests did not belong to *jus cogens*, because this norm had not been recognized and accepted as such by the international

[60] *Livre blanc sur les expériences nucléaires* (Comité Interministériel pour l'Information, June 1973). (The writer is grateful to the French 'Service d'information et de diffusion du Premier Ministre (SID)' for putting a copy of this white paper at his disposal.) At p. 1, in the Preamble, it is written that 'le Gouvernement français ne peut accepter l'argumentation présentée à la Cour internationale de justice par les gouvernements d'Australie et de Nouvelle Zélande.' (The different capitalization of the word 'gouvernement' appears in the text.)

[61] With respect to the thorny issue of jurisdiction in the *Nuclear Tests* cases, part of the French objection was based on the difference between its original declaration of 1959, recognizing the compulsory jurisdiction of the International Court under Article 36(2) of the Statute (the 'optional clause'), and the new declaration of 1966, which reserved all disputes relating to questions of national defence. (On the 'optional clause', see Merrills, 'The Optional Clause Today', 50 *B.Y.I.L.* (1979), pp. 87–116 (with a reference to the French declaration at pp. 101–2); id., 'The Optional Clause Revisited', 64 *B.Y.I.L.* (1993), pp. 197–244.) As a result of the two orders rendered by the International Court in the *Nuclear Tests* cases in 1973, France withdrew its declaration. (See Dupuy, P. M., *Droit international public*, p. 424, para. 522.) This, however, has not prevented France from voting in favour of requests for advisory opinions and submitting arguments to the International Court (Guillaume, 'Le France et la Cour internationale de Justice', *L'internationalité dans les institutions et le droit: convergences et défis. Etudes offertes à Alain Plantey* (Paris, 1995), p. 124).

[62] *Livre blanc sur les expériences nucléaires*, pp. 13–23. On the French position with respect to the main questions raised by Australia and New Zealand before the International Court, see also de Lacharrière, 'Commentaires sur la position juridique de la France à l'égard de la licéité de ses expériences nucléaires', 19 *A.F.D.I.* (1973), pp. 235–51.

community of States as a whole, as required by Article 53 of the Vienna Convention. The key passage from the French argument reads as follows:

> In effect, at least two countries have clearly expressed an opposite view: France—which adheres to this position, in the absence of real measures of world disarmament—and China. Now, these two countries, which represent many more than 800 million people, i.e. a substantial proportion of the world population, are two of the five permanent members of the Security Council.[63]

Thus, in rebuttal of a possible argument that a peremptory rule prohibiting atmospheric testing had been accepted and recognized by States belonging to different continents, different levels of development, and different ideological groups, France relied on the political power and huge population of France and China to deny the very possibility that a peremptory norm against atmospheric testing could emerge against the opposition of these two Powers.[64] This part of the French argument is further evidence of the variety and controversial nature of any attempts to define the requirement of recognition and acceptance of a norm of *jus cogens* by the international community of States as a whole.[65]

In any event, it is unnecessary to evaluate here the cogency of the French argument. The interesting point is that, while France denied the existence of a norm of *jus cogens* against atmospheric testing, almost no trace of *jus cogens* appeared in the pleadings of Australia and New Zealand before the International Court, as France itself acknowledged in its white paper.[66] Indeed, despite several references by the applicant States to the Vienna Convention on the Law of Treaties,[67] and occasional references to the 'international community as a whole' or similar expressions,[68] it was only

[63] *Livre blanc sur les expériences nucléaires*, p. 18. The French original reads as follows: 'Deux pays au moins, en effet, se sont nettement prononcés dans le sens contraire: la France—qui maintient cette position à défaut de véritables mesures de désarmement mondial—et la Chine. Or, ces deux pays, qui représentent largement plus de 800 millions d'habitants, c'est-à-dire une proportion substantielle de la population mondiale, sont deux des cinq membres permanents du Conseil de Sécurité.'

[64] In an article in which he referred to the white paper, de Lacharrière (at the time 'Directeur des Affaires juridiques au Ministère des Affaires étrangères') insisted on the fact that France and China were members of the Security Council, but he totally neglected the proportion of their respective populations. ('Tendances contradictoires en matière de consentement des états', p. 187.)

[65] See the doubts expressed, in the same sense, in section III of Chapter 3, above.

[66] 'Prenant acte de ce qu'à la différence de certains, l'Australie et la Nouvelle-Zélande ne prétendent nullement que les expériences françaises violeraient une telle règle [de *jus cogens*] . . .' (*Livre blanc sur les expériences nucléaires*, p. 17).

[67] See, for example, *I.C.J. Pleadings, Nuclear Tests*, i, pp. 511 (Article 38 of the Vienna Convention) and 512 (Article 43 of the Vienna Convention); ibid., ii, p. 130 (provisions on the Vienna Convention on the termination of treaties). New Zealand signed the Vienna Convention on 29 April 1970 and ratified it on 4 August 1971. Australia acceeded to it on 13 June 1974.

[68] See, for example, ibid., i, pp. 21 ('overwhelming majority of the community of nations') and 503 ('world community as a whole'); ibid., ii, p. 55 ('international community as a

Australia that once referred in its pleadings to the concept of *jus cogens* when quoting a remark made by Waldock during the work of codification of the law of treaties.[69]

An easy explanation of the reluctance by Australia and New Zealand to resort in their pleadings to an argument based on *jus cogens* is that the question before the International Court was not one of the invalidity of a treaty. Another explanation (and, perhaps, a more convincing one) has to do with the overall approach taken by Australia and New Zealand with respect to the concept of *jus cogens*. At the Vienna Conference, New Zealand was among the twelve States that abstained from voting on draft Article 50 (which later became Article 53 in the final text of the Vienna Convention), while Australia was among the eight States (including France) that voted against it.[70] The ground for the doubts expressed by New Zealand on the draft article on *jus cogens* was the 'risk of political misuse'.[71] Australia was even more explicit in voicing its dissatisfaction (as reflected in its vote against draft Article 50), and its representative declared that

> the Australian Government shared the difficulties of the French delegation in agreeing to become bound by a doctrine so imprecisely formulated, despite the improvements made to the wording of article 50 at the first session . . . His delegation therefore reserved its position completely and would not be able to support either article 50 or article 61.[72]

Thus, all three States involved in the disputes relating to nuclear testing in the South Pacific were critical of the formulation embodied in Article 53 of the Vienna Convention. France was now exploiting the difficult identification of recognition and acceptance of a norm of *jus cogens* by the international community of States 'as a whole' to defend its liberty to conduct atmospheric tests. On the other hand, Australia and New Zealand, while neglecting the concept of *jus cogens*, were resorting to the concept of obligations *erga omnes* in support of their views that atmospheric testing was absolutely illegal, with the consequence that France should immediately cease its tests in the South Pacific. In other words, the concepts of *jus cogens* and obligations *erga omnes* were different tools being used for opposite ends within the context of disputes affecting the most critical interests of the States involved. The strategies of Australia and New Zealand on the one hand, and France on the other, show that a party may decide to resort to one concept instead of the other, depending on whether it is on the

whole'). See also ibid., i, pp. 156–7 (extracts from statements by representatives of Fiji, annexed to the application for permission to intervene submitted to the International Court by Fiji).

[69] See section III of Chapter 9, above.

[70] *U.N.C.L.T., Off. Recs., Second Session*, pp. 106–7.

[71] *U.N.C.L.T., Off. Recs., First Session*, p. 312.

[72] *U.N.C.L.T., Off. Recs., Second Session*, p. 95. See also *U.N.C.L.T., Off. Recs., First Session*, pp. 316–17.

offensive or the defensive and how it intends to organize its argumentation. The strategy so adopted before the International Court, or an international arbitral tribunal, may have a decisive impact on the outcome of the dispute.

VI. Obligations *Erga Omnes* and *Actio Popularis*

A subject that is often discussed in connection with the concept of obligations *erga omnes* is *actio popularis*.[73] This expression indicates an action brought by a plaintiff before a court in the general interest, without any need to show an individual interest in pursuing its claim. The origins of the concept are in Roman law.[74]

Does anything similar exist in international law? In response to this question, the classic reference is a passage from the International Court's judgment in the *South West Africa* cases (Second Phase). Considering the plaintiffs' argument that the mandate for South West Africa should be interpreted in such a way that the system of supervision be effective, the International Court wrote as follows:

> Looked at in another way moreover, the argument amounts to a plea that the Court should allow the equivalent of an '*actio popularis*', or right resident in any member of a community to take legal action in vindication of a public interest. But although a right of this kind may be known to certain municipal systems of law, it is not known to international law as it stands at present: nor is the Court able to regard

[73] On *actio popularis*, see Brownlie, *Principles*, pp. 466–73; id., 'International Law at the Fiftieth Anniversary of the United Nations. General Course on Public International Law', 255 Hague *Recueil* (1995), pp. 85–9; Schachter, *International Law*, pp. 208–13; Bollecker-Stern, *Le Préjudice dans la théorie de la responsabilité internationale* (Paris, 1973), pp. 50–90; Schwelb, 'The *Actio Popularis* and International law', 2 *Israel Yearbook of Human Rights* (1972), pp. 46–56; Seidl-Hohenveldern, '*Actio Popularis* im Völkerrecht?', 14 *Comunicazioni e studi* (1975), pp. 803–13; Miaja de la Muela, 'El interés de las partes en el proceso ante el Tribunal Internacional de Justicia', ibid., pp. 525–61; Silagi, 'Die Popularklage als Fremdkörper im Völkerrecht', 4 *South African Yearbook of International Law* (1978), pp. 10–28; Jenks, 'The General Welfare as a Legal Interest', *Jus et Societas. Essays Friedmann*, pp. 151–8; Dupuy, P. M., 'Action publique et crime international de l'état: à propos de l'article 19 du projet de la Commission du droit international sur la responsabilité des états', 25 *A.F.D.I.* (1979), pp. 539–54. See also Charpentier, 'L'Affaire de la Barcelona Traction devant la Cour internationale de justice (arrêt du 5 février 1970)', 16 *A.F.D.I.* (1970), p. 311; Reisman, 'Responses to Crimes of Discrimination and Genocide', pp. 56–61; Sztucki, *Interim Measures in the Hague Court. An Attempt at a Scrutiny* (Deventer, 1983), pp. 132–6; Gray, *Judicial Remedies in International Law* (Oxford, 1987), pp. 211–15; Mbaye, 'L'intérêt pour agir devant la Cour internationale de Justice', 209 Hague *Recueil* (1988, III), pp. 316–18; Guillaume, 'Terrorisme et droit international', 215 ibid. (1989, III), pp. 401–2; Lauterpacht, E., *Aspects of the Administration of International Justice* (Cambridge, 1991), p. 63. On legal standing under various municipal and international systems, see van Dijk, *Judicial Review of Governmental Action and the Requirement of an Interest to Sue* (Alphen aan den Rijn, 1980).

[74] See *The Digest of Justinian*, iv, pp. 793–4 (*D*.47.23). On the concept and the various types of *actio popularis* in Roman law, see Casavola, *Studi sulle azioni popolari romane. Le 'actiones populares'* (Naples, 1958).

it as imported by the 'general principles of law' referred to in Article 38, paragraph 1 (*c*), of its Statute.[75]

Although the judgment that concluded the second phase of the *South West Africa* cases was adopted by the casting vote of the President, the International Court seems to have been unanimous in rejecting the admissibility of *actio popularis* in international law. For example, Judge Jessup, who appended a forceful dissenting opinion to the judgment of the International Court, expressly agreed with the majority view that *actio popularis* was not generally established in international law.[76]

The extent to which the International Court's dictum in the *Barcelona Traction* case has reversed this position is a matter of controversy. For example, in the *Nicaragua* case, Judge Schwebel remarked that the holding on the inadmissibility of *actio popularis* 'was rapidly and decisively displaced' by the International Court's dictum on obligations *erga omnes*.[77] In contrast, in his general course at the Hague Academy, Lachs remarked that 'there is a long way from the dictum of the Court to *actio popularis*'.[78] This latter view seems to be preferable in light also of a passage in the judgment in the *Barcelona Traction* case, which reads as follows:

With regard more particularly to human rights, to which reference has already been made in paragraph 34 of this Judgment, it should be noted that these also include protection against denial of justice. However, on the universal level, the instruments which embody human rights do not confer on States the capacity to protect the victims of infringements of such rights irrespective of their nationality. It is therefore still on the regional level that a solution to this problem has had to be sought; thus, within the Council of Europe, of which Spain is not a member, the problem of admissibility encountered by the claim in the present case has been resolved by the European Convention on Human Rights, which entitles each State which is a party to the Convention to lodge a complaint against any other contracting State for violation of the Convention, irrespective of the nationality of the victim.[79]

[75] *South West Africa, Second Phase,* Judgment, I.C.J. Reports 1966, p. 47, para. 88.

[76] Ibid., pp. 387–8.

[77] *Military and Paramilitary Activities in and against Nicaragua (Nicaragua* v. *United States of America),* Provisional Measures, Order of 10 May 1984, I.C.J. Reports 1984, p. 197.

[78] 'The Development and General Trends', p. 341, note 796. In the seventh part of his 'The Law and Procedure of the International Court of Justice 1960–1989" (66 *B.Y.I.L.* (1995), pp. 58–9), Thirlway leaves open the question of the relationship between obligations *erga omnes* and *actio popularis*.

[79] I.C.J. Reports 1970, p. 47, para. 91. The French original reads as follows: 'En ce qui concerne plus particulièrement les droits de l'homme, auxquels le présent arrêt a déjà fait allusion au paragraphe 34, on doit noter qu'ils comportent aussi une protection contre le déni de Justice. Toutefois, sur le plan universel, les instruments qui consacrent les droits de l'homme ne reconnaissent pas qualité aux Etats pour protéger les victimes de violations de ces droits indépendamment de leur nationalité. C'est encore sur le plan régional qu'il a fallu chercher une solution à ce problème. Ainsi, au sein du Conseil de l'Europe, dont l'Espagne n'est pas membre, le problème de la recevabilité, auquel se heurte la requête en la présente affaire, est résolu par la Convention européenne des droits de l'homme qui autorise chaque Etat partie à la convention à porter plainte contre tout autre Etat contractant à raison d'une violation de la convention sans égard à la nationalité de la victime.'

This passage makes two interesting points. The first one relates to the status of the protection against denial of justice in international law. On this issue, there is no need to expand here the considerations developed in Chapter 1, above, when it was pointed out that in the pleadings of the *Barcelona Traction* case Spain insisted that denial of justice is a damage invariably inflicted on a particular State, and not on States generally. The second point is the distinction identified by the International Court between the instruments for the protection of human rights available on the regional level and those available on the universal level. In particular, Article 24 of the European Convention on Human Rights allows every contracting party to refer to the European Commission an alleged breach of the Convention by another contracting party.[80] This reflects the existence of a 'common system of law, which may be said to be tantamount to European public law'.[81]

As the International Court acknowledged in the last quoted passage from its judgment in the *Barcelona Traction* case, the present level of integration within the international community does not allow the drawing of similar conclusions to those applicable to the system established by the European Convention on Human Rights. Hence the concept of obligations *erga omnes* does not necessarily imply the existence of a sort of *actio popularis*. In other words, the concepts of obligations *erga omnes* and *actio popularis*, though associated in some respects, are distinct and independent of one another.[82] Though indirectly, the International Court restated the point in its judgment in the *East Timor* case, when it observed in general terms that 'the *erga omnes* character of a norm and the rule of consent to jurisdiction are two different things'.[83]

So far, States have resorted to the concept of *actio popularis*, not as an alternative to showing their individual interest to bring an action, but in

[80] Article 24 reads as follows: 'Any High Contracting Party may refer to the Commission, through the Secretary-General of the Council of Europe, any alleged breach of the provisions of the Convention by another High Contracting Party.' For comment, see Pettiti, Decaux and Imbert (eds.), *La Convention europèene des droits de l'homme. Commentaire article par article* (Paris, 1995), pp. 571–8. See also Frowein, 'La Notion de victime dans le CEDH', *Studi Sperduti*, pp. 587–99; Velu and Ergec, *La Convention européenne des droits de l'homme* (Brussels, 1990), pp. 791–4.

[81] Dissenting opinion of Professor Sperduti on the admissibility of the Application relating to the 'Decision of the European Commission on Human Rights as to the Admissibility of Application No. 788/60 lodged by the Government of the Federal Republic of Austria against the Government of the Republic of Italy', 4 *Yearbook of the European Convention on Human Rights* (1961), p. 116. (The French original reads as follows: 'une communauté de droit . . . [qui] permet de parler avec une certaine approximation d'un droit public européen'.)

[82] *Oppenheim's International Law*, i, p. 5.

[83] *East Timor (Portugal* v. *Australia)*, Judgment, I.C.J. Reports 1995, p. 102, para. 29. For comment on some of the important issues raised by this pronouncement, see Dugard, '1996 and All That. The South West African Judgment Revisited in the East Timor Case', *8 African Journal of International and Comparative Law* (1996), pp. 549–63; Rosenne, 'Decolonisation in the International Court of Justice', ibid., especially pp. 571–2.

support of more traditional grounds of legal standing. In this respect, the pleadings of Australia and New Zealand in the *Nuclear Tests* cases are once again instructive. When requesting the protection of its sovereign right to the inviolability of its territory, and of its freedom of the seas, against atmospheric tests in the South Pacific, Australia insisted on its special interest in this protection, different from the general interest of all other States. Counsel for Australia expressed this special interest in the following terms:

I would not wish the Court to understand me as submitting an argument in however preliminary a form which would seek to engage France in legal responsibility to Australia merely because France has conducted atmospheric nuclear tests. That is not our primary argument. The Court must ultimately consider, in our view, France's responsibility based on the deposit of nuclear fall-out on Australian soil and its dispersion through Australian air space. Australia's primary argument is that the intrusion alone of a harmful substance violates her rights for which violation satisfaction may be awarded and that further, and additionally, the harmful substance which has intruded because of acts for which France is responsible inflicts serious, even though it may be presently incalculable, harm or damage to Australia and its population.[84]

New Zealand took an equally cautious approach to its request for protection of those rights that it claimed in common with 'all members of the international community'.[85] In the oral proceedings, it argued that a closer look at the dictum of the International Court on obligations *erga omnes* reveals the existence of two categories of these obligations. On the one hand, the obligations *erga omnes* that protect fundamental human rights are indivisible and cannot be regarded as a sum of bilateral obligations. On the other hand, the prohibition of aggression, which was originally 'bilateral and private', had then become 'multilateral, universal and public'. Having suggested this distinction, counsel for New Zealand then developed the following argument:

What consequences does such a distinction have for the judicial enforcement of universal obligations and for the judicial protection of the rights that correspond to them? The answer may well be that it has no consequences at all and that in every case where an obligation can be said to be owed to all States, every State has a legal interest in its observance. That, in fact, is the very thrust of the comments made by the Court in the *Barcelona Traction* case. Let us suppose, however, that further refinements in respect of standing are to be introduced. In that case, are there not compelling reasons for preserving, as a first priority, a universal legal interest in the performance of obligations which, by their very nature, are owed to the international community as a whole and cannot be conceived of or stated in other terms? A denial of a universal legal interest in respect of this class of obligations would necessarily entail acceptance of the unhappy situation, to which I have already referred, where

[84] *I.C.J. Pleadings, Nuclear Tests*, i, p. 479 (Argument of Mr Byers).
[85] See section III of Chapter 9, above.

rules of substantive law would be wholly devoid of any means of judicial protection.[86]

The tone of these remarks clearly indicates their tentative character. In any event, far from relying exclusively on *actio popularis*, Australia and New Zealand were very careful in presenting a fully reasoned argument on the different grounds of legal standing, and showed whenever possible a special interest that would set them apart from the international community at large.

VII. Conclusions

The analysis developed in this chapter has showed that the concept of obligations *erga omnes* is independent from both the concept of *jus cogens* and the concept of *actio popularis*.

Some aspects of the relationship between obligations *erga omnes* and *jus cogens* have been examined in terms of the relationship between norm and obligation, and of the different functions of the two concepts. In the abstract, it is impossible to establish whether the character *erga omnes* of an obligation is more or less difficult to prove than the peremptory character of a norm, as their respective processes of identification are not the same. In practice, the resort by a State to one concept or the other depends on several factors, including the circumstances of the particular case and the particular aims of the State invoking the operation of either concept.

With respect to *actio popularis*, the evidence of the independence of the concept of obligations *erga omnes* consists above all of the clear language used by the International Court in the *Barcelona Traction* case. The uncertainties still attaching to *actio popularis* are not prejudicial to the operation of the concept of obligations *erga omnes*. In practice, even when invoking the concept of obligations *erga omnes*, States tend to rely on *actio popularis* (if at all) not as an alternative, but in addition, to other grounds of legal standing.

[86] *I.C.J. Pleadings, Nuclear Tests*, ii, p. 266 (Argument of Dr Finlay).

General Conclusions

> Is there a thing of which it is said,
> 'See, this is new'?
> It has been already,
> in the ages before us.
>
> (Ecclesiastes 1,10)

Writing on one of the masterpieces in the history of painting, Gombrich has remarked that mystery 'is often the effect of a great work of art'.[1] Perhaps, the same is true of great judicial pronouncements, and certainly of the International Court's dictum on obligations *erga omnes.* The purpose of this work was to try to unravel part at least of the 'mystery' of obligations *erga omnes*.[2] While it is not for the writer to evaluate whether this purpose has been achieved, it is certainly appropriate for him to highlight the main results and implications of his work.

The separate analysis of the four examples of obligations *erga omnes* given by the International Court in its dictum, and their comparison with one another, led to the identification of five common elements, which were summarized as follows:

(1) all four examples relate to narrowly defined obligations;
(2) all four examples are essentially those of prohibitions rather than positive obligations;
(3) all four examples are those of 'obligations' in the strict sense of the term, to the exclusion of other fundamental legal conceptions;
(4) all four examples are those of obligations deriving from rules of general international law belonging to *jus cogens* and codified by international treaties to which a large number of States have become parties; and
(5) all four examples are those of obligations instrumental to the main political objectives of the present time, which in turn reflect basic moral values.[3]

Although these common elements cannot be regarded as prescriptive criteria that each obligation *erga omnes* must necessarily satisfy, they may

[1] *The Story of Art*, 16th edn. (London, 1995), p. 300. The painting in question is Leonardo's *Mona Lisa*: 'Like a living being, she seems to change before our eyes and to look a little different every time we come back to her.'
[2] See the Preface of this work, above.
[3] See section I of Chapter 8, above.

serve as a helpful starting point in evaluating other candidates of obligations *erga omnes*. This is not meant to gloss over the difficulties attaching to these common elements. For example, some of the candidates and elements of legal reasoning put forward in the international literature do not seem to be entirely consistent with the elements under numbers (1), (2), and (3).[4] As to the element indicated under number (4), the degree of evidence needed to conclude that an obligation is *erga omnes* may vary,[5] while the relationship between the concepts of obligations *erga omnes* and *jus cogens* presents several aspects that cannot readily be defined once and for all.[6] Finally, with respect to the element indicated under number (5), one should not lightly assume the existence, in the international society of the present time, of many common political objectives and universal obligations reflecting basic moral values.[7] Besides these issues, the exact definition of the rights and remedies corresponding to obligations *erga omnes* (a subject that could only be touched upon briefly in this work),[8] in many respects remains an open question.

Reasons similar to these have led Simma to write that today the concept of obligations *erga omnes* still belongs to 'the world of the "ought" rather than that of the "is"'.[9] This remark is acceptable within the strict limits indicated by Simma himself, who was mainly referring to the 'ramifications and implications' of the concept (which are still unclear or controversial), rather than the concept itself (which is now well established). In other words, the emergence of the concept of obligations *erga omnes*, like that of many other concepts of international law, may be likened to crystal growth, which 'proceeds one molecule at a time and one layer at a time. The process is slow . . .'[10] Today, it would be inaccurate to suggest that the concept of obligations *erga omnes* already has all its 'molecules' and 'layers'. At the same time, it would be equally inaccurate to infer, from the absence of several of these 'molecules' and 'layers', that the concept itself is not yet well established.

The metaphor of the crystal is useful from another angle. Quoting Justice Holmes, Dillard once observed in a separate opinion that a word is not, like a crystal, transparent and unchanged, but 'is the skin of a living thought and may vary greatly in color and content according to the circumstances

4 See sections II, III, and IV, of the same chapter.

5 See section IV of Chapter 9, above.

6 See sections II to V of Chapter 10, above.

7 See section IV of Chapter 9, above.

8 See the brief considerations on *actio popularis* developed in section VI of Chapter 10, above.

9 'Does the UN Charter Provide an Adequate Legal Basis for Individual or Collective Responses to Violations of Obligations erga omnes?', Delbrück (ed.), *The Future of International Law Enforcement. New Scenarios—New Law?* (Berlin, 1993), p. 125.

10 'Matter: Its Properties, States, Varieties, and Behaviour', *The New Encyclopaedia Britannica*, 15th edn. (Chicago, 1994), xxiii (Macropaedia), p. 622.

and time in which it is used'.[11] The words of international law, including those composing the expression 'obligations *erga omnes*', are no exception to this rule. Hence the risk that the concept may be abused and the danger, pointed out by Weil, that the 'most powerful or numerous' States may impose their will on the others.[12] The danger is even more real now than when Weil was writing about it in the eighties, since the disintegration of the socialist system, and the corresponding developments in international relations, make the appeal to obligations *erga omnes* more likely today than ever before.[13] However, on this point, as on others, one should avoid putting 'too much strain'[14] (and too many expectations) on the law, as the use and abuse of the concept of obligations *erga omnes* is essentially a political question. In any event, by making it clear in its dictum that obligations *erga omnes* are few and are such '[b]y their very nature', the International Court has contributed considerably to reducing the risk that the will of a portion (however large or strong) of the international community might be imposed on everybody.

On the basis of the analysis developed in this work, it is also possible to make two wider considerations. The first one relates to the so-called 'evidences' of the concept.[15] The concept of obligations *erga omnes* was put on the agenda by the International Court, i.e. the 'principal judicial organ' of the United Nations.[16] The concept has been acquiring new impetus through the work of codification of the law of State responsibility undertaken by the International Law Commission, i.e. a subsidiary organ of the General Assembly of the United Nations. These facts, and the very nature of the concept, indicate the close relationship between obligations *erga omnes* and the United Nations and, more generally, between the future developments of the concept and the process of 'institutionalization' of the international community.[17] While this close relationship should be acknowledged, any

[11] I.C.J. Reports 1971, p. 154, note 1. Justice Holmes's dictum appeared in *Towne* v. *Eisner*, 245 U.S. 418 (1918), p. 425. The passage is also reproduced in Jessup, 'Hardy Dillard', 23 *Virginia Journal of International Law* (1983), p. 364, note 5.

[12] 'Towards Relative Normativity in International Law?', p. 441.

[13] See Picone, 'Nazioni Unite e obblighi "*erga omnes*"' 48 *La Comunità internazionale* (1993), pp. 710–11. More generally, on the impact of ideological confrontation on the development of customary and conventional rules, see Ferrari Bravo, 'Prospettive del diritto internazionale alla fine del secolo XX', 74 *Riv.dir.int.* (1991), p. 526; id., *Lezioni di diritto internazionale*, 3rd edn. (Naples, 1992), p. 57. On the current convergence towards 'universal human values', see Vereshchetin and Mullerson, 'International Law in an Interdependent World', 28 *C.J.T.L.* (1990), p. 292.

[14] Brownlie, 'To What Extent are the Traditional Categories of *Lex Lata* and *Lex Ferenda* still viable? Presentation', p. 67.

[15] On the concept of 'evidences' of the law, see *Third Restatement*, Section 103, comment (a).

[16] See Article 92 of the Charter of the United Nations, and Article 1 of the Statute of the International Court.

[17] See Ago, 'Obligations *Erga Omnes* and the International Community', Weiler, Cassese and Spinedi (eds.), *International Crimes*, p. 238.

partial perspective (such as this or that which concentrates only on the corresponding rights of protection of obligations *erga omnes*) runs the risk of giving an inaccurate or incomplete picture of the concept, stressing certain of its aspects to the detriment of others.[18]

The second consideration relates to the approach to the concept of obligations *erga omnes* adopted in this work. As was mentioned in the Preface, the selected approach was a traditional one, with extensive references to the classic sources of international law. This approach has made it possible to highlight the novelty introduced (or, at least, confirmed and further strengthened) by the concept of obligations *erga omnes*, namely the idea that today international law does not only govern the reciprocal relations between States, but also involves considerations going beyond the mere sum of their individual interests. At the same time, in this 'new teaching' on obligations *erga omnes*,[19] there is also something that 'has been already'.[20] This is the need, which has been present since time immemorial in international relations, to search for peace and justice among States through the promotion of their common good.

[18] See section IV of Chapter 10, above.
[19] See the quotation at the beginning of Chapter 1, above.
[20] See the quotation at the beginning of these General Conclusions.

Bibliography

When preparing this bibliography, the present writer was confronted with a difficult choice. If he were to cite only the works which deal specifically and exclusively with obligations *erga omnes*, the bibliography would not do justice to the growing influence of the concept in international law. On the other hand, if he were to provide an exhaustive list of 'relevant' readings (assuming that a meaningful boundary between 'relevant' and 'irrelevant' materials can be established), the bibliography would end up providing a long, but probably useless, sequence of titles. The compromise solution that has been adopted restricts the present bibliography to the works cited in the footnotes to the text, which already reflect a considerable degree of selectivity.

For each writer, authored books precede edited ones, and both come before articles and co-authored or co-edited books. Within each category, the order of citation is chronological. For reasons of convenience, names preceded by, or beginning with, the prefixes *da*, *de*, *el*, *mac*, *mc* or *o'* (but not *van* or *von*) are listed under the initials of these prefixes. Books by unidentified authors or editors are listed under the initial letter of the first word in the title, unless the first word is a definite or indefinite article.

As a rule, the present writer has preserved the capital and lower case letters used in the titles that he has cited, even though faithfulness to the originals has resulted in inconsistent capitalization throughout the bibliography.

Abbott, W. M. and Gallagher, J. (eds.) *The Documents of Vatican II* (London, 1967).

Abi-Saab, G. 'The specificities of humanitarian law', Swinarski (ed.), *Studies Pictet*, pp. 265–79.

—— 'Cours général de droit international public', 207 Hague *Recueil* (1987, VII), pp. 9–464.

—— 'Le droit au développement', 44 *Ann. suisse* (1988), pp. 9–24.

—— 'The 1977 Additional Protocols and general inernational law: some preliminary reflections', Delissen and Tanja (eds.), *Humanitarian Law. Liber Kalshoven*, pp. 115–26.

—— 'Les sources du droit international: un essai de déconstruction', *International Law. Liber Jiménez de Aréchaga*, i, pp. 29–49.

Accioly, H. *Traité de droit international public*, French trans. Goulé of the first Portuguese edition, 1933–5, 3 vols. (Paris, 1940–2).

Acosta Estévez, J. B. Normas de *ius cogens*, efecto *erga omnes*, crimen internacional y la teoria de los circulos concéntricos', 11 *Anuario de derecho internacional* (1995), pp. 3–22.

The African slave trade from the fifteenth to the nineteenth century (Paris, 1979).

Ago, R. (ed.) *La prassi italiana di diritto internazionale, Prima Serie (1861–1887)*, i. (New York, 1970).

—— 'Positive Law and International Law', 51 *A.J.I.L.* (1957), pp. 691–733.

AGO, R. (ed.) 'La codification du droit international et les problèmes de sa réalisation', *Recueil Guggenheim*, pp. 93–131.
—— 'Droit des traités à la lumière de la Convention de Vienne. Introduction', 134 Hague *Recueil* (1971, III), pp. 297–332.
—— 'Obligations *Erga Omnes* and the International Community', Weiler, Cassese and Spinedi (eds.), *International Crimes*, pp. 237–9.
—— 'The Concept of "International Community as a Whole": A Guarantee to the Notion of State Crimes', Weiler, Cassese and Spinedi (eds.), *International Crimes*, pp. 252–3.
'Agora: What Obligation Does Our Generation Owe to the Next? An Approach to Global Environmental Responsibility', 84 *A.J.I.L.* (1990), pp. 190–212.
AGRAWALA, S. K. (ed.) *Essays on the Law of Treaties (With special reference to India)* (Bombay, 1972).
AKEHURST, M. 'Custom as a Source of International Law', 47 *B.Y.I.L.* (1974/75), pp. 1–53.
—— 'The Hierarchy of the Sources of International Law', 47 *B.Y.I.L.* (1974/75), pp. 273–85.
ALEKSIDZE, L. A. *Nekotorye voprosy teorii mezhdunarodnogo prava. Imperativnye normy jus cogens* (Tbilisi, 1982) (*Some Theoretical Problems of International Law. Peremptory Norms Jus Cogens*, in Russian, with English summary).
—— 'Legal Nature of *Jus Cogens* in Contemporary International Law', 172 Hague *Recueil* (1981, III), pp. 219–70.
ALFREDSON, G. and MACALISTER-SMITH (eds.), *The Living Law of Nations: essays on refugees, minorities, indiginous peoples and the human rights of the vulnerable groups in memory of Alte Grahl-Madsen* (Kehl, 1996).
ALLAND, D. *Justice privée et ordre juridique international. Etude théorique des contre-mesures en droit international public* (Paris, 1994).
ALLEN, C. K. *Law in the Making*, 7th edn. (Oxford, 1964).
AL-NAUIMI, N. and MEESE, R. (eds.) *International Legal Issues Arising under the United Nations Decade of International Law* (The Hague, 1995).
ALSTON, P. 'Some Notes on the Concept of the Right to Development', Prémont (ed.), *Essays Khushalani*, pp. 74–84.
AMERASINGHE, C. F. *Studies in International Law (Colombo, 1969).*
—— *Principles of the institutional law of international organizations* (Cambridge, 1996).
ANAND, R. P. 'Attitude of the Asian-African States toward Certain Problems of International Law', 15 *I.C.L.Q.* (1966), pp. 55–75.
ANDREOPOULOS, G. J. (ed.) *Genocide: Conceptual and Historical Dimensions* (Philadelphia, 1994).
ANNACKER, C. *Die Durchsetzung von erga omnes Verpflichtungen vor dem Internationalen Gerichtshof* (Hamburg, 1994).
—— 'The Legal Régime of *Erga Omnes* Obligations in International Law', 46 *Austrian Journal of Public and International Law* (1994), pp. 131–66.
ANZILOTTI, D. *Corso di diritto internazionale*, i, 3rd edn. (Rome, 1928); *Cours de droit international*, i, French trans. Gidel (Paris 1929).
—— 'Intorno agli effetti delle modificazioni del corso di un fiume sul confine fra due Stati', 8 *Riv. dir. int.* (1914), pp. 73–83.

'Appraisals of the ICJ's Decision: Nicaragua v. United States (Merits)', 81 *A.J.I.L.* (1987), pp. 77–183.

Aquinas, Thomas *Summa Theologiae*, Caramello ed., 3 vols. (Turin, 1952).

Arangio-Ruiz, G. *The United Nations Declaration on Friendly Relations and the System of the Sources of International Law (with an Appendix on the Concept of International Law and the Theory of International Organisation)* (Alphen aan den Rijn and Germantown, 1979).

—— 'Human Rights and Non-Intervention in the Helsinki Final Act', 157 Hague *Recueil* (1977, IV), pp. 195–332.

—— 'Consuetudine (consuetudine internazionale)', *Enciclopedia Giuridica*, viii (Rome, 1988), pp. 1–11.

—— 'Le domaine réservé. L'organisation internationale et le rapport entre droit international et droit interne', 225 Hague *Recueil* (1990, VI), pp. 9–484.

Arellano Garcia, C. *Derecho internacional publico*, i (Mexico City, 1983).

Ariosto, L. *Opere minori*, Segre ed. (Milan, 1954).

Aristotle *The Complete Works (The Revised Oxford Translation)*, Barnes ed., 2 vols. (Princeton, 1984).

Arrow, D. W. 'Seabeds, Sovereignty and Objective Regimes', 7 *Fordham International Law Journal* (1984), pp. 169–243.

Auburn, F. M. *Antarctic Law and Politics* (London, 1981).

Austin, J. *Lectures on Jurisprudence or the Philosophy of Positive Law*, 5th edn. Campbell (London, 1885).

'Authors Recollect Judge Lachs', Jasentuliyana (ed.), *Perspectives*, pp. 529–36.

Balladore Pallieri, G. *Diritto internazionale pubblico*, 8th edn. (Milan, 1962).

—— 'La forza obbligatoria della consuetudine internazionale', 7 *Riv. dir. int.* (1928), pp. 338–74.

Ballreich, H. 'Verträge zugunsten und zu lasten Dritter', Strupp and Schlochauer (eds.), *Wörterbuch*, iii, pp. 544–7.

Banton, M. *International Action Against Racial Discrimination* (Oxford, 1996).

Barberis, J. A. 'Réflexions sur la coutume international', 36 *A.F.D.I.* (1990), pp. 9–46.

—— 'Les règles spécifiques du droit international en Amérique latine', 235 Hague *Recueil* (1992, V), pp. 81–230.

Barboza, J. 'Necessity (Revisited) in International Law', Makarczyk (ed.), *Essays Lachs*, pp. 27–44.

Barile, G. *I diritti assoluti nell'ordinamento internazionale* (Milan, 1951).

—— *Lezioni di diritto internazionale* (Padua, 1983).

—— 'Sulle misure cautelari nell'affare degli esperimenti nucleari', 57 *Riv. dir. int.* (1974), pp. 17–28.

—— 'La structure de l'ordre juridique international. Règles générales et règles conventionnelles', 161 Hague *Recueil* (1978, III), pp. 9–126.

—— '*Obligationes erga omnes* e individui nel diritto internazionale umanitario', 68 *Riv. dir. int.* (1985), pp. 5–31.

Barros Jarpa, E. *Derecho internacional publico* (Santiago de Chile, 1955).

Basdevant, J. 'Règles générales du droit de la paix', 58 Hague *Recueil* (1936, IV), pp. 471–692.

Bassiouni, C. 'Enslavement as an International Crime', 23 *N.Y.U.J.I.L.P.* (1991), pp. 445–517.

Bastid, S. 'Observations sur la pratique du consensus', Tittel (ed.), *Multitudo. Festschrift Wengler*, i, pp. 11–25.
Battaglini, G. *La condizione dell'Antartide nel diritto internazionale* (Padua, 1971).
—— 'Il riconoscimento internazionale dei principi generali del diritto', *International Law. Essays Ago*, i, pp. 97–140.
Baxter, R. R. *The Law of International Waterways* (Cambridge, Mass., 1964).
——'Multilateral Treaties as Evidence of Customary International Law', 41 *B.Y.I.L.* (1965/66), pp. 275–300.
—— 'Treaties and Custom', 129 Hague *Recueil* (1970, I), pp. 25–106.
Beckett, W. E. 'Decisions of the Permanent Court of International Justice on Points of Law and Procedure of General Application', 11 *B.Y.I.L.* (1930), pp. 1–54.
Bedjaoui, M. *Towards a new international economic order* (Paris, New York and London, 1979).
—— (ed.) *International Law: Achievements and Prospects* (Paris and Dordrecht, 1991).
—— 'Some Unorthodox Reflections on the "Right to Development"', Snyder and Slinn (eds.), *International Law of Development*, pp. 87–116.
—— 'La "fabrication" des arrêts de la Cour internationale de Justice', *Le droit international. Mélanges Virally*, pp., 87–107.
—— 'The Right to Development', Bedjaoui (ed.), *International Law*, pp. 1177–1203.
—— 'La vision de las culturas no occidentales sobre la legitimidad del derecho internacional contemporaneo', 11 *Anuario de derecho internacional* (1995), pp. 23–62.
—— and Thierry, H. 'Future of International Law', Bedjaoui (ed.), *International Law*, pp. 1233–44.
Bello, D. A. *Principios de derecho internacional*, i (Madrid, 1883).
Bello, E. G. and Ajibola, B. A. (eds.) *Essays in honour of Judge Taslim Olawale Elias*, 2 vols. (Dordrecht, 1992).
Berg, A. 'Nuclear Tests Cases (Australia v. France; New Zealand v. France)', Heidelberg *Encycl.*, ii, pp. 216–19.
Bernardini, A. 'Qualche riflessione su norme internazionali di *jus cogens* e giurisdizione della Corte nella Convenzione di Vienna sul diritto dei trattati', 14 *Comunicazioni e studi* (1975), pp. 81–100.
Bernhardt, R. 'Corfu Channel Case', Heidelberg *Encycl.*, ii, pp. 61–4.
—— 'Custom and Treaty in the Law of the Sea', 205 Hague *Recueil* (1987, V), pp. 247–330.
—— 'Völkerrechtliche Verbote der Diskriminierung von Individuen', Jekewitz, Klein, Kühne, Petersmann and Wolfrum (eds.), *Des Menschen. Festschrift Partsch*, pp. 97–102.
—— 'Customary International Law: New and Old Problems', 19 *Thesaurus Acroasium* (1992), pp. 199–221.
Betz, J. 'Developing Countries', Wolfrum (ed.), *United Nations*, i, pp. 398–406.
Beyerlin, U. 'Rio-Konferenz: Beginn einer neuen globalen Umweltrechtsordnung?', 54 *Z.a.ö.R.V.* (1994), pp. 124–49 (in German, with English summary).
Bothe, M., Hofmann, R. and Petersmann, E.-U. (eds.) *Recht zwischen Umbruch und Bewahrung. Völkerrecht, Europarecht, Staatsrecht. Festschrift für Rudolf Bernhardt* (Berlin, 1995).

BIANCHI, A. 'Il Trattato di non proliferazione nucleare vent'anni dopo: prospettive di efficacia *ultra partes*', 100 *Studi senesi* (1988), pp. 263–326.

BIERZANEK, R. and SYMONIDES, J. *Prawo miedzynarodowe publiczne*, 3rd edn. (Warsaw, 1994).

BIRNIE, P. W. and BOYLE, A. E. *International Law and the Environment* (Oxford, 1993).

—— (eds.) *Basic Documents on International Law and The Environment* (Oxford, 1995).

BISHOP, W. W. 'General Course of Public International Law', 115 Hague *Recueil* (1965, II), pp. 151–467.

BLACKSTONE, W. *Commentaries on the Laws of England* (A Facsimile of the First Edition of 1765–1769), 4 vols (Chicago and London, 1979).

BLECKMANN, A. 'General Theory of Obligations under Public International Law', 38 *G.Y.I.L.* (1995), pp. 26–40.

BLUNTSCHLI, J. C. *Le Droit international codifié*, French trans. Lardy (Paris, 1870).

BÖCKSTIEGEL, K.-H., FOLZ, H.-E., MÖSSNER, J. M. and ZEMANEK, K. (eds.) *Law of Nations. Law of International Organizations. World's Economic Law. Liber Amicorum honouring Ignaz Seidl-Hohenveldern* (Cologne, 1988).

BÖHMER, A. 'One Hundred Years: The Kiel Canal in International Law', 38 *G.Y.I.L.* (1995), pp. 325–46.

BOKOR-SZEGÖ, H. *New States and International Law* (Budapest, 1970).

BOLLECKER-STERN, B. *Le Préjudice dans la théorie de la responsabilité internationale* (Paris, 1973).

BOS, A. and SIBLESZ, H. (eds.) *Realism in Law-Making: essays on international law in honour of Willem Riphagen* (Dordrecht, 1986).

BOS, M. *A Methodology of International Law* (Amsterdam, 1984).

BOURQUIN, M. 'La Sainte-Alliance, un essai d'organisation européenne', 83 Hague Recueil (1953, II), pp. 377–461.

BOWETT, D. W. *Self-Defence in International Law* (Manchester, 1958).

—— 'Reservations to Non-Restricted Multilateral Treaties', 48 *B.Y.I.L.* (1976/77), pp. 67–92.

——, CRAWFORD, J., SINCLAIR, I. and WATTS, A. D. 'The International Court of Justice: Efficiency of Procedures and Working Methods. Report of the Study Group established by the British Institute of International and Comparative Law as a contribution to the UN Decade of International Law', 45 *I.C.L.Q.* (1996), Supplement, pp. S1–35.

BRANDT, R. B. 'The Concepts of Obligation and Duty', 73 *Mind* (1964) pp. 374–93.

BRAUD, P. 'Recherches sur l'Etat tiers en droit international public', 72 *R.G.D.I.P.* (1968), pp. 17–96.

BRETTON, P. 'L'affaire des "otages" américains devant la Cour Internationale de Justice', 108 *J.D.I.* (1980), pp. 787–828.

BRIDGE, J. W., LASOK, D., PERROTT, D. L. and PLENDER, R. O. (eds.), *Fundamental Rights. A volume of essays to commemorate the 50th anniversary of the founding of the Law School in Exeter. 1923–1973* (London, 1973).

BRIERLY, J. L. *The Law of Nations. An Introduction to the International Law of Peace*, 3rd edn. (Oxford, 1942); 6th edn. Waldock (Oxford, 1963).

—— 'Règles générales du droit de la paix', 58 Hague *Recueil* (1936, IV), pp. 1–242.

BRIERLY, J. L. 'The Basis of Obligation in International Law', Lauterpacht, H. and Waldock (eds.), *The Basis*, pp. 1–67.
BRIGGS, H. W. *The International Law Commission* (Ithaca, N.Y., 1965).
——'Barcelona Traction: The *Jus Standi* of Belgium', 65 *A.J.I.L.* (1971), pp. 327–45.
BRILMAYER, L. *Justifying International Acts* (Ithaca, N.Y., and London, 1989).
BROMS, B. 'The Definition of Aggression', 154 Hague *Recueil* (1977, I), pp. 299–400.
BROWN, R. E., FITZMYER, J. A. and MURPHY, R. E. (eds.) *The New Jerome Biblical Commentary* (Englewood Cliffs, N.J., 1990).
BROWNLIE, I. *International Law and the Use of Force by States* (Oxford, 1963).
—— *Principles of Public International Law* (Oxford, 1966; 2nd edn. (1973); 3rd edn. (1979); 4th edn. (1990)).
—— *Loaves and Fishes: Access to Natural Resources and International Law (An Inaugural Lecture)* (London, 1978).
—— *System of the Law of Nations: State Responsibility. Part I* (Oxford, 1983).
—— *The Human Right to Development* (London, 1989).
—— (ed.) *Basic Documents on African Affairs* (Oxford, 1971).
—— (ed.) *Basic Documents on Human Rights*, 3rd edn. (Oxford, 1992).
—— (ed.) *Basic Documents in International Law*, 4th edn. (Oxford, 1995).
—— 'A Survey of International Customary Rules of Environmental Protection', Teclaff and Utton (eds.), *International Environmental Law*, pp. 1–11.
—— 'The United Nations as a Form of Government', Fawcett and Higgins, R. (eds.), *International Organization. Essays McMahon*, pp. 26–36.
—— 'Legal Status of Natural Resources in International Law (Some Aspects)', 162 Hague *Recueil* (1979, I), pp. 245–318.
—— 'Recognition in Theory and Practice', 53 *B.Y.I.L.* (1982), pp. 197–211.
—— 'The United Nations Charter and the Use of Force, 1945–1985', Cassese (ed.), *The Current Legal Regulation*, pp. 491–504.
—— 'To What Extent are the Traditional Categories of *Lex Lata* and *Lex Ferenda* still viable? Presentation', Cassese and Weiler (eds.), *Change and Stability*, pp. 66–72.
—— 'Introduction: International Law in the Second Half of the Twentieth Century', Bello and Ajibola (eds.), *Essays Elias*, i, pp. 3–20.
—— 'The Sources of the Law Governing Maritime Delimitation', *International Law. Liber Jiménez de Aréchaga*, ii, pp. 733–44.
—— 'International Law at the Fiftieth Anniversary of the United Nations. General Course on Public International Law', 255 Hague *Recueil* (1995), pp. 9–227.
BRYDE, B. O. 'Verpflichtungen Erga Omnes aus Menschenrechten', *Multilaterale Staatsverträge*, pp. 165–90.
BUCKLAND, W. W. and MCNAIR, A. D. *Roman Law and Common Law. A Comparison in Outline*, 2nd edn. revised by Lawson (Cambridge, 1965).
BUERGENTHAL, T. (ed.) *Human Rights, International Law and the Helsinki Accord* (Montclair, N.J., 1977).
BULAJIC, M. *Principles of International Development Law. Progressive Development of the Principles of International Law Relating to the New International Economic Order*, 2nd edn. (Dordrecht, 1993).
—— 'A Changing World Calls for International Development Law', Sarcevic and van Houtte (eds.), *Legal Issues*, pp. 1–22.
BUTLER, W. E. (ed.) *The Non-Use of Force in International Law* (Dordrecht, 1989).

—— '"Socialist International Law" or "Socialist Principles of International Relations"?', 65 *A.J.I.L.* (1971), pp. 796–800.
CAHIER, P. 'Le problème des effets des traités à l'égard des Etats tiers', 143 Hague *Recueil* (1974, III), pp. 589–736.
—— 'Changements et continuité du droit international. Cours général de droit international public', 195 Hague *Recueil* (1985, VI), pp. 9–374.
Cambridge Essays in International law—Essays in Honour of Lord McNair (London, 1965).
CAMPBELL, A. H. 'International Law and the Student of Jurisprudence', 35 *Transactions of the Grotius Society* (1935), pp. 113–32.
CANCADO TRINIDADE, A. A. *Direitos humanos e meio-ambiente: paralelo dos sistemas de protecao internacional* (Porto Alegre, 1993).
—— 'Co-existence and Co-ordination of Mechanisms of International Protection of Human Rights (at Global and Regional Levels)', 202 Hague *Recueil* (1987, II), pp. 9–436.
—— 'Environment and Development: Formulation and Implementation of the Right to Development as a Human Right', 3 *Asian Yearbook of International Law* (1993), pp. 15–45.
—— 'Relations Between Sustainable Development and Economic, Social and Cultural Rights: Recent Developments', Al-Nauimi and Meese (eds.), *International Legal Issues*, pp. 1051–77.
CANSACCHI, G. *Istituzioni di diritto internazionale pubblico*, 6th edn. Cansacchi and Marazzi (Turin, 1979).
CARBONNIER, J. *Droit civil. Introduction*, 24th edn. (Paris, 1996).
CARDONA LLORENS, J. 'La responsabilidad internacional por violacion grave de obligaciones esenciales para la salvaguarda de intereses fundamentales de la comunidad internacional (el "crimen internacional")', 8 *Anuario de derecho internacional* (1985), pp. 265–336.
CARELLA, G. *La responsabilità dello Stato per crimini internazionali* (Naples, 1985).
CARREAU, D. *Droit international*, 4th edn. (Paris, 1994).
CARRILLO SALCEDO, J. A. *Soberania del estado y derecho internacional*, 2nd edn. (Madrid, 1976).
—— *El derecho internacional en un mundo en cambio* (Madrid, 1984).
—— *Curso de derecho internacional publico* (Madrid, 1991).
—— *El Derecho internacional en perspectiva historica* (Madrid, 1991).
—— *Soberania de los estados y derechos humanos en derecho internacional contemporaneo* (Madrid, 1995).
CARTY, A. (ed.) *Law and Development* (Aldershot, 1992).
CASADO RAIGON, R. 'Las obligaciones "erga omnes" en el derecho internacional contemporaneo', 6 *La Ley* (29 Jan. 1985, No. 1120), pp. 1–4.
CASAVOLA, F. *Studi sulle azioni popolari romane. Le "actiones populares"* (Naples, 1958).
CASSESE, A. *International Law in a Divided World* (Oxford, 1986).
—— *Human Rights in a Changing World* (Philadelphia, 1990).
—— *Self-determination of peoples. A legal reappraisal* (Cambridge, 1995).
—— (ed.) *U.N. Law Fundamental Rights. Two Topics in International Law* (Alphen aan den Rijn, 1979).
—— (ed.) *The Current Legal Regulation of the Use of Force* (Dordrecht, 1986).

CASSESE, A. 'Consensus and Some of its Pitfalls', 58 *Riv. dir. int.* (1975), pp. 754–61.
—— 'Remarks on the Present Legal Regulation of Crimes of States', *International Law. Essays Ago*, iii, pp. 49–64.
—— 'La communauté internationale et le génocide', *Le droit international. Mélanges Virally*, pp. 183–94.
—— 'Note sull'opera di Giuseppe Sperduti', 77 *Riv. dir. int.* (1994), pp. 313–32.
—— and WEILER, J. H. H. (eds.) *Change and Stability in International Law-Making* (Berlin and New York, 1988).
CASSIN, V., DEBEVOISE, W., KAILES, H. and THOMPSON, T. W. 'The Definition of Aggression', 16 *Harvard International Law Journal* (1975), pp. 589–613.
CASTRÉN, E. J. S. 'Aspects récents de la succession d'Etats', 78 Hague *Recueil* (1951, I), pp. 379–506.
CAVAGLIERI, A. *Corso di diritto internazionale*, 3rd edn. (Naples, 1934).
—— 'Concetto e caratteri del diritto internazionale generale', 14 *Riv. dir. int.* (1921/22), pp. 289–314 and 479–506.
—— 'Règles générales du droit de la paix', 26 Hague *Recueil* (1929, I), pp. 315–583.
CAVALLI-SFORZA, L. L., MENOZZI, P. and PIAZZA, A. *The History and Geography of Human Genes*, abridged paperback edition (Princeton, 1994).
CHAMPEIL-DESPLATS, V. 'La notion de droit "fondamental" et le droit constitutionnel français', *Recueil Dalloz Sirey* (1995, No. 42), pp. 323–9.
CHARNEY, J. I. 'The Persistent Objector Rule', 56 *B.Y.I.L.* (1985), pp. 1–24.
——'Universal International Law', 87 *A.J.I.L.* (1993), pp. 529–51.
CHARPENTIER, J. 'La procédure de non objection (A propos d'une crise constitutionnelle de l'O.N.U.)', 70 *R.G.D.I.P.* (1966), pp. 862–77.
—— 'L'Affaire de la Barcelona Traction devant la Cour internationale de justice (arrêt du 5 février 1970)', 16 *A.F.D.I.* (1970), pp. 307–28.
CHAUMONT, C. 'Cours général de droit international public', 129 Hague *Recueil* (1970, I), pp. 333–528.
CHENG, B. *General Principles of Law as Applied by International Courts and Tribunals* (London, 1953; reprinted Cambridge, 1987).
—— 'How Should We Study International Law?', 13 *Chinese Yearbook of International Law and Affairs* (1994/95), pp. 214–28.
CHOWDHURY, S. R. 'Permanent sovereignty and its impact on stabilization clauses, standards of compensation and patterns of development co-operation', Hossain and Chowdhury (eds.), *Permanent Sovereignty*, pp. 42–87.
—— DENTERS, E. M. G. and DE WAART, P. J. I. M. (eds.) *The Right to Development in International Law* (Dordrecht, 1992).
CHRISTENSON, G. A. 'The World Court and *Jus Cogens*', 81 *A.J.I.L.* (1987), pp. 93–101.
—— '*Jus Cogens*: Guarding Interests Fundamental to International Society', 28 *Virginia Journal of International Law* (1988), pp. 585–648.
CHUNG, I. Y. *Legal Problems Involved in the Corfu Channel Incident* (Geneva, 1959).
CLARK, R. S. 'Crimes Against Humanity', Ginsburgs and Kudriavtsev (eds.), *The Nuremberg Trial*, pp. 177–99.
CLAUSS, I. *Die Lehre von den Staatsdienstbarkeiten historisch-dogmatisch entwickelt* (Tübingen, 1894).

COCUZZA, C. 'State Involvement in Terrorist Activities and Economic Sanctions: The Libyan Case', 7 *The Italian Yearbook of International Law* (1986–1987), pp. 190–215.

COHEN-JONATHAN, G. 'La coutume locale', 7 *A.F.D.I.* (1961), pp. 119–40.

COLARD, D. 'Premières réflexions sur le "Traité des Traités": la Convention de Vienne du 23 mai 1969', 97 *J.D.I.* (1970), pp. 264–97.

COLSON, D. A. 'How Persistent Must the Persistent Objector Be?', 61 *Washington Law Review* (1986), pp. 957–70.

COMBACAU, J. and SUR, S. *Droit international public*, 2nd edn. (Paris, 1995).

The Concept of Jus Cogens in Public International Law: Papers and Proceedings (Report of a Conference organized by the Carnegie Endowment for International Peace, Lagonissi (Greece), April 1966) (Geneva, 1967).

The Concise Oxford Dictionary of Current English, 4th revised edn. McIntosh (Oxford, 1951).

CONDORELLI, L. 'Custom', Bedjaoui (ed.), *International Law*, pp. 179–211.

—— and BOISSON DE CHAZOURNES, L. 'Quelques remarques à propos de l'obligation des Etats de "respecter et faire respecter" le droit international humanitaire "en toutes circonstances"', Swinarski (ed.), *Studies Pictet*, pp. 17–35.

CONFORTI, B. *Diritto internazionale*, 4th edn. (Naples, 1992).

—— *International Law and the Role of Domestic Legal Systems*, English trans. Provost and Van Praagh (Dordrecht, 1993).

——'In tema di responsabilità degli Stati per crimini internazionali', *International Law. Essays Ago*, iii, pp. 99–111.

'La Convention de Vienne sur le droit des traités', *Notes et Etudes Documentaires* (25 Sep. 1969, No. 3622).

CONWELL-EVANS, T. P. *The League Council in Action: A Study of the Methods Employed by the Council of the League of Nations to Prevent War and to Settle International Disputes* (Oxford, 1929).

CORNU, G. *Linguistique juridique* (Paris, 1990).

COT, J. P. and PELLET, A. (eds.) *La Charte des Nations Unies* (Paris, 1991).

COUVE DE MURVILLE, M. N. L. *Slave from Haiti: A Saint for New York? The Life of Pierre Toussaint* (London, 1995).

COWEN, D. V. *The Foundations of Freedom with Special Reference to Southern Africa* (Cape Town, 1961).

CRAVEN, M. C. R. 'The European Community Arbitration Commission on Yugoslavia', 66 *B.Y.I.L.* (1995), pp. 333–413.

CRAWFORD, J. *The Creation of States in International Law* (Oxford, 1979).

—— (ed.) *The Rights of Peoples* (Oxford, 1988).

—— 'The General Assembly, the International Court and Self-Determination', Lowe and Fitzmaurice, M. (eds.), *Fifty Years. Essays Jennings*, pp. 585–605.

CREASY, E. S. *First Platform of International Law* (London, 1876).

CROSS, R. and HARRIS, J. W. *Precedent in English Law*, 4th edn. (Oxford, 1991).

CRUSEN, G. 'Les servitudes internationales', 22 Hague *Recueil* (1928, II), pp. 1–79.

CZAPLINSKI, W. *Skutki prawne nielegalnego uzycia sily w stosunkach miedzynarodowych* (Warsaw, 1993) (*International Legal Effects of the Illegal Use of Force*, in Polish, with English summary).

DAHM, G. *Völkerrecht*, i (Stuttgart, 1958).

D'Amato, A. *The Concept of Custom in International Law* (Ithaca, N.Y., 1971).
—— 'Legal Aspects of the French Nuclear Tests', 61 *A.J.I.L.* (1967), pp. 66–77.
—— 'On Consensus', 8 *Canadian Yearbook of International Law* (1970), pp. 104–22.
Damrosch, L. F. (ed.) *The International Court of Justice at a Crossroads* (New York, 1987).
Danilenko, G. M. *Obychai v sovremennom mezhdunarodnom prave* (Moscow, 1988).
—— *Law-Making in the International Community* (Dordrecht, 1993).
—— 'The Theory of International Customary Law', 31 *G.Y.I.L.* (1988), pp. 9–47.
—— 'International *Jus Cogens*: Issues of Law-Making', 2 *European Journal of International Law* (1991, No. 1), pp. 42–65.
Da Silva Cunha, J. *Direito Internacional Publico. Introduçao e Fontes*, 5th edn. (Coimbra, 1991).
De Azevedo Soares, A. *Licoes de direito internacional publico*, 4th edn. (Coimbra, 1988).
Decocq, A. 'Le droit et la notion de crime contre l'humanité', *Revue des Sciences morales et politiques* (1992), pp. 357–72.
Degan, V. D. 'General Principles of Law (A Source of General International Law)', 3 *Finnish Yearbook of International Law* (1992), pp. 1–101.
—— 'Mixed International Jurisdictions as the Last Instances in Enforcement of Human Rights in Successor States of Former Yugoslavia', 106 *Studi senesi* (1994), pp. 323–48.
de Guttry, A. *Le rappresaglie non comportanti la coercizione militare nel diritto internazionale* (Milan, 1985).
de Hoogh, A. J. J. *Obligations 'Erga Omnes' and International Crimes. A Theoretical Inquiry into the Implementation and Enforcement of the International Responsibility of States* (The Hague, 1996).
—— 'The Relationship between *Jus Cogens*, Obligations *Erga Omnes* and International Crimes: Peremptory Norms in Perspective', 42 *Austrian Journal of Public and International Law* (1991), pp. 183–214.
de la Brière, Y. *La "Société des Nations"? Essai Historique et Juridique*, 2nd edn. (Paris, 1918).
de Lacharrière, G. *La politique juridique extérieure* (Paris, 1983).
—— 'Consensus et Nations Unies', 14 *A.F.D.I.* (1968), pp. 9–14.
—— 'Commentaires sur la position juridique de la France à l'égard de la licéité de ses expériences nucléaires', 19 *A.F.D.I.* (1973), pp. 235–51.
—— 'Tendances contradictoires en matière de consentement des Etats', *L'élaboration du droit international public*, pp. 183–203.
—— 'Aspects du relativisme du droit international', Bos and Siblesz (eds.), *Realism: essays Riphagen*, pp. 89–99.
Delbrück, J. (ed.) *The Future of International Law Enforcement. New Scenarios—New Law?* (Berlin, 1993).
Deleau, O. 'Les positions françaises à la Conférence de Vienne sur le droit des traités', 15 *A.F.D.I.* (1969), pp. 7–23.
Delissen, A. J. M. and Tanja, G. J. (eds.) *Humanitarian Law of Armed Conflict. Challenges Ahead. Essays in Honour of Frits Kalshoven* (Dordrecht, 1991).
de Martens, G. F. *Précis du Droit des gens*, i (Paris, 1831).
Denning, Lord *The Discipline of Law* (London, 1979).

DENZINGER, H. and SCHÖNMETZER, A. *Enchiridion Symbolorum definitionum et declarationum de rebus fidei et morum*, 36th edn. (Freiburg, 1976).

DE QUADROS, F. 'La Convention Européenne des Droits de l'Homme: un cas de ius cogens régional?', Beyerlin, Bothe, Hofmann and Petersmann (eds.), *Recht. Festschrift Bernhardt*, pp. 555–62.

DESCAMPS, E. E. F. 'La droit international nouveau. L'influence de la condamnation de la guerre sur l'évolution juridique internationale', 31 Hague *Recueil* (1930, I), pp. 393–559.

DE STAËL-HOLSTEIN, L. 'La doctrine des servitudes internationales et son application en Scandinavie', 3 *R.D.I.L.C.* (3rd series, 1922), pp. 424–62.

—— 'Autour de la conception juridique des servitudes internationales', 15 *R.D.I.L.C.* (3rd series, 1934), pp. 5–21.

DE TAUBE, M. 'Le statut juridique de la mer Baltique jusqu'au début du XIXe siècle', 53 Hague *Recueil* (1935, III), pp. 441–531.

DETTER, I. *The International Legal Order* (Aldershot, 1994).

DE VISSCHER, C. 'La codification du droit international', 6 Hague *Recueil* (1925, I), pp. 329–453.

DE VISSCHER, F. 'La question des îles d'Aland (*Suite*)', 2 *R.D.I.L.C.* (3rd series, 1921), pp. 243–84.

—— 'La Convention relative à la Non-Fortification et à la Neutralisation des Iles d'Aland', 2 *R.D.I.L.C.* (3rd series, 1921), pp. 568–86.

DE VISSCHER, P. 'Cours général de droit international public', 136 Hague *Recueil* (1972, II), pp. 1–202.

DE WAART, P., PETERS, P. and DENTERS, E. (eds.) *International Law and Development* (Dordrecht, 1988).

DHOKALIA, R. P. 'Problems Relating to *Jus Cogens* in the Law of Treaties', Agrawala (ed.), *Essays*, pp. 149–77.

DIACONU, I. *Normele imperative in dreptul international ('jus cogens')* (Bucharest, 1977) (in Romanian, with English summary).

—— *Curs de drept international public*, 2nd edn. (Bucharest, 1995).

DIAS, R. W. M. *Jurisprudence*, 3rd edn. (Oxford, 1970).

Dictionnaire de la Terminologie du Droit international (Paris, 1960).

DIENA, G. 'Les mandats internationaux', 5 Hague *Recueil* (1924, IV), pp. 211–65.

DIEZ DE VELASCO VALLEJO, M. *Instituciones de derecho internacional publico*, i, 10th edn. (Madrid, 1994).

—— 'El sexto dictamen del Tribunal Internacional de Justicia: Las reservas a la Convencion sobre el Genocidio', 4 *Revista espanola de derecho internacional* (1951), pp. 1029–89.

DIJK, P. (VAN) *Judicial Review of Governmental Action and the Requirement of an Interest to Sue* (Alphen aan den Rijn, 1980).

DILLARD, H. C. 'Some Aspects of Law and Diplomacy', 91 Hague *Recueil* (1957, I), pp. 445–551.

DINSTEIN, Y. *War, Aggression and Self-Defence*, 2nd edn. (Cambridge, 1994).

—— (ed.) *International Law at a Time of Perplexity. Essays in Honour of Shabtai Rosenne* (Dordrecht, 1989).

—— 'The erga omnes Applicability of Human Rights', 30 *Archiv des Völkerrechts* (1992), pp. 16–21.

DIOP, C. A. 'The unity of the origin of the human species', *Racism, science and pseudo-science*, pp. 133–7.
DOMB, F. 'Judicial Decisions of the Supreme Court of Israel Relating to the Administrated Territories', 11 *Israel Yearbook on Human Rights* (1981), pp. 349–54.
DOMINICÉ, C., PATRY, R. and REYMOND, C. (eds.) *Etudes de droit international en l'honneur de Pierre Lalive* (Basel and Frankfurt, 1993).
Le droit international au service de la paix, de la justice et du développement. Mélanges Michel Virally (Paris, 1991).
Les droits de l'homme, droits collectifs ou individuels. Acts du Colloque de Strasbourg des 13 et 14 mars 1979 (Paris, 1980).
DROZDIAK, W. 'Noted Jurist Says Bias Contains "Seeds of Genocide"', *The Washington Post*, 2 July 1995, p. A24.
DUGARD, J. *Human Rights and the South African Legal Order* (Princeton, 1978).
—— *Recognition and the United Nations* (Cambridge, 1987).
—— *International Law. A South African Perspective* (Kenwyn, South Africa, 1994).
—— 'Namibia (South West Africa): The Court's Opinion, South Africa's Response, and Prospects for the Future', 11 *C.J.T.L.* (1972), pp. 14–49.
—— 'International Human Rights', van Wyk, Dugard, de Villiers and Davis (eds.), *Rights and Constitutionalism*, pp. 171–95.
—— '1966 and All That. The South west African Judgment Revisited in the East Timor Case', 8 *African Journal of International and Comparative Law* (1996), pp. 549–63.
DUNN, L. C. *Race and Biology* (Paris, 1958).
DUPUIS, C. 'Règles générales du droit de la paix', 32 Hague *Recueil* (1930, II), pp. 5–289.
—— 'Les antécédents de la Société des Nations', 60 Hague *Recueil* (1937, II), pp. 5–108.
DUPUY, P. M. *Droit international public*, 3rd edn. (Paris, 1995).
—— 'L'affaire des essais nucléaires français et le contentieux de la responsabilité internationale publique', 20 *G.Y.I.L.* (1977), pp. 375–405.
—— 'Action publique et crime international de l'état: à propos de l'article 19 du projet de la Commission du droit international sur la responsabilité des états', 25 *A.F.D.I.* (1979), pp. 539–54.
—— 'Observations sur le "crime international de l'Etat"', 84 *R.G.D.I.P.* (1980), pp. 449–86.
—— 'A propos de l'opposabilité de la coutume générale: enquête brève sur l'"objecteur persistant"', *Le droit international. Mélanges Virally*, pp. 257–72.
—— 'The Judicial Policy of the International Court of Justice', Salerno (ed.), *Il ruolo*, pp. 61–82.
DUPUY, R. J. (ed.) *The Right to Development at the International Level—Workshop, The Hague, 16–18 October 1979* (Alphen aan den Rijn, 1980).
—— (ed.) *The New International Economic Order. Commercial, Technological and Cultural Aspects* (Workshop organized by the Hague Academy of International Law and the United Nations University, held at The Hague on 23–25 Oct. 1980) (The Hague, 1981).

—— (ed.) *The Future of the International Law of the Environment. Workshop The Hague, 12–14 November 1984* (Dordrecht, 1985).

—— 'La contribution de l'Académie au développement du droit international', 138 Hague *Recueil* (1973, I), pp. 45–74.

—— 'Communauté internationale et disparités de devéloppement. Cours général de droit international public', 165 Hague *Recueil* (1979, IV), pp. 9–232.

—— 'Thème et variations sur le droit au développement', *Mélanges Chaumont*, pp. 263–79.

—— 'Humanity and the Environment' 2 *Colorado Journal of International Environmental Law and Policy* (1991), pp. 201–4.

—— 'L'action humanitaire', Delissen and Tanja (eds.), *Humanitarian Law. Essays Kalshoven*, pp. 67–77.

DUTILLEUL, J. 'Esclavage', *Dictionnaire de Théologie Catholique*, v/1 (Paris, 1939), columns, 457–520.

The Effects of Independence on Treaties. A Handbook Published after the auspices of The International Law Association (London, 1967).

EHMKE, H., KAISER, J. H., KEWENIG, W. A., MEESSEN, K. M. and RÜFNER, W. (eds.) *Festschrift für Ulrich Scheuner zum 70. Geburtstag* (Berlin, 1973).

EIDE, A., ALFREDSSON, G., MELANDER, G., REHOF, L. A. and ROSAS, A. (eds.) *The Universal Declaration of Human Rights: A Commentary* (Oslo, 1992).

EISEMANN, P. M., COUSSIRAT-COUSTÈRE, V. and HUR, P. *Petit manuel de la jurisprudence de la Cour internationale de justice*, 4th edn. (Paris, 1984).

L'élaboration du droit international public (Colloque de Toulouse) (Paris, 1975).

EL KADIRI, A. *La position des Etats du tiers monde à la Conference de Vienne sur le droit des traités* (Rabat, 1980).

ELKIND, J. B. *Interim Protection. A Functional Approach* (The Hague, 1981).

ERICH, R. 'La question des zones démilitarisées', 26 Hague *Recueil* (1929, I), pp. 591–667.

ERLAND, O. 'Some of the Main Points in the Proposed New Law of Autonomy for Aland', 57 *Nordic Journal of International Law* (1988), pp. 251–5.

Estudios de Derecho Internacional. Homenaje al Profesor Miaja de la Muela, 2 vols. (Madrid, 1979).

Estudios juridico-sociales. Homenaje al Professor Luis Legaz y Lacambra, 2 vols. (Santiago de Compostela, 1960).

Etudes juridiques offertes à Léon Julliot de la Morandière (Paris, 1964).

FALK, R. A. *The Status of Law in International Society* (Princeton, 1970).

FASTENRATH, U. 'Servitudes', Heidelberg *Encycl.*, x, pp. 389–92.

FAUCHILLE, P. *Traité de Droit international public*, i (Paris, 1922).

FAVRE, A. *Principes du droit des gens* (Fribourg, 1974).

FAWCETT, J. E. S. *The Law of Nations*, 2nd edn. (Harmondsworth, 1971).

—— and HIGGINS, R. (eds.) *International Organization: Law in Movement. Essays in Honour of John McMahon* (London, 1974).

FENWICK, C. G. *International Law*, 4th edn. (New York, 1965).

FERENCZ, B. B. *Defining International Aggression. The Search for World Peace* (New York, 1975).

FERRARI BRAVO, L. *Lezioni di diritto internazionale*, 3rd edn. (Naples, 1992).

FERRARI BRAVO, L. 'Prospettive del diritto internazionale alla fine del secolo XX', 74 *Riv. dir. int.* (1991), pp. 525–33.

—— 'Considérations sur la méthode de rêcherche des principes généraux du droit international de l'environnement', 7 *Hague Yearbook of International Law* (1994), pp. 3–10.

FINLEY, M. I. 'Slavery', Sills (ed.), *International Encyclopedia*, xiv (New York, 1968), pp. 307–13.

FINNIS, J. *Natural Law and Natural Rights* (Oxford, 1980).

—— *Moral Absolutes. Tradition, Revision, and Truth* (Washington, D.C., 1991).

FIORE, P. *International Law Codified and its Legal Sanction or The Legal Organization of the Society of States*, English trans. Borchard (New York, 1918).

FISCHER, G. 'La zone dénuclearisée du Pacifique Sud', 31 *A.F.D.I.* (1985), pp. 23–57.

FITZMAURICE, G. G. 'The Meaning of the Term "Denial of Justice"', 13 *B.Y.I.L.* (1932), pp. 93–114.

—— 'The juridical clauses of the peace treaties', 73 Hague *Recueil* (1948, II), pp. 259–364.

—— 'Thc Law and Procedure of the International Court of Justice: General Principles and Substantive Law', 27 *B.Y.I.L.* (1950), pp. 1–41.

—— 'The Law and Procedure of the International Court of Justice, 1951–54: General Principles and Sources of Law', 30 *B.Y.I.L.* (1953), pp. 1–70.

—— 'Reservations to Multilateral Conventions', 2 *I.C.L.Q.* (1953), pp. 1–26.

—— 'The Foundation of the Authority of International Law and the Problem of Enforcement', 19 *The Modern Law Review* (1956), pp. 1–13.

—— 'The Law and Procedure of the International Court of Justice 1951–4: Treaty Interpretation and Other Treaty Points', 33 *B.Y.I.L.* (1957), pp. 203–93.

—— 'The General Principles of International Law Considered from the Standpoint of the Rule of Law', 92 Hague *Recueil* (1957, II), pp. 1–227.

—— 'Some Problems Regarding the Formal Sources of International Law', *Symbolae Verzijl*, pp. 153–76.

—— 'Judicial Innovation—Its Uses and its Perils—As exemplified in some of the Work of the International Court of Justice during Lord McNair's Period of Office', *Cambridge Essays McNair*, pp. 24–47.

—— 'The Future of Public International Law and of the International Legal System in the Circumstances of Today', *Livre du Centenaire 1873–1973*, pp. 196–329.

—— 'The Contribution of the Institute of International Law to the Development of International Law', 138 Hague *Recueil* (1973, I), pp. 203–60.

FITZMAURICE, M. A. 'International Environmental Law as a Special Field', 25 *Netherlands Yearbook of International Law* (1994), pp. 181–226.

FITZMYER, J. A. 'The Letter to Philemon', Brown, Fitzmyer and Murphy (eds.), *The New Jerome*, pp. 869–70.

FITZPATRICK, J. 'The Relevance of Customary International Norms to the Death Penalty in the United States', 25 *Georgia Journal of International and Comparative Law* (1995/96), pp. 165–80.

FLORY, M. *Droit international du développement* (Paris, 1977).

—— MAHIOU, A. and HENRY, J. R. (eds.) *La formation des normes en droit international du développement—Table Ronde franco-magrébine Aix-en-Provence, 7 et 8 octobre 1982* (Paris and Algiers, 1984).

FOCARELLI, C. 'Le contromisure pacifiche collettive e la nozione di obblighi *erga omnes*', 76 *Riv. dir. int.* (1993), pp. 52–72.

FRANCIONI, F. 'Patrimonio comune della cultura. Sovranità e conflitti armati', 106 *Studi senesi* (1994), pp. 7–21.

—— and SCOVAZZI, T. (eds.) *International Law for Antarctica* (Milan, 1987).

FRANCK, T. M. *Fairness in International Law and Institutions* (Oxford, 1995).

—— 'Word Made Law: The Decision of the ICJ in the Nuclear Tests Cases', 69 *A.J.I.L.* (1975), pp. 612–20.

FRANÇOIS, J. P. A. *Grondlijnen van het Volkenrecht*, 3rd edn. (Zwolle, 1967).

—— 'Règles générales du droit de la paix', 66 Hague *Recueil* (1938, IV), pp. 1–294.

FREESTONE, D., and DAVIDSON, S. 'Nuclear weapon-free zones', Pogany (ed.), *Nuclear Weapons and International Law*, pp. 176–216.

FRIEDMAN, L. M. *A History of American Law*, 2nd edn. (New York, 1985).

FRIEDMANN, W. G., LISSITZYN, O. J. and PUGH, R. C. *Cases and Materials on International Law* (St. Paul, Minn., 1969).

—— HENKIN, L. and LISSITZYN, O. J. (eds.) *Transnational Law in a Changing Society. Essays in Honor of Philip C. Jessup* (New York, 1972).

FROWEIN, J. A. *International Law in the Period after Decolonization* (Lagos, 1988).

—— 'Die Verpflichtungen erga omnes im Völkerrecht und ihre Durchsetzung', *Völkerrecht als Rechtsordnung. Festschrift Mosler*, pp. 241–62.

—— 'Jus Cogens', Heidelberg *Encycl.*, vii, pp. 327–30.

—— 'Collective Enforcement of International Obligations', 47 *Z.a.ö.R.V.* (1987), pp. 67–79.

—— 'La Notion de victime dans le CEDH', *Studi Sperduti*, pp. 587–99.

—— 'Reactions by Not Directly Affected States to Breaches of Public International Law', 248 Hague *Recueil* (1994, IV), pp. 345–438.

FURET, M. F. *Expérimentation des armes nucléaires et droit international public* (Paris, 1966).

—— *Le Désarmement nucléaire* (Paris, 1973).

GAJA, G. '*Jus cogens* Beyond the Vienna Convention', 172 Hague *Recueil* (1981, III), pp. 271–313.

—— 'A "New" Vienna Convention on Treaties between States and International Organizations or between International Organizations: A Critical Commentary', 58 *B.Y.I.L.* (1987), pp. 253–69.

—— 'Obligations *Erga Omnes*, International Crimes and *Jus Cogens*: A Tentative Analysis of Three Related Concepts', Weiler, Cassese and Spinedi (eds.), *International Crimes*, pp. 151–60.

Gale on Easements, 15th edn. Maurice (London, 1986).

GARVEY, J. I. 'The U.N. Definition of "Aggresion": Law and Illusion in the Context of Collective Security', 17 *Virginia Journal of International Law* (1977), pp. 177–99.

GECK, W. K. 'The Codification of International Law in the United Nations: Promoting and Obstructing Factors and their Results', 17 *Law and State* (1978), pp. 21–44.

GEORGE, R. P. (ed.) *The Autonomy of Law*. Essays on Legal Positivism (Oxford, 1996).

GIHL, T. *International Legislation: An Essay on Changes in International Law and in International Legal Situations*, English trans. Charleston (London, 1937).

GIHL, T. 'The Legal Character and Sources of International Law', 1 *Scandinavian Studies in Law* (1957), pp. 51–92.

GILBERT, G. 'The Criminal Responsibility of States', 39 *I.C.L.Q.* (1990), pp. 345–69.

GILL, T. D. *Litigation Strategy at the International Court. A Case Study of the Nicaragua v. United States Dispute* (Dordrecht, 1989).

GINSBURGS, G. and KUDRIAVTSEV, V. N. (eds.) *The Nuremberg Trial and International Law* (Dordrecht, 1990).

GINTHER, K., HAFNER, G., LANG, W., NEUHOLD, H. and SUCHARIPA-BEHRMANN, L. (eds.) *Völkerrecht zwischen normativen Anspruch und politischer Realität. Festschrift für Karl Zemanek zum 65. Geburtstag* (Berlin, 1994).

GIORGIANNI, M. *L'obbligazione (la parte generale delle obbligazioni)* (Milan, 1968).

GIRAUD, E. 'Le droit international public et la politique' 110 Hague *Recueil* (1963, III), pp. 423–801.

GIULIANO, M. 'L'ordinamento internazionale e i fiumi navigabili d'interesse internazionale', 42 *Riv. dir. int.* (1959), pp. 201–38.

—— SCOVAZZI, T. and TREVES, T. *Diritto internazionale. Parte generale*, 3rd edn. (Milan, 1991).

GLAHN, G. (VON) *Law Among Nations. An Introduction to Public International Law*, 7th edn. (Boston, 1996).

GLARE, P. G. W. (ed.) *Oxford Latin Dictionary* (Oxford, 1982).

GOLITSIN, V. V. *Antarktika: tendentsii razvitiia rezhima* (Moscow, 1989).

GOMBRICH, E. H. *The Story of Art*, 16th edn. (London, 1995).

GOMEZ ROBLEDO, A. 'Le *ius cogens* international: sa genèse, sa nature, ses fonctions', 172 Hague *Recueil* (1981, III), pp. 9–218.

GONZALEZ CAMPOS, J. D., SANCHEZ RODRIGUEZ, L. I. and ANDRES SAENZ DE SANTA MARIA, M. P. *Curso de derecho internacional publico*, 5th edn. (Madrid, 1992).

GRAEFRATH, B. (ed.) *Probleme des Völkerrechts* (Berlin, 1987).

—— OESER, E. and STEINIGER, P. A. 'Internationale Verbrechen—Internationale Delikte', 22 *Deutsche Aussenpolitik* (1977), pp. 90–101.

GRAHAM, M. W. 'The Diplomatic Recognition of the Border States. Part I: Finland', 3 *Publications of the University of California at Los Angeles in Social Sciences* (1936, No. 2), pp. i–viii and 81–230.

GRAY, C. D. *Judicial Remedies in International Law* (Oxford, 1987).

GREENBERG, J. 'Race, Sex and Religious Discrimination in International Law', Meron (ed.), *Human Rights*, ii, pp. 307–43.

GREVISSE, M. *Le bon usage. Grammaire française*, 13th edn. Goosse (Paris, 1993).

GRIEF, N. 'Nuclear Tests and International Law', Pogany (ed.), *Nuclear Weapons and International Law*, pp. 217–44.

GROS ESPIELL, H. *Derecho internacional del desarrollo* (Valladolid, 1975).

—— 'La evolucion del concepto de los derechos humanos: criterios occidentales, socialistas y del tercer mundo', 5 *Anuario hispano-luso-americano de derecho internacional* (1979), pp. 73–102.

—— 'Self-Determination and *Jus Cogens*', Cassese (ed.), *U.N. Law Fundamental Rights*, pp. 167–73.

—— 'No discriminacion y libre determinacion como normas imperativas de derecho internacional, con especial referencia a los efectos de su denegacion sobre la legitimidad de los estados que violan o desconocen esas normas imperativas', 6 *Anuario hispano-luso-americano de derecho internacional* (1981), pp. 33–81.

GROSS, E. A. '*The South West Africa Cases*: On the Threshold of Decision', 3 *C.J.T.L.* (1964), pp. 19–25.

GROSSO, G. *Le servitù prediali nel diritto romano* (Turin, 1969).

GROTIUS, H. *De jure belli ac pacis libri tres*, English trans. Kelsey of 1646 edition, Scott (ed.), *Classics of International Law* (Oxford, 1925).

GUARINO, G. *Autodeterminazione dei popoli e diritto internazionale* (Naples, 1984).

GUBIN, V. F. *Rasovaya diskriminatsiya: reaktsionnaya sushchnost' i mezhdunarodnaya protivopravnost'* (Moscow, 1979).

GUGGENHEIM, P. *Traité de Droit international public*, 2 vols. (Geneva, 1953–4).

—— 'La validité et la nullité des actes juridiques internationaux', 74 Hague *Recueil* (1949, I), pp. 195–265.

—— 'Quelques remarques au sujet de l'article 14 de la Convention européenne des droits de l'homme', *René Cassin Liber*, i, pp. 95–100.

—— *et al.* (eds.) *Répertoire suisse de droit international public. Documentation concernant la pratique de la Confédération en matière de droit international public 1914–1939*, 4 vols. (Basel, 1975).

GUILLAUME, G. 'Terrorisme et droit international', 215 Hague *Recueil* (1989, III), pp. 287–416.

—— 'Le statut de l'Antarctique: Réflexions sur quelques problèmes récents', *Humanité. Mélanges René-Jean Dupuy*, pp. 171–7.

—— 'The Future of International Judicial Institutions', 44 *I.C.L.Q.* (1995), pp. 848–62.

—— 'La France et la Cour internationale de Justice', *L'internationalité. Etudes Plantey*, pp. 119–26.

GURUSWAMY, L. D., PALMER, G. W. R. and WESTON, B. H. *International Environment Law and World Order. A Problem-Oriented Coursebook* (St. Paul, Minn., 1994).

GUTIÉRREZ ESPADA, C. *Derecho internacional publico. 1: Introduccion y fuentes*, 4th edn. (Barcelona, 1993).

The Hague Academy of International Law. Jubilee Book. 1923–1973 (Leiden, 1973).

HAIMBAUGH, G. D. 'Jus Cogens: Root & Branch (an Inventory)', 3 *Touro Law Review* (1987), pp. 203–27.

HALL, K. L. (ed.) *The Oxford Companion to the Supreme Court of the United States* (New York and Oxford, 1992).

HALL, W. E. *A Treatise on International Law*, 8th edn. Higgins, A. P. (Oxford, 1924).

HALPIN, A. K. W. 'Hohfeld's Conceptions: from Eight to Two', 44 *Cambridge Law Journal* (1985), pp. 435–57.

HANDL, G. 'Environmental Protection and Development in Third World Countries: Common Destiny—Common Responsibility', 20 *N.Y.U.J.I.L.P.* (1988), pp. 603–27.

HANNIKAINEN, L. *Peremptory Norms (Jus Cogens) in International Law—Historical Development, Criteria, Present Status* (Helsinki, 1988).

—— 'The Continued Validity of the Demilitarised and Neutralised Status of the Aland Islands', 54 *Z.a.ö.R.V.* (1994), pp. 614–51.

HANZ, M. *Zur völkerrechtlichen Aktivlegitimation zum Schutze der Menschenrechte* (Munich, 1985).

HARRIS, M. 'Race', Sills (ed.), *International Encyclopedia*, xiii (New York, 1968), pp. 263–9.

HART, H. L. A. *Essays on Bentham. Studies in Jurisprudence and Political Theory* (Oxford, 1982).

HART, H. L. A. *The Concept of Law*, 2nd edn. (Oxford, 1994).
—— 'Definition and Theory in Jurisprudence', 70 *Law Quarterly Review* (1954), pp. 37–60.
HAZARD, J. N. 'Renewed Emphasis upon a Socialist International Law', 65 *A.J.I.L.* (1971), pp. 142–8.
HEFFNER, R. D. *A Documentary History of the United States*, 5th edn. (New York, 1991).
HEFFTER, A. G. *Le Droit international public de l'Europe*, French trans. Bergson (Berlin and Paris, 1857).
HEISKANEN, V. *International Legal Topics* (Helsinki, 1992).
HELLIE, R. 'Slavery', *The New Encyclopaedia Britannica*, xxvii, pp. 288–300.
HENKIN, L. *How Nations Behave. Law and Foreign Policy*, 2nd edn. (New York, 1979).
—— *The Age of Rights* (New York, 1990).
—— *International Law: Politics and Values* (Dordrecht, 1995).
—— (ed.) *The International Bill of Rights: The Covenant on Civil and Political Rights* (New York, 1981).
—— 'National and International Perspectives in Racial Discrimination', 4 *Human Rights Journal* (1971), pp. 263–9.
—— 'Human Rights and "Domestic Jurisdiction"', Buergenthal (ed.), *Human Rights*, pp. 21–40.
—— '"Nationality" at the Turn of the Century', Beyerlin, Bothe, Hofmann and Petersmann (eds.), *Recht. Festschrift Bernhardt*, pp. 89–102.
—— 'Human Rights and State "Sovereignty" (Sibley Lecture, March 1994)', 25 *Georgia Journal of International and Comparative Law* (1995/96), pp. 31–45.
—— PUGH, R. C., SCHACHTER, O. and SMIT, H. *International Law Cases and Materials*, 3rd edn. (St. Paul, Minn., 1993).
HERCZEGH, G. *General Principles of Law and the International Legal Order* (Budapest, 1969).
HEYDTE, F. A. (von der) *Völkerrecht. Ein Lehrbuch* (Cologne, 1958).
—— 'Die Erscheinungsformen des zwischenstaatlichen Rechts: *jus cogens* und *jus dispositivum* im Völkerrecht', 16 *Zeitschrift für Völkerrecht* (1932), pp. 461–87.
HIGGINS, A. P. *The Binding Force of International Law. Inaugural Lecture in International Law at the London School of Economics and Political Science. Session 1910–11* (Cambridge, 1910).
—— 'La contribution de quatre grands juristes britanniques au droit international (Lorimer, Westlake, Hall et Holland)', 40 Hague *Recueil* (1932, II), pp. 1–85.
HIGGINS, R. *Problems and Process. International Law and How We Use It* (Oxford, 1994).
——'Aspects of the Case Concerning the Barcelona Traction, Light and Power Company, Ltd.', 11 *Virginia Journal of International Law* (1971), pp. 327–43.
—— 'Fundamentals of International Law', Jasentuliyana (ed.), *Perpsectives*, pp. 3–22.
HOHFELD, W. N. *Fundamental Legal Conceptions as Applied in Judicial Reasoning and Other Legal Essays*, Cook ed. (New Haven, 1920), pp. 23–114.
HONORÉ, T. 'Rights of Exclusion and Immunities against Divesting', 34 *Tulane Law Review* (1960), pp. 453–68.
HOOF, G. J. H. (VAN) *Rethinking the Sources of International Law* (The Hague, 1983).
HOSSAIN, K. and CHOWDHURY, S. R. (eds.), *Permanent Sovereignty Over Natural Resources in International Law. Principle and Practice* (New York, 1984).

HOSTIE, J. 'Examen de quelques règles du droit international dans le domaine des communications et du transit', 40 Hague *Recueil* (1932, II), pp. 403–523.

Humanité et droit international. Mélanges René-Jean Dupuy (Paris, 1991).

HUTCHINSON, D. J. 'Brown v. Board of Education', Hall, K. L. (ed.), *The Oxford Companion to the Supreme Court*, pp. 93–6.

HUTCHINSON, D. N. 'Solidarity and Breaches of Multilateral Treaties', 59 *B.Y.I.L.* (1988), pp. 151–215.

HYDE, C. *International Law Chiefly as Interpreted and Applied by the United States*, i (Boston, 1947).

IGNATENKO, G. V. (ed.) *Mezhdunarodnoe pravo*, 2nd edn. (Moscow, 1995).

The International Court of Justice, 3rd edn. (The Hague, 1986).

INTERNATIONAL LAW ASSOCIATION, *Report of the Sixty-first Conference held at Paris. August 26th to September 1st, 1984* (Aberystwyth, 1985).

—— *Report of the Sixty-third Conference held at Warsaw. August 21st to August 27th, 1988* (London, 1988).

—— *Report of the Sixty-fifth Conference held at Cairo, Egypt. 21 to 26 April 1992* (Cairo, 1993).

International Law at the Time of its Codification. Essays in Honour of Roberto Ago, 4 vols. (Milan, 1987).

International Law in an Evolving World. Liber Amicorum in Tribute to Professor Eduardo Jiménez de Aréchaga, 2 vols. (Montevideo, 1994).

L'internationalité dans les institutions et le droit: convergences et défis. Etudes offertes à Alain Plantey (Paris, 1995).

ISIDORUS, *Etymologiae*, Lindsay ed. (Oxford, 1911).

JAENICKE, G. 'Diskriminierung', Strupp and Schlochauer (eds.), *Wörterbuch*, i, pp. 387–92.

—— 'International Public Order', Heidelberg *Encycl.*, vii, pp. 314–18.

JANIS, M. W. *An Introduction to International Law*, 2nd edn. (Boston, 1993).

—— (ed.) *The Influence of Religion on the Development of International Law* (Dordrecht, 1991).

—— (ed.) *International Courts for the Twenty-First Century* (Dordrecht, 1992).

—— 'The Nature of *Jus Cogens*', 3 *Connecticut Journal of International Law* (1988), pp. 359–63.

—— 'The International Court', Janis (ed.), *International Courts*, pp. 13–41.

JASENTULIYANA, N. (ed.) *Perspectives on International Law (A Publication on the Occasion of the Fiftieth Anniversary of the United Nations and a Contribution to the Decade of International Law)* (London, 1995).

JEKEWITZ, J., KLEIN, K. H., KÜHNE, J. D., PETERSMANN, H. and WOLFRUM, R. (eds.) *Des Menschen Recht zwischen Freiheit und Verantwortung. Festschrift für Karl Josef Partsch zum 75. Geburtstag* (Berlin, 1989).

JENKS, C. W. 'Unanimity, The Veto, Weighted Voting, Special and Simple Majorities and Consensus as Modes of Decision in International Organisations', *Cambridge Essays McNair*, pp. 48–63.

—— 'The General Welfare as a Legal Interest', *Jus et Societas. Essays Friedmann*, pp. 151–8.

JENNINGS, R. Y. 'Recent Developments in the International Law Commission: Its Relation to the Sources of International Law', 18 *I.C.L.Q.* (1964), pp. 385–97.

JENNINGS, R. Y. 'Nullity and Effectiveness in International Law', *Cambridge Essays McNair*, pp. 64–87.
—— 'General Course on Principles of International Law', 121 Hague *Recueil* (1967, II), pp. 323–606.
—— 'Fifty Years of Hague Academy Lectures on Public International Law', *Hague Academy. Jubilee Book*, pp. 99–115.
—— 'What is International Law and How Do we Tell it When we See it?', 37 *Ann. suisse* (1981), pp. 59–88.
—— 'International Force and the International Court of Justice', Cassese (ed.), *The Current Legal Regulation*, pp. 322–35.
—— 'The International Judicial Practice of the International Court of Justice', 59 *B.Y.I.L.* (1988), pp. 31–47.
—— 'Treaties', Bedjaoui (ed.), *International Law*, pp. 135–77.
—— 'Judicial Reasoning at an International Court', *Universität des Saarlands. Vorträge Reden und Berichte aus dem Europa-Institut*, Ress ed., No. 236 (Saarbrücken, 1991), pp. 1–8.
—— 'New Problems at the International Court of Justice', *International Law. Liber Jiménez de Aréchaga*, pp. 1061–7.
—— 'The Judiciary, International and National, and the Development of International Law', 45 *I.C.L.Q.* (1996), pp. 1–12.
JESSUP, P. C. *A Modern Law of Nations. An Introduction* (New York, 1948; re-impressed in 1968 with a new Preface by the author).
—— 'Silence Gives Consent', 3 *Georgia Journal of International Law* (1973), pp. 46–54.
—— 'Hardy Dillard', 23 *Virginia Journal of International Law* (1983), pp. 363–7.
JIMÉNEZ DE ARÉCHAGA, E. 'Treaty Stipulations in Favor of Third States', 50 *A.J.I.L.* (1956), pp. 338–57.
—— 'International Law in the Past Third of a Century', 159 Hague *Recueil* (1978, I), pp. 1–344.
—— 'The Work and the Jurisprudence of the International Court of Justice 1947–1986', 58 *B.Y.I.L.* (1987), pp. 1–38.
JÖNSSON, C. *The Soviet Union and the Test Ban. A Study in Soviet Negotiating Behavior* (Lund, 1975).
JOHN PAUL II 'From this African shrine of sorrow let us implore heaven's forgiveness', *L'Osservatore Romano* (Weekly Edition in English) (4 Mar. 1992), p. 2.
JOHNSON, S. *The Earth Summit. The United Nations Conference on Environment and Development (UNCED)* (Dordrecht, 1993).
Jus et Societas. Essays in Tribute to Wolfgang Friedmann (The Hague, 1979).
JUSTE RUIZ, J. *Derecho internacional publico?* (Valencia, 1986).
—— 'Las obligaciones "erga omnes" en derecho internacional publico', *Estudios Miaja de la Muela*, i, pp. 219–33.
Justinian, The Digest of, Mommsen and Krueger eds., English trans. ed. by Watson, 4 vols. (Philadelphia, 1985).
Justinian's Institutes, Birks and McLeod eds. (London, 1987).
KAECKENBEECK, G. S. F. C. *International Rivers: A Monograph Based on Diplomatic Documents* (London, 1918).
KALSHOVEN, F., KUYPER, P. J. and LAMMERS, J. G. (eds.) *Essays on the Development*

of the International Legal Order in Memory of Haro F. Van Panhuys (Aalphen aan den Rijn and Rockville, 1980).

KAMTO, M. 'L'accession de la Namibie à l'indépendance', 94 *R.G.D.I.P.* (1990), pp. 577–634.

KAPLAN, M. A. and KATZENBACH, N. DE B. *The Political Foundations of International Law* (New York and London, 1961).

KAPOOR, S. K. *International Law*, 9th edn. (Allahabad, 1992).

KAS'IAN, N. F. *Konsensus v sovremennykh mezhdunarodnykh otnosheniyakh (mezhdunarodno-pravovye voprosy)* (Moscow, 1983).

KAUFMANN, E. 'Règles générales du droit de la paix', 54 Hague *Recueil* (1935, IV), pp. 313–615.

KELLY, C. R. 'Law of the Sea: The Jurisdictional Dispute over Highly Migratory Species of Tuna', 26 *C.J.T.L.* (1988), pp. 475–513.

KELSEN, H. *General Theory of Law and State*, English trans. Wedberg (Cambridge, Mass., 1949).

—— *International Law Studies. Collective Security under International Law* (Washington, 1957).

—— *Principles of International Law*, 2nd edn. Tucker (New York, 1966).

—— *General Theory of Norms*, English trans. Hartney (Oxford, 1991).

—— *Introduction to the Problems of Legal Theory*, English trans. Litschewski Paulson and Paulson (Oxford, 1992).

——'Théorie du droit international coutumier', 1 *Révue internationale de la théorie du droit* (1939), pp. 253–74.

KENIG-WITKOWSKA, M. M. 'The UN Declaration on the right to development in the light of its travaux préparatoires', de Waart, Peters and Denters (eds.), *International Law and Development*, pp. 381–8.

Kent's Commentary on International Law, 2nd edn. Abdy (Cambridge and London, 1878).

KISS, A. C. (ed.) *Répertoire de la pratique française en matière de droit international public*, i (Paris, 1962).

—— 'The International Protection of The Environment', Macdonald and Johnston (eds.), *The Structure and Process*, pp. 1069–93.

—— 'La contribution de la Conférence de Rio de Janeiro au développement du droit international coutumier', Al-Nauimi and Meese (eds.), *International Legal Issues*, pp. 1079–92.

—— and SHELTON, D *International Environmental Law* (New York and London, 1991).

KLEIN, E. *Statusverträge im Völkerrecht: Rechtsfragen territorialer Sonderregime* (Berlin, 1980).

—— 'Genocide Convention (Advisory Opinion)', Heidelberg *Encycl.*, ii, pp. 107–9.

KLÜBER, J. L. *Droit des gens moderne de l'Europe*, i (Stuttgart, 1819).

KLUGER, R. *Simple Justice* (New York, 1977).

KOCOUREK, A. 'The Hohfeld System of Fundamental Legal Concepts', 15 *Illinois Law Review* (1920), pp. 24–39.

KOHL, W. L. *French Nuclear Diplomacy* (Princeton, 1971).

KOJANEC, G. *Trattati e terzi stati. Limiti soggettivi di validità delle norme positive dell'ordinamento internazionale* (Padua, 1961).

KOLOSOV, I. M. and KUSNETSOV, V. I. (eds.) *Mezhdunarodnoe pravo* (Moscow, 1995).
KOOIJMANS, P. H. 'In the shadowland between civil war and civil strife: some reflections on the standard-setting process', Delissen and Tanja (eds.), *Humanitarian Law. Essays Kalshoven*, pp. 225–47.
KOS, J. S. 'Interim relief in the International Court: New Zealand and the Nuclear Test cases', 14 *Victoria University of Wellington Law Review* (1984), pp. 357–87.
KRIELE, M. 'Das Präjudiz im kontinental-europäischen und anglo-amerikanischen Rechtskreis', *La sentenza in Europa*, pp. 62–80.
KUDRIAVTSEV, V. N. (ed.) *Kurs mezhdunarodnogo prava v semi tomakh* (Moscow, 1989–93).
KUNZ, J.-L 'L'article XI du Pacte de la Société des Nations', 39 Hague *Recueil* (1932, I), pp. 683–789.
KUPER, L. *International Action against Genocide* (Minority Rights Group Report No. 53, London, 1982).
—— *The Prevention of Genocide* (New Haven and London, 1985).
—— 'Segregation', Sills (ed.), *International Encyclopedia*, xiv (New York, 1968), pp. 144–50.
LACHS, M. *The Teacher in International Law (Teachings and Teaching)* (The Hague, 1982).
—— 'The Development and General Trends of International Law in Our Time (General Course in Public International Law)', 169 Hague *Recueil* (1980, III), pp. 9–377.
—— 'Slavery: the past and the present', Delissen and Tanja (eds.), *Humanitarian Law. Essays Kalshoven*, pp. 613–25.
LAGONI, R. 'Kiel Canal', Heidelberg *Encycl.*, xii, pp. 200–2.
LAMMERS, J. G. 'General Principles of Law Recognized by Civilized Nations', Kalshoven, Kuyper and Lammers (eds.), *Essays Van Panhuys*, pp. 53–9.
LANG, J. *Le plateau continental de la Mer du Nord. Arrêt de la Cour International de Justice 20 Février 1969* (Paris, 1970).
LASSER, W. 'Stanford v. Kentucky', Hall, K. L. (ed.), *The Oxford Companion to the Supreme Court*, p. 821.
LATTANZI, F. *Garanzie dei diritti dell'uomo nel diritto internazionale generale* (Milan, 1983).
LAUTERPACHT, E. *Aspects of the Administration of International Justice* (Cambridge, 1991).
—— (ed.) *International Law. Being the Collected Papers of Hersch Lauterpacht*, 3 vols. (Cambridge, 1970/77).
LAUTERPACHT, H. *Private Law Sources and Analogies of International Law* (London, 1927).
—— *Recognition in International Law* (Cambridge, 1947).
—— *International Law and Human Rights* (London, 1950).
—— *The Development of International Law by the International Court* (London, 1958).
—— 'Implications of the *Norwegian Fisheries* Case', Lauterpacht, E. (ed.), *International Law. Collected Papers*, iii, pp. 213–17.
—— 'Codification and Development of International Law', 49 *A.J.I.L.* (1955), pp. 16–43.
—— and WALDOCK, C. H. M. (eds.), *The Basis of Obligation in International Law and Other Papers by the Late James Leslie Brierly* (Oxford, 1958).

The Law of the Sea. Exclusive Economic Zone. Legislative History of Articles 56, 58 and 59 of the United Nations Convention on the Law of the Sea (Division for Ocean Affairs and the Law of the Sea. Office of Legal Affairs) (New York, 1992).

LAWRENCE, T. J. *Essays on Some Disputed Questions in Modern International Law*, 2nd edn. (Cambridge, 1885).

LAWSON, F. H. 'Rights and Other Relations *in rem*', *Many Laws. Selected Essays* (Amsterdam, 1977), i, pp. 2–22.

LE BLANC, L. J. 'The Intent to Destroy Groups in the Genocide Convention: The Proposed U.S. Understanding', 78 *A.J.I.L.* (1984), pp. 369–85.

LE FUR, L. 'Règles générales du droit de la paix', 54 Hague *Recueil* (1935, IV), pp. 5–307.

LEMKIN, R. *Axis Rule in Occupied Europe* (Washington, 1944).

—— 'Genocide as a Crime under International Law', 41 *A.J.I.L.* (1947), pp. 145–51.

LERNER, N. *The U.N. Convention on the Elimination of All Forms of Racial Discrimination*, 2nd edn. (Alphen aan den Rijn and Rockville, 1980).

LESKY, A. *Geschichte der griechischen Literatur* (Bern, 1957–8); *A History of Greek Literature*, English trans. Willis and de Heer of the second German edition, 1963 (London, 1966).

LI HAOPEI 'Jus Cogens and International Law', *Selected Articles from Chinese Yearbook of International Law* (Beijing, 1983), pp. 41–75.

Liber Amicorum Marc-André Eissen (Brussels and Paris, 1995).

LISSITZYN, O. J. 'International Law and the Advisory Opinion on Namibia', 11 *C.J.T.L.* (1972), pp. 50–73.

LISZT, F. (VON) *Das Völkerrecht systematisch dargestellt* 12th edn. Fleischmann (Berlin, 1925); *Le Droit international. Exposé systématique*, French trans. Gidel and Alcindor of the ninth German edition, 1913 (Paris, 1927).

Livre du Centenaire 1873–1973. Evolution et perspectives du droit international, Institut de Droit International (under the auspices of) (Basel, 1973).

LORIMER, J. *The Institutes of the Law of Nations. A Treatise of the Jural Relations of Separate Political Communities*, i (Edinburgh and London, 1883).

LOWE, V. and FITZMAURICE, M. (eds.) *Fifty Years of the International Court of Justice. Essays in Honour of Sir Robert Jennings* (Cambridge, 1996).

LOWE, V. and WARBRICK, C. (eds.) *The United Nations and the Principles of International Law. Essays in memory of Michael Akehurst* (London and New York, 1994).

LUKASHUK, I. I. *Mekhanizm mezhdunarodno-pravovogo regulirovaniia* (Kiev, 1980).

—— *Funktsionirovanie mezhdunarodnogo prava* (Moscow, 1992).

—— *Mezhdunarodnoe pravo v sudakh gosudarstv* (Saint Petersburg, 1993).

LUSTIGER, J. M. 'La personne devant le Cardinal Archevêque de Paris', *Recueil Dalloz Sirey* (1995, No. 2), pp. 6–9.

MACDONALD, R. St. J. (ed.) *Essays in Honour of Wang Tieya* (Dordrecht, 1993).

—— 'Fundamental Norms in Contemporary International Law', 25 *Canadian Yearbook of International Law* (1987), pp. 115–49.

—— 'The Principle of Solidarity in Public International Law', Dominicé, Patry and Reymond (eds.), *Etudes Lalive*, pp. 275–307.

—— and JOHNSTON, D. M. (eds.) *The Structure and Process of International Law: Essays in Legal Philosophy Doctrine and Theory* (The Hague, 1983).

—— MATSCHER, F. and PETZOLD, H. (eds.) *The European System for the Protection of Human Rights* (Dordrecht, 1993).

MacGibbon, I. C. 'Some Observations on the Part of Protest in International Law', 30 *B.Y.I.L.* (1953), pp. 293–319.

Magallona, M. M. 'The Concept of *Jus Cogens* in the Vienna Convention on the Law of Treaties', 51 *Philippine Law Journal* (1976), pp. 521–42.

Makarczyk, J. *Principles of a New International Economic Order* (Dordrecht, 1988).

—— (ed.) *Essays in International Law in Honour of Judge Manfred Lachs* (The Hague, 1984).

Mamiani, T. *D'un nuovo diritto europeo* (Turin, 1859).

Mani, V. S. *International Adjudication: Procedural Aspects* (The Hague, 1980).

—— 'The Advisory Opinion in Namibia Case: A Critique', 11 *Indian Journal of International Law* (1971), pp. 467–80.

Manlii Severini Boetii Opera Omnia, ii (Paris, 1847).

Mann, F. A. *Foreign Affairs in English Courts* (Oxford, 1986).

—— 'The Doctrine of *Jus Cogens* in International law', Ehmke, Kaiser, Kewenig, Meessen and Rüfner (eds.), *Festschrift Scheuner*, pp. 399–418. (This article is now reproduced in Mann, F. A., *Further Studies in International Law* (Oxford, 1990), pp. 84–102.)

Manning, W. O. *Commentaries on the Law of Nations*, revised edn. Amos (London and Cambridge, 1875).

Marchisio, S. 'Servitù (diritto internazionale)', *Enciclopedia del diritto*, xlii (Milan, 1990), pp. 342–55.

Marek, K. 'Contribution à l'étude du jus cogens en droit international', *Recueil Guggenheim*, pp. 426–59.

—— 'Criminalizing State Responsibility', 14 *Revue belge de droit international* (1978–79), pp. 460–85.

Margolis, E. 'The Hydrogen Bomb Experiments and International Law', 64 *Yale Law Journal* (1954–55), pp. 629–47.

Marino Menéndez, F. M. *Derecho Internacional Publico. Parte general* (Madrid, 1993).

Maritain, J. 'Autour de la nouvelle déclaration universelle des droits de l'homme (Introduction aux textes réunis par l'Unesco, juillet-août 1948)', *Les droits de l'homme*, Mougel ed. (Paris, 1989), pp. 125–37.

Markesinis, B. S. and Deakin, S. F. *Tort Law*, 3rd edn. (Oxford, 1994).

Martino, R. R. 'All human needs must be respected (Intervention of Archbishop Martino at the UN Conference on Environment and Development)', *L'Osservatore Romano* (Weekly Edition in English) (17 June 1992), p. 13.

May, H. G. and Metzger, B. M. (eds.) *The New Oxford Annotated Bible with the Apocrypha* (New York, 1977).

May, W. E. *An Introduction to Moral Theology* (Huntington, Indiana, 1994).

Mbaye, K. 'Le droit au développement comme un droit de l'homme', 5 *Revue des droits de l'homme* (1972), pp. 503–34.

—— 'L'intérêt pour agir devant la Cour internationale de Justice', 209 Hague *Recueil* (1988, III), pp. 223–346.

—— 'Introduction (Human Rights and Rights of Peoples)', Bedjaoui (ed.), *International Law*, pp. 1043–58.

McCaffrey, S. '*Lex Lata* or the Continuum of State Responsibility', Weiler, Cassese and Spinedi (eds.), *International Crimes*, pp. 242–4.

McClane, J. B. 'How Late in the Emergence of a Norm of Customary Law May a

Persistent Objector Object?', 13 *ILSA Journal of International Law* (1989), pp. 1–26.

McDougal, M. S., Lasswell, H. D. and Chen, L. *Human Rights and World Public Order. The Basic Policies of an International Law of Human Dignity* (New Haven and London, 1980).

—— and Reisman, W. M. *International Law in Contemporary Perspective: The Public Order of the World Community. Cases and Materials* (Mineola, New York, 1981).

—— and Schlei, N. A. 'The Hydrogen Bomb in Perspective: Lawful Measures for Security', 64 *Yale Law Journal* (1954–55), pp. 648–710.

McGoldrick, D. 'Sustainable Development and Human Rights: An Integrated Conception', 45 *I.C.L.Q.* (1996), pp. 796–818.

McKean, W. A. *Equality and Discrimination under International Law* (Oxford, 1983).

—— 'The Meaning of Discrimination in International and Municipal Law', 44 *B.Y.I.L.* (1970), pp. 177–92.

McNair, A. D. *Dr Johnson and the Law* (Cambridge, 1948).

—— *The Law of Treaties* (Oxford, 1961).

—— 'So-called State Servitudes', 6 *B.Y.I.L.* (1925), pp. 111–27.

—— 'The Function and Differing Legal Character of Treaties', 11 *B.Y.I.L.* (1930), pp. 101–5.

—— 'The Stimson Doctrine of Non-Recognition', 14 *B.Y.I.L.* (1933), pp. 65–74.

—— 'Treaties Producing Effects "Erga Omnes"', *Scritti Perassi*, ii, pp. 27–30.

McWhinney, E. *Judge Shigeru Oda and the Progressive Development of International Law. Opinions (Declarations, Separate Opinions, Dissents) on the International Court of Justice, 1976–1992* (Dordrecht, 1993).

—— *Judge Manfred Lachs and Judicial Law-Making. Opinions on the International Court of Justice, 1967–1993* (The Hague, 1995).

Mélanges offerts à Charles Chaumont. Le droit des peuples à disposer d'eux-mêmes. Méthodes d'analyse du droit international (Paris, 1984).

Mélanges offerts à Henri Rolin. Problèmes de droit des gens (Paris, 1964).

Mendelson, M. 'State Acts and Omisssions as Explicit or Implicit Claims', *Le droit international. Mélanges Virally*, pp. 373–82.

—— 'The International Court of Justice and the sources of international law', Lowe and Fitzmaurice, M. (eds.), *Fifty Years. Essays Jennings*, pp. 63–89.

Menzel, E. 'Aland-Inseln', Strupp and Schlochauer (eds.), *Wörterbuch*, i, pp. 21–4.

Mercier, C. *Les Servitudes Internationales* (Lausanne, 1939).

Meron, T. *Human Rights and Humanitarian Norms as Customary Law* (Oxford, 1989).

—— (ed.) *Human Rights in International Law: Legal and Policy Issues*, 2 vols. (Oxford, 1984).

—— 'The Meaning and Reach of the International Convention on the Elimination of All Forms of Racial Discrimination', 79 *A.J.I.L.* (1985), pp. 283–318.

—— 'On a Hierarchy of International Human Rights', 80 *A.J.I.L.* (1986), pp. 1–23.

—— 'The Geneva Conventions as Customary Law', 81 *A.J.I.L.* (1987), pp. 348–70.

Merrills, J. G. *Anatomy of International Law. A Study of the Role of International Law in the Contemporary World*, 2nd edn. (London, 1981).

—— *The Development of International Law by the European Court of Human Rights* (Manchester, 1988).

MERRILLS, J. G. *International Dispute Settlement*, 2nd edn. (Cambridge, 1991).
—— 'On Teaching International Law', 10 *The Journal of the Society of Public Teachers of Law* (New Series, 1968–69), pp. 169–77.
MERON, T. 'The Optional Clause Today', 50 *B.Y.I.L.* (1979), pp. 87–116.
—— 'The Optional Clause Revisited', 64 *B.Y.I.L.* (1993), pp. 197–244.
MIAJA DE LA MUELA, A. *Aportacion de la Sentencia del Tribunal de la Haye en el caso Barcelona Traction (5 de febrero de 1970) a la jurisprudencia internacional* (Valladolid, 1970).
—— '"Ius cogens" y "ius dispositivum" en Derecho internacional publico', *Estudios Legaz y Lacambra*, ii, pp. 1121–53.
—— 'El interés de las partes en el proceso ante el Tribunal Internacional de Justicia', 14 *Comunicazioni e studi* (1975), pp. 525–61.
MIATELLO, A. *L'arme nucléaire en droit international* (Berne, 1987).
MIK, C. 'On the Specific Character of State Obligations in the Field of Human Rights', 20 *P.Y.I.L.* (1993), pp. 113–36.
MODEEN, T. 'Aaland Islands', Heidelberg *Encycl.*, xii, pp. 1–3.
MONACO, R. *Manuale di diritto internazionale pubblico*, 2nd edn. (Turin, 1971).
—— 'Cours général sur des Principes de droit international public', 125 Hague *Recueil* (1968, III), pp. 93–336.
MOORE, J. B. *History and Digest of International Arbitrations to which the United States has been a Party*, iii and iv (Washington, D.C., 1898).
MORELLI, G. *Nozioni di diritto internazionale*, 7th edn. (Padua, 1967).
—— 'Norme dispositive di diritto internazionale', 11 *Riv. dir. int.* (1932), pp. 388–404 and 483–508.
—— 'A proposito di norme internazionali cogenti', 52 *Riv. dir. int.* (1968), pp. 108–17.
—— 'Norme c.d. fondamentali e norme cogenti', 64 *Riv. dir. int.* (1981), pp. 509–10.
MORENO QUINTANA, L. M. *Tratado de derecho internacional*, 3 vols. (Buenos Aires, 1963).
MOSLER, H. *The International Society as a Legal Community* (Aalphen aan den Rijn and Germantown, 1980).
—— 'Ius cogens im Völkerrecht', 25 *Ann. suisse* (1968), pp. 9–40.
—— 'International Legal Community', Heidelberg *Encycl.*, vii, pp. 309–12.
MOVCHAN, A. P. *Kodifikatsiia i progressivnoe razvitie mezhdunarodnogo prava* (Moscow, 1972).
—— *Mezhdunarodnyi pravoporiadok* (Moscow, 1996).
—— 'Sovremennyi mezhdunarodnyi pravoporiadok', Graefrath (ed.), *Probleme*, pp. 257–62 (in Russian, with English summary).
MÜNCH, I. (VON) 'The Wimbledon', Heidelberg *Encycl.*, ii, pp. 293–6.
MULLERSON, R. A. 'Sources of International Law: New Tendencies in Soviet Thinking', 83 *A.J.I.L.* (1989), pp. 494–512.
—— and TUNKIN, G. I. (eds.) *International Law* (Moscow, 1990).
Multilaterale Staatsverträge erga omnes und deren Inkorporation in nationale IPR-Kodifikationen—Vor- und Nachteile einer solchen Rezeption (Heidelberg, 1986).
MURASE, S. 'Perspectives from International Economic Law on Transnational Envirornmental Issues', 253 Hague *Recueil* (1995), pp. 283–431.

NAHLIK, S. E. 'Traités internationaux et Etats tiers. Historique d'une codification', 4 *Thesaurus Acroasium* (1977), pp. 9–30.
NAKATANI, K. 'The Functions and the Legality of Economic Sanctions under International Law—A Study of the Legal Consequences of International Wrongful Acts', (published in Japanese in six parts in vols. 100 and 101 of *Kokka Gakkai Zassi—The Journal of the Association of Political and Social Sciences* (1987 and 1988)).
—— 'Economic Sanctions and Compliance: Theoretical Aspects' (paper submitted to the American Society of International Law/Japanese Association of International Law/Canadian Council of International Law (ASIL/JAIL/CCIL) Joint Meeting—Atlanta, 25 Mar. 1996).
NASTASE, A. 'The Right to Peace', Bedjadui (ed.), *International Law*, pp. 1219–31.
The New Encyclopaedia Britannica, 15th edn. (Chicago, 1974; 1994) (Macropaedia).
NGUYEN QUOC DINH, DAILLIER, P. and PELLET, A. *Droit international public*, 5th edn. (Paris, 1994).
NICIU, M. I. *Dreptul international public*, i (Iasi, 1992).
NIEBUHR, G. 'Baptist Group Votes to Repent Stand on Slaves', *New York Times*, 21 June 1995, p. A1.
NINCIC, D. 'Les implications générales juridiques et historiques de la Déclaration d'Helsinki', 154 Hague *Recueil* (1977, I), pp. 45–102.
NYS, E. 'Le concert européen et la notion de droit international', 1 *R.D.I.L.C.* (2nd series, 1899), pp. 273–313.
OBIETA, J. A. *The International Status of the Suez Canal*, 2nd edn. (The Hague, 1970).
O'CONNELL, D. P. *State Succession in Municipal Law and International Law*, 2 vols. (Cambridge, 1967).
—— *International Law*, 2nd edn., 2 vols. (London, 1970).
—— *The International Law of the Sea*, Shearer ed., 2 vols. (Oxford, 1982–4).
—— 'A Re-consideration of the Doctrine of International Servitude', 30 *The Canadian Bar Review* (1952), pp. 807–18.
—— 'The Law of Nature and the Law of Nations: Where does the Church Stand To-day?', 48/49 *Law and Justice* (1975), pp. 48–66.
ODA, S. 'The International Court of Justice Viewed from the Bench (1976–1993)', 244 Hague *Recueil* (1993, VII), pp. 9–190.
—— and OWADA, H. 'Annual Review of Japanese Practice in International Law XV (1976–77)', 28 *Japanese Annual of International Law* (1985), pp. 59–176.
OELLERS-FRAHM, K. 'United States Diplomatic and Consular Staff in Tehran Case', Heidelberg *Encycl.*, ii, pp. 282–6.
—— 'Comment: The erga omnes Applicability of Human Rights', 30 *Archiv des Völkerrechts* (1992), pp. 28–37.
—— 'Die Einsetzung des "Internationalen Tribunals über Kriegsverbrechen im ehemaligen Jugoslawien" durch den Sicherheitsrat', Beyerlin, Bothe, Hofmann and Petersmann (eds.), *Recht. Festschrift Bernhardt*, pp. 733–51.
OGISO, M. 'Japan and the UN Convention on the Law of the Sea', 25 *Archiv des Völkerrechts* (1987), pp. 58–81.
OPPENHEIM, L. *International Law. A Treatise*, Lauterpacht, H. ed., i (6th edn., London, 1947; 8th edn., London, 1955) and ii (7th edn., London, 1952).

Oppenheim's International Law. Peace, i, 9th edn. Jennings and Watts (London, 1992).

ORAA, J. *Human Rights in States of Emergency in International Law* (Oxford, 1992).

ORLIN, T. S. 'The Prohibition of the Death Penalty: An Emerging International Norm?', Rosas, Helgesen, and Gomien (eds.), *Human Rights*, pp. 136–73.

ORREGO VICUNA, F. *Antarctic Mineral Exploitation. The Emerging Legal Framework* (Cambridge, 1988).

OSAKWE, C. 'Socialist International Law Revisited', 66 *A.J.I.L.* (1972), pp. 596–600.

OTT, D. H. *Public International Law in the Modern World* (London, 1987).

Our Common Future (World Commission on Environment and Development) (Oxford, 1987).

Oxford English Dictionary, 2nd edn. (Oxford, 1989).

PADELFORD, N. J. and ANDERSSON, K. G. A. 'The Aaland Islands Question', 33 *A.J.I.L.* (1939), pp. 465–87.

PARRY, C. *The Sources and Evidences of International Law* (Manchester, 1965).

—— (ed.) *A British Digest of International Law*, 2b (London, 1967).

PARTSCH, K. J. 'Discrimination', Macdonald, Matscher and Petzold (eds.), *The European System*, pp. 571–92.

PASTOR RIDRUEJO, J. A. *Curso de derecho internacional publico y organizaciones internacionales*, 6th edn. (Madrid, 1996).

PATHAK, R. S. and DHOKALIA, R. P. (eds.) *International Law in Transition. Essays in Memory of Judge Nagendra Singh* (Dordrecht, 1992).

PATON, G. W. *A Textbook of Jurisprudence*, 4th edn. Paton and Derham (Oxford, 1972).

PAUST, J. J. 'The Complex Nature, Sources and Evidences of Customary Human Rights', 25 *Georgia Journal of International and Comparative Law* (1995/96), pp. 147–64.

PEIRANO BASSO, J. 'Naturaleza y fundamento del derecho internacional publico', *International Law, Liber Jiménez de Aréchaga*, i, pp. 181–208.

PELLET, A. *Le droit international du développement*, 2nd edn. (Paris, 1987).

—— 'Note sur la Commission d'arbitrage de la Conférence européenne pour la paix en Yougoslavie', 37 *A.F.D.I.* (1991), pp. 329–48.

—— 'L'activité de la Commission d'arbitrage de la Conférence européenne pour la paix en Yougoslavie', 38 *A.F.D.I.* (1992), pp. 220–38.

—— 'L'activité de la Commission d'arbitrage de la Conférence internationale pour l'ancienne Yougoslavie', 39 *A.F.D.I.* (1993), pp. 286–303.

PÉREZ DE CUÉLLAR, J. *Anarchy or Order. Annual reports 1982–1991* (New York, 1991).

PEREZ LUNO, A. E. *Los derechos fundamentales*, 2nd edn. (Madrid, 1986).

PERROTT, D. L., 'The Logic of Fundamental Rights', Bridge *et Alii* (eds.), *Fundamental Rights*, pp. 1–17.

PETERS, P., SCHRIJVER, N. and DE WAART, P. 'Responsibility of States in Respect of the Exercise of Permanent Sovereignty over Natural Resources: An Analysis of Some Principles of the Seoul Declaration (1986) by the International Law Association', 36 *Netherlands International Law Review* (1989), pp. 285–313.

PETERSMANN, H. 'The Right to Development in the United Nations: An Opportunity for Strengthening Popular Participation in Development. Programs and Prospects', Jekewitz, Klein, Kühne, Petersmann and Wolfrum (eds.), *Des Menschen. Festschrift Partsch*, pp. 125–40.

PETTITI, L. E., DECAUX, E. and IMBERT, P. H. (eds), *La Convention européenne des droits de l'homme. Commentaire article par article* (Paris, 1995).

PHILLIMORE, R. *Commentaries upon International Law*, 2nd edn. (London, 1873); 3rd edn., i (London, 1879).

PICONE, P. (ed.) *Interventi delle Nazioni Unite e diritto internazionale* (Milan, 1995).

—— 'Diritto internazionale dell'economia e costituzione economica dell'ordinamento internazionale', Picone and Sacerdoti (eds.), *Diritto internazionale dell'economia*, pp. 31–105.

—— 'Obblighi reciproci ed obblighi *erga omnes* degli Stati nel campo della protezione internazionale dell'ambiente marino dall'inquinamento', Starace (ed.), *Diritto internazionale*, pp. 15–135.

—— 'Recensione: Lauri Hannikainen, *Peremptory Norms* (jus cogens) *in International Law. Historical Developments. Criteria. Present Status*, Helsinki, Finnish Lawyers' Publishing Company, 1988, pp. XXXII-781', 73 *Riv. dir. int.* (1990), pp. 791–5.

—— 'Nazioni Unite e obblighi "*erga omnes*"' 48 *La Comunità internazionale* (1993), pp. 709–30.

—— 'Recensione: Claudia Annacker, *Die Durchsetzung von erga omnes Verpflichtungen vor dem Internationalen Gerichtshof*, Hamburg, 1994, Verlag Dr. Kovac, pp. XXII–146', 77 *Riv. dir. int.* (1994), pp. 1118–22.

—— 'Interventi delle Nazioni Unite e obblighi *erga omnes*', Picone (ed.), *Interventi*, pp. 517–78.

—— and SACERDOTI, S. (eds.) *Diritto internazionale dell'economia. Raccolta sistematica dei principali atti normativi internazionali ed interni con testi introduttivi e note* (Milan, 1982).

PICTET, J. S. *Development and Principles of International Humanitarian Law* (Dordrecht, 1985).

—— (ed.) *Commentary. III Geneva Convention Relative to the Treatment of Prisoners of War* (Geneva, 1960).

PINCKAERS, S. T. *Ce qu'on ne peut jamais faire. La question des actes intrinsèquement mauvais. Histoire et discussion*, 2nd edn. (Fribourg and Paris, 1995).

PIZA ESCALANTE, R. E. 'La "opinion juris" como fuente autonoma del derecho internacional ("opinio juris" y "jus cogens")', 9 *Anuario hispano-luso-americano de derecho internacional* (1987), pp. 131–94.

PODESTA COSTA, L. A. and RUDA, J. M. *Derecho internacional publico*, updated edn., 2 vols. (Buenos Aires, 1984).

POGANY, I. (ed.) *Nuclear Weapons and International Law* (New York, 1987).

PORTER, J. (ed.) *Genocide and Human Rights: A Global Anthology* (Washington, 1982).

POST, H. H. G. 'Some Curiosities in the Sources of the Law of Armed Conflict Conceived in a General International Legal Perspective', 25 *Netherlands Yearbook of International Law* (1994), pp. 83–117.

POTTER, P. B. 'The Doctrine of Servitudes in International Law', 9 *A.J.I.L.* (1915), pp. 627–41.

POUND, R. *An Introduction to the Philosophy of Law*, 2nd edn. (New Haven and London, 1954).

—— 'Hierarchy of Sources and Forms in Different Systems of Law', 7 *Tulane Law Review* (1933), pp. 475–87.

PRATT, J. T. and MACKENZIE, W. W. *Law of Highways*, 21st edn. Parrish and Lord De Mauley (London, 1967).

PRÉMONT, D. (ed.) *Essays on the Concept of a "Right to Live" in Memory of Yougindra Khushalani* (Brussels, 1988).

PROVOST, R. 'Reciprocity in Human Rights and Humanitarian Law', 65 *B.Y.I.L.* (1994), pp. 383–454.

PUSTA, C. R. 'Le statut juridique de la mer Baltique à partir du XIXe siècle', 52 Hague *Recueil* (1935, II), pp. 109–89.

QUADRI, R. *Diritto internazionale pubblico*, 5th edn. (Naples, 1968).

—— 'Cours général de droit international public', 113 Hague *Recueil* (1964, III), pp. 237–483.

QUÉNEUDEC, J.-P. 'La notion d'Etat intéressé en droit international', 255 Hague *Recueil* (1995), pp. 339–462.

QUIRK, R., GREENBAUM, S., LEECH, G. and SVARTIK, J. *A Comprehensive Grammar of the English Language* (London, 1985).

Racism, science and pseudo-science. Proceedings of the symposium to examine pseudo-scientific theories invoked to justify racism and racial discrimination, Athens, 30 March to 3 April 1981 (Paris, 1983).

RAGAZZI, M. 'Introductory Note to "Conference on Yugoslavia Arbitration Commission: Opinions on Questions Arising from the Dissolution of Yugoslavia"', 31 *I.L.M.* (1992), pp. 1488–90.

—— 'Consuetudine internazionale, principi generali e norme di *jus cogens* nella dottrina sovietica (anche in rapporto all'Atto di Helsinki)' (Thesis for the J.D. degree (Laurea in Giurisprudenza), University of Ferrara, Faculty of Law, academic year 1983/84).

RAMCHARAN, B. G. 'Equality and Nondiscrimination', Henkin (ed.), *The International Bill of Rights*, pp. 246–69.

RAO, T. S. R. 'International Custom', 19 *Indian Journal of International Law* (1979), pp. 515–21.

RAY, J. 'Des conflits entre principes abstraites et stipulations conventionnelles', 48 Hague *Recueil* (1934, II), pp. 631–707.

RAZ, J. *The Concept of a Legal System*, 2nd edn. (Oxford, 1980).

Recueil d'études de droit international en hommage à Paul Guggenheim (Geneva, 1968).

Recueil sur les sources du droit en l'honneur de F. Geny, 3 vols. (Paris, 1935).

REDGWELL, C. 'Universality or Integrity? Some Reflections on Reservations to General Multilateral Treaties', 64 *B.Y.I.L.* (1993), pp. 245–82.

REHNQUIST, W. H. *The Supreme Court. How It Was, How It Is* (New York, 1987).

REID, H. D. *International Servitudes in Law and Practice* (Chicago, 1932).

REISMAN, W. M. 'Responses to Crimes of Discrimination and Genocide: An Appraisal of the Convention on the Elimination of Racial Discrimination', 1 *Denver Journal of International Law and Policy* (1971), pp. 29–64.

—— 'Chinese Fallout', *The Nation*, 8 Jan. 1977.

René Cassin Amicorum Discipulorumque Liber. Problèmes de protection internationale des droits de l'homme, 4 vols. (Paris, 1969–72).

RESCHER, N. *Moral Absolutes. An Essay on the Nature and Rationale of Morality* (New York, 1989).

RESHETOV, I. A. 'Development of Norms of International Law on Crimes Against Humanity', Ginsburgs and Kudriavtsev (eds.), *The Nuremberg Trial*, pp. 199–212.

Restatement of the Law. The Foreign Relations Law of the United States (As Adopted and Promulgated by The American Law Institute at Washington, D.C. May 14, 1986), 2 vols. (St. Paul, Minn., 1987).

REUTER, P. *La Convention de Vienne sur le droit des traités* (Paris, 1970).

—— *Droit international public*, 6th edn. (Paris, 1983) (7th unaltered edn., Paris, 1992).

—— *Introduction to the Law of Treaties*, English trans. Mico and Haggenmacher (London and New York, 1989).

—— *Le développement de l'ordre juridique international: écrits de droit international* (Paris, 1995).

—— 'Principes de droit international public', 103 Hague *Recueil* (1961, II), pp. 425–656.

REZEK, J. F. *Direito internacional publico. Curso elementar*, 2nd edn. (Sao Paulo, 1991).

RIALS, S. *La déclaration des droits de l'homme et du citoyen* (Paris, 1988).

RIEDEL, E. 'Standards and Sources. Farewell to the Exclusivity of the Sources Triad in International Law?', 2 *European Journal of International Law* (1991, No. 2), pp. 58–84.

RIGAUX, F. 'Le crime d'Etat. Réflexions sur l'article 19 du projet d'articles sur la responsabilité des Etats', *International Law. Essays Ago*, iii, pp. 301–25.

RIGO SUREDA, A. *The Evolution of the Right of Self-Determination. A Study of United Nations Practice* (Leiden, 1973).

RIPERT, G. 'Les règles du droit civil applicables aux rapports internationaux (Contribution à l'étude des principes généraux du droit visés au Statut de la Cour permanente de Justice internationale)', 44 Hague *Recueil* (1933, II), pp. 565–664.

RIVIER, A. *Principes du Droit des gens*, i (Paris, 1896).

ROBERTS, A. and GUELFF, R. (eds.) *Documents on the Laws of War*, 2nd edn. (Oxford, 1989).

ROBERTSON, A. H. and MERRILLS, J. G. *Human Rights in the World. An introduction to the study of the international protection of human rights*, 3rd edn. (Manchester and New York, 1989, reprinted with minor revisions 1992).

ROBINSON, H. *The Genocide Convention. A Commentary* (New York, 1960).

RODLEY, N. S. 'Human Rights and Humanitarian Intervention: The Case Law of the World Court', 38 *I.C.L.Q.* (1989), pp. 321–33.

RÖLING, B. V. A. 'The 1974 U.N. Definition of Aggression', Cassese (ed.), *The Current Legal Regulation*, pp. 413–21.

ROLAND, H. and BOYER, L. *Locutions latines du droit français*, 3rd edn. (Paris, 1993).

ROLIN, H. 'La pratique des mandats internationaux', 19 Hague *Recueil* (1927, IV), pp. 493–628.

RONZITTI, N. *Rescuing Nationals Abroad Through Military Coercion and Intervention on Grounds of Humanity* (Dordrecht, 1985).

—— 'La disciplina dello jus cogens nella Convenzione di Vienna sul diritto dei trattati', 15 *Comunicazioni e studi* (1978), pp. 241–99.

—— 'Use of Force, Jus Cogens and State Consent', Cassese (ed.), *The Current Legal Regulation*, pp. 147–66.

RONZITTI, N. 'Trattati contrari a norme imperative del diritto internazionale?', *Studi Sperduti*, pp. 209–72.

ROSAS, A., HELGESEN, J. and GOMIEN, D. (eds.) *Human Rights in a Changing East–West Perspective* (London and New York, 1990).

ROSENNE, S. *The Law of Treaties: A Comparative Guide to the Legislative History of the Vienna Convention* (Leiden and Dobbs Ferry, 1970).

—— *The Law and Practice of the International Court*, 2nd revised edn. (Dordrecht, 1985).

—— *Developments in the Law of Treaties 1945–1986* (Cambridge, 1989).

—— *The World Court. What it is and how it works*, 5th revised edn. (Dordrecht, 1995).

—— 'Bilateralism and Community Interest in the Codified Law of Treaties', Friedmann, Henkin and Lissitzyn (eds.), *Transnational Law. Essays Jessup*, pp. 202–27.

—— '"On Defining International Aggression. An Exercise in Futility". A book review of Benjamin B. Ferencz, "Defining International Aggression. The Search for World Peace"', 12 *Israel Law Review* (1977), pp. 401–5.

—— 'Publications of the International Court of Justice', 81 *A.J.I.L.* (1987), pp. 681–96.

—— 'The President of the International Court of Justice', Lowe and Fitzmaurice, M. (eds.), *Fifty Years. Essays Jennings*, pp. 406–23.

—— 'Decolonisation in the International Court of Justice', 8 *African Journal of International and Comparative Law* (1996), pp. 564–76.

ROSENSTOCK, R. 'Crimes of States—an Essay', Ginther, Hafner, Lang, Neuhold and Sucharipa-Behrmann (eds.), *Völkerrecht. Festschrift Zemanek*, pp. 319–34.

ROSS, A. *A Textbook of International Law. General Part* (London, 1947).

ROUCOUNAS, E. J. 'Le traité et les Etats tiers (Quelques approches subjectives et objectives)', 17 *Revue Hellénique de Droit International* (1964), pp. 299–365.

ROUSSEAU, C. *Principes généraux du droit international public*, i (Paris, 1944).

—— *Droit international public*, 5 vols. (Paris, 1971–83).

ROVINE, A. W. 'The World Court Opinion on Namibia', 11 *C.J.T.L.* (1972), pp. 203–39.

ROXBURGH, R. F. *International Conventions and Third States. A Monograph* (London, 1917).

ROZAKIS, C. L. *The Concept of Jus Cogens in the Law of Treaties* (Amsterdam, 1976).

RUBIN, A. P. 'The International Legal Effects of Unilateral Declarations', 71 *A.J.I.L.* (1977), pp. 1–30.

RUCZ, C. 'Les mesures unilatérales de protection des droits de l'homme devant l'Institut de droit international', 38 *A.F.D.I.* (1992), pp. 579–628.

RUDA, J. M. 'Reservations to Treaties', 146 Hague *Recueil* (1975, III), pp. 95–218.

—— 'Some of the Contributions of the International Court of Justice to the Development of International Law', 24 *N.Y.U.J.I.L.P.* (1991), pp. 35–68.

RUDOLF, W. 'New States and International Law', 21 *Law and State* (1980), pp. 47–73.

RUZIÉ, D. *Droit international public*, 12th edn. (Paris, 1996).

SAHOVIC, M. 'Le concept du crime international de l'Etat et le développement du droit international', *International Law. Essays Ago*, iii, pp. 364–9.

SAITO, Y. 'Judge Tanaka, natural law and the principle of equality', Alfredsson and Macalister-Smith (eds.), *The Living Law: essays Grahl-Madsen*, pp. 399–408.

SALERNO, F. (ed.), *Il ruolo del giudice internazionale nell'evoluzione del diritto internazionale e comunitario* (Padua, 1995).

SALMON, J. J. A. 'Faut-il codifier l'état de necessité en droit international?', Makarczyk (ed.), *Essays Lachs*, pp. 235–70.

—— *Salmond on Jurisprudence*, 12th edn. Fitzgerald (London, 1966).

SALVIOLI, G. 'I terzi nel diritto internazionale', 12 *Riv. dir. int.* (1918), pp. 229–41.

—— "La jurisprudence de la Cour permanente de Justice internationale', 12 Hague *Recueil* (1926, II), pp. 5–113.

—— 'Les règles générales du droit de la paix', 46 Hague *Recueil* (1933, IV), pp. 1–164.

SANDS, P. *Principles of international environmental law I. Frameworks, standards and implementation* (Manchester, 1995).

—— 'International Law in the Field of Sustainable Development', 65 *B.Y.I.L.* (1994), pp. 303–81.

SARCEVIC, P. and VAN HOUTTE, H. (eds.) *Legal Issues in International Trade* (London, 1990).

SARIN, M. L. 'The Protection of the Human Environment in a Divided World and International Law', Bello and Ajibola (eds.), *Essays Elias*, i, pp. 197–264.

SCELLE, G. *Précis de droit des gens. Principes et systématique*, 2 vols. (Paris, 1932–4).

—— 'Essai sur les sources formelles du droit international', *Recueil Geny*, iii, pp. 400–30.

SCERNI, M. 'La procédure de la Cour permanente de Justice internationale', 65 Hague *Recueil* (1938, III), pp. 565–681.

SCHABAS, W. A. *The Abolition of the Death Penalty in International Law* (Cambridge, 1993).

SCHACHTER, O. *Sharing the World's Resources* (New York, 1977).

—— *International Law in Theory and Practice* (Dordrecht, 1991).

—— 'How Effective are Measures against Racial Discrimination', 4 *Human Rights Journal* (1971), pp. 293–310.

—— 'International Legislation', Sills (ed.), *International Encyclopedia*, vii, pp. 551–8.

—— 'The Role of the Institute of International Law and its Methods of Work', *Livre du Centenaire*, pp. 403–51.

—— 'Principles of International Social Justice', *Jus et Societas. Essays Friedmann*, pp. 249–77.

—— 'The Evolving International Law of Development' 15 *C.J.T.L.* (1976), pp. 1–16.

—— 'Philip Jessup's Life and Ideas', 80 *A.J.I.L.* (1986), pp. 878–95.

—— 'In Defence of International Rules on the Use of Force', 53 *The University of Chicago Law Review* (1986), pp. 113–46.

—— 'Disputes Involving the Use of Force', Damrosch (ed.), *International Court*, pp. 223–41.

—— 'Entangled Treaty and Custom', Dinstein (ed.), *International Law. Essays Rosenne*, pp. 717–38.

—— 'The Greening of International Law', *Humanité. Mélanges René-Jean Dupuy*, pp. 271–7.

SCHACHTER, O. 'United Nations in the Gulf Conflict', 85 *A.J.I.L.* (1991), pp. 452–73.
—— 'Human Rights and Economic Development', Bello and Ajibola (eds.), *Essays Elias*, i, pp. 389–98.
—— and SERWER, D. 'Marine Pollution Problems and Remedies', 65 *A.J.I.L.* (1971), pp. 84–111.
SCHINDLER, D. 'Die erga omnes-Wirkung des humanitären Völkerrechts', Beyerlin, Bothe, Hofmann and Petersmann (eds.), *Recht. Festschrift Bernhardt*, pp. 199–211.
SCHMALBERGER, T. *In Pursuit of a Nuclear Test Ban Treaty: A Guide to the Debate in the Conference on Disarmament* (New York, 1991).
SCHRAG, P. G. *Global Action: Nuclear Test Ban Diplomacy at the End of the Cold War* (Boulder, 1992).
SCHREUER, C. 'Capital Punishment and Human Rights', Beyerlin, Bothe, Hofmann and Petersmann (eds.), *Recht. Festschrift Bernhardt*, pp. 563–77.
SCHWARZENBERGER, G. *International Law as Applied by International Courts and Tribunals*, i (London, 1957).
—— 'International jus cogens?', 45 *Texas Law Review* (1965), pp. 455–78.
SCHWEBEL, S. M. 'Aggression, Intervention and Self-Defence in Modern International Law', 136 Hague *Recueil* (1972, II), pp. 411–98.
—— 'Human Rights in the World Court', 24 *Vanderbilt Journal of Transnational Law* (1991), pp. 945–70.
SCHWEISFURTH, T. *Sozialistisches Völkerrecht? Darstellung—Analyse—Wertung der sowjetmarxistischen Theorie vom Völkerrecht 'neuen Typs'* (Berlin, 1979).
——'International Treaties and Third States', 45 *Z.a.ö.R.V.* (1985), pp. 653–74.
SCHWELB, E. 'The International Convention on the Elimination of All Forms of Racial Discrimination', 15 *I.C.L.Q.* (1966), pp. 996–1059.
——'The *Actio Popularis* and International law', 2 *Israel Yearbook of Human Rights* (1972), pp. 46–56.
'Scintillae iuris'. Studi in memoria di Gino Gorla, 3 vols. (Milan, 1994).
SCOBBIE, I. 'Towards the Elimination of International Law: Some Radical Scepticism about Sceptical Radicalism', 61 *B.Y.I.L.* (1990), pp. 339–62.
—— 'Discontinuance in the International Court of Justice: the Enigma of the *Nuclear Tests* cases', 41 *I.C.L.Q.* (1992), pp. 808–40.
SCOTT, J. B. (ed.) *The Hague Peace Conferences of 1899 and 1907. A Series of Lectures Delivered Before the Johns Hopkins University in the Year 1908*, ii (Baltimore, 1909).
Scritti di diritto internazionale in onore di Tomaso Perassi, 2 vols. (Milan, 1957).
SÉFÉRIADÈS, S. 'Principes généraux du droit international de la paix', 34 Hague *Recueil* (1930, IV), pp. 181–489.
SEIDL-HOHENVELDERN, I. *International Economic Law*, 2nd edn. (Dordrecht, 1992).
—— *Völkerrecht*, 8th edn. (Cologne, 1994).
—— 'Der Barcelona-Traction-Fall', 22 *Österreichische Zeitschrift für öffentliches Recht* (1971), pp. 255–310.
—— '*Actio Popularis* im Völkerrecht?', 14 *Comunicazioni e studi* (1975), pp. 803–13.
—— 'The Charter of Economic Rights and Duties of States', *Studi Balladore Pallieri*, ii, pp. 550–6.
La sentenza in Europa. Metodo, tecnica e stile (Padua, 1988).

SERENI, A. P. *Diritto internazionale*, 4 vols. (Milan, 1956–65).

SETTE CAMARA, J. 'Behind the World Bench', *International Law. Liber Jiménez de Aréchaga*, pp. 1069–79.

SHAHABUDDEEN, M. *Precedent in the World Court* (Cambridge, 1996).

SHAKER, M. 'The Moscow Test Ban Treaty', 27 *Revue égyptienne de droit international* (1971), pp. 41–58.

SHARP, R. H. *Nonrecognition as a Legal Obligation 1775–1934* (Liège, 1934).

SHAW, M. N. 'Genocide and International Law', Dinstein (ed.), *International Law. Essays Rosenne*, pp. 797–820.

SHESTAKOV, L. N. *Imperativnye normy v sisteme sovremennogo mezhdunarodnogo prava* (Moscow, 1981).

SHIHATA, I. F. I. *The Power of the International Court to Determine its own Jurisdiction: Compétence de la Compétence* (The Hague, 1965).

—— 'The Treaty as a Law-Declaring and Custom-Making Instrument', 22 *Revue égyptienne de droit international* (1966), pp. 51–90.

SILAGI, M. 'Die Popularklage als Fremdkörper im Völkerrecht', 4 *South African Yearbook of International Law* (1978), pp. 10–28.

SILLS, D. L. (ed.) *International Encyclopedia of the Social Sciences*, vii (New York, 1972), xiii and xiv (New York, 1968).

SIMMA, B. *Das Reziprozitätselement in der Entstehung des Völkergewohnheitsrechts* (Munich, 1970).

—— (ed.) *The Charter of the United Nations. A Commentary* (Oxford, 1994).

—— 'The Antarctic Treaty as a Treaty Providing for an "Objective Regime"', 19 *Cornell International Law Journal* (1986), pp. 189–209.

—— 'Does the UN Charter Provide an Adequate Legal Basis for Individual or Collective Responses to Violations of Obligations erga omnes?', Delbrück (ed.), *The Future of International Law*, pp. 125–46.

—— 'International Human Rights and General International Law: A Comparative Analysis', 4 *Collected Courses of the Academy of European Law* (1993, II), pp. 153–236.

SINCLAIR, I. M. *The Vienna Convention on the Law of Treaties*, 2nd edn. (Manchester, 1984).

—— *The International Law Commission* (Cambridge, 1987).

—— 'The Impact of the Unratified Codification Convention', Bos and Siblesz (eds.), *Realism: essays Riphagen*, pp. 211–29.

—— 'State Responsibility and the Concept of Crimes of States', Weiler, Cassese and Spinedi (eds.), *International Crimes of State*, pp. 223–5.

SINGH, G. 'The Greenhouse Effect—Need for Legal Control', Pathak and Dhokalia (eds.), *International Law. Essays Nagendra Singh*, pp. 149–59.

SINGH, N. 'Address of welcome delivered by the President of the International Court of Justice, Judge Nagendra Singh, to His Holiness Pope John Paul II on the occasion of the latter's visit to the Court on 13 May 1985', *The International Court of Justice*, pp. 138–40.

—— 'Right to Environment and Sustainable Development as a Principle of International Law', Bello and Ajibola (eds.), *Essays Elias*, i, pp. 181–95.

SLONIM, S. *South West Africa and the United Nations: An International Mandate in Dispute* (Baltimore and London, 1973).

SMETS, P.-F. *Les effets des traités internationaux à l'égard des Etats tiers* (Paris, 1965–6).

SMITH, A. E. *Colonists in Bondage, White Servitude and Convict Labor in America, 1607–1776* (Chapel Hill, N.C., 1947).

SMITH, H. A. (ed.) *Great Britain and the Law of Nations*, i (London, 1932).

SMITH, J. C., *Legal Obligation* (London, 1976).

SNYDER, F. and SLINN, P. (eds.) *International Law of Development: Comparative Perspectives* (Abingdon, 1987).

SÖDERHJELM, J. O. *Démilitarisation et neutralisation des Iles d'Aland en 1856 et 1921* (Helsingfors, 1928).

SÖRENSEN, M. *Les sources du droit international. Etude sur la jurisprudence de la Cour permanente de justice internationale* (Copenhagen, 1946).

—— (ed.) *Manual of Public International Law* (London, 1968).

—— 'Principes de droit international public', 101 Hague *Recueil* (1960, III), pp. 1–254.

SPERDUTI, G. *La fonte suprema dell'ordinamento internazionale* (Milan, 1946).

—— *Lezioni di diritto internazionale* (Milan, 1958).

—— *Il dominio riservato* (Milan, 1970).

—— 'Les obligations solidaires en droit international', Makarczyk (ed.), *Essays Lachs*, pp. 271–5.

Staatsrecht-Völkerrecht-Europarecht, Festschrift für Hans-Jurgen Schlochauer (Berlin, 1981).

STARACE, V. (ed.) *Diritto internazionale e protezione dell'ambiente marino* (Milan, 1983).

—— 'La responsabilité résultant de la violation des obligations à l'égard de la communauté internationale', 153 Hague *Recueil* (1976, IV), pp. 265–317.

Starke's International Law, 11th edn. Shearer (London, 1994).

STARKMAN, P. 'Genocide and International Law: Is there a Cause of Action?', 8 *ASILS International Law Journal* (1984), pp. 1–65.

STEIN, T. L. 'The Approach of the Different Drummer', 26 *Harvard International Law Journal* (1985), pp. 457–82.

STEINER, H. J. and ALSTON, P. (eds.) *International Human Rights in Context. Law, Politics, Morals. Texts and Materials.* (Oxford, 1996).

STONE, J. *Aggression and World Order. A Critique of United Nations Theories of Aggression* (London, 1958).

—— 'Holes and Loopholes in the 1974 Definition of Aggression', 71 *A.J.I.L.* (1977), pp. 224–46.

STREIT, G. 'Les grandes puissances dans le droit international', 2 *R.D.I.L.C.* (2nd series, 1900), pp. 5–25.

STROZZI, G. 'I "principi" dell'ordinamento internazionale', 47 *La Comunità internazionale* (1992), pp. 162–87.

STRUPP, K. and SCHLOCHAUER, H.J. (eds.) *Wörterbuch des Völkerrechts*, 2nd edn., 3 vols. (Berlin, 1960–2).

Studi in onore di Giorgio Balladore Pallieri, 2 vols. (Milan, 1978).

Studi in onore di Giuseppe Sperduti. Fonti internazionali e rapporti fra ordinamenti, l'individuo nel diritto internazionale, altri contributi (Milan, 1984).

SUBEDI, S. P. 'The Doctrine of Objective Regimes in International Law and the Competence of the United Nations to Impose Territorial or Peace Settlements on States', 37 *G.Y.I.L.* (1994), pp. 162–205.

SUCHARITKUL, S. 'The Role of the International Law Commission in the Decade of International Law', 3 *Leiden Journal of International Law* (1990, No. 3, Special Issue December 1990), pp. 15–42.

SUDRE, F. 'Droits intangibles et/ou droits fondamentaux: y a-t-il des droits prééminents dans la Convention européenne des droits de l'homme?', *Liber Eissen*, pp. 381–98.

SUENENS, L. J. *Le Roi Baudouin. Une vie qui nous parle* (Ertvelde, 1995).

SUR, S. 'Sources du droit international. La coutume', *Jurisclasseur de droit international* (1989), 'Fascicule 13'.

SWINARSKI, C. (ed.) *Studies and essays on international humanitarian law and Red Cross principles in honour of Jean Pictet* (Geneva and The Hague, 1984).

Symbolae Verzijl présentées au Professor J. H. W. Verzjil à l'occasion de son LXXième anniversaire (The Hague, 1958).

'Symposium. Earth Rights and Responsibilities: Human Rights and Environmental Protection', 18 *Yale Journal of International Law* (1993), pp. 213–411.

SZTUCKI, J. *Jus Cogens and the Vienna Convention on the Law of Treaties* (Vienna, 1974).

—— *Interim Measures in the Hague Court. An Attempt at a Scrutiny* (Deventer, 1983).

—— 'Some Questions Arising from Reservations to the Vienna Convention on the Law of Treaties', 20 *G.Y.I.L.* (1977), pp. 277–305.

Tableau des Résolutions adoptées (1957–1991), Institut de Droit International (under the auspices of) (Paris, 1992).

TABORY, M. *Multilingualism in International Law and Institutions* (Alphen aan den Rijn and Rockville, 1980).

TAKANO, Y. *Einführung in das Völkerrecht*, German trans. Richter of the second Japanese edition, 1969 (14th reprint, 1977), 3 vols. (Cologne, 1979–92).

TANAKA, K. 'Du droit international au droit mondial', *Etudes Julliot de la Morandière*, pp. 547–70.

—— 'Some Observations on Peace, Law, and Human Rights', Friedmann, Henkin and Lissitzyn (eds.), *Transnational Law. Essays Jessup*, pp. 242–56.

TANZI, A. *L'immunità dalla giurisdizione degli agenti diplomatici* (Padua, 1991).

TARUFFO, M. 'Dimensioni del precedente giudiziario', *'Scintillae iuris'*, i, pp. 383–404.

TAYLOR, T *The Anatomy of the Nuremberg Trials* (New York, 1992).

—— 'The Nuremberg War Crimes Trials', 450 *International Conciliation* (1949), pp. 243–371.

TECLAFF, L. A. and UTTON, A. E. (eds.) *International Environmental Law* (New York, 1974).

TÉNÉKIDÈS, G. 'L'action des Nations Unies contre la discrimination raciale', 168 Hague *Recueil* (1980, III), pp. 269–487.

TETTAMANZI, D. *Verità e libertà. Temi e prospettive di morale cristiana* (Casale Monferrato, 1993).

THIERRY, H. 'L'évolution du droit international. Cours général de droit international public', 222 Hague *Recueil* (1990, III), pp. 9–186.

—— COMBACAU, J., SUR, S. and VALLÉE, C. *Droit international public*, 3rd edn. (Paris, 1981).

THIRLWAY, H. W. A. *International Customary Law and Codification* (Leiden, 1972).
—— 'The Law and Procedure of the International Court of Justice 1960–1989', 60 *B.Y.I.L.* (1989), pp. 1–157.
THIRLWAY, H. W. A. 'The Law and Procedure of the International Court of Justice 1960–1989', 61 *B.Y.I.L.* (1990), pp. 1–133.
—— 'Reflections on the Articulation of International Judicial Decisions and the Problem of "Mootness"', Macdonald (ed.), *Essays Wang Tieya*, pp. 789–812.
—— 'The Law and Procedure of the International Court of Justice 1960–1989', 66 *B.Y.I.L.* (1995), pp. 1–96.
THOMAS, J. A. C. *Textbook of Roman Law* (Amsterdam, 1976).
THORNBERRY, P. *International Law and the Rights of Minorities* (Oxford, 1991).
TIEWUL, S. A. 'International Law and Nuclear Test Explosions on the High Seas', 8 *Cornell International Law Journal* (1974), pp. 45–70.
TITTEL, J. (ed.) *Multitudo Legum Ius Unum. Festschrift für Wilhelm Wengler zu seinem 65. Geburtstag*, 2 vols. (Berlin, 1973).
TOMUSCHAT, C. 'Equality and non-discrimination under the International Covenant on Civil and Political Rights', *Staatsrecht. Festschrift Schlochauer*, pp. 712–16.
—— 'Das Recht auf Entwicklung', 25 *G.Y.I.L.* (1982), pp. 85–112 (in German, with English summary).
—— 'Obligations Arising for States without or against Their Will', 241 Hague *Recueil* (1993, IV), pp. 195–374.
TOUSCOZ, J. *Droit international* (Paris, 1993).
TREVES, T. 'Military Installations Structures, and Devices on the Seabed', 74 *A.J.I.L.* (1980), pp. 808–57.
—— 'La Déclaration des Nations Unies sur le renforcement de l'efficacité du principe du non-recours à la force', 33 *A.F.D.I.* (1987), pp. 379–98.
—— 'Codification du droit international et pratique des Etats dans le droit de la mer', 223 Hague *Recueil* (1990, IV), pp. 9–302.
TRIGGS, G. (ed.) *The Antarctic Treaty Regime: Law, Environment and Resources* (Cambridge, 1987).
TRUYOL Y SERRA, A. *Los derechos humanos. Declaraciones y Convenios internacionales*, 3rd edn. (Madrid, 1982).
—— *Histoire du droit international public* (Paris, 1995).
—— 'Théorie du droit international public. Cours général', 173 Hague *Recueil* (1981, IV), pp. 9–444.
TUNKIN, G. I. *Theory of International Law*, English trans. Butler (London, 1974).
—— 'Jus Cogens in Contemporary International Law', 3 *The University of Toledo Law Review* (1971), pp. 107–18.
—— 'International Law in the International System', 147 Hague *Recueil* (1975, IV), pp. 1–218.
UDINA, M. 'La succession des Etats quant aux obligations internationales autres que les dettes publiques', 44 Hague *Recueil* (1933, II), pp. 669–773.
ULLOA, A. *Derecho internacional publico*, 4th edn. (Madrid, 1957).
UNGER, R. F. *Völkergewohnheitsrecht—objectives Recht oder Geflecht bilateraler Beziehungen: Seine Bedeutung für einen "persistent objector"* (Munich, 1978).
The United Nations and Apartheid 1948–1994 (New York, 1994).

URIBE VARGAS, D. 'La troisième génération des droits de l'homme', 184 Hague *Recueil* (1984, I), pp. 355–76.

URRUTIA, F.J. 'La codification du droit international en Amérique', 22 Hague *Recueil* (1928, II), pp. 81–236.

VALENCIA-OSPINA, E. 'The International Court of Justice and International Environmental Law', 2 *Asian Yearbook of International Law* (1994), pp. 1–10.

VALI, F. A. *Servitudes of International Law*, 2nd edn. (London, 1958).

VALTICOS, N. 'Des parallèles qui devraient se rejoindre: les méthodes de contrôle international concernant les conventions sur les droits de l'homme', Beyerlin, Bothe, Hofmann and Petersmann (eds.), *Recht. Festschrift Bernhardt*, pp. 647–61.

VALTIERRA, A. *Peter Claver. Saint of the Slaves*, English trans. Perry and Woodward (Westminster, Maryland, 1960).

VASCIANNIE, S. 'Part XI of the Law of the Sea Convention and Third States: Some General Observations', 48 *Cambridge Law Journal* (1989), pp. 85–97.

VATTEL, E. (de) *The Law of Nations or the Principles of Natural Law Applied to the Conduct and to the Affairs of Nations and of Sovereigns*, trans. Fenwick of 1758 edition, Scott (ed.) *Classics of International Law* (Washington, D.C., 1902; reprinted New York and London, 1964).

VELU, J. and ERGEC, R. *La Convention européenne des droits de l'homme* (Brussels, 1990).

VERDROSS, A. (VON) *Die Quellen des universellen Völkerrecht. Ein Einführung* (Freiburg, 1973).

—— 'Forbidden Treaties in International Law', 31 *A.J.I.L.* (1937), pp. 571–7.

—— 'Jus Dispositivum and Jus Cogens in International Law', 60 *A.J.I.L.* (1966), pp. 55–63.

—— and SIMMA, B. *Universelles Völkerrecht*, 3rd edn. (Berlin, 1984).

VERESHCHETIN, V. S. and MULLERSON, R. A. 'International Law in an Interdependent World', 28 *C.J.T.L.* (1990) pp. 291–300.

VERHOEVEN, J. *La Réconnaissance internationale dans la pratique contemporaine* (Paris, 1975).

—— 'Le crime de génocide. Originalité et ambiguïté', 24 *Revue belge de droit international* (1991), pp. 5–26.

VEROSTA, S. 'International Law in Europe and Western Asia between 100 and 650 A.D.', 113 Hague *Recueil* (1964, III), pp. 491–613.

VERZIJL, J. H. W. *International Law in Historical Perspective*, iii (Leiden, 1970).

VIERDAG, E. W. *The Concept of Discrimination in International Law with Special Reference to Human Rights* (The Hague, 1973).

—— 'Some Remarks about Special Features of Human Rights Treaties', 25 *Netherlands Yearbook of International Law* (1994), pp. 119–42.

VILLIGER, M. E. *Customary International Law and Treaties* (Dordrecht, 1985).

VINOGRADOFF, P. *Villeinage in England: Essays in English Medieval History* (London, 1892; reprinted 1927).

VIRALLY, M. 'Vers un droit international du développement', *11 A.F.D.I.* (1965) pp. 3–12.

—— 'The Sources of International Law', Sörensen (ed.), *Manual*, pp. 116–74.

—— 'Réflexions sur le "jus cogens"', 11 *A.F.D.I.* (1966), pp. 3–29.

—— 'Panorama du droit international contemporain. Cours général de droit international public', 183 Hague *Recueil* (1983, V), pp. 9–382.

VITTA, C. 'La défense international de la liberté et de la moralité individuelles', 45 Hague *Recueil* (1933, III), pp. 557–666.

VITTA, E. 'Le traité multilatéral peut-il être considéré comme un acte législatif?', 6 *A.F.D.I.* (1960), pp. 225–38.

Völkerrecht als Rechtsordnung. Internationale Gerichtsbarkeit. Menschenrechte. Festschrift für Hermann Mosler (Berlin, 1983).

Völkerrechtlicher Vertrag und Drittstaaten (Treaties and Third States) (in German, with English Summaries of the Reports) (Heidelberg, 1988).

WALDOCK, C. H. M. 'The Anglo-Norwegian Fisheries Case', 28 *B.Y.I.L.* (1951), pp. 114–71.

—— 'The Regulation of the Use of Force by Individual States in International law', 81 Hague *Recueil* (1952, II), pp. 451–517.

—— 'General Course on Public International Law', 106 Hague *Recueil* (1962, II), pp. 1–251.

WALLACE, C. D. 'Barcelona Traction Case', Heidelberg *Encycl.*, ii, pp. 30–3.

WALLACE, R. *International Law. A Student Introduction*, 2nd edn. (London, 1992).

WANG TIEYA 'The Third World and International law', MacDonald and Johnston (eds.), *The Structure and Process*, pp. 955–76.

—— 'International Law in China: Historical and Contemporary Perspectives', 221 Hague *Recueil* (1990, II), pp. 195–370.

WEERAMANTRY, C. G. 'The Teaching of Human Rights', 1 *Sri Lanka Journal of International Law* (1989), pp. 79–111.

—— 'An Appreciation of Judge Nagendra Singh', Pathak and Dhokalia (eds.), *International Law. Essays Singh*, preliminary essay (vi).

—— 'The International Court of Justice in the Age of Multiculturalism', 36 *Indian Journal of International Law* (1996, No. 2), pp. 17–38.

WEIL, P. 'Towards Relative Normativity in International Law?', 77 *A.J.I.L.* (1983), pp. 413–42.

—— 'Le droit international en quête de son identité. Cours général de droit international public', 237 Hague *Recueil* (1992, VI), pp. 9–370.

WEILER, J. H. H., CASSESE, A. and SPINEDI, M. (eds.) *International Crimes of State. A Critical Analysis of the ILC's Draft Article 19 on State Responsibility* (Berlin and New York, 1989).

WEISBURD, A. M. 'The Effect of Treaties and Other Formal International Acts On the Customary Law of Human Rights', 25 *Georgia Journal of International and Comparative Law* (1995/96), pp. 99–146.

WEISS, B. E. *In Fairness to Future Generations: International Law, Common Patrimony and Intergenerational Equity* (Tokyo and Dobbs Ferry, 1989).

——'The Planetary Trust: Conservation and Intergenerational Equity', 11 *Ecology Law Quarterly* (1984), pp. 495–581.

WENGLER, W. *Völkerrecht*, 2 vols. (Berlin, 1964).

WESTLAKE, J. *International Law*, i (Cambridge, 1910), ii (2nd edn., Cambridge, 1913).

WHEATON, H. *Elements of International Law: with a Sketch of the History of the Science* (Philadelphia, 1836).

WHITE, G. E. *The American Judicial Tradition. Profiles of Leading American Judges*, expanded edn. (New York and Oxford, 1988).

—— *The Marshall Court and Cultural Change 1815–1835*, abridged edn. (New York and Oxford, 1991).

WHITEMAN, M. '*Jus Cogens* in International Law, with a Projected List', 7 *Georgia Journal of International and Comparative Law* (1977), pp. 609–26.

WIECEK, W. M. 'Antelope, The', Hall, K. L. (ed.), *The Oxford Companion to the Supreme Court*, p. 34.

WILBERFORCE, R. 'Some Aspects of the Anglo-Norwegian Fisheries Case', 38 *Transactions of the Grotius Society* (1953), pp. 151–68.

WILLIAMS, C. 'Slavery (and the Church)', *New Catholic Encyclopedia*, xiii (New York, 1967), pp. 281–2.

WILLIAMS, J. F. 'La doctrine de la réconnaissance en droit international et ses dévéloppements récents', 44 Hague *Recueil* (1933, II), pp. 203–313.

WILLISCH, J. *State Responsibility for Technological Damage in International Law* (Berlin, 1987).

WINIARSKI, B. 'Principes généraux du droit fluvial international', 45 Hague *Recueil* (1933, III), pp. 75–217.

WOLFF, C. *Jus gentium methodo scientifica pertractatum*, English trans. Drake of 1764 edition, Scott (ed.), *Classics of International Law* (Oxford, 1934).

WOLFKE, K. *Custom in Present International law*, 2nd revised edn. (Dordrecht, 1993).

—— '*Jus Cogens* in International Law (Regulations and Prospects)', 6 *P.Y.I.L.* (1974), pp. 145–62.

——'Some Reflections on International Environmental Law-Making and Enforcement', 8 *P.Y.I.L.* (1976), pp. 33–53.

WOLFRUM, R. 'Purposes and Principles of International Environmental Law', 33 *G.Y.I.L.* (1990), pp. 308–30.

—— (ed.) *United Nations: Law, Policies and Practice*, new, revised English edn., 2 vols. (Munich and Dordrecht, 1995).

WOOLSEY, L. H. 'The Tacna-Arica Settlement', 23 *A.J.I.L.* (1929), pp. 605–10.

The World Charter for Nature, European Council for Environmental Law (under the auspices of) (Berlin, 1986).

WRIGHT, Q. *Mandates under the League of Nations* (Chicago, 1930).

WYK, D. (VAN), DUGARD, J., DE VILLIERS, B. and DAVIS, D. (eds.) *Rights and Constitutionalism. The New South African Legal Order* (Kenwyn, South Africa, 1994).

WYROZUMSKA, A. 'Problem istnienia w prawie miedzynarodowym publicznym sluzebnosci miedzynarodowego', 7 *Acta Universitatis Lodziensis. Folia Iuridica* (1982), pp. 71–96 (in Polish, with English summary).

—— 'Treaties Establishing Territorial Regimes', 15 *P.Y.I.L.* (1986), pp. 251–76.

YANAI, S. and ASOMURA, K. 'Japan and the Emerging Order of the Sea—Two Maritime Laws of Japan', 21 *Japanese Annual of International Law* (1977), pp. 48–114.

YASSEEN, M. K. 'L'interprétation des traités d'après la Convention de Vienne sur le droit des traités', 151 Hague *Recueil* (1976, III), pp. 1–114.

YEPES, J. M. 'La contribution de l'Amérique latine au développement du droit international public et privé', 32 Hague *Recueil* (1930, II), pp. 691–799.

—— 'Les problèmes fondamentaux du droit des gens en Amérique', 47 Hague *Recueil* (1934, I), pp. 1–143.

ZACKLIN, R. (ed.) *The Process of Change in International Law (Report of a Conference organized by the Carnegie Endowment for International Peace, Geneva, 1963)* (Geneva, 1965).

ZACKLIN, R. 'The problem of Namibia in International Law', 171 Hague *Recueil* (1981, II), pp. 225–340.

ZEMANEK, K. 'State succession after decolonisation', 116 Hague *Recueil* (1965, III), pp. 181–300.

—— 'The United Nations Conference on the Law of Treaties Between States and International Organizations: The unrecorded history of its "general agreement"', Böckstiegel, Folz, Mössner and Zemanek (eds.), *Law of Nations. Liber Seidl-Hohenveldern*, pp. 675–7.

ZICCARDI, P. 'Règles d'organisation et règles de conduite en droit international. (Le droit commun et les ordres juridiques)', 152 Hague *Recueil* (1976, IV), pp. 119–376.

—— 'Il diritto nell'insegnamento di Roberto Ago', 78 *Riv. dir. int.* (1995), pp. 305–17.

ZICCARDI CAPALDO, G. (ed.) *Repertory of Decisions of the International Court of Justice (1947–1992)*, 2 vols. (Dordrecht, 1995).

ZOLLER, E. 'L'affaire du personnel diplomatique et consulaire des Etats-Unis à Teheran', 84 *R.G.D.I.P.* (1980), pp. 973–1026.

ZOUREK, J. 'Enfin une Définition de l'Agression', 20 *A.F.D.I.* (1974), pp. 9–30.

ZWEIGERT, K. and KÖTZ, H. *Introduction to Comparative Law*, 2nd edn., English trans. Weir, 2 vols. (Oxford, 1987).

Index

(This index does not list either personal names (listed in the Bibliography) or the names of cases and documents (listed in their respective Tables))